PETER MAY & JACKIE MARTIN

KNOCKOUT

FIRST CERTIFICATE

TEACHER'S BOOK

OXFORD

UNIVERSITY PRESS

Oxford University Press
Great Clarendon Street, Oxford OX2 6DP

Oxford   New York
Athens   Auckland   Bangkok   Bogotá
Buenos Aires   Calcutta   Cape Town   Chennai
Dar es Salaam   Delhi   Florence   Hong Kong
Istanbul   Karachi   Kuala Lumpur   Madrid
Melbourne   Mexico City   Mumbai   Nairobi
Paris   São Paulo   Singapore   Taipei   Tokyo
Toronto   Warsaw

and associated companies in
Berlin   Ibadan

OXFORD and OXFORD ENGLISH
are trade marks of Oxford University Press

ISBN 0 19 4533654

© Oxford University Press 1999

Printed in Hong Kong

www.oup.co.uk

Acknowledgements

The authors and publisher are grateful to those who
have given permission to reproduce the following
extracts and adaptations of copyright material:

p124 Foods That Harm, Foods That Heal © 1996.
Permission granted by Reader's Digest Association
Limited; pp199,128 Fact File Sport by Peter Brooke-Ball.
Copyright © Grisewood & Dempsey Ltd. 1991; p131
'Michelangelo CEO' by William Wallace. © 1994 New
York Times Co. Reprinted by permission; p143 AA
Essential Explorer: China by Christopher Knowles © The
Automobile Association 1995; p153 The Colourful World
of Birds by Euan Dunn, published by Octopus Books ©
1976 Hennerwood Publications Limited; p200 Law
Without a Lawyer by Fenton Bresler, published by Sinclair
Stevenson. Copyright © 1995 Fenton Bresler; p202
'Antonia Bellanca' by Nilgin Yusuf. Appeared in *RED
Magazine* September 1998; p203 'Red stars' by Kate
Hamilton. Appeared in *RED Magazine* September 1998;
p187 'Breakfast cereal eaters get head start on the day'
by Jeremy Laurance. Appeared in *The Times* 5 April 1997
© Times Newspapers Limited, 1997; p195 'Riverboats
aground as drought takes grip' by John Vidal, 2 April
1997 © *The Guardian*.

Photography:
ImageBank: p21/L D Gordon (meditating), Joe Patronite
(soccer), Eric Schweikardt (balloon), John P. Kelly
(aeroplane)

Illustration:
Peter Cornwall p212

Contents

The *Knockout First Certificate* Course

INTRODUCTION

Components

The *Knockout First Certificate* course consists of the Student's Book, the Teacher's Book and two audio cassettes, plus the Workbook and a free cassette. The With-Key edition of the Workbook contains answers and transcripts.

Rationale

The course is purpose-written for the revised Cambridge First Certificate in English. It can be used with learners of whatever age or cultural background, in any country and in monolingual or multilingual classes.

It is particularly suitable for students who have studied English for 500–600 hours and are now beginning the academic year leading up to the exam. They are likely to have quite a good level of receptive and productive language skills, to be familiar with many of the main grammatical structures of English and to have a reasonable range of basic vocabulary items at their disposal.

They are, however, also liable to make fairly frequent errors (including some of a quite basic nature) when speaking or writing, have difficulty fully understanding spoken or written texts, know insufficient vocabulary to be able to communicate completely accurately and appropriately, and lack knowledge about the exam and the best ways to tackle FCE task-types.

The course aims to overcome these and other difficulties by assuming that:

- pair and group work is essential in the First Certificate classroom
- learning is assisted when students work out rules or identify patterns for themselves
- students learn best when they work with materials that are relevant to their own lives
- they should have an opportunity to activate new language by using it in realistic situations
- the development of accuracy and fluency are both vital for success at First Certificate
- reinforcement of what they have learnt is necessary if they are to remember and use it
- they need to find effective learning strategies suited to their own way of studying
- they should be encouraged to learn outside the classroom and shown how to do so
- self-assessment focuses minds on what they can do now and how they can do more
- cultural awareness is an important factor in developing language abilities
- students want and need to see how they are progressing compared to the exam standard
- they can best learn about First Certificate in task-based activities that demystify the exam
- they want and need to study and practise every possible FCE exam task-type
- all First Certificate exam tasks can be used with a teaching, not just a testing, purpose
- students can gradually become more independent learners as the course progresses.

The Student's Book

THE CONTENTS PAGES

These four pages provide an overview of the course. They are particularly useful for cross-referencing topics, skills work and extra features such as the Exam Study Guide (see below).

The Exam: Outline of the Examination

These pages provide an overview of First Certificate. For each part of every paper, there are page references to help both you and your students find the pages in the Student's Book that give information and offer suggestions on that task-type.

THE UNITS

Each unit deals with one or more of the topics that may occur in the exam. The order of sections within each unit remains basically the same, although in some units there are two Reading texts and one Listening, while in others there are two Listenings and one Reading. The first two pages in every unit, however, always feature a Reading text as an introduction to the theme.

Each double-page spread can be treated as a complete teaching unit, which may be suitable for a single lesson. On the last page there is always a Study Check which focuses on what students have learned in the unit. There are also a number of useful extra features such as Exam Study Guides, Common Errors boxes and First Certificate Facts boxes, which are explained in detail below. The ten pages of each unit are likely to need between about six and nine hours of class time to complete.

UNIT SECTIONS

Vocabulary

Some units begin with a Vocabulary section as a lead-in to the topic and the Reading section to follow. The expressions presented will normally be relevant to both, and of sufficiently high level to be challenging, but at the same time within the range of language required for success at First Certificate. Recycling and testing of new lexical items is a constant feature of the course, not only within the Student's Book but also in the Teacher's Book (Further Practice, Unit Tests and Progress Tests) and Workbook.

Special attention is paid to those areas of vocabulary learning which are specifically tested in FCE. For example, in Paper 3 (Use of English) these include affixes, parts of speech and compound words (word formation), collocations (multiple-choice cloze), reference words (open cloze), and reporting verbs (key word transformation).

Students are constantly encouraged to use new lexis in their writing and speaking, and guidance is given on how to develop communication strategies to help them improve their vocabulary while engaging in oral activities, as well as the reading and listening skills needed to work out new expressions from context. In all exam-style activities, however, the vocabulary load is maintained at the level that students can reasonably expect to find in the First Certificate exam itself. Extra topic-related vocabulary is presented and practised in the Teacher's Book Further Practice section.

Speaking

The Speaking heading is sometimes used for oral lead-ins to Reading and Listening sections, but more commonly for sections that focus on FCE Paper 5 Speaking. All four parts of the First Certificate oral paper are covered at least twice, with special attention paid to confidence-building, as for many students this part of the exam can be daunting if they are not properly prepared for it.

Pair and group work is an integral part of the course, partly because of its importance in helping to build general communicative skills but also because candidates will have to work collaboratively with a partner in the exam itself. Naturally, the students who have had plenty of practice working in pairs in class tend to be better prepared for the FCE Paper 5 format.

There are also many other activities in sections such as Grammar, Reading and Vocabulary where pairs, groups and the class as a whole can develop their speaking skills. A special feature of the course is the use of information-gap activities as a means of learning about the exam itself through discussion. See, for example, Use of English (Part 3) in Unit 1. For ways of encouraging students to practise speaking outside the classroom, see the Unit 8 Exam Study Guide.

Reading

There is a Reading section on the first two pages of every unit, and some units also include a second Reading. All four parts of Paper 1 are covered at least five times, and the possible variations within the exam format (for example headings or summaries, missing sentences or paragraphs) are all systematically dealt with. A wide range of text sources (newspapers and magazine articles, advertisements, fiction, etc.) is used, reflecting the diversity of the material used in the exam itself.

These sections usually begin with a gist-reading activity before moving on to the exam task. As with

other FCE tasks, there is often guidance and in some cases – especially in the first half of the course – assistance is given (see 'Help boxes' below). The task focus varies from reading for the main points to reading for detail, and from studying text structure to looking for specific detail. Students are also trained to deduce overall meaning and to work out the meanings of individual words and phrases by using contextual clues.

The three basic task-types used, as in the exam, are multiple matching, multiple choice and gapped text. All texts and tasks comply with the examiners' guidelines in terms of length and level of vocabulary, so it is advisable to tell students that although there may well be some expressions that they do not understand, the questions will not focus on lexical items above First Certificate level. As with all the other FCE task-types, students are encouraged to discover as much as they can about how the exam works, and how they can improve their performance. For ways of encouraging extensive reading outside the classroom, see the Exam Study Guide in Unit 4. Additional exam-style reading texts can be found in the Teacher's Book Further Practice section.

Grammar

A high degree of grammatical accuracy is of course essential for success in FCE, and the wide grammar syllabus in the Student's Book is supplemented by additional points and extensions in the Further Practice in the Teacher's Book. As students at this level will probably already have studied many of these structures, *Knockout* often uses an inductive approach to grammar input. This means that students work out or complete rules for themselves by, for instance, matching definitions with examples, or filling in missing words in an explanation. For more complex grammar points, however, where a majority of the class are likely to find an inductive approach too demanding, a short explanation is given in the traditional way.

Following the presentation, controlled practice activities lead into freer practice, often with a follow-up in the Study Check. As with vocabulary, there is substantial recycling of structure later in the unit, in subsequent units and in the Teacher's Book, where grammar points are also tested (Unit Tests and Progress Tests). Grammar sections often lead into Use of English sections, where further practice is given in key word transformations, error correction and so forth. Revision of individual student's problem areas is the focus of the Unit 14 Exam Study Guide, while the Index of Grammar and Functions (see below) is particularly useful for cross-referencing to other sections that deal with the same, or related, structures.

Use of English

All five parts of Paper 3 are dealt with at least three times each in specific Use of English sections, with further practice of some task-types in other sections such as Grammar. Language from Grammar, Vocabulary and Phrasal Verbs sections is often given more coverage here. The Further Practice activities in the Teacher's Book contain more Use of English work in every unit, with alternatives to the standard format to provide variety and/or a step-by-step approach to the exam tasks.

Listening

All units contain one or two Listening sections, and in each there is a First Certificate task. The four parts of Paper 4 are all practised at least five times each. Help is given in earlier units as all texts and tasks are at FCE level; this provides a gentle introduction to exam-authentic tasks and helps build students' confidence in their ability to follow what they hear and answer the questions.

Pre-listening may include visuals to set the scene, vocabulary work to lighten the lexical load or a focus on the task-type to help students find out how it works and how to approach it. The main listening tasks consist of texts taken, as in the exam, from a wide range of sources involving one or more speakers. They include conversations, discussions, interviews, features, instructions, phone calls, lectures, reports and so on. The task focus varies from understanding the gist, main points or detail, to listening out for specific information or deducing meaning.

It is advisable to warn students in advance that on the recordings, as in the FCE exam, they probably won't understand every word – but that they are not expected to and will not need to in order to complete the tasks successfully. Full tapescripts are included in the Teacher's Book. For ways of encouraging extensive listening outside the classroom, see the Unit 7 Exam Study Guide.

Writing

All FCE Writing task-types are covered, with the Part 1 transactional letter the focus of the section in five units. There is at least one section dealing with each of the Part 2 tasks, which include articles, reports, compositions, non-transactional letters and writing about set books. A key element of the writing syllabus is the use of model answers, which appear either as part of the unit or in the Exam Revision Section at the back of the book.

Students are encouraged throughout the course to check their own (and each other's) work for mistakes. This is the focus of the Exam Study Guide in Unit 6 and Unit 9, where they identify their most frequent errors, think about what kinds they are and decide why they make them. To this end it is helpful if students keep all their written work for future use. There are further writing tasks in Study Check (see below), and in the Further Practice section in the Teacher's Book.

Phrasal Verbs

Many units contain a Phrasal Verbs section. Each presents and practises the most frequently-occurring and useful combinations of adverb particles with one particular verb in a variety of activities. The verbs studied in this way include *get, look, put, give, take, bring* and *turn*. Many others appear, especially in vocabulary, post-reading and post-listening activities, and a full list of the phrasal verbs used in the course can be found in the Index of Phrasal Verbs on page 187 of the Student's Book.

Study Check

The final section in every unit, Study Check, enables students to revise and review what they have learned by working through both oral and written activities. There is usually a second FCE Writing task with further guidance on how to approach it, and there is often freer practice of structures presented in Grammar sections earlier in the unit.

UNIT BOXES

Exam Study Guide

In many units, this feature encourages students to think about their exam preparation and find new ways of practising their language skills. These learner training activities, specially adapted for FCE students, are designed to help them become more independent learners and encourage them to take more responsibility for their own progress towards success in the exam, and with language learning in general. Activities range from self-assessment to planning timing in the exam, plus a focus on each of the main skills, vocabulary, error analysis and revision. It may be best to check in advance what the activities consist of, as occasionally students may need to prepare for them by, for example, collecting together samples of their past written work.

Help boxes

In earlier units, these boxes give valuable advice on what to look out for when tackling exam tasks. They also make these tasks a little easier, as all exam material in Knockout is set at the standard of the exam itself and this might otherwise prove daunting at the beginning of the course.

First Certificate Facts

These boxes give useful information about the exam itself, by focusing on points which answer the questions that students often ask, or wonder about.

Common Errors

Common Errors boxes highlight mistakes that First Certificate students frequently make. These are often grammar points that they will already have studied at a lower level but which may still cause difficulties. The recommended way of using these boxes is as follows:

1 Students working individually or in pairs study the incorrect sentence and identify the error.
2 They rewrite the sentence correctly, noting down the mistake.
3 After checking their corrected version with the Grammar Reference, they read the relevant grammar input.
4 This can be followed up with class feedback.

EXAM SKILLS

A key feature of *Knockout* is its approach to exam tasks and how to tackle them. Instead of giving lists of details and exam tips, this course actively involves students in learning how First Certificate task-types work by presenting information and advice in the form of task-based activities. For example, rather than being given columns of Do's and Don'ts, they have to decide whether they should or should not do certain things, basing their answers on what they have found out in an information-gap activity (earlier units) or on what they have already learned about the task-type (later units). FCE tasks themselves, such as cloze and word formation, are often used as a means of making learning about the exam more challenging. In many tasks, students are shown how questions and answers work, and are encouraged to think through the process for themselves in order to gain an insight into what the examiners are looking for. In fact, learning about the exam is treated in much the same way as learning about language: through guided discovery, practice with the techniques and discussion with other students.

GRAMMAR REFERENCE

The main structures presented and practised in each unit are explained, with further examples, in the corresponding unit of the Grammar Reference. Students should use it from the beginning of the course to check their answers to the questions in the Common Errors boxes, and can also refer to it for self-study and revision purposes.

EXAM REVISION SECTION

Another unique feature of this book is the Exam Revision Section, which contains questions and tasks focusing on every part of the five FCE papers. There are also model answers to any Writing tasks that do not have sample texts in the units where they are presented.

During the *Knockout* course, students will have learned an enormous amount about the exam and how to approach it, but inevitably they will have forgotten some of the advice and suggestions – just as they will not remember everything about the grammar and vocabulary they have studied. In order to re-activate this knowledge, it is suggested that shortly before students take the exam they work their way through the activities in the Exam Revision Section. These consist of a wide range of exercise types that can be done quickly and easily. The questions focus on the exam instructions, exam techniques and the language needed for successful completion of exam tasks, and students should use the Index of Exam Task-types to check their answers in the relevant part or parts of the Student's Book. They are, in effect, writing their own exam tips. There is a key in the Teacher's Book on page 106.

INDEX OF EXAM TASK-TYPES

This index can be used both in conjunction with the Exam Revision Section and for cross-referencing to other parts of the book where help and/or guidance is given.

INDEX OF PHRASAL VERBS

This contains the phrasal verbs at or close to FCE level that are used in written contexts in the Student's Book. It includes multi-part verbs in Reading texts, Grammar activities, etc., plus any that need to be written in by students. You may want to point out the following:

- the meaning given against each one is only intended as a rough guide
- for many of the verbs listed, other meanings are possible
- the context on the page referred to should be checked for the exact meaning to be understood
- verbs which are presented and practised in Phrasal Verbs sections are highlighted
- the page reference normally refers to the first time the item appears in the course unless it is included in a Phrasal Verbs section, in which case the latter reference is given.

INDEX OF IRREGULAR VERBS

This index lists the verbs normally considered to be within the range of vocabulary required for success at FCE level, plus any other irregular verbs featured in the Student's Book.

INDEX OF GRAMMAR AND FUNCTIONS

All the structures presented and practised in the Student's Book are included here, either under their grammatical name, the specific words used or as a way of expressing a language function.

CASSETTES

The two audio cassettes contain all the listening texts from the 15 Units in the Student's Book. Full tapescripts appear at the relevant points of the teaching notes in the Teacher's Book. Cassette 2, side 2 contains the recording for Further Practice Pronunciation activities and the Practice Test.

SUPPLEMENTING THE STUDENT'S BOOK

The various components of *Knockout First Certificate* – including the Exam Revision Section in the Student's Book, the Further Practice and Follow-ups in the Teacher's Book, plus the enormous amount of relevant material in The Workbook – form a complete FCE course which in most circumstances will not need supplementing.

This does not preclude, of course, the possibility of adapting the material to the needs of a particular class or to your own teaching style. Indeed, it is strongly hoped that the approach to First Certificate preparation used in this course will lead to experimentation with new ways of using this and other classroom material. Students, too, should be encouraged to extend their learning beyond that of the tasks set in class and for homework.

The Teacher's Book

The Teacher's Book is an integral part of the course. It contains a large amount of teaching and testing material – much of it photocopiable – plus extensive guidance on how to exploit both this and the material in the Student's Book.

TEACHER'S NOTES

There are detailed teaching notes designed to help you and your students make the best possible use of *Knockout First Certificate Student's Book*. They include the following features:

- For every activity, the suggested procedure for using the material, often including recommended classroom focus (teacher–students, student–student, groups, individuals working alone, etc.).
- A complete key, with suggested or possible answers given where more than one is possible.
- Full transcripts of the Listening texts that are used in the Student's Book.
- Notes on special difficulties, including vocabulary items and the cultural background.
- Explanations and the corrected forms for the Common Errors boxes in the Student's Book.
- Alternative ways of exploiting the material and adapting it to the particular needs of your students. These are marked VARIATION.
- Further tasks that can be used, if you wish and if time allows, to extend the activity. They often involve speaking or writing fluency practice. These are marked FOLLOW-UP.
- Cross-references to relevant parts of the course, including the Teacher's Book Further Practice and the Workbook.
- Reminders at the end of units to give the Unit Test and, where relevant, the Progress Test.

FURTHER PRACTICE

For each unit of the Student's Book there is a corresponding set of photocopiable extra activities in the Teacher's Book. This material complements that in the unit, for example by expanding grammar points and extending vocabulary areas presented in the Student's Book unit and providing a range of useful back-up material such as discussion questions, additional writing tasks and 5-minute activities all based around the unit theme. For each unit there is a combination of the following activities:

- Lead-in activities and Discussion questions to stimulate ideas and provide extra speaking practice
- Vocabulary exercises to widen the lexical input
- Grammar sections which expand the points presented in the Student's Book
- alternative Use of English skills-building activities
- Reading texts providing additional exam practice
- Pronunciation work on key areas of difficulty, including intonation, sentence stress and linking
- Further Writing tasks based on the unit theme
- 5-minute activities which can be used as fillers and fun activities

The Teacher's Notes includes references suggesting at which stage some of these activities could be used.

Recordings for the pronunciation activities are at the end of the Class Cassettes. An answer key follows the Further Practice Section.

UNIT TESTS

There are fifteen photocopiable Unit Tests, one to follow each unit. They consist of a wide variety of non-exam task-types that test the grammar and

vocabulary presented in that unit of the Student's Book. The recommended time limit for each test is 30 minutes. They are easy to mark, using the answer key provided.

PROGRESS TESTS

The four photocopiable Progress Tests, to be given after Units 4, 8, 12 and 15, each contain four Use of English exam-style tasks plus an FCE Writing task, with three options in the case of Part 2 questions. They test the language presented in all the foregoing units, so that while Test 1 focuses on structure and lexis from Units 1–4, Test 2 covers that from Units 1–8, and so on. It should be made clear to students that all these tasks are at FCE level and therefore it is to be expected that in the early tests they would get relatively low scores, but that these should rise as they progress through the course. The recommended time allowed for each complete test (including 45 minutes for the writing question) is two hours. A full key is provided.

PRACTICE TESTS

There is a complete First Certificate Practice Test at the end of the Teacher's Book. The recordings are at the end of the Class Cassettes.

The Workbook

The Workbook includes 15 units corresponding to those of the same name and number in the Student's Book. They contain:

- Activities that present and practise more topic-related vocabulary, including phrasal verbs, often in a lighthearted and entertaining way. Answers are given in the With-Key edition.
- First Certificate Reading featuring all the Paper 1 task-types, with extensive guidance.
- First Certificate Listening with guidance and advice, covering all the Paper 4 task-types. The recordings are on the free cassette which accompanies the Workbook and full transcripts are provided in the With-Key edition.
- Further controlled practice activities covering the grammar presented in the Student's Book. These concentrate more on production rather than recognition.
- More practice with all the First Certificate Use of English task-types. They often focus on topic-related vocabulary and structures presented in the corresponding unit of the Student's Book.
- Further guided writing practice, often with sample texts, covering all the types of task (including Set Books) occurring in both parts of Paper 2.
- Skills Development boxes. These give advice on how to develop the language skills necessary for success at First Certificate level.
- Exam Tips boxes. These give useful advice on how to answer particular parts of exam questions.
- Common Errors boxes. These focus on common grammatical areas. Full explanations are given in the With-Key edition.

After each Unit there is a Grammar Check section, where students note down their own examples of structures which have been presented and practised.

In addition, following each of Units 11–15 there are two extra pages that focus on one of the five exam papers: Unit 11 – Reading, Unit 12 – Writing, Unit 13 Use of English, Unit 14 – Listening, Unit 15 – Speaking. Each of these contains the following:

- *How to succeed* sections giving advice on what the First Certificate examiners will be looking for.
- *What the examiners say* boxes containing suggestions made by the examiners themselves on how you can get better marks.
- *Marking* information. This section tells you how marks are given, including the number of marks for different kinds of questions or parts of the Paper.
- *What not to do*. Hints on what to avoid doing during the exam.
- *Make a note of it*. Personalisation sections where students can record what they need to remember to do, any special difficulties they have, useful language, and so on.
- Survival Skills boxes containing essential advice for that Paper.
- Checklist boxes packed with further useful tips for each part of the Paper.

At the end of the Workbook there is a complete model interview with visuals, including detailed advice and a range of activities to familiarise students with the structure of Paper 5 and the types of questions they may be asked. The recording of the model interview is on the free cassette accompanying the Workbook and a complete transcript is included in the With-Key edition, following the answers to the Practice Test.

1 In fitness and in health

SPEAKING *p8*

❶ Get students to ask and answer in pairs, and then elicit scores. If necessary, explain terms such as *jogging* (in some languages they may use the Anglicism *footing*) and *martial arts* (elicit internationally-known disciplines such as *judo*, *karate*, *kung fu* and *t'ai chi*). Opinions on scores may vary according to culture (on red meat, holidays and visiting the doctor, for example) and students' experience – or lack of it – of the activities mentioned. Encourage discussion of variables: *it depends* how much fruit, *as long as* you don't take pills instead of eating good food, *provided you* also do other kinds of exercise, and so on.

❷ Tell them to note down their own additions to the list (prompts here might include swimming, eating vegetables, avoiding stress, not getting sunburnt, etc.) and then ask pairs for their ideas. Ask them to discuss what advice they would give to each of age groups a–c.

READING: multiple matching *pp8–9*

❶ This activity introduces the topic of the Reading text and feeds in vocabulary, nearly all of which appears in the text in some form. Highlight any words that may cause your students pronunciation difficulties, such as *strength* and *tough*, or the /ɪ/ sound in *fit*, *skill* and *kick*. Pairs discuss the questions and then report back to the class.

❷ | **ANSWERS:** 1F 2F 3F 4T 5F 6F |

❸ 1 If students are new to multiple matching, show them an example from a past paper or book of practice tests. Ask them what the difference is between a *heading* and a *summary*. Point out that there is always one extra sentence that they do not need to use, in order to avoid the jigsaw effect.

NOTE: *Jigsaw effect* – if there is an equal number of headings/summaries and paragraphs, the last one falls into place like the final piece of a jigsaw and therefore tests nothing.

Students could do this ordering activity in pairs. Point out that for the present purposes, 'summary' and 'heading' are used interchangeably.

| **ANSWERS:** 4 3 2 7 8 6 1 5 |

NOTE: As with any ordering exercise or test, remember to give credit for the right links (4–3, 3–2, 2–7, 7–8, 8–6, 6–1, 1–5) rather than correct numerical sequence, otherwise a single mistake means all subsequent answers are 'wrong'.

2 The underlining task provides advance practice for another Reading task: gapped texts in Part 3 of Use of English, where students have to use both the content and linguistic clues to replace sentences or complete paragraphs.

| **POSSIBLE ANSWERS:** 2 this example paragraph 3 Next 4 first impression 5 Part 2 6 remaining 7 again 8 Each time |

NOTE: There is a focus on reference words in Reading tasks in Unit 11.

❹ Focus on the instructions, in particular the mention of summaries rather than headings, and then on the underlined clues, pointing out that these do not occur in the exam. Remind students not to worry too much about any individual words or phrases that they might not understand.

| **ANSWERS:** 1G 2C 3A 4D 5F 6B Not needed: E |

VARIATION: With a strong class, ask why E is not needed. ANSWER: there is no reference to misuse (although in fact all reputable Taekwondo clubs insist that their members swear an oath never to do so).

❺ This could be done in pairs or groups, with perhaps a class roundup at the end.

VARIATION: If anyone in the class has personal experience of a martial art, ask him or her to tell the rest of the class about it and then take questions.

WORKBOOK: Part 1 pp8–9; Focus On Reading p72.

GRAMMAR: present tenses *p10*

❶ Begin by ensuring that everyone understands the terms 'present simple' and 'present continuous' (students might previously have learned the terms 'simple present' and 'present progressive') and knows which is which. Students then match rules a–j and sentences 1–10, working either in pairs or alone. Point out that use j (irritating things) needs to be used with words like *always*, *constantly*, *continually* and *forever*.

| **ANSWERS:** 1d 2c 3i 4a 5g 6j 7h 8b 9e 10f Place: a sports centre |

VARIATION: Begin by putting the examples on the board and elicit rules a–j with the students' books closed.

COMMON ERRORS

'Where are you from, Nikos?' 'I'm coming from Athens.' The correct form is: *I come from Athens.*

② Students may be aware of the restrictions on certain verbs – for example they should not say 'I'm understanding the question' – but without knowing why, especially if their first language does not have a present continuous form, or the rules of usage are different. You may want to begin by eliciting 'stative' (or 'state') verbs and asking the class if they can identify what those they suggest have in common. They then do the activity, alone or in pairs.

> **ANSWERS:**
> 1 Perception: hear, taste, smell
> 2 Appearance: appear
> 3 Thinking: believe, imagine, know, suppose, understand, remember, wish
> 4 Likes and dislikes: hate, dislike, love, prefer, admire, need, want
> 5 Possession: belong, possess, keep, have

VARIATION: With a weaker class, tell them the number of verbs they need to find for each category.

③ Explain that the few statives that are used in the continuous change their meaning to refer to an active form of behaviour (in the case of *think*, mental activity). Pairs study and do the exercise, then go through the answers with the class. If necessary, explain in more detail, for example *tasting*: testing it to see if he likes it.

> **ANSWERS:**
> 1 considering   2 action, not possession   3 action of sniffing   4 not returning it to its owner

VARIATION: With a strong class, explain that the use of *have* as in 'have a sleep', etc. is largely delexical (i.e. has little or no meaning in itself, but is used with a noun to indicate that someone does something), and corresponds closely to the verb 'sleep'. Point out that this is a very common usage in spoken language and elicit more examples (*give a smile, take a photo, give an answer*).

④ The emphasis now shifts to verbs that are often used in both present tense forms. Make sure that everyone understands *stretch* and *reach* and point out that these six questions practise all ten uses presented in activity 1.

> **ANSWERS:** 1 helps, is helping   2 try, are trying
> 3 think, I'm thinking   4 I'm reaching, reach
> 5 starts, I'm starting   6 go, I'm going
> The speaker does weight training.

⑤ Elicit the type of use each represents.

> **ANSWERS:** 1 c, g   2 b, j   3 b, i   4 h, e   5 d, f
> 6 a, i

FOLLOW-UP: Give freer practice by getting pairs to tell each other what their friends, brothers and sisters are probably doing at the moment, and what they are doing later. Then they choose one person and describe his or her daily routine, possibly contrasting it with that of the speaker.

WORKBOOK: Present tenses p10.

FURTHER PRACTICE: Present tenses p109.

USE OF ENGLISH: key word transformations *p11*

① You could start by pointing out the relevance of this activity to everyday speaking and writing, in the sense that we often look for alternative ways of saying the same thing. Focus attention on the instructions, checking understanding (e.g. What is 'the word given' in the example? Answer: *impossible*) and go through the example, pointing out the need to keep the first person plural in the second sentence. Explain that, as every question tests two things, they should always do as much as they can as they may get one out of two possible marks.

② This activity helps students to find out about the exam through discussion, and also practises question forms with and without *do*, but particularly with modals and *be*. Tell the 'B' students to read the text on p164 carefully, making a mental note of the information in it. Explain that the points are not necessarily in the same order as in Student A's questions, so they must absorb them, rather than attempting to match lines in the text to questions. When pairs have finished, go through the answers with the class, ensuring that everyone has the correct answers and the reasons for them written down.

> **ANSWERS:** 1 ✓   2 ✗ You must never put six words.
> 3 ✓   4 ✗ You cannot cross out any of the words printed.   5 ✗ You must never change the key word or leave it out.   6 ✓   7 ✓   8 ✗ They count as one.

VARIATION: When pairs have finished correcting the statements, tell them to compare the register of the two sources of the same information, noting that the language in the Revision Section text is more formal than that used in the statements. Ask why this is so: they should be able to answer that the statements are more in the style of spoken language, while reference material tends to be more 'serious' in tone.

③ Point out that in exam questions there is no connection between the structures tested on any one paper, and of course the required number of words will not be given in brackets! Go through the answers, making sure that everyone understands all the 'extra' words and changes (with correct positioning) that need to be made, such as *her* in 1 and *definitely* in 3.

> **ANSWERS:**
> 1 this land belongs to her   2 is planning to
> 3 is definitely keeping   4 isn't very interested in
> 5 takes off at   6 running quickly improves
> 7 does she play particularly well   8 am seeing him briefly   9 as soon as I finish   10 is/are always losing matches

WORKBOOK: Key word transformations p10; Focus On Use of English p88.

FURTHER PRACTICE: Key word transformations p110.

VOCABULARY: parts of the body p12

1 Elicit answers, demonstrating where the parts of the body are located if necessary. Some of them will be heard on the Listening recording. Pairs then describe past injuries and how they happened. Encourage discussion of any caused while training or doing exercise, as this is one of the topics covered in the next activity and in the Listening to follow.

2 As usual with gap-fill activities, ask the class to read quickly through the text first for gist. Set a simple task, such as thinking of a title for it, and elicit suggestions after they have had a minute or two to read it through. Point out that the eleven words are all used on the Listening recording and tell students to fill in the gaps in the text, working individually. Encourage them to use the contextual clues to work out the correct answers: e.g. in question 2, an antonym of *tense* is needed, in 3 the gap is followed by a definition (*in other words…*), as is 4 (*another way of saying…*), while in 5 there is an example (*like…*) and in 6 another definition (*This is known as…*). Highlight the pronunciation of any that your students may find difficult to recognize when they hear them (e.g. *breathe*, *rhythm*).

> **ANSWERS:** 1 warm-up 2 loose 3 strain
> 4 endurance 5 skills 6 co-ordination
> 7 skipping 8 stiff 9 breathe 10 rhythm

WORKBOOK: Vocabulary pp6–7.

LISTENING p13

1 Point out that the focus of the Listening in this Unit is understanding the gist of the text. Stress the importance, when listening to dialogue, of students always knowing who they are listening to: in this case it is always either to Cheryl or Josephine. Allow time for the class to look at the instructions and questions, before playing the recording twice. Go through the correct answers and elicit reasons why the distractors are wrong.

> **ANSWERS:** 1C 2A 3C 4B 5C 6B

2 Pairs discuss these questions, which activate lexis from the text and from both parts of Vocabulary on p12.

> **SUGGESTED ANSWERS:** good for legs, stomach/ tummy, bottom, upper body (plus mind-body co-ordination and stamina); can damage knees, joints, calf, Achilles' tendon, back

WORKBOOK: Part 4 pp7–8; Focus On Listening p96.

TAPESCRIPT

Cheryl: As a child, I remember skipping for hours on end, singing silly songs and competing for the neighbourhood championship title. Back then, I didn't think about the health or fitness benefits, but the current revival of interest has brought this favourite childhood pastime out of the playgrounds and into the grown-up world of high-tech health clubs and gyms. An exercise that has been a favourite with boxers and other athletes for many years, skipping is an excellent workout. It not only tones legs, tummies and bottoms, it also builds upper body strength and improves mind-body co-ordination while building stamina. Such is the level of interest now, there are even professional skipping teachers and skipping fitness videos. Josephine Mason is a skipping instructor based in Wales and she's developed a technique she calls Rhythm Skipping. Can you tell the listeners about it, Josephine?

Josephine: Yes, well, it's a series of rope routines set to music and performed at different speeds. The basic techniques are different from boxing skipping where the feet are hardly lifted off the ground. Instead, with Rhythm Skipping, the knees are lifted up high to the chest and toes are pointed to stretch the stomach, hips and bottom muscles. The balls of the feet should take the impact and the knees should be loose. Because the jumping action of skipping is hard on the joints, you should wear good trainers, or even boxing boots, to protect the lower calf and Achilles' tendon, which will strain under the body weight.

Cheryl: I should point out that I've already been for my first session, I went the other day, but I made the mistake of thinking it was going to be child's play. I hadn't warmed up properly and there was a sharp pain from my stiff knees once we started.

Josephine: Yes, as with all fitness programmes your muscles and joints should be fully warm and stretched beforehand to help reduce the risk of injury. Also, because skipping is high-impact, anyone with previous injuries, back pain or trouble with their joints should avoid any skipping, however harmless it may seem.

Cheryl: And it does look quite easy doesn't it? I mean, when the experts do Rhythm Skipping it looks effortless, but now I've tried it for myself I know it's not. In fact at first, I felt like a clown skipping a country dance in big, floppy shoes. The changing rope speeds or 'rhythms' need a surprising amount of skill and my two left feet kept getting caught in the rope so …

Josephine: You have to remember that Rhythm Skipping is about mind and body. It takes practice because each basic jump requires rhythm, balance, endurance, co-ordination and skill.

Cheryl: Well I certainly did find that as soon as I stopped worrying and trying so hard, the movements came naturally and I started having fun. It was a bit like circuit training – skipping in two-minute bursts with short breaks in between. To my embarrassment, I began puffing almost immediately and two minutes began to seem like a very long time indeed. But I knew it was doing me good and I stuck at it.

Josephine: I'm pleased to hear it!

Cheryl: Skipping, then, is great for either outdoor or indoor workouts, it's cheap and it's a portable way to keep fit while travelling. The routines you do can be complicated or simple, you can vary the speed and you can even personalize your routine to your very own needs.

SPEAKING p13

❶ Explain the format of the Speaking part of the exam (two candidates and two examiners, only one of whom speaks to the candidates). Students then read the text and pairs fit the missing questions and statements into the gaps. You may want to point out that this activity has some similarities to Part 3 of FCE Reading. When they have finished, check the answers and elicit more examples for each gap.

ANSWERS: 1G 2B 3C 4F 5A 6D 7E

❷ This is a potentially useful ice-breaking activity for the start of the course, so it might be a good idea to place students with different partners.
If students have any difficulty forming the questions, point out that do is used whenever what, which or who is the object of the sentence. Question forms:
• What's your name and where do you come from?
• Which part of town do you live in?
• Where are you studying? / Where do you work?
• Why are you preparing for First Certificate?
• How do you usually spend your evenings?
• What are you doing after the lesson?

❸ You may want to warn students that if examiners feel that candidates are trying to recite prepared speeches they will intervene and move the conversation on. Practising likely topics, though, is a perfectly valid form of preparation and students could have the good fortune to find that what they have done actually comes up in the exam. For this activity, it is essential that students write their questions, and with a weaker class it is probably a good idea to check these before they move on to the speaking part.

SUGGESTED ANSWERS: 1 Where do people do X? 2 What equipment is needed?   3 Who can do X? 4 How can you avoid getting hurt?   5 In what way is X good for you?   6 How long have you been doing X?

Students then use what they have written as a framework for what they say about their favourite form of exercise or other hobby.

VARIATION: Students do activity 3 as a role play, with their partners acting as examiners. However, you should make it clear that in the exam it will of course be the examiner who is asking the questions, not the other candidate. You may once again wish to mix students with new partners.

WORKBOOK: Focus On Speaking p104.

READING: gapped text pp14–15

❶ Ensure that everyone reads the instructions carefully by asking questions such as What is the article about? What has been taken out of the text? and What do you have to do with them?
Students work individually, reading the advice and text. Go through the answers when everyone has finished.

ANSWERS: 1D 2A 3F 4E 5G 6B

VARIATION: Also focus on language clues like These scientists and this diet. Then, when you are checking the answers, elicit more such as This discovery, Unlike and The results. See Unit 11 for more on reference words.

❷ This could be done in pairs or as a class discussion. Ask if the content of the article has made anyone think of making changes to their eating habits.

WORKBOOK: Focus On Reading p72.

WRITING: a transactional letter p15

❶ This activity give a basic introduction to the compulsory transactional letter (the Writing section in Unit 8 covers it in greater detail). Students should read the first paragraph and then discuss where each of the five words goes. Use the inclusion of e.g. in sentence 2 to point out that commonly used abbreviations like this and others such as NB and etc. may appear in the input text(s). You might also want to elicit other salutations like Dear Sir or Madam/ Yours faithfully (needed for activity 2 below).

ANSWERS: 1 addresses   2 ending   3 copy (odd words or phrases are acceptable)   4 unnecessary 5 formal (semi-formal is usually enough)

❷ Let students read the introduction, text and notes. Answer any questions. Elicit the function of the letter (to give information) and its purpose (to create international awareness of attitudes to health in the students' own country).

VARIATION: With a younger class, it may be advisable first to discuss some of the topics in groups or as a class.

❸ Style/register is dealt with in more detail in Unit 2 Writing, but it may be worth eliciting some of the features of formal/informal language now. Remind students that they do not have to try to bring in all these uses of the present tenses: they are just suggestions. Mark their completed work for content, organization, range, style and effect on the target reader.

WORKBOOK: Writing p11; Focus On Writing p80.

GRAMMAR: countable and uncountable nouns *p16*

❶ Students work together on their answers, correcting common mistakes like 'people is' and focusing on the unlikeliness of someone on a diet eating a whole turkey as a 'very light lunch', etc. Check that they have identified and corrected the mistakes, but also that they have not wrongly 'corrected' other expressions (by putting *a pollution* or *on diet*, for example).

ANSWERS: 1 People are   2 just turkey   3 a lot of hard exercise   4 correct   5 have bad luck
6 news item/story or item of news   7 such bad behaviour   8 Few players   9 correct
10 speaks very good

❷ The examples are taken from the previous Reading text. Begin by eliciting a definition of 'countable' and 'uncountable' (some students may know them as 'count' and 'uncount' nouns from certain grammar books) and then asking the class for examples of both.

Ask about the 15 words, paying particular attention to those that may have countable equivalents in the students' first language: *evidence*, possibly. Point out that most illnesses (such as *measles*, *bronchitis*, etc.) are normally uncountable in English, and that the internationally-used word *toast* is not countable in its country of origin (the same is true of others such as *camping* and *parking*).

ANSWERS: countable: island, beaches, diet, herbs, bowl, cakes, secrets
uncountable: health, diet, pasta, toast, bread, evidence, butter, cancer

❸ Students work in pairs or individually. Then go through the answers with the class.

ANSWERS:
a a/an, many, few, a few, a large number of, each, every
b much, little, a little, a great deal of, a large amount of, large amounts of
c all, a lot of, plenty of, lots of
  Not often in positive statements: many, much, few, little

Point out the restrictions on *plenty of* (positive connotations only), as well as the usefulness of *a lot of* and the less formal *lots of* if the rules are hard to remember!

Students then write phrases such as *plenty of toast, a few beaches, a little bread*. Point out that some of the nouns (*health, diet,* etc.) are unlikely to follow any of these expressions.

COMMON ERRORS

We have a lovely weather in my country.
The correct form is: *We have lovely weather in my country.*

❹ Emphasize the fact that *oils* (like *foods* and *fats*, also from the Reading text) is far less common than the uncountable use. Remind the class of the risk of misunderstanding and absurdity, possibly quoting examples such as *I'd like a spaghetti, please; the supermarket is now selling an ostrich*, and then allow time for pairs to discuss the differences between the expressions.

ANSWERS:
1 time (concept) – a time (an occasion)
2 fish (in general) – a fish (specific, whole one)
3 hair (all) – a hair (one only)
4 oil (in general) – oils (varieties)
5 business (activity) – a business (company)
6 room (space) – a room (part of a house)
7 cold (sensation) – a cold (illness)
8 iron (the metal) – an iron (for clothes)
9 wood (material) – woods (varieties/forest)
10 tin (the metal) – a tin (a can)

VARIATION: With an advanced class you could elicit more examples (*have some melon/have a melon, the risk of disease/infectious diseases*, etc.).

❺ Students work in pairs, then report back to the class. Suggest that they learn these in pairs, so that when they are writing or speaking they have a grammatically correct alternative they can use.

ANSWERS:
information – a report
shopping – a purchase
education – a course
medicine – a pill
scenery – a view
traffic – a vehicle
advice – a suggestion
luggage – a suitcase
cash – a coin
travel – a journey
vocabulary – a word
homework – an exercise
work – a job
accommodation – a room

❻ Point out that these expressions are another way of avoiding mistakes with uncountables. After you have gone through the answers, elicit further phrases – possibly using the words in activities 2 and 4 (*a piece of bread, a bit of glass*, etc.). You may also want to look at more precise expressions such as *a slice of toast*; if so, see the Grammar Reference on p169.

POSSIBLE ANSWERS: a <u>piece</u> of information/
advice/luggage/work; a <u>bit</u> of information/
shopping/traffic/advice/cash/homework/work; an
<u>item</u> of information/shopping/luggage/vocabulary

NOTE: If the students' first language is Greek or of
Latin origin, there may be common L1 cognates that
are countable, possibly including *information*,
luggage and *work*. Elicit as many as possible and
make sure students note them down.

WORKBOOK: Countables and uncountables p10.

EXAM STUDY GUIDE *p17*

This activity is the first of many Learner Training
features in the course. It also provides further
practice with present verb forms. It is important
that students do this exercise alone. Tell them to
refer back to the list of mistakes when they are
doing productive skills work in the future.

FOLLOW-UP 1: When they have finished, a check
(possibly by a show of hands) on the results should
provide some useful feedback on students'
perceptions, aims and problems.

FOLLOW-UP 2: Return to this (completed) table in Unit
6 on p63 (Exam Study Guide), telling students to
compare their thoughts then and now.

STUDY CHECK *p17*

❶ Partners ask each other, practising the question
forms of present tenses and un/countable nouns
from Grammar of the unit. You could ask pairs to
feed back to the class any ideas for exercise or eating
that sound particularly useful.

❷ Use the criteria mentioned for Writing on p15 to
mark their completed work. Report writing is dealt
with in detail in Unit 5.

VARIATION: Before they begin doing their report,
students write their plan for the content for you to
check.

**Students now do Unit Test 1 on p168 of this book.
The answers are on p214.**

2 Thrills and frights

SPEAKING p18

❶ Do 1 as a teacher-class focus, discussing the difference between rational and irrational fears, then allow time for pairs to order the pictures in 2 before they report back to the class. Elicit possible cognates in 3 such as 'claustrophobia', 'arachnophobia', etc., pointing out the /f/ sound of 'ph' in phobia, as well as the form *afraid/scared/frightened/terrified of* (the dark, flying, thunder, snakes, heights and so on).

WORKBOOK: Vocabulary p12.

❷ Elicit the answers and ask the class if they think any of these are typical of America or are more general fears.

FOLLOW-UP: Elicit fears that have not already been mentioned, such as cats, old age or speed. Depending on the culture(s) the students are from, and current events, you may wish to develop areas such as war, drought, famine or political/social instability. Get students to give some historical or cultural background to explain them, and find out whether or not people tend to talk openly about their fears, and why.

❸ Ask the class what they think. A range of answers is possible: a need for excitement, bravado, bonding in a shared danger, the challenge of overcoming fears, 'it's great when it stops', etc. It is important to elicit here, at the very least, 'rollercoaster' and 'big dipper'. 'Water jump' and 'haunted house' also feature later in the unit.

FURTHER PRACTICE: Vocabulary p111.

READING: multiple matching and multiple choice pp18–19

❶ This exercise practises the format of FCE Reading Part 1, but with highlighted clues to show students the kind of information they will need to look for in the exam paper. Point out that there may be more than one clue to each answer.

> **ANSWERS:** 1E 2D 3C 4H 5G 6B 7A

WORKBOOK: Part 1 pp14–15; Focus On Reading p72.

❷ The multiple-choice questions practise the format of FCE Reading Part 2 and take students through the main points of the text. Students are guided to the relevant information by the Help box. When the class have finished the task, check their answers.

> **ANSWERS:** 1D 2A 3A 4A 5C 6B

FOLLOW-UP 1: Ask the class to identify the exact words in the text that helped them decide on their answers. If time allows, also go through the

distractors. In question 1, for example, students explain that The Forbidden Valley is the name given to the exact place where Nemesis is, that Alton Towers is a theme park and that The Corkscrew is an older rollercoaster in the same park. You might want to explain that *stall* in *stall turn* means a sudden stop.

FOLLOW-UP 2: In this optional Vocabulary activity, students use both the contexts in the Reading text and the definitions given here to work out the meanings of the words:
Match these words from the text with definitions 1–10, as in the example:
to bury (line 9) to hang (line 13) loop (line 5)
to plunge (line 38) to claim (line 6) track (line 12)
to house (line 12) to rock (line 23) roll (line 18)
to bend (line 23)

   Example: *to blast*: destroy by using explosives
 1 .... : make something become curved
 2 .... : enclose in order to protect
 3 .... : rails for trains or fairground rides
 4 .... : a circular movement
 5 .... : say something is a fact
 6 .... : be held only at the top
 7 .... : a curve that crosses itself
 8 .... : put in the ground and cover
 9 .... : shake from side to side
10 .... : suddenly go down

> **ANSWERS:**
> 1 bend 2 house (elicit the /z/ pronunciation of 'house' as a verb) 3 track 4 roll 5 claim
> 6 hang 7 loop 8 bury 9 rock 10 plunge

FURTHER PRACTICE: Nouns and verbs p112.

❸ Do this as a class discussion or in pairs, asking for volunteers to describe any particularly good rides they have been on, or other ways of being scared for fun.

WORKBOOK: Focus On Reading p72.

GRAMMAR: the indefinite and definite article p20

❶❷❸ Possibly give other uses of *a* such as: a single countable noun after *with* or *without* – working without a break, the job was done with a computer; parts of the body – he broke a finger, twisted an ankle, etc. (but perhaps elicit why 'he hurt a nose' is unacceptable).

> **ANSWERS:** 1 1d 2c 3a 4b

Rule for *an*: b – an umpire, a hobby, an MA, an honour, a uniform, an honest answer. Stress that it is the sound, not the spelling, which is important. Further examples: an RP Accent, a unique feeling, an heiress, etc.

COMMON ERRORS

First elicit the answer and then tell students to check with the Grammar Reference. Answer: *The thief was sent to prison for 10 years.* In common expressions, such as *at school, in hospital, to church* there is no definite article after the preposition, particularly when we are referring to the normal use of a building or other place.

4 Students work in pairs. Check they have identified all the errors before matching them with the rules. Point out that in a few cases, more than one rule can be given as the answer.

ANSWERS:
 1 I think the (2.3) most exciting game in the (2.2) world is (3.4) cricket.
 2 He is working as a (1.3) shop assistant in (3.3) Oxford Street.
 3 Everyone just wants to have (3.2/3.4) fun at the (2.2) seaside.
 4 The (2.6) train from Madrid to Seville travels at nearly 200 miles an (1.4) hour.
 5 She's doing an (1.1) MA in modern languages at a (1.1/1.2) well-known university.
 6 You don't often hear bands playing the (2.5) violin at (3.1) rock concerts.
 7 She reckons the (2.7) parachute was the (2.3) best thing ever invented.
 8 Some say it is an (1.2) expensive sport, but the (2.4/3.4) equipment can be cheap.
 9 We were hit by a (1.1) storm and floods. Two days later the (2.1) storm ended.
 10 To go to the (2.4) same place it happened would be a (1.2) bad mistake.

VARIATION: With a weak class, you could tell them first to underline the nouns in each sentence.

5 Students work individually and then compare answers in pairs. Go through as a class.

ANSWERS: 1 0 2 the 3 a 4 0 5 0 6 0
7 a 8 the 9 the 10 the 11 the 12 an
13 the 14 the 15 the 16 the 17 0 18 a
19 0 20 a

WORKBOOK: The indefinite and definite article p16.

USE OF ENGLISH: multiple-choice cloze *p21*

1 This section introduces FCE Paper 3 Part 1. After the class have studied the various kinds of collocation (point out that other collocations are possible in the examples, for instance *television featured/covered* and *badly hurt*), elicit more of each type, possibly writing some of them up on the board. Questions 1–8 could be done fairly quickly as a teacher-class focus, but pause on any that are typical mistakes made by your students and get them to make a special note.

You may also want to ask the class which type of collocation each one is.

ANSWERS:
 1 interested in (preposition)
 2 riding a motorbike (verb + noun)
 3 on foot (preposition)
 4 last long (verb + noun)
 5 low safety standards (adjective + noun)
 6 holds the world record (verb + noun)
 7 consists of (preposition)
 8 take FC (verb + noun)

2 1 Students work alone on this gist-reading activity. You may want to give clues to the source (article in the travel section of a newspaper), for instance pointing out the advice to visitors at the end. Elicit some suggestions for a title.

2 This focuses on collocations and makes the gap-filling task a little easier by highlighting complete expressions. Students work individually, then compare answers with their partners and finally with the class.

ANSWERS: 1B 2B 3A 4B 5D 6A 7B 8B 9D 10A
11B 12A 13B 14A 15B

WORKBOOK: Multiple-choice cloze p16.

FURTHER PRACTICE: Multiple-choice cloze p112.

EXAM STUDY GUIDE *p22*

This focuses on listening strategies. Stress the importance of doing **a** and **c**: activities 1 and 2 below are practical examples of these. Ask the class why the other three are not good ideas. Possible reasons: **b** there isn't time, and there's no link between the four parts anyway; **d** concentrate more on overall meaning, main points, attitudes, etc.; **e** concentrate throughout both opportunities to hear it.

LISTENING *p22*

1 Students work in pairs and groups, thinking about all aspects of the subject. You may want to prompt with aspects such as equipment, fears, sort of people. When their lists are finished, elicit ideas and put the useful words on the board. The scientific name *speleology* may be a cognate.

2 Stress to the class the importance of developing the habit of asking themselves prediction questions before every listening task, thus creating a framework of what they will hear.

Let students discuss what they already know in pairs first: caves in their country/equipment needed/the kind of people who go caving/the dangers/the fears, etc. Then elicit these and also the answers to the three questions: two speakers; perhaps she feels 'cold', 'wet', 'happy', 'tired', possibly 'exhausted', 'excited', even 'relieved', etc.; numbers/measurements/geographical location. Check that everyone understands the language used in the questions, possibly highlighting *ladder* and *depth*.

❸ This task follows FCE Part 2 format (taking notes on the main points). Play twice.

> **ANSWERS:** 1 childhood   2 heights   3 floor/ground   4 100 feet   5 water   6 water
> 7 weather   8 back   9 south-east France
> 10 5,000 feet/about 1 mile

❹ Pairs or groups discuss first, then report back to the class on their feelings and any interesting sports that have come up. Encourage the use of expressions heard on the tape.

WORKBOOK: Part 2 pp13–14; Focus On Listening p96.

TAPESCRIPT

Interviewer: Here we are on a very damp and windswept hillside somewhere near Ingleton in the Yorkshire Dales, and I have with me Karen Jackson, who is a keen potholer. Karen – the first and most obvious question: why caves?

Karen: Well it all goes back to childhood days when I used to do a bit of rock climbing, and I wasn't too bad at it – the only trouble was that whenever I got more than about 20 feet off the ground and looked down I started to get all dizzy and panicky so I more or less gave it up. Then one very dark night we were out hill walking and somehow we ended up on the edge of a kind of a precipice, so someone of course made a joke about me being scared of heights and I just said 'I'm OK as long as I can't see the bottom' and everyone laughed and that was that. But later I talked about it to a friend and she said 'Why don't you try caving then?'

Interviewer: But surely there are some pretty long drops underground too?

Karen: Oh sure, but the point is that when you've got any real depth below you the light from your lamp just won't reach the floor so it doesn't worry you!

Interviewer: And how exactly do you get down that far? And perhaps more importantly, how do you get back up again?

Karen: Well for pitches – drops – under about 100 feet we use wire-rope ladders which are quite easy to carry rolled up, and for greater depths than that we go down on a single rope. Obviously we leave them in place for when we come back up again, though climbing using a rope is hard work and takes practice.

Interviewer: I'm still not convinced, though, of *why* you do it? What's the appeal?

Karen: I think in my case it's partly using a skill I've got that otherwise would be wasted, but also it's because there's a special world down there. It's so clean and quiet – just the sound, sometimes, of rushing water – and the temperature stays just about the same all year round. And you reach caverns and when you look around everything's shiny in those limestone colours, but really I suppose the biggest thrill is the feeling of achieving something. Especially when you've come through passages with water right up to the roof, where you just have to hold your breath, duck right down into the flooded section and hope you find air on the other side.

Interviewer: And what happens if you don't?

Karen: Well any sensible caver will have studied underground maps of the system and will know exactly the distances involved and what the water level usually is.

Interviewer: But couldn't that change, and trap people?

Karen: Yes, it can, and that's why you have to keep a careful eye on the weather forecast before you go underground. A sudden thunderstorm and a whole system can flood in minutes.

Interviewer: And the inevitable question: what about claustrophobia? Half a mountain on top of you and the risk of getting stuck in a hole two feet across with the water rising? Don't you ever think about what *might* happen? Earthquakes, for instance?

Karen: Well, as I said you have to take precautions, like always letting someone above ground know when you're due back, but really you have to be rational about these things and remind yourself that the rock you're going through probably hasn't moved for millions of years so it's not very likely to start doing so now! And if the worst came to the worst and you did get into difficulties, well, the cave rescue people are marvellous – though you'd feel a bit silly if you had to be dragged out feet first by a bunch of blokes!

Interviewer: Yes, right, not a happy thought. But tell me – just one last question – what's your dream cave, a sort of inverted Everest I suppose, that you'd really like to explore?

Karen: I think that would probably be the Reseau Jean Bernard, in south-east France.

Interviewer: And how deep's that?

Karen: 5,000 feet, about a mile.

Interviewer: Thanks, Karen – and good luck!

SPEAKING *p23*

❶❷❸ If necessary, explain the situation in the exam, with one examiner directing the conversation while another assesses. Point out that in Part 3 the candidates are largely on their own, and should where possible address their comments only to each other. Stress that the aim is not the product – successfully completing the task – but the process: speaking English effectively while trying to do so. Check all the expressions on the map are understood. Ensure students follow the guidelines given. When they have finished, ask the class about any difficulties they had with vocabulary, etc., and provide feedback on what you have heard.

FOLLOW-UP: Extend this activity into a Speaking Part 4 (a three-way discussion of matters related to the theme of Part 3), either in pairs (the two candidates) or in groups of three, with a third student taking the role of examiner. He or she could ask questions such as: What safety precautions should climbers/cavers/walkers take? What equipment is needed? Why do people go on survival courses/climb mountains/go hill walking? Which of these activities are popular in your country? Where do people go to do them?

WORKBOOK: Focus On Speaking p104.

PHRASAL VERBS: *get* *p23*

Begin by eliciting examples of phrasal verbs and putting them on the board. You could give a further example by asking a few students 'What time did you *get up* this morning?' They do the exercise individually, and then compare answers in pairs and with the class.

> **ANSWERS:** 1 got into 2 get up 3 get off
> 4 get up to 5 getting on 6 get together
> 7 got away with 8 got over 9 get through
> 10 get by

WORKBOOK: Phrasal verbs *get* p13.

VOCABULARY: films *p24*

This activity introduces words that will be needed later in the unit, including lexis from the Reading text on the next page. Students could use dictionaries or check with others in groups. Highlight pronunciation, and word stress as you go through the answers with the class, allowing time for students to write in the words.

> **ANSWERS:** 1 pictures 2 performance 3 shot
> 4 reviews 5 scene 6 edit 7 script 8 plot
> 9 screen 10 suspense 11 release 12 audience
> 13 casting

FOLLOW-UP: Elicit and/or introduce more film expressions.

READING: multiple choice and gapped text *pp24–25*

❶ The aim here is to activate words from Vocabulary and to prepare students for the Reading text. Find out which are the most popular films among the class as a whole.

❷ As sometimes happens in Part 4 of FCE Reading, this activity uses multiple-choice questions (in this case 1–4 respectively) to identify the source, choose a title, infer and focus on the writer. The difference here is that students have to justify their choice in writing rather than just use inspired guesswork.

> **ANSWERS:** 1C 2B 3C 4B

VARIATION: Discuss the differences between the four text-types in question 1, and ask who has seen the films in question 3. Ask someone to give a quick description of *Alien*.

WORKBOOK: Focus On Reading p72.

❸ This activity practises the format of Part 3 FCE Reading. To focus on cohesive devices, clues are highlighted in the text and the task of matching them to the sentences added. Students work individually, check in pairs and then with the class.

> **ANSWERS:** 1D 2B 3G 4A 5E 6C

❹ This activity (following on from Phrasal Verbs on p23) practises two-part verbs from the Reading text by getting students to match them with their meanings, but with the added help of different contexts (including topic-related vocabulary such as *director* and *cartoons*). Students work in pairs. Encourage them to look back at the text for further clues to the meanings.

> **ANSWERS:** 1e 2g 3d 4h 5b 6c 7f 8a

❺ Let pairs discuss, or elicit the answers.

GRAMMAR: participle adjectives *p26*

❶ Go through the examples (the *-ing* ones are from the Reading text on page 18–19) and get the class to work in pairs, before eliciting the words (*amazing*, *tired*, etc.) that may cause spelling problems. Write these on the board.

FOLLOW-UP: Elicit more words that form adjectives in the same way, such as *relax*, *confuse*, *horrify*, *disgust*, *embarrass* (check these last two are not false cognates), *depress*, *irritate*, *exhaust*, *satisfy*, *refresh*, *infuriate*, *threaten*, *tempt* (point out this has a positive *-ing* form but the *-ed* form can be negative).

❷ The skill required is similar to that of Use of English Part 5 (word formation), but here the students have to choose the word from the list before they modify it. This should be done in pairs and then checked as a class.

> **POSSIBLE ANSWERS:**
> 1 thrilling 2 alarming 3 amazing
> 4 fascinating 5 tired 6 bored 7 surprised
> 8 exciting 9 disappointed 10 astonishing

❸ This exercise gives an opportunity for active use. Pairs compare work. Check for errors.

WRITING: an informal letter *pp26–27*

❶ Elicit more features of informal letters, such as: missing out pronouns and other words; exclamation marks; PS at the end, etc.

❷ The focus is on key factors in letter-writing that will be specified in the instructions for FCE Paper 2: why, how, who and to whom. Point out that *appropriate style* in this case means informally, and highlight other important words in the instructions: *first time, friend, did, felt* and *letter*. Elicit possible deficiencies in task completion if any of these words is ignored. For example, not to write about something done 'for the first time' could produce a text about something the student often does, written entirely in the present simple instead of the anticipated past forms.

Students work in pairs to find and correct the mistakes. You may want to tell them that they are all examples of the grammar points presented in this Unit (four articles and two participle adjectives). Tell them to ignore the spaces above and below the text for the moment. Go through the answers with the class.

> **ANSWERS:** amazing; a very friendly instructor; the grass; terrified; on the ground; it was wonderful fun

❸ Students work in pairs. Elicit the answers and put the answers to **b** on the board. Point out that there are of course other ways of expressing the same ideas and elicit some, such as **a** 'I'm writing to tell you about…', **b** 'to start with/then/later/afterwards' and **c** 'I'm looking forward to hearing from you'.

> **ANSWERS:** 1 I must tell you about…
> 2 First/Then/After that/At last
> 3 Please write soon…

❹ Ask which are the more informal ones and which would be appropriate for the letter in activity 2 (*Dear* (first name); *Yours/Best wishes/Regards/Love*). Point out that *Love from* is possible. Students then fill in the spaces individually. Check what – and where – they have written. Make sure they haven't, for example, put their name at the top right, their surname before their first name or the name of the town and the date at the bottom of the page.

❺ This exercise practises matching informal letter formulaic expressions with their functions, and should be done in pairs. Go through the answers with the class.

> **ANSWERS:** a4 b6 c1 d2 e8 f3 g5 h7

❻ Again students work in pairs, before checking as a class.

> **ANSWERS:** 1h 2b 3f 4d 5a 6e 7c 8g

❼ Students work individually. Collect in their work. Their comments about their own progress might provide some useful feedback.

WORKBOOK: Writing p17; Focus On Writing p80.

STUDY CHECK *p27*

❶ This exercise gives freer oral practice based on the theme of the Unit. You might want to ask some pairs which films or programmes they talked about, and find out what the rest of the class think of them.

❷ A final letter-writing task gives students – especially shy ones – an opportunity to ask any questions they were afraid to ask in open class, and can provide more feedback. Decide what degree of formality/informality you would prefer in students' letters, and tell them.

Students now do Unit Test 2 on p169 of this book. The answers are on p214.

3 Looking ahead

SPEAKING *p28*

❶ This should be done fairly quickly, as the exam technique of comparing photos is dealt with in more depth on p33. Be ready to supply vocabulary where necessary (*test tubes*, etc.). The picture on the left shows Jerry Lewis in *The Nutty Professor*.

❷ Encourage pairs to make a list of scientists, such as Frankenstein, and prompt with the names of other films and TV programmes they might have seen, such as *The Lost World*, *The X-Files* or *The Outer Limits*. A lot of countries still show episodes of old series like *The Avengers*, which often include just the kind of stereotyped scientists mentioned in the Reading text.

VARIATION: With young students, ask them to compare the pictures with the way they study science at school. Prompt, if necessary, with questions: What is/was the most interesting thing about school science? What kind of equipment do/did the school labs have? Which of the photos is more similar to them? etc.

READING: multiple matching *pp28–29*

❶ Explain to the class that the purpose of this exercise is to activate in English the same reading skills that they would probably use in their first language before beginning to read an article. Whenever students are about to read a text, remind them to ask themselves questions about their existing knowledge of the topic and to try to predict the content.

❷ Remind the class that this kind of help is not given in the exam and that it is here to demonstrate the sort of thing they will have to look for.

VARIATION: Before they start reading, ask the class which of these films they have seen, and elicit brief comments on how they remember their portrayal of scientists.

ANSWERS: 1F 2B 3D 4C 5G 6A 7 and 8 C/D 9G
10A 11E 12 and 13 A/B

❸ Pairs fill in the definitions, using both contexts – the text and sentences 1–7 – as clues. Highlight the pronunciation of any likely to cause difficulties, such as *research* and *breakthrough*.

ANSWERS: 1 authentic   2 genetics
3 breakthrough   4 absent-minded
5 unconcerned   6 jargon   7 research

❹ Do as a discussion at pair, group or class level.

WORKBOOK: Part 3 p20; Focus On Reading p72.

USE OF ENGLISH: word formation *p30*

NOTE: Many English affixes may be cognates, or translate directly from the students' first language, but some very common ones like -*less* (often mistakenly assumed to have a comparative rather than absolute meaning) and *out*- (sometimes taken to be a reference to place) can confuse.

❶ Go through these with the class and elicit more examples (*useless*, *postmodern*, *actor*, etc.).

ANSWERS: -*less* negative; *post*- after (time); *non*-negative; -*or* person

❷ Pairs put the affixes into the sets and then report back to the class.

ANSWERS:
1 Negative: un-, dis-, anti-, il-, in-, ir-, im-
2 Size or amount: out-, under-, micro-, over-, hyper-, super-, mega-
3 People: -ee, -er, -eer
4 Time: pre-, post-
5 Positions: trans-, inter-

❸ Go through the names of all the planets, practising the pronunciation (the words themselves may be cognates in the students' L1, but they might be pronounced quite differently).

Most answers have affixes already presented, apart from *technological* (see Vocabulary page 32).

ANSWERS: 1 impossible   2 countless   3 basic
4 successful   5 outer   6 unknown   7 endless
8 scientists   9 outlive   10 disappear

FOLLOW-UP: Elicit the meanings of the affixes that are used, and ask the class what changes in part of speech have been made.

ANSWERS: 0 p, negative, adj   1 p, negative, adj
2 s, negative, adj   3 s, adj   4 s, adj   5 s, position, adj   6 p, negative, adj   7 s, negative, adj
8 s, people, noun   9 p, amount, verb
10 p, negative, verb

WORKBOOK: Focus On Use of English p88.

GRAMMAR: the future *p31*

The first example is taken from the word formation text above.

❶ 1 Let students study 1–9 briefly, then ask for the answers.

ANSWERS: 1 future continuous
2 present continuous   3 *will* future
4 future perfect   5 *going to* future
6 present simple   7 present simple
8 *will* future   9 future perfect continuous

VARIATION: Refer students back to the use of the present simple and present continuous for future meanings in Unit 1, p10. Then elicit an example of each of the six tenses here with future meaning.

2 Tell pairs to work these out, then go through the answers with the class, possibly eliciting more examples. Point out that there may be more than one answer in some cases, for example 7 could be b or d.

SUGGESTED ANSWERS:
1c   2b   3f   4a   5g   6e   7b/d   8i   9h

2 Point out that 'error' is used here to include expressions that do not sound natural. Students work in pairs. Then ask why each (except 6) is wrong and elicit the reason why the mistakes in numbers 1 and 10 give the wrong impression of the speaker's intentions.

In 1 it appears that he or she has already made a decision. In 10 it appears that a spontaneous negative decision (*I'll wash my hair*) has been made in response to an invitation or suggestion.

ANSWERS: 1 I'll go   2 will be appearing   3 you finish/you've finished   4 leaves   5 I'll buy/I'm going to buy   6 correct   7 are in lower   8 I'll be using   9 he'll try   10 I'm washing/I'm going to wash

3 Point out that these are in Use of English Part 3 format. Ask why, for the first question, *Linda will have her sixteenth birthday on Wednesday* is wrong (the answer uses six words).

ANSWERS: 1 will be sixteen on   2 you planning to do anything/anything for   3 you after I talk/after I've talked   4 think they will be arriving   5 be 2020 before we see   6 have been studying it

4 These could be done orally in pairs or else students could write down their comments. You may want to elicit some or all of their answers, asking the class what they think are the best ideas, suggestions or excuses.
Likely forms: 1 …does…leave…   2 I'll be (-ing)…
3 I'm (-ing)…   4 I'm going to…/I'll…   5 I'm/we're going to…   8 I'll have…

NOTE: Encourage the use of *probably, possibly, perhaps*, etc. Depending on class level, you might also want to introduce the forms *I might/may/should be doing* and *I may/might/should have done*.

WORKBOOK: The future p21.

VOCABULARY: affixes *p32*

1 Go through these quickly with the class. The meanings of most of them should already be known,

but the important thing is that students associate each of the suffixes with one part of speech, and also that they are given more word formation practice.

ANSWERS: 1 adjectives   2 nouns   3 adverbs
4 adjective
electrical: electricity, electrically
industrial: industrially, industrialization, industrialist, industrialism
visual: visually, visualize
technological: technologically, technologist
employment: unemployment, employer, employee
environment: environmentally, environmentalist, environmentalism
equipment: equip
apparently: apparent
automatically: automatic
particularly: particular
powerful: power, powerfully

2 Let pairs study these and then check their answers. Elicit the word meaning 'inability to sleep' (*insomnia* – used in Listening, possibly a cognate).

FOLLOW-UP: Elicit or give more examples of the affixes not previously practised, for example: *portable – drinkable, acceptable* or *faulty – noisy, hairy*.

LISTENING *p32*

Make sure everyone understands these three points, by using the exam task in 2 as an example if necessary.

1 Pairs discuss. Take any questions and then check the answers: 4 and 7 before, and 1, 2, 3, 5 and 6 while.

2 Students work individually. You might want to give the class an example of suggestion 7 in practice, by eliciting words connected with each of the three appliances in Question 1; words actually used in the recording – such as *pocket/handbag, sound, call, speak, dial, number* and *hands* – may well come up. Play the recording right through (each situation is repeated).

ANSWERS: 1C   2B   3A   4A   5A   6C

VARIATION: Stress the importance of bearing in mind all of points 1–7. With a strong class you could also suggest they pay particular attention to the following:
Question 1: 7, Question 2: 7, Question 3: 3, Question 4: 5, Question 5: 2, Question 6: 5.

WORKBOOK: Focus On Listening p96.

TAPESCRIPT

One
This is a particularly neat one here. It'll fit easily into your pocket or handbag and weighs just 50 grams, but it's powerful enough and the sound quality is excellent. To make a call all you have to do is just say the name of the person you want to speak to and it dials the number automatically, which is great if for some reason you've got your hands full!

Two

This full-time position consists of writing reports and scientific articles about new medicines. Candidates should have a university degree in biochemistry and have experience in the writing of scientific material in English. He or she will be fluent in spoken and written English and also have a good level of Spanish. Knowledge of either Greek or Polish would be an asset.

Three

If you sometimes feel that dropping off to sleep is a bit like turning a switch off, then that is very much what it is like, according to recent research. It seems that in the part of the brain called the hypothalamus there's a group of nerve cells that behave quite differently from all the others when we nod off, in that they actually become more active. Their job, apparently, is to turn off the systems in the brain that operate when we are awake – so if you suffer from insomnia, it could be that this switch is faulty.

Four

A couple of years ago I always used to take my laptop on the train with me, but then I realized that it may be the fashion but the thing was fragile and underpowered – and wherever I went. I was at risk of losing thousands of pounds worth of equipment. So one day I decided to forget about the glorified typewriter and move on to much simpler word-processing technology: a bag of books, a handful of biros and a stack of lined A4 paper.

Five

– 'Have you got one of those special tapes, you know one of those you're supposed to run when the picture on the telly's gone all fuzzy?'
– 'Oh, right, a head cleaner cassette – but are you sure that's what you need?'
– 'Yeah 'cause it says here that after 200 hours of playing tapes you should use one – and we've been watching a different film every night for nearly two years now.'

Six

If we continue with this mad race for more and more technological progress, without a thought for the unfairness it is bound to cause, then we're going to end up with a new class division just as bad as that brought about by the industrial revolution in the nineteenth century. Except that this time the people with the computers in the rich countries won't even know that the poor exist because they will spend all their time communicating by PC with other rich people.

SPEAKING *p33*

Go through the introduction, checking that everyone understands the exam procedure.

❶ The topic follows on from that of the last Listening text. Further practice is given with future forms. You may want to monitor conversations, providing feedback when they have finished.

❷ Monitor as above.

WORKBOOK: Focus On Speaking p104.

LISTENING *p34*

❶ The aim is to encourage students always to think about the topics they are about to hear discussed on the recording. Encourage the use of different ways of expressing opinions, pointing out the relative formality of *In my opinion* and *I believe (that)* but the informality of *If you ask me*.

VARIATION: Give more examples of predictions, perhaps a more optimistic one:
'I think we'll do all our shopping by e-mail. We'll look at the goods on the shop's website, make our choice and then send our order, which will be delivered to our house.'
Or one that foresees little change in the future:
'If you ask me, most people will still be going to the same shops and markets they always went to.'

❷ Emphasize that the aim is successful completion of the exam task, and that listening for similar predictions to their own is a means of helping to achieve this, not a separate activity.

ANSWERS: 1D 2C 3E 4F 5B

WORKBOOK: Part 3 p19; Focus On Listening p96.

❸ Allow time for pairs to discuss and then do a quick class round-up.

FOLLOW-UP: Ask the class which predictions they agreed/disagreed with most strongly.

TAPESCRIPT

One

I certainly think that before too long we'll see the results of research into fabrics that reduce stress and others that contain scent, as well as materials that have medicinal properties. Manufacturers will be able to do this by putting tiny, micron-sized bubbles into, say, dresses or shirts, and filling them with 'smart' technologies, so that they release fragrances, vitamins or other medications that can be absorbed through our skin from the fibres.

Two

All this equipment to keep you in touch with the outside world has its price. You'll continually have to be buying the latest technologies and paying for expensive updates if you want to send and receive text, pictures and sound at full speed. You'll find yourself saving up all the time to be able to afford it, while connection charges keep going up and the government thinks up more and more ways of taxing the airwaves.

Three

Technology will allow us to escape from the city to the country and do our jobs there. With less commuting, the metropolitan centres will free themselves from the human gridlock of the nine-to-fivers. Perhaps one day we will look back, laugh and shake our heads when we remember that, as part of every weekday, we used to waste so much time and energy trapped in little steel boxes that took us to and from our offices. We even had a name for it: 'rush hour'.

Four
People will choose equipment to fit their lifestyles and needs, and makers will respond to that demand. The consumer will have control over everything. Ovens will become voice-activated so that we only have to touch the voicebox panel at the top of the device and say: 'Lasagne for four and an apricot flan, please.' Five minutes later, a computerised voice will announce: 'Meal prepared'.

Five
I don't think there'll be that much change really, apart from making space for the obligatory mod cons. Our lifestyle may be changing but the problem is that at the root of our deepest instinct is the desire to live in a rose-covered cottage; so the sorts being built, and apparently most in demand, have traditional designs and layouts. We'll still be living in a way that would be readily recognizable to the ancient Romans.

VOCABULARY: suffixes *p34*

❶ Before students begin, elicit the pronunciation of subjects 1–10, ensuring correct word stress: bi<u>o</u>logy, <u>chem</u>istry, etc. You may need to help with the pronunciation of cognates that are pronounced quite differently in the students' L1. Elicit the answers, with correct word stress, when pairs have finished.

> **ANSWERS:** 1 biologist 2 chemist 3 physicist
> 4 geologist 5 ecologist 6 mathematician
> 7 astronomer 8 engineer 9 mechanic
> 10 computer scientist

VARIATION: Depending on the age and/or level of the class, you might want to add more subjects such as *anthropology*, *biochemistry* and so on.

❷ This could be done in groups. Encourage the use of a range of future forms: *will be doing*, *will have done* as well as *will*. Point out that their notes will be needed for Writing, which follows.

WORKBOOK: Vocabulary p18.

WRITING: a discursive composition *p35*

❶ You may want students first to look at the sample composition on p163. Pairs study the text and replace the sentences: 1B 2C 3A. Check comprehension before moving on by asking questions like 'What should you put in the third paragraph?' If necessary, explain the drawback of arguing point by point as follows: it often involves using a lot of contrastive sentences that require a wide range of linking expressions to avoid becoming highly repetitive.

❷ Students work individually, following the advice in the nine points.

Point out that the reader is specified as 'the teacher', which is sometimes the case in FCE questions of this type, so tell them what style you want them to write in. For more linking expressions, see Unit 14 Writing (Discursive composition – opinion). You may wish to suggest to students that, if they find it difficult to think of ideas on both sides of the argument (particularly any they personally disagree with) in the exam itself, it may be best for them to choose another question to answer.

VARIATION: You may want to prompt students with the following:
Think of the good and bad things that scientific and technological progress may bring about. Consider the branches of science and technology listed in Vocabulary 1 above, and how they might affect aspects of life such as education, sports and hobbies, travel, social and family relationships, the environment, health, language learning, entertainment and the media. Think back to topics A–F in Listening above. Also consider the possibility, mentioned by the last speaker in Listening, that not a lot will change in the way that many people live.

WORKBOOK: Writing pp22–23; Focus on Writing p80.
FURTHER PRACTICE: *too* and *enough* p115.

COMMON ERRORS

> *I think the future will be enough different.*
> The correct form is: *I think the future will be quite different.*

GRAMMAR: *make* and *do* *p36*

❶ Elicit the answers: 1 do 2 make (which could also be explained by saying 'we *make* something that wasn't there before').

❷ Students do this activity quickly, as they will either know them or they won't. Go through the answers with the class.

> **ANSWERS:** make a discovery   do harm
> make a promise   make certain   do damage
> make an attempt   make a plan   make an excuse
> do better   do their best   do an experiment
> make a choice   make a suggestion   make progress
> make notes   make an effort

❸ Students work alone. Elicit answers and/or check written work, then ask if they know any other expression with *do* or *make*.

❹ Further practice with prefixes. These could be elicited.

> **ANSWERS:** do too much, do again, do better than (somebody else), unfasten or remove the effects of

Ask what the noun 'remake' means (it may also be used in the students' L1 for new versions of old films).

USE OF ENGLISH: open cloze
pp36–37

❶ Students are probably familiar with this task-type, but may find some of the answers to questions 1–10 surprising. Allow time for pairs to work these out, take any questions and then go through the answers.

> **ANSWERS:** 1C 2E 3D 4G 5H 6B 7A 8J 9F 10I

❷ Students work alone. This activity continues the process of encouraging students to acquire the habit of predicting text content, this time by getting them to form their own questions. Possible answers: What is its general topic? – future developments in science and technology; What kind of things do you think will be a little late? – scientific/technological breakthroughs. You could also ask: *What kind of things will its main points be?* Answer: *predictions*.

❸ Students work alone. Further practice is given with *too*, *do*, *make* and *will*. Point out that the parts of speech given here are among the most frequently tested in this task-type. Give examples if any of the terms (e.g. 'quantifier') are not known to some students. Check both the answers and part of speech of each one.

> **ANSWERS:** 1 out (phrasal verb particle)
> 2 to (preposition)   3 least (adverb)   4 however/
> though/nevertheless (adverb)   5 which (relative)
> 6 according (preposition)   7 more (quantifier)
> 8 it (pronoun)   9 on (preposition)
> 10 too (quantifier)   11 the (article)
> 12 into (preposition)   13 until/unless
> (conjunction)   14 away (phrasal verb particle)
> 15 will (modal)

The photo shows Woody Allen in *Sleeper*.

WORKBOOK: Open cloze p22; Focus On Use of English p88.

FURTHER PRACTICE: Open cloze p115.

STUDY CHECK *p37*

❶ Give pairs plenty of time to discuss these, including a change of Student A/B role if they are interacting well. Perhaps have a class roundup of volunteers' comments at the end.

❷ 1 Ensure that this is done quickly, with just a list of topics noted down. Further examples: war, pollution, crime, drugs, overcrowding.
  2 You may want to mention that one of the topics they choose will also be set as a writing task later, as this may affect their preferences. With a weak class, prompt with expressions such as:
Yes, but… I know, but… I'm not so sure,… But don't you think…?

❸ Refer students back to Writing on p35 for advice on how to organize and write a 'for and against' essay.

Students now do Unit Test 3 on p170 of this book. The answers are on p214.

4 Taking it easy

SPEAKING AND VOCABULARY p38

1 Let students think about these questions, discuss them in pairs or groups and note down their answers. Then when they look at the text in Reading below, they can compare with the UK figures given for men and women (for categories **a**, **b** and **d**).

2 Students write down their answers. Go through them with the class, allowing time for students to add those they hadn't thought of. If students don't know the English names, getting them to describe board games such as Ludo or Snakes and Ladders can provide useful speaking practice.

If necessary, prompt as follows: music – playing the guitar, outdoor activities – rambling, books – science fiction, keeping pets – looking after a cat, board games – draughts (chess is featured on p40), card games – poker (the name may be used in the students' L1), electronic games – CD Rom, Game Boy, etc. Students then find out which is the most popular in their group by taking it in turns to ask the others about each category. You may want groups to report back to the class to find out which are the most popular overall.

WORKBOOK: Vocabulary p24.

3 It is important that students do part 1 quite quickly, so remind them not to spend too long trying to think of an example for every one. Allow time for them to draw up lists, compare and try to convince their partners that they would enjoy the same kind of reading. Don't encourage discussion of individual books at this stage as this is the focus of Reading 1 below.

NOTE: Asking the class about their overall likes and dislikes could provide useful information if you are thinking of recommending certain types of free-time reading during the course.

READING: multiple matching pp38–39

1 Students work in pairs, practising question forms. Suggest that they look at the photographs for ideas: do they read in any of those places? If there is time, you could ask the class for the names of any books or other reading material that students have particularly enjoyed, and encourage others to make a note of the details.

FOLLOW-UP: If you feel the class need more practice with prediction work, tell them to look at the title of the text and the two lines below it. Then they ask their partners what they think the article will be about. Ask the class what the words *read* and *page-turners* tell them about the meaning here of *leaf*. Also ask if anyone understands both meanings of the title, pointing out that puns are often used by writers

of articles (see Writing on p45) to attract the reader's attention.

2 Students work alone. Remind them that writing their own headings is good reading skills training.

> **SUGGESTED ANSWERS:** 1 Change your free-time habits   2 You can read wherever you are
> 3 If necessary, be brutal   4 Choose your author
> 5 You don't have to finish every book
> 6 Don't read late at night   7 What will reading do for you?

When students have suggested their own answers, give them the following headings to match.
A Don't be afraid to give up
B Treat them badly if you have to
C Is reading worth it?
D Carry a book about
E Finding the time at home
F When not to read
G Buy it, don't borrow it
H Deciding what to read
I We realize we should read

> **ANSWERS:** 1E 2D 3B 4H 5A 6F 7C

3 Do as a pair, group and/or class discussion.

WORKBOOK: Focus On Reading p72.

EXAM STUDY GUIDE

Give help where necessary, for example with the names of books written by authors they mention, how easy they are to read, where to find them, etc. You could write up on the board the addresses of English bookshops, libraries, etc., and might also want to suggest they try books on audio cassette. The answer to 7, given that FCE can use texts from a wide variety of sources, is virtually any kind of reading material, though preferably it should be just a little above the student's current level so that he or she practises a range of word attack and text attack skills.

VARIATION: With a class that has experience of working with readers, ask them what grade would suit them, for example 2,000, 3,000, 4,000 or 5,000 headwords. These numbers of headwords (i.e. the vocabulary used) correspond approximately to those used in Grades 2–5 of the *Oxford Progressive English Readers*, designed for teenagers/young adults from Intermediate level (Grade 1) to Advanced (Grade 5).

GRAMMAR: frequency adverbs *p40*

❶ If there is time, elicit more examples and put them on the board or OHP. Let pairs work on deciding the rules.

ANSWERS: usually 1 before the main verb 2 after *be* 3 after the modal, before the main verb

❷ Pairs discuss these. Feed in expressions like 'just above' and 'right below'.

ANSWERS: nearly always; generally/usually/ regularly/normally; often/frequently; sometimes; occasionally; hardly ever/rarely/seldom/almost never

❸ Elicit the names of the pieces in chess, plus key words such as 'check'. Point out that there are other possibilities to the suggested answers below, such as 2 'Usually, the first piece …' but that the <u>safest</u> place is that indicated in activity 1 and recommended in the answer. The game is chess.

SUGGESTED ANSWERS:
1 The player with the white pieces always starts.
2 The first piece to move is usually a pawn, but it could be a knight.
3 White sometimes begins by attacking the black king.
4 Black may sometimes reply by bringing its queen into play.
5 The player that loses their queen seldom wins the game.
6 After the queen, the strongest piece is generally the rook, or 'castle'.
7 The bishop can never move sideways, only diagonally.
8 When pieces threaten the king, the attacker must always say 'check'.
9 A king in a weak position rarely escapes 'checkmate' against a good player.

GRAMMAR: *must, have to and should* *p40*

❶ If necessary, give more examples of each, stressing the difference between the internal obligation, i.e. the speaker's authority in the case of 'must' and the external obligation/authority often present when 'have to' is used. The complete difference in meaning between 'mustn't' and 'don't have to' also needs to be highlighted.

ANSWERS: 1b 2a 3c 4f 5g 6e 7d

❷ You might also want to mention 'ought not to', 'are to' and 'aren't to'.

ANSWERS: a ought to   b you've got to
c needn't/don't need to/haven't got to

❸ Students do this individually. Go through the answers with the class (question 8 recycles 'worth'; 10 recycles 'give up').

POSSIBLE ANSWERS:
1 You should have lessons.
2 No, you've got to have an opponent.
3 You shouldn't spend so much.
4 You ought to take up a hobby.
5 You don't have to have a garden.
6 You mustn't do that!
7 Yes, you have to buy one.
8 No, they don't need to be very old.
9 You must get another one.
10 You haven't got to be a brilliant artist to paint.

❹ Perhaps have a class round-up of suggestions when pairs have finished.

WORKBOOK: *must, have to* and *should* p28.

COMMON ERRORS

Must you to go so soon? Modal verbs are followed by the base infinitive of a verb (without *to*) so the correct form is: *Must you go so soon?*

USE OF ENGLISH: key word transformations *p41*

Remind students that in the exam a much wider range of structures is tested and that they will not have the help given here. Emphasize the importance of correct word order in the answers.

ANSWERS: 1 are seldom   2 regularly visit his
3 hardly ever loses   4 rarely goes on
5 nearly/almost always goes fishing   6 you ought to come   7 must not take photographs
8 really have to be left   9 you don't have to
10 don't always need to

WORKBOOK: Focus On Use of English p88.

LISTENING *p42*

❶ Students work in pairs. Go through the answers with the class.

ANSWERS:
Before you listen: 2, 4, 5
While you listen: 1, 6, 7, 8, 9, 11, 12
After you listen: 3, 10

❷ Students do this quickly in pairs. Some may be cognates or international words. Go through the answers, asking for examples of those in group 1. If time allows, ask students to contrast pop and rock, chant and singing, etc.

ANSWERS:
1 kinds of music: pop opera techno reggae classical chant rock
2 words used in music: notes tune symphony rhythm chord
3 equipment for listening to music: cassette-recorder CD player

3 Students work alone. Play the recording through twice. Go through the answers and the prompts with the class.

4 Students discuss in pairs. Finish by asking volunteers to tell the class which they have chosen. If several mention the same song, ask why they think it has that effect.

WORKBOOK: Part 2 p25; Focus on Listening p96.

TAPESCRIPT

Pres: We've been hearing for what seems like a long time about the crisis in the music business: how record sales are falling, fewer recording contracts being offered, less cash available for promotion and all that kind of thing, but the fact remains that it is still a huge industry, isn't it?

Jeff: Yeah, it's massive; it's one of this country's major foreign currency earners and it provides a tremendous number of job opportunities for young people in an exciting and ever-changing world where some of them, at least, can use their creative talents to the full.

Pres: And what have been the biggest changes in recent times?

Jeff: I suppose one of the most significant ones has been the way so many different kinds of music have appeared. I mean, there used to be a few mainstreams like classical, pop and jazz, but now everything's broken up and multiplied into all sorts of different styles, so that if you go into a music store nowadays you see sections aimed at every imaginable ethnic and social group within society; from symphonies, operas and chant through salsa, blues and country to rap, techno, reggae, drum'n'bass and trip-hop.

Pres: And music's everywhere: you couldn't get away from it even if you wanted to, could you?

Jeff: Right, I mean it's there in so many places that sometimes we don't even notice it, but it's being used to make us behave in particular ways, and that worries some people.

Pres: Such as?

Jeff: Well take supermarkets, for instance. They've discovered that they can get us to buy more, and more of certain products, just by playing the right music while we shop. Or firms that get their staff to work harder by making sure they listen to the right tunes all day long.

Pres: Yes, it does sound a bit sinister.

Jeff: Well I suppose it's nothing new, really. After all, some kind of music has been used since ancient times to stop people noticing how boring their work really is, and to create a group spirit when taking on difficult tasks.

Pres: As in sports, too.

Jeff: Yes, that's right. That's why we have songs specially written for our football teams, in the hope of encouraging the players to win important matches, as well as all this singing of national anthems before international games. Have you noticed how, nowadays, every team attempts to sing louder than the other during the pre-match *God Save the Queen*, *Marseillaise*, or whatever? It's a battle cry by any other name, really.

Pres: But surely music can bring on a whole range of emotions, not just aggressive ones? I mean, restful pieces of music can help insomniacs fall asleep, some people find they can concentrate better if they listen to particular rhythms and so on.

Jeff: Yes, but the point is these forms are usually chosen by individuals because they want to alter – or intensify – their mood. And this is one of the most wonderful things about music, that you can actually change the way you feel just by putting the record of your choice on your stereo, cassette-recorder or personal CD player. As soon as you hear the first few notes, or the opening chords, they go straight to your emotions and everything around you is transformed. The world suddenly looks different and the great thing is that you, no matter how sad and lonely you were feeling, have brought it all about by yourself.

Pres: There also seems to be a close link to memory, too.

Jeff: Yeah, maybe it's the closeness of its rhythms to those of the human body in terms of heartbeat and breathing, but some rock music in particular seems to press the memory buttons, perhaps a long time after that specially sad or happy event which you associate with it. If you're in your teens you may have mixed feelings about this, but there's every likelihood that when – maybe 30 years or more from now – you hear certain songs again, you'll remember exactly where you were, how you felt and who you were with. Or who you were wishing you were with.

SPEAKING *p43*

1 If necessary, prompt with places such as lifts, supermarkets and airports; as well as when you are holding on the phone, watching TV ads and so on.

VARIATION: Play the first minute of the Listening text again and tell the class to make notes on the places and situations that are mentioned. For the second part of the task, you could feed in more vocabulary such as *hymns*, *carols* and *jingles*, and broaden the scope to include music that other people listen to, e.g. children: *lullabies*, *nursery rhymes*, etc.

2 This focus on the exam skills needed for Part 3 of FCE Speaking also provides further practice with three of the modals presented in this Unit. Students do the exercise in pairs.

> **ANSWERS:** 1 should   2 should   3 shouldn't
> 4 shouldn't   5 should   6 should   7 shouldn't
> 8 shouldn't   9 shouldn't   10 don't have to
> 11 shouldn't   12 should   13 should
> 14 shouldn't   15 don't have to

3 The advice from 2 above is applied in this Paper 5 Part 3 task. It also provides an opportunity to use expressions from Listening. If *compilations* is not a cognate in the students' L1, explain that it means things like 'Hits of the 90s', 'Twenty All-time Hip Hop Greats', etc.

WORKBOOK: Focus On Speaking p104.

READING: gapped text *pp44–45*

1 Allow time for discussion and then go through the answers with the class. Identify the singers and names of the bands if the class can't, and ask if they know any of their songs. You could also ask in what ways they have influenced modern bands. Another possible question: 'Are you fed up with hearing people of your parents' generation saying how much better music was back then?'

> **ANSWERS:** 1 David Bowie   2 The Beatles
> 3 The Rolling Stones   4 Rod Stewart
> all first famous in the 1960s

2 Discuss briefly as this topic will be dealt with in greater depth later in the Unit.

VARIATION: With a weak class, do the activity below as a pre-reading task. Write the text on the board, the OHP or a worksheet. When students have written in their answers, go through with the class. Highlight pronunciation, especially in the cases of any words borrowed from English in the students' L1.

These expressions are from the Reading text. Use each once to fill in the gaps.

hits performance tour sponsorship stage
record company single

> There was an excited audience of over 50,000
> people to watch the (1) .... by possibly the
> biggest stars of the moment in rock music. They
> played all their best-known (2) .... as well as
> their latest (3) .... , staying on (4) .... for
> more than two hours. The concert formed part of a
> world (5) .... which includes concerts in over 30
> countries. Their (6) .... expect a big
> boost to sales of their new album and (7) ....
> by a major clothes manufacturer will bring in even
> more cash.

> **ANSWERS:** 1 performance   2 hits   3 single
> 4 stage   5 tour   6 record company
> 7 sponsorship

3 Let students read this alone, then remind them of the usefulness of always looking at the example question, both to get the feel of the text and – over the course – to become familiar with correct answers. This applies to other parts of the Reading paper, too. Students do the exam task. Point out that the clues are there to train them to look for clues for themselves, and are not, of course, a feature of the exam paper. Do not take too many questions on vocabulary items at this stage, as in the exam they will almost certainly have to match headings, summaries, sentences or paragraphs without understanding every word in them. For example, it is probably sufficient for students to appreciate that *balding* in sentence A is connected with *old* and contrasts with *slim*, *hair*, etc. without having to know the exact meaning. These could be dealt with after the exam task has been done.

> **ANSWERS:** 1H 2F 3A 4D 5G 6C 7E

4 This activity helps to consolidate understanding of the main points of the text, practise multiple matching, and provide a partial model for the Writing section to follow. After pairs have done the exercise, go through the answers: paragraph 1 should be 7, 5 should be 1 and 7 should be 5.

5 This could be done in pairs or groups, with a class round-up to follow.

WORKBOOK: Part 4 pp26–27; Focus On Reading p72.

WRITING: an article *p45*

1 The Reading text is used as a model article for this focus on one of the task types in FCE Writing Part 2. Students could underline the relevant parts of the text and note down their answers. Go through them with the class.

> **POSSIBLE ANSWERS:** Beginning: to involve the
> readers   Organization: to deal with different
> aspects of the topic   Style: It is not formal
> Ending: to make readers think

VARIATION: With a strong class, ask what kind of contrast the writer uses in the title. Answer: smash hits/megabores and sixties/today.

2 Students work individually. You could check that everyone has decided who the subject of the article will be before moving on to the next activity.

3 4 Students do these alone. Their plan could be in the form of a 'rise of' mini-biography, progressing from the singer's/band's background, socio-economic and musical influences, their early days, what the student and other people like about them, their music and then their future. Stress the importance of using linking expressions to create a cohesive text. Answers to first two questions in 4: International music magazine; young people.

VARIATION: With a young class, or students who do not have much experience of writing articles, look at their plans before they start writing. Point out that paragraphs in this kind of informal article tend to be short (often covering one main point each, as in the Reading text) and arranged so as to hold the reader's interest.

5 If students do this for homework, suggest they swap completed essays for checking before the next lesson. The phrasal verb *give in* is recycled in the rubric.

WORKBOOK: Writing p29; Focus On Writing p80.

GRAMMAR: comparative and superlative forms *p46*

1 This activity requires students to complete the rules and use phrases they have already worked with as their examples. It could be done in pairs. Check everyone has the right answers.

> **ANSWERS:**
> 2 paler/larger; -r; palest/largest; -st; the finer points/their latest hits
> 3 consonant; hotter/flatter; hottest/flattest; slimmer and fitter/the biggest stars
> 4 drier/busier; driest/busiest; the easiest ones/ you're even luckier
> 5 more; more fantastic /more beautiful; most; most fantastic /most beautiful; choose the most suitable heading/more complex and challenging
> 6 less/more; least/most; better/worse; best/worst; the worst of all/CDs are better than records

Students read the explanations in the second part and ask any questions. You may want to give – or elicit – more examples.

COMMON ERRORS

You're a better musician than I. If there is no verb after the pronoun, the object pronoun must be used. The correct form is: *You're a better musician than me/I am.*

2 Students could do these in pairs or individually. Go through the answers:

> **ANSWERS:** 1 to a better concert than   2 isn't as good as   3 far more expensive than   4 isn't quite as creative

3 Students do these in pairs or groups. If there is time, elicit more sentences.

FURTHER PRACTICE: Comparatives using *the …, the …* p118.

USE OF ENGLISH: multiple-choice cloze *p47*

1 Pairs or groups discuss the question, which is answered in the text in 2.

2 This begins by looking at the example. The highlighting of collocations follows on from the main focus on this task type in Unit 2, where ten collocations were given. Students do the exercise

alone or in pairs. Go through the answers with the class and tell them to write down the collocations in their vocabulary notebooks.

> **ANSWERS:** 1C 2D 3A 4D 5C 6D 7B 8A 9A 10A 11B 12D 13B 14A 15C

VARIATION: Point out that sometimes the four choices have similar meanings, for example *journey*, *travel*, *trip* and *voyage*, but only one fits the text. Focus attention on question 1. Explain or elicit the fact that all four words mean 'people that pay attention to something', but ask what. Tell the class to match A, B, C and D with one of these: sport, radio, events, television.
Then they decide which of them best fits the context of the paragraph.

> **ANSWERS:** A events   B sport   C television D radio. Suggest students approach similar questions in future in this way.

WORKBOOK: Word formation p28; Focus On Use of English p88.

STUDY CHECK *p47*

1 1 Students do this individually. Check their written work.

2 Monitor pairs to check that the forms presented in the Unit have been assimilated, giving feedback where necessary after they have finished.

2 If necessary, point out that students are expected to compare the music from their own country with music sung in English or other foreign languages. Refer students back to the guidelines for making plans for writing articles on p45. You may want to let the class discuss the four points listed as preparation for the writing task. Another point that could be considered is whether the prices charged by foreign acts for albums, videos, concert tickets and so on are higher, and what the class think of this.

Students now do Unit Test 4 on p171 of this book. The answers are on p214.
Then they do Progress Test 1 on p183 of this book. The answers are on p217.

5 Home and away

VOCABULARY: living conditions *p48*

❶ Pairs or groups quickly make lists in each of categories 1–3. Go through with the class. The expressions given will be needed for the Reading text and/or elsewhere in the Unit. This activity could also be done in pairs or groups. Take questions and when the class have finished go through the three groups, paying attention to meaning (a *cooker* is not a person, for instance) and pronunciation (*ceiling*, *cupboard*, etc.).

> **ANSWERS:**
> 1 Places: detached house, terraced house, villa, cottage, semi-detached house, apartment.
> 2 Parts: landing, airing cupboard, ceiling
> 3 Items: mattress, freezer.

VARIATION: With a weaker class, words that also appear later in the Unit and could be introduced here include *flat*, *caravan* (1) and *fridge*, *carpets*, *dishes* (3).

WORKBOOK: Vocabulary p30.

❷ Elicit the difference in meaning: *homework* is associated with studies; *housework* with domestic chores like cleaning and washing dishes; *household* with looking after a house and the people who live there, or to refer collectively to the family or group of people who live there. The second and third words are used in Reading below.

❸ Let pairs discuss this and then elicit the answers: they all have a connection with renting property; the tenant pays rent and a deposit to the owner or landlord/landlady, bills to the phone company, etc.

FOLLOW-UP: Here is an optional speaking activity, which could be done in pairs or groups. Encourage students to think about house-sharing situations from films or TV, such as *Friends*.

1 What do you think the people who share the house in the picture might disagree about?
Think about the following, for example: *They might argue about who has which room.*
• rooms • noise • the phone • the TV • rules
• the rent • bills • music • smoking
• cleaning • washing the dishes • the bathroom
• boyfriends/girlfriends

2 Now imagine you are sharing a flat with people of your own age. Which of the things above could cause most trouble? What would you say to the people responsible?
Example: *Would you mind not making so much noise?*
Can you think of any other things that would annoy you?
Is there anything that you do which might annoy other people? Be honest!

VARIATION 1: With a weaker class, you could expand some or all of the points:
• making too much noise • taking too long in the bathroom • not cleaning the bath or shower
• playing music that you don't like • staying on the phone too long • not paying the rent • making rules that others must obey • refusing to wash the dishes • using your things without permission
• smoking in the flat • arguing over what TV channel to watch • arguing over the phone bill

VARIATION 2: With an older, or more advanced, class you could add more sources of potential conflict, e.g. not telling you about phone messages, coming in very late at night, inviting people to stay at the flat, causing danger to health or safety, parties.

FURTHER PRACTICE: Vocabulary p120.

READING: multiple choice *pp48–49*

❶ Students read individually. This follows on from Reading in Unit 2, where students choose the best of four titles. Elicit suggestions after a timed 120 seconds.

❷ You may want to explain that a part of the text is 'not tested' if none of the answers are to be found there and none of the distractors relate to that part. Point out that all the questions in this exercise test the ability to read for specific information: in the case of global, or general, questions (see p24), all of the text is of course relevant. Students do the exam task alone.

> **ANSWERS:** 1B 2A 3B 4D 5A 6A 7D 8C

VARIATION: With an advanced class you might want to add this task: read the parts in brackets, underline anything you don't understand and move on quickly. When you have finished the exercise, look back at these parts and discuss with your partner how much time you saved by not worrying about things you did not need to know.

❸ Pairs discuss. When they have finished, ask the class what they think, and whether the writer's experiences in 'Room to let' have influenced them at all!

WORKBOOK: Part 2 pp32–33; Focus On Reading p72.

GRAMMAR: past tenses *pp50–51*

❶ Allow time for students to think about each of 1–3 and/or discuss with their partners. Elicit the answers, including contracted forms (*We'd leave*, etc.) in 3, and highlight the pronunciation of past tense verb endings and the modals *used to* and *would*. Emphasize the point about not using the past continuous in 3 if L1 interference causes your students to make this mistake. Also point out that we only use *would* in this way for actions, not states.

> **ANSWERS:**
> 1 a I moved to London   b We usually left messages   c My bed was on the landing
> 2 We didn't use to leave messages; Did we use to leave messages?
> 3 a I wasn't going out with anyone   b we were sipping/she was questioning   c she was hanging

COMMON ERRORS

> *These days I (usually) stay with friends.* There is no present form of *used to*. The present simple or the present simple plus a frequency adverb is used instead.

VARIATION: With a weaker class, you may want to expand on the point about *would*. If so, give an example: We could write *We would leave messages*, but only with an expression that indicates the past, like *in those days* or *when we shared a flat*. Ask the class why. Answer: because it is clear from the context that it refers to the past, rather than being a conditional.

FOLLOW-UP: Point out that we normally pronounce *was* and *were* using their weak forms – *she was* [wəz] *hanging*, *they were* [wə] *working* – and ask when might we use their strong forms: [wɜː] and [wɒz].

> **ANSWER:** to stress the word in some way, for example to contradict somebody who says 'she wasn't hanging' or 'they weren't working'.

❷ 1 Give students no more than a couple of minutes to read this, and let them discuss the title with their partners. Reasons: spending the night far (deep) underground/having a good (deep) sleep.

VARIATION: With a strong and/or older class, use this as an example of the widespread use of puns in the titles of English articles, news reports, etc. If you have time, give more examples ('Mad cow talks in Brussels', etc.). Ask the class if the press in their country do this and, if possible, get them to translate a few examples. This will probably prove quite difficult to do, and should help create awareness of the difficulties involved in understanding the double meanings of English titles. Focus on this when you are working with authentic material, reminding students that a title (including those of FCE texts) may contain more information than first meets the eye.

2 Emphasize the need to study whole sentences before they write their answers, as these can depend on more than just the phrase where the space occurs. Students then fill in the gaps on their own. Check the answers with the class, asking for reasons where appropriate (e.g. Q1: there is no continuous form of *mean*).

> **ANSWERS:** 1 meant   2 needed   3 allowed
> 4 went   5 were   6 created   7 remained
> 8 had to   9 varied   10 was walking   11 could
> 12 hit   13 became   14 were going/had gone
> 15 woke up   16 turned into   17 was shrinking
> 18 were   19 spent   20 slept

VARIATION: With some classes, you may want to elicit approximate centigrade and metric equivalents for the measures used before students begin.

❸ Students do these alone or in pairs.

> **ANSWERS:** 1 used to live there
> 2 she would always laugh   3 use to live in that
> 4 wasn't planning   5 while we were having
> 6 didn't use to have

❹ Before students do this (individually), tell them whether other students will be reading their sentences, as it may affect the amount of personal detail they give. You may want to suggest they use *would* as well as *used to* but, if so, remind them not to use *would* for states. When they have finished, check their writing for accuracy.

❺ You may want to introduce the topic by mentioning a relevant film, such as *The Money Pit*. Remind students they can change the order of the clauses, to give 'I was chatting on the phone when the bath water overflowed' or 'The bath water overflowed when I was chatting on the phone', and the difference in emphasis that this can create. For the last part of this activity, you could give some examples of disasters that have occurred to you, particularly any that happened in the students' own country!

WORKBOOK: Past tenses p33.

FURTHER PRACTICE: *used to* p121.

PHRASAL VERBS: *look* p52

❶ Students look at the nine sentences in a minute or so. Elicit the answer B.

❷ Students do these in pairs. Point out that the Listening text below contains several of these phrasal verbs. Be ready to take topic-related vocabulary questions (*surveyor*, *lawyer*, *purchase*, *manager*, *mortgage*, etc.). Go through the answers with the class when they have finished and make sure everyone has the correct ones written in.

> **ANSWERS:** 2 through – examine one by one
> 3 up – search for information   4 for – try to find
> 5 over – inspect   6 into – investigate   7 after – take care of   8 forward – anticipate with pleasure
> 9 out – be careful to avoid

WORKBOOK: Phrasal verbs *look* pp30–31.

LISTENING pp52–53

❶ This activity helps students to find out about the exam through discussion. Student A fills in gaps individually (allow only two or three minutes for this – either they know the answers already or they don't), while B reads the text in the Listening section at the back of the book. The most important element of this activity is learning about the exam task, but it also previews contrast links (see Grammar on p55) and the open cloze (see Use of English on p57), although you might want to point out to the class that in the exam the cloze tests only grammatical and lexico-grammatical items. Tell the 'B' students to read the text carefully, making a mental note of the information in it. Explain that the points are not necessarily in the same order as in Student A's questions. When pairs have finished, go through the answers with the class, ensuring that everyone has the correct answers and understands all the exam information and advice.

> **ANSWERS:** 1 different   2 connection   3 might
> 4 same   5 hand   6 function   7 six   8 one
> 9 introduction   10 predict   11 vocabulary
> 12 twice   13 end   14 therefore   15 second

❷ The aim of these questions is to help students think about the content of the texts and relate the ideas to their own experiences. Suggest that students ask themselves similar questions whenever they do this kind of listening exercise.

VARIATION: With a weaker class, explain that the answers relate directly to what the five speakers on the recording say. With stronger classes, it is probably best not to point this out until after they have done the exercise as it may make the task too easy.

❸ After students have read the instructions, encourage them to think about any experiences of their own with noisy neighbours (not just at home, but on holiday, staying with friends, etc.), what they have heard and what they have read about the subject. Play the recording twice.

> **ANSWERS:** 1E 2F 3D 4B 5A

❹❺ Students discuss in pairs.

WORKBOOK: Part 3 p32; Focus On Listening p96.

TAPESCRIPT

One
Try to avoid bad neighbours in the first place. Call round at the house you are looking at as many times as is reasonable and at varying times of the day. Talk to the milkman, the postman and the newsagent. Look at the number of bells on neighbouring front doors to see if the house is divided into flats, which could be noisier. Look out for pubs, nightclubs and football stadiums in that part of town.

Two
It certainly isn't a problem of minor importance. In the past year alone there have been three killings, one suicide, several arson attacks and thousands of fights after disputes about noise between neighbours. Only this week a woman admitted breaking down the door of the church next door to silence the bells, and a dispute about a fence was settled with a chainsaw.

Three
The biggest myth is that once you get away from the town everything is peace, quiet and rural bliss. It isn't, of course. You should always first look round the district to make sure you're not going to be near a farm with cockerels or something. And stud farms, racing stables and dairies all start at the crack of dawn, which means an early wake-up for everyone.

Four
The environmental health department of the local council will look into cases where people are being disturbed by noisy neighbours and nowadays can take action. Since the Noise Act was passed anyone causing a nuisance by playing loud music between eleven at night and seven in the morning risks an on-the-spot fine of £100 and can have their hi-fi equipment confiscated there and then.

Five
The best thing is to give them a taste of their own medicine. Go to a sound system suppliers and pick up a couple of industrial speakers – relatively small ones will do – and set them up against the adjoining wall. When you play your own particular favourites the sound level next door could top 115 decibels and what's worse they'll only hear the bass tones. Something with a repetitive beat would make it even more nauseating.

SPEAKING p53

❶ You may need to explain a few of the terms used in the table: *pop into*, *inflict*, *terrible argument*, *report to*. Students do this in pairs and then report back to the class.

VARIATION 1: The class discuss whether the figure in each case is likely to be higher or lower in their own country. You might want to take a vote, or get students to do a class survey, on some or all of these points to see how the class's attitudes compare with those as measured by the UK survey. To avoid stereotyping, you could suggest reasons for any differences, for example: types of housing, types of community, family structure, climate, etc.

VARIATION 2: If time permits, here are some more findings they could discuss.

Can rely on immediate neighbours to help in times of trouble:	74%
Strongly agree that people have a duty to be good neighbours:	54%
Immediate neighbours are considerate:	81%

Neighbours have a key to your home when
you are away: 45%
Immediate neighbours are a bit eccentric
or odd: 15%
Completely trust immediate neighbours: 56%

❷ Students work in pairs. Check for correct
formation of questions from the prompts. Remind
them that in the exam they can only talk about what
the examiner asks them about, although they may be
able to expand on points and touch on related topics.

VARIATION: With a weaker class, give some or all of
these prompts to help them answer their partners'
questions:
• how quiet, lively or noisy the neighbourhood is
• social problems such as crime, vandalism and drugs
• whether housing is old or modern, mostly houses
  or flats
• how friendly people are; whether there are a lot of
  young people or old people
• which of these are close to your home: school/
  university/your workplace, shops, sports facilities,
  cafés and restaurants, parks, a hospital, facilities for
  children (nurseries, swings, etc.), a library, meeting
  places (bars, discos, youth clubs, etc.), somewhere
  to learn English
• public transport and roads
• how other places compare with where you live
  now.

WORKBOOK: Focus On Speaking p104.

READING: multiple choice p54–55

❶ Point out that where the exam text is taken from
fiction, no title will be given. Allow a timed maximum
of two minutes for individual gist reading, without
taking any questions, and then discuss students'
suggestions. The extract is from *The Rose of Tibet* by
Lionel Davidson, written in 1962 and set in India.

❷ Students answer individually.

ANSWERS: 1C 2C 3B 4B 5B 6A

❸ Elicit the meanings of the words in 1 and 2 after
pairs have had some time to work them out. You may
want to go through the clues in the text for some or
all of them. Point out that *couldn't stand* is a virtual
synonym for *couldn't bear*. For the words in 3, ask
what they have in common before eliciting more
precise explanations. Point out that in **c** and **d** the
similar words are not the same part of speech.

ANSWERS: a unrefined or not well finished
b levels of a building   c bad smell
d very/too bright   e not clean

❹ Elicit reactions to the first question and possible
explanations for the second, such as unemployment,
urban overcrowding, inadequate housing provision
and lack of social security. Answers to the third
question can relate to past or present.

FOLLOW-UP: Possible follow-up questions include
'Why do you think the people seemed happy, despite
the awful conditions? Where do you think conditions
like that still exist today?'

WORKBOOK: Part 2 pp32–33; Focus On Reading p72.

GRAMMAR: contrasting ideas p55

❶ Students could fill in the gaps in pairs. Check that
everyone has the correct answers before moving on.

ANSWERS: 1 but   2 although   3 in spite of
4 however

❷ Tell students both to think about the meanings of
the clauses and to look back at the grammar of the
examples in exercise 1 above. Elicit the answers

ANSWERS: 1e 2c 3f 4a 5b 6d

COMMON ERRORS

She was late. So was I, though. Though, but not
although, can be used to contrast at the end of a
separate sentence.

There is further practice with these forms in Use of
English and Study Check on p57.

❸ Students show each other their sentences and
explain the background to each one.

FOLLOW-UP: Here are some optional key word
transformations. As well as practising the target
structures within the exam format, this activity gives
further practice of phrasal verbs with *look*, and past
tense forms. Students do these individually and then
check with their partners. Advise students to be
careful with Question 6: the key word is *through*, not
'though'!

1 They had to sleep in the street, in spite of the
  falling temperature.
  although
  They had to sleep in the street,
  .... falling.

2 Despite having a job, he couldn't afford the rent.
  even
  He couldn't afford the rent .... a job.

3 Despite looking everywhere for the keys, she
  couldn't find them.
  though
  She couldn't find the keys, ...
  them.

4 We found a place to live even though everyone
  said it was impossible.
  despite
  We found a place to live .... everyone said
  it was impossible.

5 Although the law changed, landlords were still
  evicting people.
  spite
  Landlords were still evicting people ....
  in the law.

6 Although we examined all the figures, we didn't
  spot the mistake.
  through
  Despite .... the figures, we didn't spot
  the mistake.

> **ANSWERS:** 1 although the temperature was
> 2 even though he had   3 though she looked
> everywhere for   4 despite the fact that   5 in
> spite of the change   6 looking/going through (all)

WRITING: a report p56

❶ Students work in pairs, identifying examples of techniques used.

> **ANSWERS:** all ticked except points 4 and 11

❷ If there is time, groups – or the class as a whole – could discuss these points.

❸ You may want to elicit names of sections, and possibly encourage students to make certain choices, for example younger students could concentrate on 'pocket money', 'rooms' and 'essential possessions'. Point out that there is no compulsion to use all the techniques, but that in many respects the text is a useful model.

❹ There is an opportunity here for students to use grammar practised in this unit and Unit 4. Approximate expressions: check that everyone understands the meanings of these, if necessary by giving/eliciting contextualized examples.

VARIATION: With a weaker class, you might want to start with basic approximate forms such as *about*, *more than* and *less than*.

WORKBOOK: Writing p35; Focus On Writing p80.

USE OF ENGLISH: open cloze p57

❶ Students work alone. Elicit the answers, stressing the importance of quick reading and brief answers if this is to be a useful first stage of cloze technique. When the class have filled in all the gaps, get them to compare their comprehension 'before and after'. They may be surprised to find how much of an incomplete text they have understood. Point out that this is to some extent a 'real-world' skill as we sometimes have to cope with unclear handwriting, fuzzy faxes, etc., and that a high proportion of texts containing difficult expressions can also be understood.

> **POSSIBLE ANSWERS:**
> 1 No family support; lack of self-belief; employers put off by appearance; cannot be contacted easily
> 2 She found out more about human nature; the experience enabled her to open her mind.

FOLLOW-UP: Encourage students to ask themselves similar questions whenever they do gap-filling exercises of any sort in the future.

You may like to discuss the photo with students, asking if this is a familiar sight where they live, how they react to people like this etc. Draw their attention to the type of shop and the sign, and the contrast with the person.

❷ Many of the items tested here are forms presented and practised in this unit and Unit 4. Go through the answers with the class after they have filled in as many gaps as they can.

NOTE: If possible, let students put the answers into the spaces, as it makes the activity far more task-authentic if they can actually complete the text rather than write the answers on a separate piece of paper.

> **ANSWERS:** 1 an/per   2 However   3 for   4 if
> 5 such   6 than   7 but   8 being   9 should
> 10 who   11 Although   12 anywhere   13 on
> 14 ever   15 was

WORKBOOK: Multiple-choice cloze p34; Focus On Use of English p88.

STUDY CHECK p57

❶ Check written work for accuracy.

❷ Monitor conversations and provide feedback when they have finished.

VARIATION: Give pairs the following instructions: tell your partner what your family or friends were doing when you arrived home yesterday, and what you were doing when others came in. If you live alone or didn't see anyone, say what your classmates were doing when you arrived for the lesson, and what you were doing when others got here.

❸ If students are unfamiliar with 'homeswap', ask them what might be the pros and cons of exchanging your home with somebody else for a short period. Elicit more points to put in the report, especially any that are relevant to the students' own culture.

Students now do Unit Test 5 on p172 of this book. The answers are on p214.

6 If it tastes good

SPEAKING *p58*

Students first work individually and then form groups to compare answers. They could also suggest reasons for any patterns that emerge. Groups then report back to the class on the results. Elicit answers to the follow-up questions after the questionnaire.

VOCABULARY: food and cooking *p58*

1 Elicit the answer – they are all associated with eating quickly – and special features: the informality of *(have a) bite to eat*, the negative connotations of *junk food* contrasted with *convenience food* (the term used by the industry). Allow several minutes for students to note down examples. Tell them to think of fast eating in general – bowl of cereal, a sandwich, a piece of cake and a glass of milk, a bar of chocolate, etc. – rather than try to find examples in each category, as several overlap in meaning.

2 They are all methods of cooking. Students will probably be able to translate these directly once they know exactly what they mean, so it is probably best to elicit and clarify them directly rather than let pairs spend too long on trying to work them out. Groups or pairs make lists of examples. Also elicit (or present) the names of the equipment used in each case.

ANSWERS: boil – in water at 100°C, e.g. eggs, vegetables; fry – in a frying pan, with oil or fat, e.g. fish, sausages; grill – direct heat, usually from above, e.g. toast, meat; roast – in an oven or over a fire, especially meat and chicken; bake – in an oven, especially cakes and bread; steam – above the water, e.g. vegetables, rice

FURTHER PRACTICE: Vocabulary and speaking p123.

READING: multiple matching *p59*

1 Ensure the class do not start reading beyond the title at this stage. Elicit answers without saying whether they are right or wrong yet. You could also ask why they think so. Tell them to read the whole text. Set a time limit of two minutes and then ask for the answers.

ANSWERS: Britain (most)   Italy (least)

2 Students work individually. Point out that the Help approach (matching *Wh-* words in headings to certain types of paragraph) can often be used with other texts (a *Why* b *What/Which*).

ANSWERS: 1H 2A 3C 4D 5F 6E 7B
Not needed: G

3 If there is time, broaden this into a class discussion.

FOLLOW-UP: Groups discuss the third question in 1 above (*How do you think your own country compares?*). If students are at all slow to decide on this, prompt by suggesting that they think back to the results of the survey in Speaking. They could also estimate how many burger restaurants there are in their capital city – bearing in mind that in London, for instance, there are many hundreds.

WORKBOOK: Part 1 pp38–39; Focus On Reading p72.

FURTHER PRACTICE: Multiple matching p124.

GRAMMAR: conditionals (1 and 2) *p60*

1 The first example is taken from the Reading text on p59. Allow time for pairs to study and then go through the answers. With a strong class, elicit more examples of each type.

ANSWERS: 1a 2c 3b. Verb forms: 1 present simple/*will* future   2 past simple/*would* conditional 3 past simple/*would* conditional. Names: 1 1st conditional   2 2nd conditional   3 2nd conditional

2 Students work in pairs. Check their answers and revise any points that are not clear.

ANSWERS: 1 ✓ 2 ✓ 3 if we arrive 4 ✓ 5 I'd buy 6 ✓ 7 I'd make 8 ✓ 9 if they kept 10 if it were/was

3 Stress the unlikelihood of people intentionally keeping food at body temperature, or heating most liquids to 132°C.

ANSWERS: 1B 2C 3D 4A

4 If necessary, prompt with practical alternatives – 'I'll ask for cereal instead', 'I'll politely say "No thank you"', etc. – especially if your students are likely to be staying with host families! You could add more, such as *lunch consists of a sandwich* or *there is fried meat for breakfast*.

5 Students write their answers individually. With a weaker class, do the first one as an example, e.g. If I ate too much *cake*, I *would get very fat.*
Possible prompts: 2 sweets, meals 3 fruit, protein 4 meat, breakfast 5 water, liquids 6 coffee, beer 7 chocolate, snacks 8 my lunch, a big meal. Check for accuracy.

6 Prompt, if necessary, with 1 *I'd eat tinned…* 2 *I'd drink ouzo, I'd try paella* 3 *I'd eat even more burgers* 4 *I'd drink tea all the time*, etc.

FOLLOW-UP: Add other situations such as *If you were staying in France or Italy, If you were South American,* etc., or relate them to the students' own country: *If you were Basque, Catalan, Galician,* etc.

WORKBOOK: Conditional forms p39.

USE OF ENGLISH: word formation *p61*

❶ Students read the introduction, ask any questions they might have and then do the task.

> **ANSWERS:** a 5 b 8 c 4 d 1 (some may suggest 4 should be last)

Pairs or groups could discuss what they decided and justify their answers.

❷ This activity revises the names of parts of speech (and the phrase *part of speech,* which will be needed) and gives examples of some of the kinds of changes that can be expected.

1 Point out that both prefixes and suffixes are possible (as well as changes to the internal spelling of the word, for example changing *strong* to *strengthen*).

> **ANSWERS:** noun, adjective, adverb

VARIATION: With a strong class the list could be extended to *successor, succession* and *successive.*

2 Students write the forms and parts of speech as they did with *succeed.*

> **ANSWERS:** care/carefulness (noun), careful, careless (adjective), carefully, carelessly (adverb). Stronger students may also come up with (un)caring (adjective) and (un)caringly (adverb)

❸ Point out that in this exercise the answers have been filled in for students to analyse. (If students are not familiar with the task-type, refer them to the instructions in exercise 4 below.) Pairs or individuals do 1 and 2, then go through all the answers with the class.

> **ANSWERS:** 0 *-ibility,* noun – noun   1 *-al,* noun – adjective   2 *-hood,* noun – noun   3 *-tion,* verb – noun   4 *in-,* verb – noun   5 *-ance,* verb – noun   6 *-ably,* verb – adverb   7 *-arently,* verb – adverb   8 *-ce,* verb – noun   9 *-ment,* verb – noun   10 *-ments,* verb – (plural) noun

❹ Students do the exercise individually, then compare answers with their partners. Check when they have finished, and ask for responses to the content of the text.

> **ANSWERS:** 1 especially   2 lively   3 frequently   4 helping   5 musical   6 mouthfuls   7 background   8 dangerous   9 attention   10 warnings

WORKBOOK: Word formation p40; Focus On Use of English p88.

FURTHER PRACTICE: Word formation p125.

VOCABULARY: smelling and tasting *p62*

❶ Students could do these in pairs or groups. Elicit or point out differences in connotation: an *aroma* or *fragrance* is usually pleasant, while a *smell* or *odour* can be good or bad. A number of these words are used in the Listening below.

> **ANSWERS:**
> a tongue (n), bite (n and v), flavour* (n and v), lick (v), swallow (v), sip (n and v), chew (v), taste (n and v), texture (n) *But see Listening 1 below.
> b smell (n and v), odour (n), aroma (n), fragrance (n), sniff (n and v)

VARIATION: With a younger class, ask individual students to demonstrate verbs such as *bite, swallow, sip, chew* and *sniff.*

FOLLOW-UP: Ask which of the words end in a /ə/, and which one both begins and ends with this sound. Then highlight and drill their pronunciation. Answers: *flavour, odour* and *texture* end in /ə/; *aroma* both begins and ends with a schwa.

❷ Students work in pairs. Give an example, if necessary, of a simile – such as *cabbage smells like old socks.*

WORKBOOK: Vocabulary p36.

LISTENING *p62*

❶ Let pairs discuss this for a minute and then elicit the answers: we partially lose our sense of taste; because the senses of taste and smell are closely linked; 'flavour', therefore, is really a result of the interaction of taste and smell.

❷ This is an FCE Part 2 Listening task, so students should do this exercise individually. The help that is given follows on from the focus on parts of speech in word formation on p61. The text contains several conditional forms.

> **ANSWERS:** 1 half a cup   2 fresh   3 brown   4 two tablespoons   5 chop up   6 mix   7 cover   8 cut up   9 sweet   10 slices.

WORKBOOK: Focus On Listening p96.

TAPESCRIPT

As anyone with a cold knows, if the nose isn't working, food won't taste as good. That's because the brain mixes taste and smell sensations to produce one complex perception that we call 'flavour'. One way to simulate the effect of an absence of food odour is by holding your nose whenever you taste something.

Also, the aromas of most foods are usually complex mixtures of several individual aromatic chemicals. The odour of strawberries, for example, is made up of compounds that can also be found in green peas, brown sugar and apples. If you sniff all three together, the smell will be of strawberries.

Here's how you can experiment with odours. Firstly, the materials. Take some green peas: about half a cup should do. For this experiment to work they really must be fresh, not frozen. You also need half an apple, peeled and without its core. The final ingredient is brown sugar: two tablespoons should be enough. In addition, you will need a coffee cup or mug as well as a piece of cardboard big enough to cover the cup.

Now the method. Begin by using a sharp knife to chop up the apple. Then place all the ingredients in a blender or a food processor and mix them together. Put the result in the cup and then cover it with the cardboard. Ask somebody to identify the odour but slide back the cardboard only enough to let the other person sniff. Don't let him or her see what's inside because the strange colour and texture will send clues that prevent identification.

As a separate experiment, cut up some of the remaining apple, hold your nose and place it on your tongue. Roll it around a bit to taste it but don't chew. If you're like most people who taste the apple without the aid of their noses, you'll find that the fruit is sweet – a sensation your tongue picks up by itself – but bland, as it lacks the complex flavour associated with apples. Pinching your nose reduces the air flow through the nasal cavity, where the smell receptors are situated. Then release your nose and see whether the flavour changes. When you do this, air can flow to these receptors, even from within the mouth, carrying the aroma of apple. Old apples lack flavour because their aromas have evaporated.

As a further experiment, try the same procedure with slices of pear or other fruit. With their noses held, many people can't tell the difference between one fruit and another, unless they chew and get clues from the texture. Incidentally, if you chew during this experiment, you will probably release a more powerful odour that can reach the smell receptors even if you're holding your nose.

WRITING: an article *pp62–63*

❶ Let pairs discuss these questions and then check that they all have the correct answers.

ANSWERS:
1 in the hope that your article will be printed
2 a description of a meal from your country or abroad – ingredients, cooking instructions and serving suggestions   3 people in other countries, who presumably are interested in cooking

❷ You may want to tell students to look at the final instructions in 5 ('He or she should try to guess what the dish is') as the reason for not writing the name yet. It should also encourage them to write a clearly laid-out plan. If you feel there is a likelihood that they are all going to write about the same dish – moussaka, cocido, pizza or whatever – suggest they choose a slightly less common one (you could encourage this by saying that there is more chance of

something different being chosen to be read out to the rest of the class at the end of the activity).

With students who are already competent writers in English it is probably advisable to stress that these are suggested guidelines, not a prescriptive list which must be followed in every detail. Less skilled writers, however, may well benefit from initially using this kind of structure as a framework, especially if they are encouraged to build on it by adding their own points. With all classes it is important to go through the vocabulary exercises in parts 2 and 3. Finally, students read each other's plan quickly and try to decide what dish it is.

VARIATION 1: Leave time at the end of the lesson for students to write their plans and for you to check what they intend to write before they go off and do the task for homework. (This can be extended to other writing tasks.)

VARIATION 2: In a multicultural class, suggest that if students cannot identify the dish they could say if it is similar to a dish from their own or another country.

NOTE: You may want to ensure that students at least recognize basic UK/US measures such as *pint*, *pound* (*lb*) and *ounce* (*oz*), and mention that some people (and recipes) still use the Fahrenheit scale for temperatures.

❸ Students work alone. Emphasize the importance of always following point one (why/what/who) whenever they are writing a text. Remind them they can now use the name of the dish in their text!

❹ When they have done their articles (or before the end of the lesson if they are going to do them for homework) refer students to the Exam Study Guide feature below. Pairs could also check each other's work in class.

VARIATION: Ask the class which dishes the readers of texts found the most appetizing, and get the readers or writers to give the recipe, possibly orally, to the rest of the class. A good speaker could do this as a dictation exercise.

WORKBOOK: Writing pp40–41; Focus On Writing p80.

EXAM STUDY GUIDE *p63*

The Learner Training feature aims to create the habit of systematic checking of written work. The activity practises structures presented in this unit.

ANSWERS: A 2 was sleeping   B 9 in bed
C 8 despite/in spite of   D 1 bookshop   E 4 These
F 3 I am   G 5 on TV   H 6 I'd like   I 10 Greek,
Spanish   J 7 where

FOLLOW-UP: Check the students' lists. You may find it useful to take a copy for future remedial and/or revision work. A new list could be drawn up near the end of the course, and the findings compared.

PHRASAL VERBS: *put* p64

❶ Point out that there are many other phrasal verbs with *put*, and other meanings of the verbs practised here, but that these ten are among the most useful. The questions should be done quickly as students will either know these or they won't: it is in the nature of phrasal verbs that their component parts may not be a reliable guide to their overall meaning (e.g. *put up with*).

ANSWERS: 1a 2b 3a 4a 5a 6b 7a 8b 9a 10a

❷ It is probably best, at this stage of the course, to avoid too much discussion of the grammar of phrasal verbs, but it might be worth pointing out the simple rule that three-part verbs (verb + adverb + preposition) like *put up with*, *go on about*, etc. cannot be separated in this way.

POSSIBLE ANSWERS:
1   Oh, I've just put it away.
2   Well she certainly looks as if she's put on weight/put weight on!
3   No, we've put it off till next week.
4   Yes, you can put this one on/put on this one.
5   Oh, I'm sorry; I'll put it out now/put out my cigarette now.
6   Yes, they've put up the price/put the price up.
7   The smell puts me off.
8   Yes, I'll put you through.
9   No, I'm not going to put up with it any more.

❸ Encourage pairs to think about their daily routine, starting with early in the morning: staying in bed (*put off getting up*, *put on the radio*), getting dressed (*put on clothes*, *make-up*, etc.), making breakfast (*put the kettle*, *the toaster*, etc. *on*), having breakfast (*put on the table*, *put away afterwards*), leaving the house (*put the heating off*, *put the lights out*, etc.).

VARIATION: Pairs use phrasal verbs with *put* to say what members of their family do each day. They include the above and add references to how they are affected by other people, for example irritating habits (*can't put up with*, *put me off*, etc.).

WORKBOOK: Phrasal verbs *put* p36.

GRAMMAR: *unless, as long as, provided* pp64–65

COMMON ERRORS

No matter how much I eat, I'm always hungry. No *matter* is followed by *what*, *where*, etc. to say that something is always true or always happens irrespective of circumstances. For a contextualized example, refer students back to the last sentence of the Reading text on p59.

FURTHER PRACTICE: *no matter what*, *whatever*, etc. p123.

❶ Elicit the answers and point out variations like *provided that* and *on condition (that)*. You may want to point out that *as long as* is more emphatic than *if*, while *provided/providing*, etc. are rather more formal.

ANSWERS: 1b 2a 3a

❷ Students could discuss these in pairs.

POSSIBLE ANSWERS: 1 you drink   2 you don't
3 you are a   4 I'll have/I'll order that
5 will be served   6 won't harm

FOLLOW-UP: With an imaginative class, one student could provide their own prompts and their partner would complete the sentence.

❸ Depending on the students' cultural background, you may want to choose who is paired with whom for this activity, or else leave them with their usual partner. Further practice with *must/have to/need* is given here (you may wish to refer students back to Unit 4). Students change roles so that both practise the forms.

VARIATION: In certain societies it may be useful to remind the class that this is a light-hearted and purely imaginary activity. You could also add to the conditions depending on local values, for example by specifying 'There must be no alcohol' or, in other cultures, that there should be plenty!

USE OF ENGLISH: key word transformations p65

Point out that where a second kind of change is not required it is because the conditional form itself is more complex. In Question 1, for example, *as long as* is needed, while Question 5 entails the use of both the *were/was* and the *would* parts of the sentence. This activity gives further practice with the phrasal verbs from p64 and also introduces more 'restaurant' vocabulary such as *cancel*, *charge* and *tip*. Weaker students could work on 1–8 in pairs.

ANSWERS: 1 stay as long as you   2 provided (that) you brush   3 you put on your clothes/you put your clothes on   4 didn't charge (us) such   5 weren't/wasn't full I would/I'd   6 put me off eating unless   7 tip the waiter unless   8 less whisky if I were. You may want to ask the class what the 'second change' was in the relevant questions: 3 phrasal verb 4 grammar 6 phrasal verb 7 vocabulary 8 grammar

VARIATION: With a lower-level class, you may want to start by giving the example of Question 3, pointing out that a phrasal verb is needed.

WORKBOOK: Focus On Use of English p88.

LISTENING p66

1 This is a cultural awareness activity so there are no 'correct' answers. Encourage comparison with habits in English-speaking countries, including both similarities and any differences such as: far fewer courses, having vegetables as part of the main course, wine more for special occasions, sweet dessert only, cheese after the sweet. Also encourage discussion about why these differences exist: climate, local produce, timetable, attitudes to food, etc.

2 Pairs go through the courses, explaining anything that their partners may not know, and describing the taste of things they have not tried. Make sure they get the names of the drinks right.

3 'Yes'/'No' questions are similar in many ways to 'True'/'False' questions, so a lot of the advice on p76 in Unit 7 applies to both types. Students study the instructions, explanation and example. Then they listen twice to the recording and write in their answers. Go through the answers and take any questions. Transcribed extracts from the text will be used in Speaking below.

> **ANSWERS:** 1 No 2 No 3 No 4 No 5 Yes
> 6 No 7 Yes

VARIATION: Tell a weaker class that at least three of the answers are 'Yes' and at least three 'No' (without giving precise numbers of Yes and No answers at this stage as it would make the final choice obvious – the jigsaw effect).

WORKBOOK: Part 1 p37; Focus On Listening p96.

TAPESCRIPT

Kathy: OK then, for starters how about some lovely soft black olives, and er – let me see – a slice of tortilla: do you know what I mean?

Phil: Is that Spanish omelette?

Kathy: Yes, that's right, with potatoes mixed in. It'd be tasty warm, but really delicious if we left it to cool down.

Phil: I'd like oysters, too. Fresh with real lemon juice they're the perfect appetizer.

Kathy: Not for me. I had some once and I was ill for the whole weekend. Put me off oysters for life, they did. But I tell you what I'd really like: a few of those huge shellfish we had in Galicia. Remember?

Phil: Yeah, and that white wine we had with it, it was so light and dry: *vinho verde*, that was it...

Kathy: Sorry, what was that?

Phil: *Vinho verde*. You know, that Portuguese wine.

Kathy: Ooh, yes, I'd like some of that again. With a glass of really cool mineral water as well.

Phil: Good idea. But back to food, though. How would you like some asparagus, fresh of course, with mayonnaise?

Kathy: Mmm, yes. And perhaps to follow that I'd have one, or maybe two, of those cheese rolls they have in France, you know, a lump of fresh goat's cheese wrapped in thin bacon or ham or something like that.

Phil: Yes, I know the things you mean, they're really tasty.

Kathy: And to go with that I'd have a bowl of really crisp mixed salad. Lovely!

Phil: I think by then we'd be getting a little fed up, I mean full up and it'd be time to start thinking about the main course.

Kathy: Yes, but I'd still like to have a drop of soup, perhaps the Italian one – you know – with lots of fresh veg and tomatoes and olive oil, with cheese scattered on top...

Phil: Minestrone.

Kathy: Yes, that's it. Yum. Ooh, this is really starting to make my mouth water!

Phil: Mine too, but what about the next...

Kathy: Yeah, we'd have been guzzling for ages by now. Right, so let me think – I know, I'd have a moussaka, oven-baked so that fantastic cheese sauce is just turning brown.

Phil: Nice. But I think I'd go for the hottest curry I could find, that's to say a really spicy one. Do you know what kind I mean?

Kathy: Yeah, a vindaloo sounds like what you're after. A bit too spicy for me but if you can handle it, fine.

Phil: Well I'd have a little Indian side-salad and perhaps a bowl of yoghurt to help cool things down a bit. And plenty of ice-cold beer, perhaps a couple of those really nice Belgian ones.

Kathy: Sounds OK. But I think I'd stick with the white wine 'cause it'd go really well with some of my favourite cheeses, like old Manchego, or mature English ones.

Phil: So you'd have cheese before the dessert?

Kathy: Sure. It's only in the UK that people have a savoury course after the sweet! And then we could start thinking about all those goodies like cream cakes with jam, and chocolate fudge cake...

Phil: And then the longest siesta ever.

Kathy: Just what I was thinking.

SPEAKING pp66–67

1 It may be useful to get pairs first to discuss the communication strategies they use in their mother tongue. In many cultures, they are likely to find they are very similar to the seven listed here. If they can think of more, get them to explain so that you can give them the nearest equivalents in English. You could also give the terms in brackets next to the answers, as some may be cognates in the students' first language(s).

2 Students work in pairs. Elicit the meaning of *veg* in F, i.e. *vegetables*.

> **ANSWERS:** B 2 (hesitating) C 6 (asking for clarification) D 1 (approximating) E 3 (self-correcting) F 4 (paraphrasing) G 7 (clarifying)

VARIATION: With a strong class, elicit more examples of each strategy.

❸ Stress that this is not a writing task, that they are making notes for oral work to follow. Also make sure pairs read the points *before* they start talking.

VARIATION: Suggest that pairs bear in mind the turn-taking of the speakers in Listening (you may want to play the recording again to highlight this) if it is something they find difficult. Remind them that they will have to take turns speaking in the exam.

FOLLOW-UP: Each pair in turn describes their ideal meal to the rest of class, who would then vote on which is the best.

WORKBOOK: Focus On Speaking p104.

STUDY CHECK *p67*

❶ Students do these individually. Check their written work for accuracy.

❷ Refer pairs to the pictures. Point out that this is the kind of decision-making task they will do with another candidate in Part 3 of FCE Speaking. Monitor their speaking and give feedback when they have finished.

WORKBOOK: Focus On Speaking p104.

❸ This is very much a personal ideal, so it is probably best for students to work on this alone. Again, you may want to look at their writing plans before they start. When you are correcting their work, highlight any habitual mistakes that they should have picked up at the checking stage.

Students now do Unit Test 6 on p173 of this book. The answers are on pp214–15.

7 This sporting life

READING: multiple matching *pp68–69*

❶ Refer students to the picture of the bowling alley. Ask the questions, possibly following up with 'Why is it called that?' (tenpin bowling) and 'Why do you think it started there?' (the USA). You could also briefly discuss its popularity or otherwise in the students' country, the reasons for this, and who plays it – or just likes to 'hang out' in bowling centres.

❷ Focus on the scorecard, checking that everyone understands the word 'score' in this context. Students work in pairs or groups to fill in the labels and decide how many pins were knocked down. All the target words are fairly frequent in general use, so it might be advisable to contrast their ordinary meaning with their specific meaning here.

> **ANSWERS:** 1 pins 2 lane 3 gutter 4 aisle
> 5 3 6 7 7 10

❸ This activity provides both advice on FCE Reading Part 4 and an introduction to relative clauses (which are dealt with in detail in the pages that follow: do not go too deeply into their grammar and usage at this stage).
  Students could do the activity in pairs. Clarify any points they might raise. For instance: if they ask about 'questions that have answers in more than one section' (3A), refer them to Questions 14 and 15 in the exam task which follows.

> **ANSWERS:** 1D 2C 3A 4B

NOTE: You may want to point out that in Part 4 one or more multiple-choice questions testing overall comprehension is possible – if unlikely.

VARIATION: An alternative after gist reading is to look at all the questions, which can help students avoid wasting time on irrelevant parts of the text.

❹ Students do this alone, using the help given, although you may want them to compare answers when they have finished.

> **ANSWERS:** 1C 2D 3A 4C 5A 6D 7B 8C 9D 10A
> 11D 12B 13D 14/15 B/C (where there are two
> possible answers, they are interchangeable)

❺ Pairs answer the question. Then ask the class as a whole what they think.

FOLLOW-UP: Pairs discuss which of the four centres they would like most, which least, and why. Then they report back to the class. Ask if bowling centres sound like good places to go (not just for the bowling) and, with students who have already been, how prices in their country compare with those in the UK (give local currency equivalents if necessary).

WORKBOOK: Part 2 pp44–45; Focus On Reading p72.

GRAMMAR: *can, could, may* and *might* *p70*

Tell students to read the grammar explanation carefully. The restrictions on the use of *can* may not exist for the equivalent word(s) in their first language, and they might expect a future form for some of the uses involving the other modals. Give and elicit more examples if necessary. Point out that *mayn't* is very rare, and that the opposite of *must be* is *can't be*, not *mustn't be*.

❶ Students work in pairs. Go through the correct forms as a class and point out that further practice is given with these forms in Use of English and later in the Unit.

> **ANSWERS:** 1 correct 2 might not (mightn't) or
> may not 3 might, may or could 4 might not
> (mightn't) or may not 5 might, may or could
> 6 correct 7 might, may or could 8 can't, cannot,
> couldn't or could not

❷ Students do these individually.

> **ANSWERS:** 1 possible they won't be/they will not
> be 2 can usually repair 3 next time it may not
> 4 might not actually be doing 5 couldn't/can't
> possibly win

WORKBOOK: *can, could, may* and *might* p45.

GRAMMAR: relative clauses *pp70–71*

Let students read the explanation and the examples. Elicit more relative pronouns used in defining relative clauses (*who, which* and *whose*, but not *whom* at this stage: see Common Errors below), then do the same for non-defining (*who, whose*). You may want to give or – with higher levels – elicit, examples with *where* (*the place where we met*), and *when* (*the time when it happened*).

COMMON ERRORS

The person to whom I wrote has not replied. In more formal contexts, *whom* is often used instead of *who* when it is the object of the verb in the relative clause. When, in these circumstances, it follows a preposition we nearly always use *whom*. In everyday conversation we would probably say *The person (who) I wrote to has not replied.*

❶ The extracts are in the order they appear in the text, so if students want more context they can refer back to Reading 4. Allow plenty of time for pairs to decide on their answers, then check their writing and/or go through the answers with the class. Pay more attention to **c** than **d**, as it is probably more useful for students to be able to identify relative clauses without a relative pronoun (which may not happen in their first language) than to learn how to omit them from their own writing and speaking (which makes little real difference to their communicative ability).

> **ANSWERS:**
> 1 who first organized professional bowling – defining
> 2 whose bowling roots are in Ohio – non-defining
> 3 which walked around talking to the kids – non-defining
> 4 we found – defining, 'that' added
> 5 which made it difficult for new bowlers,– non-defining
> 6 which we visited – defining, 'which' crossed out
> 7 who is from Texas – non-defining
> 8 I've ever been to in the States – defining, 'that' added
> 9 when the Super Bowl puts on a disco – non-defining
> 10 which made for a much better atmosphere – non-defining

FOLLOW-UP: Highlight the pronunciation of non-defining relative clauses, particularly those enclosed by commas. Explain that as they contain extra, non-essential information, the speaker often pauses and then says them quickly and more quietly than the rest of the sentence. Extracts 2 and 7 are good examples of this, but you might want to give some of your own, and elicit more from stronger students.

❷ Students do these in pairs or groups, noting down their answers. Ask what sport is referred to (tennis) and then go through the answers, taking vocabulary questions at the same time.

> **ANSWERS:**
> 1 repetition of subject 'he': *the player who won*
> 2 correct
> 3 'what' incorrect: *the shot (that/which) he likes*
> 4 object 'it' repeated: *that she prefers.*
> 5 correct
> 6 non-defining, only one mother possible, so commas needed: *her mother, who was also a player, is*
> 7 'that' used in non-defining relative clause: *which was very exciting*
> 8 *that* or *which,* not 'where', or without 'on'
> 9 correct
> 10 non-defining with no relative pronoun: *the champion, whose first shot*

VARIATION: With a more advanced class, focus on Question 9. Point out that it is more common, especially in spoken language, to put the preposition ('to') at the end of the relative clause, rather than before the relative pronoun ('I don't know to which player the umpire was speaking'). Give more

examples (*the court which they played on, the incident I was telling you about,* etc.) and elicit the more formal variation. See also the Grammar Reference on p175.

❸ Stress that the answers can contain either defining or non-defining relative clauses. Ensure that pairs work independently until they have written all their answers. Check written work for complete accuracy.

> **ANSWERS:** The meanings are identical or very similar, except for Question 3: the first implies that he was shouting as he ran onto the court while the second indicates he was already shouting before he did so. Sport: basketball.
> 1 The court, which is 26 metres long, is 14 metres wide. The court, which is 14 metres wide, is 26 metres long.
> 2 Jones, who was the best player, scored 12 points. Jones, who scored 12 points, was the best player.
> 3 The spectator who ran onto the court during the time-out was shouting.
>   The spectator who was shouting ran onto the court during the time-out. Different
> 4 The players who are extremely tall find it easiest to score.
>   The players who find it easiest to score are extremely tall.
> 5 Pushing an opponent, which is called a personal foul, is not allowed.
>   Pushing an opponent, which is not allowed, is called a personal foul.
> 6 The free throw which was given in the last minute decided the match.
>   The free throw which decided the match was given in the last minute.

VARIATION: With a weaker class, give clues as to which are which by telling the class to put a comma after 'court' in Question 1 and 'Jones' in Question 2.

❹ Point out that the answers to these questions are 'open': encourage students to write whatever they most readily associate with the sports mentioned.

> **POSSIBLE ANSWERS:** 1 which is popular in the USA
> 2 I love/hate most   3 who play rugby   4 which can be dangerous   5 I don't/I try to   6 which is a cycle race   7 who want to be champions
> 8 which started in Greece

❺ Remind pairs that the aim is to elicit relative clauses, possibly with a few examples like *I don't enjoy watching sports that are violent* or *I don't like doing the sports we played at school.* Monitor conversations, noting topics to avoid in future discussions, writing, etc.

LISTENING *p72*

Point out that in their first language the students almost certainly follow the same procedure of thinking about what they already know about a topic before they listen to (or read) something else about it, and then compare and contrast the new information with their existing knowledge.

Emphasize that what they hear in FCE Listening, and therefore in material that prepares them for it, may be about fairly familiar topics, but it will nearly always contain 'new' aspects of, or angles on, those topics. They are very unlikely, for example, to be given a text about the marathon that lists well-known facts about how it started and so on.

FOLLOW-UP: Tell the class to think back to information in previous listening activities which has surprised them, and to discuss it with their partners. If students are slow in deciding which activities to talk about, refer them to those in earlier units which have generated most discussion about the content of the texts.

❶ Students practise forming and answering questions, e.g. *What's she been doing? She's been running in a marathon.* You may want to point out that they will be referring back to the questions in activity 3. The woman has just run 26.2 miles.

VARIATION: With an older or more advanced class, ask more specific questions such as:
During the race, do runners need much more oxygen, energy, or water?
How do they make sure they get enough of each?
What do you think happens if they don't?
What else can happen to the human body during a marathon?
What long-term effects can marathon running have on people?

❷ Give students a minute to look at the questions and remind them not to write more than four words for each answer. Then play the recording twice, while students fill in their answers individually. Go through the answers, ensuring that everyone writes in a correct one for each question.

> **ANSWERS:** 1 height   2 running shoes
> 3 frequency   4 (approximately) 4 hours
> 5 about 20 miles   6 pasta, bread, bananas
> 7 about the same   8 5 litres   9 boiling point
> 10 longer/more active/healthy lives

❸ Students may find they had misconceptions about a number of points, particularly about the amount of energy a marathon runner uses up, what they eat beforehand, how essential sweating is, how healthy marathon-running is and what happens to the human body (it shrinks). Ask the class what they found predictable in the text, and what was surprising.

WORKBOOK: Part 2 p43; Focus On Listening p96.

TAPESCRIPT

Every runner reaching the finishing line in the Marathon will have taken about 30,000 strides, with each foot hitting the pavement 15,000 times. Each of these foot-to-pavement impacts will send a force that is the equivalent of 2.5 times the runner's body weight up through the legs and lower back, placing huge strains on the skeleton and muscular system.

For a 70-kilo runner, this is equivalent to a total impact of more than five million kilograms passing through the lower limbs and back by the time the race is over. It is this impact with the ground that causes a compression of the spine, and this is the reason why so many competitors finish the race one centimetre shorter than they started it.

Fortunately for runners concerned about a loss of stature, this shrinkage is only temporary and they should wake up back to their normal height after a good night's sleep.

Damage caused by this impact can also be reduced by wearing quality running shoes and by training for long-distance running, which will actually strengthen limbs and joints.

Shortly after the starter gun sounds, the runners have to change their breathing, increasing both its depth and frequency. This is because marathon running requires a continuous supply of oxygen to the working muscles to produce the energy needed to keep moving. At rest, most people only need to supply the muscles with about three units of oxygen per minute – one unit is equivalent to one millilitre of oxygen per kilogram of body weight.

For those at the front of the race, who are running at speeds in excess of 12 mph, this demand increases twentyfold to about 60 units a minute. Even the runners towards the back of the field, completing the distance in approximately four hours, need about 35 units of oxygen a minute, a level seldom if ever achieved by those who do little more than sit behind a desk, drive a car and watch television.

Something else that marathon runners need lots of is energy, which comes from the calories eaten in their diet. Our muscles get energy from two main sources – carbohydrate and fat – and while most people have enough reserves of fat to be able to complete 40 marathons, one after the other, we only have enough carbohydrates to run rather less than one.

This results in the well-known 'wall', the feeling of running on empty that affects most runners once they have done about 20 miles. To delay the point at which carbohydrate stores are exhausted, many runners follow carbohydrate-loading regimens in the run-up to a marathon, frantically filling up with pasta, bread and bananas in an effort to increase their carbohydrate stores.

Curiously, those at the front and those near the back will need roughly the same amount of energy to carry them from the start to the finish of the race, regardless of how long it takes to complete. Studies on marathon runners have shown the energy demand of running 26.2 miles is about 2,500 calories – roughly three-quarters of the total daily energy intake for most people.

Like a car, marathon runners need water as well as fuel. On a warm day, most runners can expect to lose up to five litres of fluid, mainly from sweating. Unless this is countered by frequent drinks en route, dehydration will quickly occur.

When this happens, runners lose the ability to keep cool by sweating, and unless the body can lose heat efficiently by sweating, temperature levels rise rapidly. If any runner at the front of the field suffers a breakdown in this system of heat loss, they will produce enough heat to raise their body temperature to boiling point by the 10-mile mark.

Before anyone who has toyed with the idea of training for and running in a marathon becomes completely disillusioned and starts thinking about something less strenuous, say snooker or darts, it is worth remembering the positive health benefits that are the reward for regular exercise and training.

Those who complete marathons will have a lower incidence of heart attacks (compared with the general population), lower blood pressure and a reduced risk of life-threatening strokes. They can also expect a longer life and should remain healthy and active for far longer than those who watch races from the safety of their armchairs before heading off to the pub for a lunchtime pint.

VOCABULARY: compound words
pp72–73

❶ Point out the use of relative clauses in the definitions. Let pairs discuss these questions before you go through the answers with the class.

> **ANSWERS:** adjectives – 70-kilo, long-distance; nouns – lunchtime, running shoes, sports research centre

Adjectives are formed by adding an adjective to a noun, often with a hyphen. Nouns are formed by joining two words (with or without a hyphen), or by two or more separate words. English adjectives (like *70-kilo*) do not have plural forms, but *sports* is a noun. Highlight common problems like *records shop* and *fourteen-years-old boy*, eliciting corrections and explanations (here, the nouns *record* and *year* are used adjectivally, so there is no pluralization). Mention that the rules determining whether a compound is hyphenated, or whether it is one or two words, are very involved. It is best for students to check which form to use in their dictionary – preferably a recent edition as, over time, some compounds can change from one to another. They can also vary from writer to writer.

VARIATION: With a more advanced class, ask how single compound words are stressed: normally, those beginning with an adjectival form stress the second word (old-<u>fashi</u>oned, narrow-<u>mind</u>ed) and those beginning with a noun stress the first (<u>spring</u>time, <u>ice</u>-skating).

❷ Students do this in pairs. They should remember some at least of these from the recording; otherwise they will probably be able to work out most of them from the meanings and the prompts.

> **ANSWERS:** 1 finishing line 2 well-known
> 3 boiling point 4 heart attack
> 5 life-threatening

❸ These could be done orally or, if more practice with relative clauses is needed, written and checked for accuracy. There are some general expressions so that students realize that compound nouns and adjectives are also widely used outside sports contexts.

> **POSSIBLE ANSWERS:** a person who plays volleyball, work (that) you do at home, a car that is used in races, a stick used for playing hockey, shelves where books are kept, a person who lifts weights (in competition), a place where people can park their cars, a person who teaches sports, a cup which is used for drinking tea, a board which is used to surf, a person who has fair hair, a person who plays football in the First Division, a person who uses the left hand rather than the right, a machine which is used to dry the hair, a race in which people walk 20 kilometres, mail that is sent electronically

❹ Students work in pairs. When the class have finished, elicit as many different compounds as possible, and check written work.

> **POSSIBLE ANSWERS:** bus stop, bus driver; tennis player, badminton player; classroom, classmate; good-looking, good-natured; rugby ball, football; ice-skates, roller-skates; toothpaste, toothache; schoolteacher, schoolchildren; golf course, golf club; gold medal, medal-winner; first place, First Certificate

VARIATION: With a weaker class, make it a matching activity by choosing suitable words that go with some or all of the ten listed and putting them on the board in jumbled order, for example: skates, children, room, teacher, paste, etc.

❺ Stress that the use of relative clauses is optional, in order to keep the exercise moving quickly. Encourage students to give more general, background information first and lead gradually towards the more specific.

WORKBOOK: Vocabulary p42.

FURTHER PRACTICE: Vocabulary p126.

GRAMMAR: punctuation *p73*

❶ Begin by eliciting the names and main uses of commas, full-stops, colons (to show that what follows is a list, an example or a summary of what has gone before, or to introduce a contrasting idea) and semi-colons (for a pause halfway in length between that of a comma and a full-stop). Some learners may have difficulties with the use of commas in participle constructions and non-defining relative clauses (see Grammar on p42), and Greek speakers may have trouble with the form of the semi-colon. If necessary, refer students to the use of the hyphen in compound adjectives (opposite).

There may be a tendency to use « » instead of inverted commas (quotation, or quote, marks), and Spanish speakers may use inverted question/ exclamation marks at the beginning of sentences.

Students work in pairs or groups and then report back to the class. Go through the answers, and ask what – if any – punctuation marks and uses in their own language they have written in.

The apostrophe may not exist in some languages, and the slash is included partly because of its increasingly common use in IT. Point out that we sometimes call brackets *parentheses*, which may be a cognate.

ANSWERS: - hyphen, to join words   ? question mark, at the end of a question   ' apostrophe, possessive/missing letter(s)   ( ) brackets, to enclose information   / slash, to give alternatives
! exclamation mark, to show surprise, anger, etc.
" " inverted commas, to indicate direct speech

Don't go through too many examples from the Reading text: eliciting one or two should be enough.

POSSIBLE ANSWERS: video-game, child-friendly; so how do British bowling alleys compare to their American counterparts?; It's, I've; (when the Super Bowl puts on a disco); It's truly a great place for the entire family to go!; : 'I was smiling from the time I walked in the door until the time I walked out.'

VARIATION: With a more advanced class, elicit or explain other uses of these signs, such as inverted commas for TV programme titles, slang, irony, etc.

❷ Students may not expect differences in the use of capitals and as a result not quite know what is going on when the use of a small letter in their written work is highlighted as a mistake (they may even wonder whether the problem is one of spelling). It is worth pointing out, then, that at First Certificate level forms such as *next november*, *my italian friend* and *she speaks french* are regarded as errors.

Groups discuss 1–10 and fill in the table. Also ask the class if the first person singular subject pronoun ('I', in English) starts with, or is, a capital, and whether any other personal pronouns are capitalized in their language. In some cases the second person polite form may be written with a capital and students could carry this over into English by writing 'You' in all sentence positions.

ANSWERS: in English, usually all have capitals except 9 (only the topic words are capitalized) and 10. Other languages will vary, but some European languages do not use capitals for nationalities, languages, months, days of the week, equivalents of the word 'street' (e.g. *rue de France*), or any but the first word of book and film titles. Some may, on the other hand, capitalize nouns in general (e.g. German).

NOTE: Particularly with younger groups, it may be advisable to have a 'serious' newspaper or book written in the students' first language so that any disputes about correctness can quickly be settled!

WRITING: a report *p74*

This task is similar to one type of task used in FCE Writing Part 2.

❶ Allow a minute or so for individuals to think about this.

❷ Students should be able to divide the task up into four sections:
a describing the activity b why it will be popular
c good points d bad points.
You may want to check this before moving on to the next stage.

❸ These are suggestions only, many of them based on points dealt with in the Listening text about the marathon. You may want to suggest other points to consider.

VARIATION: Advanced students could brainstorm more ideas here.

❹ This is a good opportunity for students to try out the use of relative clauses. Suggest, as with other 'new' grammar points, that if they are experimenting but are not sure whether what they have written is right, they put a question mark in the margin for your attention. Also encourage them to practise using any forms of punctuation that they tend to find difficult.

❺ Pay particular attention when you look at their work to any habitual errors and any involving the grammar and punctuation/capitalization points from this Unit.

WORKBOOK: Writing p47; Focus On Writing p80.

VOCABULARY: prepositional phrases with *in* *p74*

❶ Point out that these are just some, although among the most common of the many expressions with *in*. You could mention that they often come after the verb, or the object of the verb if there is one. For emphasis they are sometimes at the beginning of the clause or sentence, but this is complicated by the fact that a number of them would not normally be placed there.

With a strong class elicit, or give, more (e.g. *in tears*) – but don't bother with purely positional expressions like 'in the room'. Warn against being fooled by potential 'false friends' like *in particular/in private*. As with other exercises of this type, remind students that although a phrase may appear to fit more than one gap ('in fact' could fit in Question 9, but 'in other words' would not work in Question 2) they have to look at all the questions before they can be sure that any single one has the correct answer. Draw attention to the use of inverted commas to show that each is a personal opinion.

ANSWERS: 1 in danger   2 in fact   3 in public
4 in half   5 in common   6 in private   7 in particular   8 in trouble   9 in other words
10 in love Not needed: in the end

❷ When you have been through the answers to activity 1, allow time for pairs to discuss each of the comments in turn. Each student then writes a sentence using *in the end*, for example:

In the end, the Olympics will be completely commercialized.
They will stop athletes using drugs in the end.
In the end, (my country) will have the best team in the world.
There'll be nothing but sport on TV in the end.
Give pairs more time to discuss these, and perhaps have some or all reported back to the class.

FURTHER PRACTICE: Prepositional phrases with *at*, *by* and *on* p127.

COMMON ERRORS

The winners celebrated at the end of the match. We use *at the end* to mean 'when it finished' but *in the end* when we want to say 'finally, after a lot of difficulties or uncertainties', e.g. *It was a hard match but in the end they were the winners.*

USE OF ENGLISH: error correction
p75

If your students have not practised an error correction activity before, you may want to refer them to the Skills Development in the Workbook. Students look at the Help box and do the exercise alone. Further practice with relative pronouns and prepositional phrases with 'in' (*in time*, *in bed*, etc.) is given. You may want to focus on 'in the bed' if it is a common error carried over from the students' first language. Ask the class to explain the use of punctuation in the text, especially exclamation marks and the apostrophe in *Where're* (informal speech). Refer students to the grammar reference if they find *wish* confusing.

ANSWERS: 1 was 3 in 4 been 7 by 8 of 9 had 11 for 12 it 13 being 14 the 15 who

VARIATION: With a weaker class, you could give further clues by telling them what part of speech some or all of the incorrect words are.

WORKBOOK: Error correction p46; Focus On Use of English p88.

FURTHER PRACTICE: Error correction p127.

PHRASAL VERBS: *give* *p75*

❶ The example is taken from the Error Correction text above. Elicit the meaning: stop trying (to find it). Students could do the exercises in pairs. Point out that other phrasal verbs with 'give' exist, but these are probably the most common.

ANSWERS: 1C 2F 3A 4G 5D 6B 7E

VARIATION: With a more advanced class, ask which of the phrasal verbs in 1–7 are separable, i.e. which can put the object before the second part, for example *When are you going to give that racket you borrowed back?* Answer: all except Question 3, where there is no object.

❷ Once the meanings have been established in activity 1, pairs decide on the best answers. The phrasal verb *cut down* in answer g is recycled from Unit 4.

ANSWERS: a5 b4 c6 d2 e1 f3 g7

❸ Pairs practise asking and answering, using all seven phrasal verbs.

COMMON ERRORS

Give back the ball you borrowed or *Give the ball you borrowed back*. The object has been included twice.

EXAM STUDY GUIDE *p76*

With some classes, you could introduce a third category of 'fairly sure', and/or do the activity on a percentage basis: from 100% ('completely sure') through 50% ('fairly sure') to 0% ('totally unsure'). Suggest that students follow a mixture of the advice given (as they should always do if their answers fall into more than one category).

Warn students against reading too much into a single exercise (seven questions with a 50/50 chance of being right in the case of the exercise on this page), as it is unlikely to give a usefully representative sample of either questions or answers.

Look at the categories ticked by students and make a note for future planning and reference. This approach can also be used with reading and Use of English tasks. Point out the use of inverted commas in the quotes. You could add to the suggestions here by using your knowledge of the students' country. For example, by telling them the local times of programmes on the World Service, BBC World TV, MTV, etc. that are relevant to their age group and interests, and that have useful language content. Point out the importance of regular listening, rather than one-offs that are not likely to help very much. Mention the addresses of bookshops and libraries that sell or lend 'talking books', TV programme guides, magazines with film reviews and so on. Record from the radio/TV while you are in English-speaking countries, and don't forget the commercials or, better still, programmes featuring lots of funny/clever ads. When groups have finished, ask a spokesperson from each one to report the best ideas back to the class, and make a note of them yourself.

LISTENING *p76*

❶ Student A quickly answers the eight points while B reads the text on p166. Suggest they look at the format of the instructions and questions in activity 3 below, as these are typical of the kinds used in FCE. When the class have finished, go through all eight points. Answer: 7 is incorrect – it is always one or the other and it is better to guess than to leave a blank.

❷ Elicit answers when groups have discussed these questions. Ensure everyone keeps a note of the football words, some of which may be cognates. Answers: Football. She has to referee matches using whistle, red and yellow cards, make sure everyone follows the rules, stop play to award free kicks, penalties, throw-ins, etc. Age 13 – perhaps point out that she referees junior matches played by boys and girls. With her training, experience and confidence, players probably react no worse than with any other referee.

❸ Students do the listening task individually. The advice relates back to the Exam Study Guide above; if students seize on the expression 'Come on, ref' and stop listening for any more on that point, they may miss the correction the speaker makes ('Come on, reds'). Play the tape twice and then go through the answers.

> **ANSWERS:** 1F 2T 3F 4F 5T 6F 7T

WORKBOOK: Focus on Listening p96.

TAPESCRIPT

Interviewer: Abigail, at 13 you're the youngest qualified female referee in the country. How did it happen?

Abigail: Well, since I was little I'd always loved playing football but I was starting to get fed up with the way the others at school were behaving. They wouldn't let me have the ball and they kept swearing at me – and that was my own side. So my dad suggested I should go on a refereeing course he'd spotted in Exeter, which was run by the Football Association.

Interviewer: And you passed both the oral and the written exams with flying colours, I believe. How old were you then?

Abigail: I was just twelve. Now I've got to wait till I'm fourteen to be fully registered, but then I can start really doing things!

Interviewer: And with your single-mindedness I'm sure you'll go right to the top. But let's just go back to when you began. How did you feel when you first refereed a match? Was it a frightening experience?

Abigail: Well, it was cold and wet and I must admit I was very nervous, at least until I blew the first whistle. After that I think my mum suffered more than me.

Interviewer: Was she there, at the game?

Abigail: Yes, she was on the touchline. She was really wound up and she told me later that she thought she could hear the opposition manager yelling 'Come on, ref!' every two minutes. It wasn't until way into the second half that she realized he was shouting 'Come on, reds!'.

Interviewer: Tell me, how many yellow and red cards have you shown, and how did the players react?

Abigail: I've only ever shown one, and it was a yellow. And it was in a school 'friendly'!

Interviewer: What happened when you did that?

Abigail: After I had booked him the rest of the players decided that they wanted to get their name in my book and they all started kicking one another, but I refused to play that game and kept my cards in my pocket.

Interviewer: So already you're capable of applying commonsense rather than the letter of the law, which many of your seniors find impossible, I must say. And talking of seniors, do you ever get to watch the professional game, or are you too busy with training and your own matches?

Abigail: Well, now and then I do, but I always seem to end up spending as much time watching the referee as the game. Even at Plymouth Argyle, which is my favourite team.

Interviewer: How do you react to all the criticism that the modern referee has to endure? What about the endless scrutiny on TV of controversial decisions?

Abigail: The referee's always right.

Interviewer: But why are you prepared to be the target of all the nasty comments you know you're going to get? Surely it can't be very pleasant?

Abigail: My mum says I just like being in charge but it's not that. I suppose it's because there are things I want to do. What I really dream about is doing the Cup Final, with the world's TV cameras there.

Interviewer: Perhaps one day you will. If so I don't think there's much chance that you'll be compromised by the presence of Plymouth Argyle.

Abigail: Oh, I don't know!

Interviewer: Abigail, thanks for talking to us.

Abigail: Thank you.

SPEAKING *p77*

❶❷❸ Remind the class that this task is similar to Part 2 of FCE Speaking. You may want to put students into different pairs where there is more likelihood that one will prefer to talk about team sports and the other about tennis.

Encourage students to find not only differences but also similarities, for instance: both games played with a round ball, team sports, all men, penalties/free throws, noisy young fans, popular in Mediterranean countries and so on. Feed in vocabulary where necessary (if none of these are exactly your favourite sports, you might want to ask a colleague before the lesson for some basic expressions!). If you are not sure of the meanings of some of the terms, elicit them. Get students to begin with forms such as 'It's when …, or conditionals and relative clauses as suggested in the Student's Book.

Remind the class that Student B's comments on A's pictures, and vice versa, should be fairly short, as in the exam.

Stage 5 could enable Student A to say whether he or she prefers to see amateur as opposed to professional sport – especially if this is an issue in the student's country.

WORKBOOK: Focus On Speaking p104.

STUDY CHECK *p77*

1 When groups have finished, they report back to the class. Take a class vote or count the number of groups that have voted for each person, sport, etc., making a note of their likes and dislikes for future reference. The use of the present perfect with *ever* previews the main grammar focus of the next Unit.

2 Students work individually. Encourage the use of the grammar, vocabulary and punctuation presented in this Unit.

Students now do Unit Test 7 on p174 of this book. The answers are on p215.

8 In the spotlight

You could begin the Unit with this optional Vocabulary activity:
Put these words into pairs with the same meaning, e.g. *recording* and *tape*.

> recording show comedy cartoons shock humour idiotic programme tape moronic offend animations

Students match these quickly in pairs. Point out that the words are all used in the reading text. They are introduced here as they may be useful in the Speaking section that follows. You may want to add some pairs of words from the text that are not directly related to the topic: *sofa*/*couch*, *film*/*movie*, etc., although the latter two (and other words that overlap with TV, like *script* and *casting*) have already appeared within the topic of Cinema (Unit 2). With a weak group, point out (or begin by eliciting) the part of speech of each word, especially those, like *show* and *shock*, that can be either verb or noun. Go through the meanings when pairs have finished.

> **ANSWERS:** show/programme, comedy/humour, idiotic/moronic, cartoons/animations, shock/offend

SPEAKING *p78*

This could be done as a whole-class warm-up. Elicit the names of the programmes (they may of course be different in the students' first language) and those of the main characters (and their English pronunciation).

> **ANSWERS:** the Flintstones, the Simpsons, Tom and Jerry, Beavis and Butthead

Ask which channel they are usually on. Check the names and pronunciation of international TV channels (and highlight the word 'channel', not 'canal' or 'chain' for TV station). Check whether these (or similar cartoons) are shown in English or dubbed into the local language, and possibly also the times if students seem very keen on any of them. Elicit words they associate with each, like 'family' (the *Simpsons*) and 'dinosaurs' (the *Flintstones*), and ask – if the class answer 'children' in response to the question about age group – whether adults enjoy them too, and *vice versa*.

Ask the class if they know anyone like, for example, Bart Simpson and what makes characters like that believable (or not). Ask if there are people who copy them, how and with what results. Find out whether they think any copying of cartoon characters is conscious or not, and what it can lead to – especially Beavis and Butthead or similar, but also the effect the violence in, say, *Tom and Jerry* might have on children. Ask about the sort of messages these programmes send out in terms of stereotyping,

attitudes to other people, to animals, to work, to studying and so on. With a younger class, you could ask whether their parents stop them watching any of these programmes, and why.

VARIATION: With an advanced, or older, class, ask what kind of humour each is, presenting or eliciting expressions like 'satirical', 'slapstick', 'witty' and 'black humour'. You may want to ask why we find certain things funny and others not, the differences between individuals and between cultures, and whether such conflicts as those between cat and mouse (*Tom and Jerry*) represent 'universal' humour. If so, ask if there are any others.

READING: gapped text *pp78–79*

❶ Remind students that sometimes the exercise consists of replacing sentences and sometimes entire paragraphs, but that it is always one or the other, not a mixture of missing sentences and missing paragraphs. Also point out that (in the case of sentences) they can be taken from anywhere in the paragraph. Allow time for students to read the information and possibly refer them back to previous Part 3 (sentence) activities in Units 2 and 4 for examples.

Students read the instructions and advice individually, asking any questions they may have. Remind them that looking at the example and deciding why it is right is always an excellent way of 'tuning into' the text and the task. Point out the importance of looking for various kinds of links – especially meaning, grammar and vocabulary. The use of 'all of which' as a clue relates back to the grammar in Unit 7 (relatives); the focus on inverted commas relates back to Punctuation (also in Unit 7). Students then work through the text and questions in a maximum of about 20 minutes (they will, however, need to work slightly faster than this in the actual exam: the total time allowed for the four Parts of Paper 1 is 75 minutes, of which some time must be left for transferring answers to, and/or checking, the answer sheet). Go through the answers, but do not take any vocabulary questions for the moment.

> **ANSWERS:** 1F 2A 3B 4C 5D 6G Not needed: E

❷ It is important that students use the context to decide on the meanings, rather than just make inspired guesses. Elicit a more detailed description of *couch potatoes* (people who spend all their time sitting on the sofa, presumably watching TV) and perhaps ask what, therefore, a *mouse potato* does, or doesn't, do (spends all day sitting looking at a PC screen).

> **ANSWERS:** full-length / not shortened, sitcoms / TV comedy series, couch potatoes / lazy people, simple-minded / unintelligent, spin-off / series derived from, pop culture / art forms for ordinary people

Elicit examples of *pop culture* and *sitcoms* (= 'situation comedies': showing the same characters in a particular situation, often weekly); perhaps also any *spin-offs* that students might know. If necessary, refer students back to Compound Words in Unit 7.

❸ You could give an example of how to use the context for the first word: *critics* is contrasted with 'supporters' and 'fans' in the same sentence. Elicit the rest, pointing out that they are all related to the topic and therefore may well be useful later on in the Unit.

> **POSSIBLE ANSWERS:** critics – opponents; casting – selecting; animations – cartoon films; credits – list of names at the end of a film; scripts – dialogue; commentary – observations on the action

❹ Finish with a brief class discussion if the exchange of opinions among pairs is lively.

WORKBOOK: Part 3 pp50–51; Focus On Reading p72.

FURTHER PRACTICE: Gapped text p131.

GRAMMAR: the present perfect
pp80–81

❶ 1 The example is taken from the Reading text on p79. Students first establish that the tense of 'appeared' is the past simple, and that 'has been' is the present perfect. Then they should decide that the first event happened in 1993 (elicit or point out 'at a definite point in the past'), and that the debate started at some time in the past between 1993 and the time of writing and is still going on. Ask the class what they decided about the third question: if they say 'the present simple' or 'the past simple', point out that neither is possible in English in this sentence. Do not attempt to explain why at this point, as this is the focus of the next part of the activity.

2 Students discuss this in pairs.

> **ANSWER:** A; not 'this year' or similar, so it's not B; no mention of obvious present results, so it can't be C; we know that it started in 1993, so it isn't D

3 Focus attention on uses B, C and D and allow pairs a minute or two to work these out. Go through the answers and then give (or, with a strong class, elicit) more examples of each use, for instance 'I've been to New York twice this year' (B), 'I've lost my pen'(C), 'There's been an accident' (D).

> **ANSWERS:** a C   b D   c B

❷ This part focuses on meaning C of the present perfect. Point out that once the TV headline had been given, the news item would probably be in the past simple:
A plane has made an emergency landing. No-one was hurt in the incident, which took place ...

> **SUGGESTED ANSWERS:** 1 A teenager has saved a child from the river.   2 A local hero has won the World Championship.   3 The voters have elected a new government for the next five years.
> 4 A storm has hit the Atlantic coast and homes have been damaged.   5 A bomb has exploded in the city centre but nobody has been hurt.
> 6 A student has passed the exam with the highest-ever score.

VARIATION: With an advanced class, extend this to more complicated headlines.

❸ Students discuss these in pairs. Point out, especially to a younger or weaker class, that 'January', 'Friday', etc. could equally well be 'June' or 'Tuesday' and so on.

> **ANSWERS:**
> 1 recently, this month, since January, so far this year, already
> 2 last year, last Friday, while I was listening, a few days ago, when it happened

❹ This activity concentrates on the use of *for* and *since* to express meaning A. You may want to give / elicit more examples. It also revises relative clauses (non-defining) from Unit 7. Students do these individually – unless they need to ask other students questions about the dates (if no-one knows, suggest they guess). When they have finished writing, they compare their sentences (and opinions) with their partners. Some of the verbs (*enjoy/watch*, *hate/ avoid*) are interchangeable, but what is lexically more important is the introduction of more media expressions like *satellite dish*, *teletext*, *broadcast*, *quiz show* and *soap*. Go through the answers with the class as usual, making a note for future reference of what particularly interests, bores or simply turns students off.

> **POSSIBLE ANSWERS:** 1 have watched, over a year
> 2 has been, 1980   3 have followed, it started
> 4 have enjoyed, two years   5 have hated, I was a child

COMMON ERRORS

I've known her for five years. During is used to indicate when something took place (morning / afternoon / evening / night, months, seasons, years, decades, centuries); *for* for how long it took.

❺ This exercise practises use D of the present perfect. Elicit more changes, based if possible on the local situation, e.g. 'The number of homes with cable TV has increased'; 'A well-known media tycoon has bought two of the biggest channels'. Rather than have students write what they believe to be untrue, let them use individual verbs more than once. The answers will be student-specific, and several of the verbs are interchangeable, but here are some possibilities:

POSSIBLE ANSWERS:
1 Programmes in general have got worse.
2 The amount of advertising has dropped.
3 The number of channels has increased.
4 Picture quality has improved.
5 The number of video recorders has risen.
6 The price of TV sets has fallen.
7 Programmes for young people have changed.
8 The number of programmes in English has stayed the same.

6 The initial aim here is to practise short forms using *ever/yet/already/still*, so encourage brief exchanges first and allow longer discussions about individual programmes only when you are satisfied they have mastered these forms. Tell students also to try to persuade each other to watch or listen to programmes they haven't seen/heard 'yet'.

7 Point out that questions requiring the use of the present perfect are quite common in FCE Use of English Part 3. Let individuals or pairs have plenty of time to think and write before you go through the answers.

ANSWERS: 1 hasn't been on TV 2 best documentary I've ever 3 haven't watched it for 4 worst series they've ever 5 have run out of 6 have been able to see

8 1 Students work in pairs.

VARIATION 1: With younger learners, you may want to give short prompts ('bus strike', 'bank robbery', 'earthquake') to get pairs started, possibly writing them up on the board. They should then produce simple forms such as 'There's been a bus strike'.

VARIATION 2: Stronger students could give more details without using time expressions or other tenses: 'There's been chaos throughout the city centre and the emergency services have been seriously affected.' B could then ask questions such as 'What did people do?', to which A replies (also using the past simple), for example, 'Many of them walked to work'.

2 Ideally, students talk about their extra listening, reading, etc. as suggested in the Exam Study Guide boxes (for speaking ideas, see the last page of this Unit), but they could also mention skills practice set for homework. Follow-up questions and answers as in 1.

FURTHER PRACTICE: Present perfect or past simple? p130.

VOCABULARY: the arts *p82*

1 Students work in pairs. Check when they have finished, eliciting more in all categories, though pointing out that 'music' in this context relates to that in opera, ballet and other forms of dance (for music in general, see Unit 4).

ANSWERS: 1 exhibition, portrait, abstract, sculpture, shade, watercolours, sketch, canvas, art gallery, drawing, frame, oil painting, carving, landscape 2 opera house, concert hall, ballet, ballerina, tenor, stage, applause, soprano, audience 3 masterpiece, creative

2 Pairs describe and give reasons.

WORKBOOK: Vocabulary p48.

FURTHER PRACTICE: Vocabulary and speaking p129.

LISTENING *p82*

1 Point out that this kind of multiple-matching task sometimes occurs in the exam and stress the importance of always knowing which person they are listening to. The Help here should introduce them to the voices and roles. Play the recording twice. Students work individually. Go through the answers.

ANSWERS: 1R 2K 3K 4R 5T 6K 7T

2 You could suggest they consider whose comments, the mother's or the teacher's, are more likely to help Kate in terms of her art and her life in general.

FOLLOW-UP: Students describe a famous work of art to their partners, who have to guess what it is. They could choose anything artistic: a painting, a famous sculpture or statue, etc. Tell them not to reveal the name or too many clues at the beginning.

WORKBOOK: Part 4 p49; Focus On Listening p96.

TAPESCRIPT

T: You've always enjoyed drawing, I think, Kate, haven't you?

K: Yes, even when I was a kid I liked to do sketches on bits of paper: I'd just start drawing something simple and then it'd get more complicated and I'd just carry on until I'd done something I liked the look of.

R: Yes, we'd be forever coming across drawings around the house, she'd been doing drawings like that since she was six, and of course I saw things her friends had drawn when they were together, but somehow Kate's were quite different.

T: In what way?

R: I think somehow they weren't, well, the only way I can put this is that they weren't *childish*, I mean you could see immediately what they were.

T: They weren't just rough shapes, then?

R: No, there was much more to them than that, and they seemed to have a sort of *depth* about them, too.

K: I think what my mum's saying is that they were three-dimensional, with shading and perspective and things like that.

T: And how did you feel about this?

R: Well, to be honest her father and I weren't really sure what to think, with her being so young and…

T: And what are your feelings now, Mrs Ray?

R: Oh nowadays I realize that's what she wants to do, and she does it very well so it's up to her.

K: I wish! You're always telling me I'm spending too long in my room, I don't eat properly and all the rest of it!

R: But it's true! Some days in the school holidays we don't see you from dawn to dusk, and as for your friends – well, pretty soon I'm sure they'll just give up trying to ring you and make friends with someone else.

T: Can I just say that this sounds quite typical of highly creative individuals; they often do have a tendency to neglect relationships with family and friends, though of course this doesn't mean they feel any less close to them.

R: But surely it isn't normal for a girl of fourteen to be getting up and going out at half past five, when it's still dark – which is what she's started doing lately.

K: You know why I do that, Mum, I've explained it all before. I have to get out early, to get some fresh air and exercise, to walk for a hour or so until I start to feel a bit tired and then when I get back and sit down the ideas just seem to start to flow and more often than not I'll do some decent work.

T: Well once again that seems to be a fairly common pattern, with the artist finding that the best new ideas come when she's half-thinking about something else, not concentrating too much on *trying* to create something original. So I really wouldn't worry, Mrs Ray, your daughter seems to me …

GRAMMAR: present perfect continuous *p83*

❶ Let students do the task quickly and then elicit the answer: … present perfect … present participle … .

VARIATION: With a weak class, give or elicit more examples of the affirmative form plus negatives and interrogatives.

❷ Don't spend too long on the activity, or analysing the answers (a2 b3 c1), as in some cases the uses can overlap ('You've been working on that for ages and it's still only half done!'), but you may want to give/ elicit more examples and ask which categories they fall into.

❸ Students work in pairs. Ask why 6 is wrong but 9 is right: different meanings of 'have' ('possess' in 6 but delexical in 9). Take any questions on theatre vocabulary and go through the answers.

> **ANSWERS:** 1 Nobody's recognized her yet.
> 2 I've always wanted to study drama.   3 correct
> 4 I think I've lost my ticket for tonight.   5 correct
> 6 This town has had a theatre for centuries.
> 7 Shakespeare isn't easy, but I've understood so far.
> 8 They've stopped putting good plays on TV recently.   9 correct   10 I've liked his acting since I was a child.

VARIATION: With a weak class, refer them back to Unit 1 grammar and point out that the same restrictions on stative verbs in the present continuous apply to other continuous forms.

❹ Students do this individually. Refer them back to activity 3 on p80 if they have difficulties deciding between simple past and perfect forms. Go through the answers with the class.

> **ANSWERS:** 1 went   2 have admired   3 spoke
> 4 have been waiting   5 have been studying
> 6 told   7 have seen   8 was   9 said
> 10 have been looking   11 have been thinking

FOLLOW-UP: Point out that some verbs can be used in either the present perfect or the present perfect continuous without much difference in meaning, for example:
She's worked in the theatre for years. She's been working in the theatre for years.
Explain that other verbs like this include *live*, *rain*, *stay*, *study* and *wait*, and tell students to make an example sentence for each ('We've been living here for years,' etc.), either written or spoken.
Then ask them what these verbs have in common.

> **ANSWER:** they all refer to something that is continuous anyway

WORKBOOK: Present perfect forms pp51–52.

USE OF ENGLISH: word formation *p83*

❶ This activity follows on from the use of present or past participles to form perfect tenses. See also Participle Adjectives on p26. Students fill in the missing words, referring to the instructions in activity 2 below if necessary. Check the answers (1 fascinating; 2 amazed) and which is the present participle (*fascinating*) and which is the past participle (*amazed*).

❷ You may want to refer students back to the focus on Use of English Part 5 on p61, as well as the advice on affixes on p30, before students do this activity individually. Check for correct spelling, especially for answers 3, 5 and 9 (dropping the 'e' from the base word).

> **ANSWERS:** 1 favourite   2 discussion   3 raising
> 4 following   5 providing   6 faced   7 acting
> 8 performances   9 producing   10 powerful

WORKBOOK: Multiple-choice cloze p52; Focus On Use of English p88.

WRITING: a transactional letter *pp84–85*

❶ Students work in pairs. Remind them that this question is compulsory and that there is no choice of titles. With an advanced class point out that basically the tasks fall into two main groups: responding to a request for action or initiating action.

The aim of the activity is to make students aware of the range of possibilities that exists, and to prepare them for activities 2 and 3 below. If students ask, tell them that: **a** 3 is the maximum number of texts, **b** 'linked' means annotated, with arrows or lines pointing to the relevant parts of the text, **c** 'other' might include leaflets, etc., **d** 'other' could be boss, neighbour, etc., **e** 'other' might be 'very informal' or 'intimate' (relative, etc.), but not 'very formal' or similar, **f** 'other' could include 'correct', etc.

> **ANSWERS:** b linked   c advert, note   d company, stranger   e semi-formal   f complain

❷ In pairs, they write in the four other notes handwritten on the 'Channel Extra' text, if necessary drawing a line to indicate the part of the text that means the same, which they should underline. Highlight media expressions in the letter, such as 'classic', 'commercial breaks' and 'updates', and take any other questions on the language used. There are potentially useful forms like 'I am afraid (that)', 'up to the standard', 'to make matters worse' and 'hour after hour'. Go through the answers (and/or check written work if you feel they may have made mistakes).

> **ANSWERS:** Ads always interrupting/*spoilt by all the commercial breaks*; Not the sports popular here/*in this country we do not think of baseball or American football as top sports*; Not in original language/*translated*; Same reports again and again/*same stories repeated hour after hour*

VARIATION: With a strong class, ask them for alternative ways of expressing each point.

❸ Remind students that the basic guidelines for Paper 2 Part 1 were given in Unit 1: you may want them to refer back to these (and their own notes and writing) before continuing. Point out that the first eight points here apply to all transactional letters, the ninth just to letters of complaint. Allow pairs to read the points quickly and ask if there is anything they don't understand, then give them sufficient time to check the letter carefully.

> **ANSWERS:** With the exception of 7 (ticking as each mentioned), all the points are covered. The writer adds the suggestion (8) that the reader should cancel and refund.

❹ Emphasize that the text, like similar ones in the exam, is an extract, not a complete letter. Students work individually, seeking help with any comprehension difficulties. Particularly with weaker classes, go through the 'Before you write' points before they put pen to paper:

> **SUGGESTED ANSWER:** Analyse: d friend
> e informal   f inform
> Possible key words: arts, theatre, art galleries, museums, concert, opera, ballet, what's on, how easy, how much, let me know, first visit, haven't been, artists, TV, play, long way, costs.
> Possible plan/purpose: 1st paragraph – thank friend for letter/say why writing
> 2nd/3rd/4th paragraphs – build on key words in notes and text, possibly add more information
> 5th paragraph – express hope that information will be useful/look forward to seeing friend

Possible useful expressions: *I think you'd enjoy*; *I'm sure you'll have a good time*, etc. Highlight the pronunciation of the key words, especially any that look the same as those in the students' first language (possibly *theatre*, *opera*, *ballet*, for example) but may be pronounced quite differently. Elicit the meaning of 'play' in this context. Remind students of the need to use *been*, not 'gone' when forming the first person, present perfect of *to go* ('I have gone' is a highly unlikely form).

While students write, answer any vocabulary questions they might have. For 'music' words, refer them back to Unit 4. Allow a few minutes for them to check their work after they finish, looking particularly, as always, for any habitual errors. Tell them also to put themselves in the place of the reader, and imagine whether they would feel they had been given the information they requested in a friendly and helpful manner. The word *role* should be familiar from 'roleplay', but make sure students understand it as it appears again (in a different, but related, context) in the rubric of Listening on p86.

Pairs show each other their lists of common mistakes while they check one another's work.

WORKBOOK: Writing p53; Focus On Writing p80.

LISTENING *p86*

This section follows on from the Part 1 focus in Unit 3, which dealt with questions on factual information. The focus in Unit 12 will be on questions about mood, attitude and feeling, while Unit 15 will look at questions that ask about purpose.

Explain or elicit what is meant here by 'role': somebody's position in a social situation which entails a certain kind of behaviour and way of speaking. Ask students to think about the different forms of address, for example, that are used in their first language depending on whether people are talking to their boss, a stranger or a friend; the head teacher or a fellow pupil, etc. There is likely to be an even more clearly marked distinction than in English, as they will probably use different pronouns (*tú/usted*, *tu/vous*, etc.) and verb forms in the second person.

Begin the activity by telling the class to work through Questions 1 and 2 (there is no recording for these two) and discuss the answers in pairs.

1 You may want to ask for examples of speech that would be unlikely if the secretary were talking to her boss ('Look…', 'just because you couldn't be bothered…', etc.). The use of the third person indicates a third party who is not the listener. 'Tins, brushes and paint' indicate a decorator. 'She' is probably the secretary's boss.

ANSWER: B

2 Pairs should decide that 'This' indicates that the speaker is actually in the place. Remind them always to pay particular attention, when the question is 'Where…?', to what accompanies expressions of place.

ANSWER: A

3–8 Tell students to read the advice carefully, stressing the importance of not answering too quickly on the basis of incomplete or misleading information. One occurrence of the present perfect that needs special care is *I've flown across here* in Question 6, which does not state a definite time but could be construed as meaning the speaker is still in a plane, leading to an incorrect choice of A as the answer. Play the recording in the usual way, bearing in mind that in Part 1 each separate text is played twice consecutively. Go through the answers.

ANSWERS: 3A 4C 5A 6B 7A 8B

VARIATION: With a strong class, elicit the words that act as 'distractors' from the correct answer, for instance in 2: *station*, *railway*.

WORKBOOK: Focus On Listening p96.

TAPESCRIPT
Three
…so I wonder, Frank, if you could possibly have a look at the motor for me? I'd take it to the garage but you know how much they charge just for a mechanic to stick his nose under the bonnet, and as for the guy I bought it from – well, he just keeps saying 'it never gave *me* any trouble' and it's really a waste of time talking to him. I've tried just about everything I can do myself without any luck but I'm sure it's something really simple and I know you've always been pretty good with things like that – ever since you fixed my bike when we were kids, in fact!

Four
Man: Come on, let's go in, we've been waiting for ages.
Woman: Let's hang on for just a minute or so. We said we'd meet them here and the play doesn't start for another half hour, after all.
Man: Well I don't see why we can't meet them in the bar and then go straight to our seats all together. What's the point of having an evening at the theatre if we're going to spend half our time standing on the pavement?

Woman: Look, why don't you go in and have a drink now, and I'll stay here for a bit longer, just in case they turn up?
Man: OK, see you soon.

Five
Yes, I know it'd mean I wouldn't be able to go to school that day, but the exams are over and it really doesn't matter that much; loads of people are taking days off whenever they feel like it and the teacher doesn't say, well, a thing. Kylie's with me now and *her* mum says she can go, and you know how strict she is. But this really is something special, it's Swan Lake and you know how much I've always wanted to go to the ballet, so please, just this once…

Six
The view from up here, on a clear day like this, really is quite breathtaking. You can actually see right across the forest, the rivers and the hills to both the east and the west coast, and to the south the famous six peaks across the Straits are clearly visible. I've flown across here, of course, so I knew roughly what to expect, but that was at 30,000 feet and I never imagined how incredible the landscape would be from this height. And somehow it's even more magical when you've paused to look out from the fiftieth floor, then from the hundredth and finally, when you reach the very top, you get to see the whole fantastic panorama.

Seven
No, I'm afraid we've got nothing at all left for tomorrow evening or Saturday, we're completely booked up. If you leave it with me I might be able to find you something for early next week, perhaps for an afternoon performance, but that all depends on people cancelling and returning their tickets so it's by no means certain. All I can suggest, then, is that you give me your name and a contact phone number, and if anything comes up my colleague or I will give you a ring. How does that sound?

Eight
Woman: I like that one. The colours really are something special. Where did you find it?
Man: Oh, in a little shop down one of those side streets behind the city centre. Got it pretty cheaply. In fact the new frame cost almost as much.
Woman: And yet it sort of brightens up the whole place, doesn't it? It's amazing what one good painting can do – especially in a room like this.
Man: Yeah, that's why I chose it, really. I spend a lot of time in here: reading, listening to music and that.

SPEAKING *p87*

❶ Begin by asking the class what they know about Part 1 of Speaking, and how to approach it. Mention the short dialogue at the beginning, where the Interlocutor introduces himself/herself and the Assessor, and checks the identity of the candidates. You may want to point out that they are being assessed right from the moment they go into the exam room, so there is no question of 'waiting for the exam to start' before they begin to speak good English! Remind them always to say 'Hello', 'Good Morning' or something similar when they walk in.

Students do the activity in pairs, with the emphasis more on creating the right message in each case rather than absolutely correct sentences, although it does provide practice with notes similar to the work they have been doing in Writing. Go through the answers with the class, giving and/or eliciting more suggestions and information where you think necessary.

SUGGESTED ANSWERS:
There are two examiners, one talks to you and the other assesses you.
Listen carefully to the examiner's questions.
Ask for a repetition (of the question) if you don't understand.
The longer your answers are, the better.
Don't speak too quietly.
Speeches learnt before the exam are not allowed/ You are not allowed to make...
The main aim is to get used to your partner and the examiners.
Each candidate speaks for a maximum of about 2 minutes.

---

❷ Students work individually. Point out that this is the likely order of the categories in the exam. Put a time limit on this and encourage students not to spend too much time on any one category. With weaker students, you could prompt with some of the following:

1 Your home town
Where are you from? Where do you live now? How long have you lived there? What do you like and dislike about living there? If you have lived anywhere else, what are the main differences between the two places?

2 Your family
How many brothers and sisters do you have? How well do you get on with them? Do you spend much time with your cousins? What kinds of things do you talk about with your parents, aunts and uncles and grandparents?

3 Your work or studies
What do you enjoy most and least about your job, school or university? What qualifications do you (or did you) need to get for your job, for university or for the job you want to do? Where would you most like to study or work?

4 Your leisure activities
What is your favourite hobby, sport or cultural activity? How did you become interested in it? What sort of TV programmes do you like to watch? What kinds of music do you like to listen to? How do you usually spend your holidays?

5 Your future plans
What are your aims for the next few years? How will learning English help you achieve them? What do you think you will be doing and where will you probably be living in five years' time? How do you think you will spend your free time then?

The six points are loosely based on the criteria used by the examiners. Stress that they will be marked positively, i.e. that they will be given credit for what they demonstrate they are capable of doing, rather than simply having marks deducted for mistakes. Students fill in the table individually, although with some classes you may feel they would benefit from also asking their partners for a second opinion. In any event, make a note of the students' self-assessment and repeat the activity later in the course, getting the class to compare their evaluations then and now.

Elicit more suggestions for speaking practice, and add any of your own based on your local knowledge, for example places where English-speakers – including people using English as a *lingua franca* – tend to go in the evening, language conversation groups and advertisements (often in English-language magazines, bookshops and clubs) for language lesson exchange.

❸ Put students into groups that are not usually together, as otherwise many of the questions will lack authenticity. Monitor the conversations, ensuring that 'Candidates' do not just give 'Yes/No' or other single-word answers, but expand on and illustrate the points they are asked about. The 'Assessors' write down their marks: have a look at these before the Candidate sees them.

FOLLOW-UP: Let the Candidates leave the groups and talk to other Candidates about how it went – just as they might after the real exam – while Examiners and Assessors discuss the marks and any other useful comments they want to make. The original groups then reform and the mark sheets are given, other feedback provided and Examiners/Assessors can point out any difficulties they may have had, such as Candidates speaking too quietly or not enough, using L1 words and so on. Candidates could also comment on the Examiners' performance: relevance of the questions, manner, etc. ... Groups could then report back to the class, but only on general difficulties they face and their possible solutions rather than commenting on individual students.

WORKBOOK: Focus On Speaking p104.

STUDY CHECK *p87*

❶ Students work individually. They could also write about what these people have achieved, not managed/been able to do, seemed about to do and wanted to do.

VARIATION: More advanced students could imagine what they have felt like doing and what they have been thinking of doing, where they have been thinking of going and so on.

❷ With some classes you may want to tell them before they start that this is for individuals only: they won't have to show their sentences to other students, otherwise some may be inhibited by the personal nature of experiences, or by not wanting to seem boastful. Remind the class that this use of the present perfect means 'some time in my life' and therefore need not refer to recent events. Collect their work for correction.

❸ Point out that to tell the story of a TV programme, play, etc. we often use the present simple, but mixed with present perfect forms to give background ('She lives alone but she's been going out with a man who ...'). When the compositions have been written and corrected, you could ask the writers of some of the better ones to read them out to the class, without mentioning the name of their choice of subject. The class have to listen and try to identify the programme, play, etc.

FOLLOW-UP: For further practice with the present perfect continuous, put the following sentences on the board or OHP and get the class to reply using the verb in brackets.
Example:
They're not making any mistakes. (rehearse) – *They've been rehearsing*.
1 The audience look very happy. (laugh)
2 Why are the heroine's eyes all red? (cry)
3 You seem very tired today. (work)
4 They're carrying some heavy things. (shop)
5 You're looking very hot. (dance)
6 How can you be so sure you'll pass? (study)

This focuses on use 3 (see activity 2 on p83) of the present perfect continuous. Students write their answers and then compare. Go through them with the class, and then elicit similar replies by asking, for example: Why have you brought an umbrella? – 'It's been raining'; What's that book doing there? – 'I've been reading it'; or Why is my hand covered in chalk? – 'You've been writing on the board'.

> **SUGGESTED ANSWERS:** 1 They've been laughing.
> 2 She's been crying.   3 I've been working hard.
> 4 They've been shopping.   5 We've been dancing.
> 6 I've been studying a lot.

VARIATION: Students say similar things about their partners and the classroom. Their partners answer using the present perfect continuous. If pairs are slow finding things to talk about, prompt by pointing at anything in the classroom that has changed, including objects that you have brought with you, such as realia ('We've been talking about it'), homework ('You've been correcting it') or belongings such as a coat ('You've been wearing it').

Students now do Unit Test 8 on p175 of this book. The answers are on p215.
Then they do Progress Test 2 on p187 of this book. The answers are on p217.

9 What happened next?

VOCABULARY: crime *p88*

1 Groups first match cuttings and crimes, then decide on the name for each type of criminal. In some languages, the cognates of *crime* and *criminal* refer only to murder/er, so if this is the case in your students' L1, begin by eliciting definitions of one or both words. These texts introduce more topic-related vocabulary that will be needed later on in the Unit.

> **ANSWERS:** 2 vandalism/vandal   3 blackmail/er
> 4 shoplifting/er   5 theft/thief   6 smuggling/er
> 7 burglary/ar   8 terrorism/ist   9 kidnapping/er
> 10 murder/er

VARIATION: With a weak class, check that all groups have reached agreement on the correct meanings of the ten expressions. If not, elicit them from other groups before they proceed to match them with the newspaper extracts.

FOLLOW-UP: Think of other crimes, such as bag-snatching or forgery, and describe them to the class, who must say what each one (and the corresponding word for the criminal) is.

2 Let students work these out individually or in pairs, as there are plenty of clues in both the names of the punishments and contexts 1–6. As you go through the answers with the class, you could ask the class which of them are currently used in their country, and possibly which they think are humane/cruel or useful/useless.

> **ANSWERS:** 1 fine (point out that the verb form is the same)   2 death (also 'capital punishment', 'execution')   3 jail (or 'prison') sentence
> 4 suspended sentence (if the concept is not known in the students' country, explain that if the criminal offends again within a certain time period – often two years – s/he will have to serve not only the suspended prison term but also any other sentence imposed for the subsequent offence)
> 5 community service   6 life imprisonment (with some classes you may need to explain that in certain countries there have been cases of murderers sentenced to 'life' being released after less than ten years, whereas people convicted of offences against property have served much longer terms)

WORKBOOK: Vocabulary p54.

READING: multiple matching *p89*

1 Allow time for students to read the information, and answer any questions.
   Do not go into the grammar used to indicate event order at this stage, as this (the past perfect and

linking expressions) will be the subject of the following pages. The first events in this story are described in paragraph 2.
   Allow no more than 20 minutes for students to do the exam task; possibly less as this is quite a short text. Go through the answers.

> **ANSWERS:** 1F 2G 3B 4H 5C 6E 7A
> Not needed: D

2 Prompt, if necessary, with questions from Vocabulary, as well as:
Should the fact that no-one was physically hurt be taken into account?
Does it really make a difference that the gun wasn't real? (presumably the staff were just as scared)
Is a crime against a rich institution like a bank less serious than one against people?
Should a carefully premeditated ('professional') crime carry a particularly severe sentence?
Does the sort of man who abandons his dog deserve all he gets?

WORKBOOK: Part 4 pp56–57; Focus On Reading p72.

FURTHER PRACTICE: Multiple matching p135.

GRAMMAR: past perfect *p90*

1 The example of the past perfect – some students may know this tense as the pluperfect – is taken from the Reading text. It is formed by using *had* + past participle of main verb; the negative is *had not run* or *hadn't run* (not *didn't have run* or similar).

2 Point out that past simple/past perfect can be either order, as therefore can the first and second actions/situations.

> **ANSWERS:** 1 had caught (1), thought (2)
> 2 had been (1), remembered (2)
> 3 he'd left (1), realized (2)

Another example in the text: He's the one who *noticed* that you'*d left* your dog tied up outside.

3 It is possible in activity 1 (*had been running*), but not in any of these uses of the past perfect verbs in activity 2.

4 Students do the task individually or in pairs.

> **ANSWERS:** 1 ✓   2 a …guards noticed the tunnel, several prisoners had escaped   3 b had surprised
> 4 a They (had) arrested…they released
> 5 a were worried…had increased   6 ✓

5 Tell students to read quickly through the text for gist. Point out that in some cases more than one tense is possible, but that certain answers are more likely. When they have finished, check understanding of topic-related vocabulary (*judge*, *deny*, *trial*, *witnesses*).

> **SUGGESTED ANSWERS:** 1 told 2 had given
> 3 said 4 had owned 5 had been 6 had been
> performing 7 had neglected 8 added
> 9 had denied 10 had cost

VARIATION: With a strong class, get them to decide on the fairness of the sentence as they gist read, giving you their answer after one or two minutes at the most.

FOLLOW-UP: Ask the class what similarities there are with the story in Reading of the dog that led police to the bank robber, and why tales like this are popular. You might also want to ask which of the two stories is true and which has been made up: the answer is that this one is true but the one on p89 is fictional.

❻ Point out that this time they have to imagine the situation and choose the verbs for themselves, as well as give the correct form of them.

> **ANSWERS:** 1 had had 2 had heard 3 had
> broken/opened 4 hadn't put/turned/switched
> 5 had opened 6 had gone 7 had been coming
> 8 had been dreaming. Elicit the word 'nightmare'.

WORKBOOK: Past perfect forms p58.

GRAMMAR: narrative time links *p91*

❶ Most of these linking expressions have already appeared in this Unit. When you have checked the answers you may want to elicit or give more examples. Ask the class which other word in activities 1–4 means the same as 'detained' (*arrested*).

> **ANSWERS:** 1 by the time 2 once/as soon as
> 3 just before 4 as soon as/once

C O M M O N   E R R O R S

> *When he had made sure nobody was around he
> went in*. With time conjunctions we normally use a
> past perfect if the subjects of the two clauses are
> the same.

❷ This activity has three main purposes: to provide controlled practice with time links, to present more 'crime and punishment' vocabulary, and to provide a framework of the legal process in English law into which that vocabulary can fit and therefore make sense (you may want to point this out with some classes). It also gives another example of the 'and then something went wrong' type of crime story in preparation for the Writing task on p93. With a weaker class, you may want to introduce some of the words first, or at least take questions while they work on the activity in pairs. Check and if necessary practise pronunciation, especially of items like *lawyer*, *trial*, *bail*, *guilty* and *judge*.

> **ANSWERS:** 1f 2h 3i 4g 5b 6d 7c 8a 9e

❸ Students study the introduction, examples and the questions.

> **ANSWERS:** past perfect and past simple, in that
> order.

Then they do the activity, possibly in pairs.

> **POSSIBLE ANSWERS:**
> 1 They'd no sooner broken in than security cameras
>   started filming them.
> 2 They'd hardly opened the safe when the alarm
>   went off.
> 3 They'd hardly taken any of the money before
>   they had to escape.
> 4 Their getaway car had hardly gone round the
>   corner when the police arrived.

FOLLOW-UP: Practise with more examples. If students have difficulty remembering which is followed by 'when' and which by 'than', remind them that 'sooner' is a comparative and must therefore take 'than'.

VARIATION: With a very advanced class, focus on the inverted, rather literary variations *Hardly had the guard opened the door when the gang struck* and *No sooner had they climbed over the fence than the alarm went off*. Then tell them to rewrite their answers to 1–4 using these forms.

> **POSSIBLE ANSWERS:**
> 1 No sooner had they…
> 2 Hardly had they…
> 3 No sooner had they…
> 4 Hardly had their…

❹ Point out that overuse of the past perfect in a narrative can seem unnatural, and that in text and speech we avoid this, often by using time links. Remind them to use the adverb 'afterwards', not the preposition 'after' on its own. Students write their answers and compare with their partners. Check their written work and/or elicit answers from the class.

> **POSSIBLE ANSWERS:** 1 crashed into a wall
> 2 somebody realized who he was 3 fired back
> 4 they raced off 5 started selling heroin
> 6 there were fewer burglaries

❺ When pairs have decided on the main points of their story, they form a group of four with another pair. They then take turns telling the other pair what happened. Monitor conversations for accurate use of the target structures.

VARIATION: Here is an alternative activity to give to the class:
'Work in pairs. Think of a famous crime in your country's history or recently in the news, or else a well-known one in a book or film. Without mentioning who did it or exactly where, tell your

partner what happened. Where you can, use time links, the past perfect, the past perfect continuous and the past simple. You could begin with any preparations the criminals had made and then describe each step. Your partner must guess which crime you are talking about.'

If you think some of the class may have difficulties thinking of a suitable crime, write the names of some well-known cases (at least three or four) on the board for students to choose from. You might want to suggest that as long as they keep to the main facts they can be fairly economical with the truth when it comes to giving details. When everyone has finished, find out which crimes were discussed, and ask why they are so well known.

LISTENING p92

❶ Let groups try to work out for themselves which laws the signs refer to (see questions A–F in Activity 3 below for the answers), but if necessary take any vocabulary questions and briefly discuss the cultural background to these laws. Don't, however, get involved in making lengthy distinctions between 'crimes' and 'misdemeanours', 'laws' and 'by-laws' and so on: they will probably prove very difficult to explain or translate and the legal system in the students' country is likely to be quite different from that in English-speaking societies anyway. It should be sufficient to establish whether each action can be officially punished or not, and whether this is also the case in their country.

FOLLOW-UP 1: Students may describe a situation where many or all of these things are illegal but the laws are rarely enforced, or simply unenforceable – in other words, everybody ignores them and the authorities have given up. Groups could discuss the rights and wrongs of this.

FOLLOW-UP 2: Groups talk about what the penalty should be for repeat offenders, and how it should (or should not) differ in the case of, for example, the under-age drinker and the adult who sells them the drinks.

❷ Remind the class that, unlike Listening Part 1, there is a common theme here so it is correspondingly easier to home in on the situation. Allow only about 30 seconds for them to decide on the places, as they will not have much time to look at the questions in the exam. Ask what they think the places are, but do not at this stage say whether they are right as this would detract from the exam authenticity of the task.

> **ANSWERS:** A in a cinema   B on the railway or underground, or possibly the bus   C in the street   D in the street   E in the street   F in a pub

❸ Play the recording twice. Go through the answers, confirming correct suggestions for where the incidents took place and then ask what clues they heard, e.g. B: *fare*, *queueing*, *pay at the other end*.

> **ANSWERS:** 1D 2B 3C 4F 5E Not needed: A

❹ Ask the class whether they have been influenced by anything the speakers said. You may want to take a class vote on whether each individual should be prosecuted, and then try to reach a consensus on any punishments.

FOLLOW-UP: Ask the class if there are any laws in their country which they think are unfair, why they think this and what should be done about these laws. Issues to discuss here could include whether the police pick on young people; who is more 'to blame' (the bar staff or the young person) if someone is drinking under-age; 'What would happen if everyone did that?' as an argument, and so on. On the subject of punishments, refer students back to the list on p88, possibly adding relevant ones such as probation, conditional discharge, etc., explaining, if necessary, what they entail. They could discuss what sort of distinction should be made between offenders who didn't know they were breaking the law and those who did, but felt – like the graffiti artist – that the law was unjust. Discuss laws relevant to the students' age group and the culture they are from. Choose from (for example): laws that discriminate against women or ethnic groups; conscription; minimum age limits for driving, marrying, signing contracts, voting, etc. You could also ask pairs to tell each other the story of any brushes with the law they have had.

VARIATION: Ask which of the speakers have received fair and unfair treatment, and if the class were the judges, what punishment (if any) they would give each of them.

WORKBOOK: Focus On Listening p96.

TAPESCRIPT

One
Well, I was just walking along minding my own business when this policeman came up to me and said he was arresting me. At first I didn't know what he was on about but then he said he'd seen me eat a bar of chocolate and throw away the wrapper. Can you believe it? In fact it'd been a complete accident: I'd been digging the return half of my train ticket out of my coat pocket at the time, so I wasn't really thinking about what I was going to do when I finished my Mars bar, but it was a windy day and suddenly a gust caught the wrapper and sent it sailing away behind me. And there I was, being treated like some sort of juvenile delinquent!

Two
So I've just wasted a whole afternoon hanging around this lousy place – I mean, you can't even get a drink here – and I've been fined £80, and on top of all that I've now got a criminal record all because of a £2 fare that I was going to pay anyway. It's incredible, isn't it? With the city full of real villains why do they have to waste their time chasing after law-abiding people whose only crime

is that they can't spend half the morning hanging around queueing, and fully intend to pay at the other end? And they call this Justice.

Three
I was on my way home from the cinema the other night when a police car stopped and these two coppers waved me down. They said they'd nearly run into me and that I was 'a danger to other road users', or some stuff like that. One of them said he'd warned me about the same thing a couple of nights before but I told him that was rubbish, he must have got me mixed up with someone else. Anyway, they took my name and address and said that if I didn't get 'em fixed and they saw me again I'd be in trouble, so I said 'Don't you mean if you don't see me?' but they didn't laugh much.

Four
How on earth was I supposed to know they shouldn't have been there? Someone else must've ordered for them. I can't go round everyone asking to see their birth certificates and if they don't come up to the bar themselves I just don't see them, specially when the place is packed out with people who've just come out of the cinema next door. And even if they do, how are you supposed to tell what age they are? On a Friday night they're all dressed up with somewhere else to go, and if that means a club they're bound to have made sure they look old enough.

Five
It's ridiculous, really. In any other country I'd be regarded as someone who makes a valuable contribution to brightening up our inner cities, not someone to be persecuted and prosecuted like this. I had two experts from the local college who told the court my work had real artistic value, but the magistrates still fined me £100 for defacing a public building and said I had to pay £300 towards the cost of cleaning it off. The people who dreamt up that law must be complete and utter…

SPEAKING p92

This section continues the theme of unfairness in the legal system and links it to Writing below. Tell pairs to take their time thinking up a story, possibly making notes to use when they speak. If there is time, volunteers tell their stories to the class, who could vote on the best one.

WRITING: a narrative p93

1 Remind the class that in Part 2 of Writing the tasks vary from exam to exam, and although story writing is quite a frequent option there is no guarantee that this (or any other Part 2 task type) will appear on any given exam paper. The note expansion task, which is similar to that used in CAE, could be done in pairs. Allow plenty of time for this, as the information the notes contain is important. It also provides practice with abbreviations.

POSSIBLE ANSWERS:
  2 Attract the reader's attention and make him or her want to read on.
  3 Say where and when it happened, giving background information using the past continuous.
  4 Describe the main characters and their relationships with each other.
  5 Use a paragraph for each main part of the story and put the events in a logical sequence.
  *6 Include some direct speech to bring the characters to life and create variety.
  7 Use the past perfect and past simple for events, joining them with time links.
  8 Do not write about too many events because the maximum number of words is 180!
  9 End the story with an explanation, a mystery or a surprise for the reader.
 10 Check your work, especially narrative tenses as one mistake can lead to others.
  * You may want to point out that the examiners do not necessarily look for direct speech.

2 Encourage students always to analyse Writing instructions in this way.

ANSWERS: the organizers of a short story competition, presumably to win, a 120–180 word story, 1st person, beginning

3 Students work individually, writing down short answers.
Here are two more questions they could ask themselves:
– Is it about a big crime or a 'minor' offence like those in Listening?
– If you were falsely accused, was it a mistake or was it intentional?

VARIATION: With a weaker class, check for understanding of distinctions such as awaiting trial/ convict, unfair law/false accusation and mistake/ intentional.

4 1 Tell students to do this quickly, using their answers to the Reading task to help them if necessary. Each stage corresponds roughly to a paragraph of *A policeman's best friend*.

ANSWER: g d a b c e f h

2 Advise students to use about four paragraphs, possibly but not necessarily with some of the stages from 1 above.
3 With lower-level students it may be advisable to suggest they follow chronological order, but beginning with the words given, for example, should provide more practice with narrative tense sequences.
4 Remind students of the importance of working from their notes as they write.

WORKBOOK: Writing p59; Focus On Writing p80.

VOCABULARY: transport p94

1 You might want to make it clear that the topic area has moved on from crime to transport. Opinions may vary from country to country on what constitutes a common way of travelling, with students of some nationalities suggesting, for instance, *tram*, while others might mention *horse*, *skis* or even *camel* (see Use of English on p96). Possibly the most frequently referred to will be the following: bus, train, bicycle, car, motorbike, underground, coach, ship/ferry/boat, plane, taxi and, of course, on foot. When pairs have finished, go through the lists as a class making sure that everyone has noted down all of them. Accept any others that students actually use, say *skateboard* or *roller blades*, but not ones that cannot by any stretch of the imagination be regarded as common, like *submarine*.

VARIATION: To practise frequency adverbs, draw a table like the one below on the board or OHP, and get students to copy it into their notebooks. Pairs ask one another about each form of transport and fill in their answers. Example:
How often do you travel by bus?   *Every day, really.*
And how often do you go by bus?   *Oh, occasionally.*

	You	Your partner
Every day	_____	_____
Often	_____	_____
Sometimes	_____	_____
Occasionally	_____	_____
Never	_____	_____

Introduce the difference between *drive* (a car, a bus) and *ride* (a bike, a horse). Encourage less brusque responses than simply a frequency adverb: 'Only occasionally, I think', 'Well, sometimes' (although students write in just the name of the means of transport: *bus*, *train*, etc.).

2 Check comprehension of the terms and then let pairs discuss these, using several adjectives for some forms of transport if they wish. Pairs write down the opposites, then repeat the above.

POSSIBLE ANSWERS: expensive, cold, unhealthy, inconvenient, dangerous, unreliable, uncomfortable, slow, tiring, boring, unsociable/lonely, inflexible (i.e. doesn't always go where you want it to go)

VARIATION: With an advanced class, elicit more adjectives.

3 Elicit these quickly, pointing out that they are all used in the Listening text.

ANSWERS: cabin staff – plane, service station – car, coach, lorry, etc., gridlock – car, etc., terminal – plane, boarding card – plane

4 Tell the class that most of these expressions are used in the Listening below. When pairs have decided which go into which groups, go through the answers, possibly as collocations with *flight*, *airline* or *ticket* (also for other forms of transport). Give examples of the use *dear*: a bit dear, rather dear, etc.

ANSWERS: cheap – cut-price, economy, budget, bargain; expensive – full-fare, full-price, dear

This vocabulary will also be useful in Unit 10 (shopping, consumer issues).

WORKBOOK: Vocabulary p54.

COMMON ERRORS

We left our bikes and continued on foot. Although we say *by bike, car, train, plane, ship,* etc., with *foot* we use *on*.

FURTHER PRACTICE: Vocabulary p133.

LISTENING p94

1 If you are in a country where there are these large differences in ticket prices, ask the class to name some of the small airlines that offer cheap fares, as well as the names of some big international carriers like BA, Lufthansa, Iberia, Olympic, etc. If not, explain briefly the situation in other countries (no booking, no frills, cheap fare, versus full-price ticket with all the trimmings).

2

ANSWERS: 1B 2B 3C 4C 5A 6A 7C

WORKBOOK: Part 4 p55; Focus On Listening p96.

TAPESCRIPT

Pres: Now we turn to the question of value for money in the air. We sent James on a return flight to Greece, the lucky man, but on a different airline each way. On the way out he flew with a cut-price airline, but we won't say which because all the budget operators charge about the same for their European destinations, and it wouldn't be fair to single one out. Coming back he was with one of the big carriers, but again it will remain anonymous as a ticket from BA, Olympic or whoever costs more or less the same – which is probably part of the problem. Anyway, James, tell us how the outward flight went.

James: Well, the first thing I noticed was that there was no ticket. I just turned up at Terminal 2, paid the very friendly person at the counter and was given a boarding card. It was quick and easy and an hour later I was sitting on the plane, which was ready to take off.

Pres: And what was the plane like?

James: This was the first drawback because it was a bit small and every seat was taken. Added to that was the fact that you're not given a seat number so I hadn't been able to ask to sit next to the emergency exit, which I usually do because someone of my height needs the extra space in front. That meant a four-hour journey with very little leg-room.

Pres: What about the cabin staff?

James: I didn't see much of them, in fact, which in some ways was a welcome change from all the fussing about and bringing you this and that which seems to take up so much time on other flights I've been on. Probably it was because there were only three staff on the plane compared with the usual six when they have to cater for first class as well.

Pres: And the catering itself?

James: Minimal. A cup of coffee, better than usual on a plane I must say, and a couple of biscuits. I'd foreseen that though, and brought sandwiches with me, so it didn't really matter.

Pres: How about your arrival there?

James: We were a bit late – there'd been an air traffic control hold-up of some sort in London – and then of course the pilot parked about as far away from the terminal as it was possible to go. Then we had to wait standing on the bus in the heat while someone who'd left his camera on the plane went back to look for it, so by the time we actually got into the building our luggage had already arrived. But I was out of the airport and on my way into Athens within about half an hour of the time I'd reckoned on.

Pres: OK, we'll skip your stay there, which I'm sure was marvellous, and pick up the story on the way back. Tell us what happened from when you checked in with your full-price ticket.

James: Well actually the story begins before then, because on my way out to the airport we'd been stuck in an almighty traffic jam and the taxi driver thought we weren't going to make it in time. Now if that had happened and I'd been flying with an economy airline I would've had to wait until Wednesday for the next flight out. But with a full-fare ticket in my pocket I knew there'd be another plane later the same day, so I suppose you could say that not worrying about that was worth a bit.

Pres: And not having to worry about your report being late, either. Anyway, go on.

James: Well, in the end I just made it in time. The check-in was all a lot more formal, and so were the staff, but they gave me some free labels for my luggage…

Pres: Wow.

James: …and much more importantly, the plane was a lot bigger. A DC10, I think, compared to the 737 on the way out. There was plenty of room, partly because it was half empty…

Pres: Aha.

James: …and there were half a dozen smartly turned-out staff. The food was OK: the usual cold meat and salad followed by the customary unidentifiable dessert that nobody ever eats, plus a not-bad glass of beer and a drinkable cup of tea. Certainly nothing special, though.

Pres: But they got you home on time.

James: They got me into *Heathrow* on time, yes. My wife picked me up in her new car and we headed for London, only to run straight into another huge jam, this time on the M25 motorway.

Pres: And the cost?

James: £85 on the way out and, would you believe, £460 on the way back.

Pres: So there you have it. Unless you're an outsize person, make a habit of missing flights or collect luggage labels, the choice seems pretty clear.

3 There are nine examples of the past perfect.

SPEAKING p95

1 Point out that the examiners do not want to hear candidates repeating the same things they said in Part 3 of the exam, so the conversation must move on to other areas of the topic. Pairs match example sentences a–d with rules 1–4. Elicit/give more examples when they have done this.

ANSWERS: 1b 2d 3a 4c

2 Pairs correct the mistakes orally (and also in writing if they obviously have difficulty with them).

ANSWERS: 1 What do you feel about this? 2 Do you think you could say that again? 3 Which of them are you keen on? 4 Correct 5 Can you tell me what you think? 6 Sorry, what did you say?

3 Pairs practise the question forms. Encourage the use of past perfect forms for events leading up to the situation depicted, past continuous for the background and a mixture of past perfect, past continuous and past simple for the events afterwards, with suitable time links. Listeners encourage the speakers, where necessary, by using questions similar to (particularly past tense forms of) those in 2 above.

FOLLOW-UP: Suggest students say what they *would have done*, without getting involved in discussion of complete 3rd conditional sentences at this stage (that can wait until Unit 12), unless your class is quite advanced in terms of level.

VARIATION: With a not-very-imaginative class, prompt with some anecdotes of your own, based on one of the photos, another picture in the book or elsewhere.

WORKBOOK: Focus On Speaking p104.

FURTHER PRACTICE: *Yes/no* questions p134.

PHRASAL VERBS: *take* p96

This activity gives further practice with narrative tense sequences and time links. Students should also be encouraged to look out for the kinds of clues they concentrate on here when they are working with narrative reading texts.

❶ Elicit the meanings of the verbs from Listening: leave the ground (aircraft); occupy (also time). In the first of the next two sentences, *took off* means the same as *removed*, while in the second *took up* is almost the opposite of *stopped playing*, but ask students to explain in more detail: *took off* = *removed* = the opposite of 'put on'; *took up* means 'adopt as a hobby or pastime'.

❷ Let pairs discuss these and write down a phrase for each of 1–10. When they have finished, elicit answers and possibly more examples of each of the underlined verbs.

> **SUGGESTED ANSWERS:** (clues in brackets)
> 1 took after = was very similar to (looked just like)
> 2 took on = accepted (nobody else wanted to do)
> 3 take on = employ (reducing its workforce)
> 4 take in = fully understand an idea (only just suggested/needed some time)
> 5 took back = returned (bought it/stopped working)
> 6 take to = begin to like (reserved)
> 7 took over = got control of (bought/firm)
> 8 took away = subtracted (added up/calculate)
> 9 took down = made a note of (every word the teacher said)
> 10 taken in = tricked (fraud)

VARIATION: An alternative way to do this activity, particularly with a slower class, is to give them the meanings jumbled up and get them to match them with each verb: accept   was very similar to   subtracted   tricked   got control of   begin to like   made a note of   employ   fully understand an idea   returned

❸ Point out that this pattern is not really practicable with every one of the verbs, e.g. *take after* (1) and *take to* (6), but in most cases they should be able to practise the patterns from Grammar on pp90–91. Encourage a variety of forms (the past perfect continuous is possible in some cases).

USE OF ENGLISH: open cloze *p96*

❶ Test-wise students are aware of many of these recurring alternative answers: the aim of this section is to impart this knowledge to all students without them necessarily having to do vast numbers of cloze tests to find out for themselves.

1 and 2 Students read individually. Elicit the answer to the examples: the gaps could be filled by 1 *as*, *when* or *while*; 2 *the/those*. Remind students that if they give more than one answer, they will not even get one mark unless every alternative is correct.

VARIATION: Students look back at open cloze exercises they have done earlier in the course and find more examples of alternative correct answers. Other common ones (not in the text) include: *but/while/whereas, will/shall, would/should, would/could, which/that, till/until, to/towards, may/might/could, called/named, each/every*.

❷ 1 Students work in pairs. Elicit possible answers (in text): arid, rain, landscape, dunes, sandstorm, rock, nature, camels. Also dry, hot/heat, sun, etc.

2 Students work alone, then compare answers with their partners. Go through them as a class, eliciting every possible answer.

> **ANSWERS:** 1 for   2 rise   3 every   4 like
> 5 because/as/since/where   6 on   7 without
> 8 where   9 so/this/that   10 to   11 such
> 12 most/really   13 in   14 on   15 which/that

WORKBOOK: Word formation p58.

FURTHER PRACTICE: Open cloze p134.

EXAM STUDY GUIDE *p97*

Preparation: In the lesson before the one when you plan to do this activity, refer students back to Unit 6 and ask them to find their list of 'top 6 mistakes' from Exam Study Guide on p63. Tell them to look through their written work since then and update their list.

1 If necessary give examples of each reason for mistakes before students do the task alone. Elicit the answers.

> **ANSWERS:** 1D 2A 3B 4C

Suggest students put 4C into practice by writing a question mark in the margin of their written work when they are trying something out, though of course reminding them not to do this in exam conditions.

2 It is important that students realize that the reason for each mistake here depends on the individual, and will normally change as they progress. Elicit answers and allow the class to agree/disagree with each other.

> **POSSIBLE ANSWERS:** (but person specific)
> 1 It's snowing! B   2 have A   3 driving D
> 4 when you arrive B   5 plane to get B
> 6 He had no sooner C   7 to have sunk D
> 8 women A/B

3 Working alone, students use their updated lists from 'Preparation' above.

STUDY CHECK *p97*

❶ Students work individually, planning their stories. Suggest that it could be a comedy in which everything goes wrong, like Steve Martin's *Trains, Planes and Automobiles*, a thriller like one of the James Bond movies or a human interest story in which one or more people travel a great distance to achieve happiness. Pairs comment on each other's speaking and both think about why they made certain mistakes.

2 The aim of this activity is to revise the past perfect, past perfect continuous and time links. Prompt, if necessary, with suggestions such as 'I'd learned how to use the simple past' or 'I'd used *Headway Intermediate*'. Make a note of any activities they'd enjoyed for future reference when planning lessons.

3 The instructions provide a lot of scope for giving background information and flashbacks, so students should be able to practise using the grammar from this Unit, as well as vocabulary from the 'crime and punishment' pages. Finally, encourage everyone to think about the reasons for their mistakes, as suggested in the Exam Study Guide.

Students now do Unit Test 9 on p176 of this book. The answers are on p215.

10 Appearances and reality

SPEAKING *p98*

❶ Groups exchange opinions about the pictures and then draw up two lists. If necessary, prompt with some or all of these categories: women's clothes, men's clothes, hairstyles, cosmetics, footwear, perfume, aftershave, headgear, jewellery, eyewear, tattoos, piercing.

❷ This is an FCE Speaking Part 2 activity. Remind pairs that in the exam A should talk about his or her photos for one minute, while B's comments on A's pictures should be much briefer.

❸ This is the theme of the Reading text to follow, so do this as a quick whole-class discussion.
Q1: Prompt with *They look* + adjective, *Young people think…*
VARIATION: With a more advanced class, suggest forms such as *They look as though/if they… They give the impression…*, etc.
WORKBOOK: Focus On Speaking p104.

READING: multiple choice *pp98–99*

❶ Students quickly scan the text to find *trainers, tiny shorts, knee-length black boots, mini-skirts, tight jeans, T-shirts, high-heeled shoes, patterned tights, slim-fit shirts, striped jackets, woollen suit, cotton blouse*. Then they put them into the two categories (which will be student specific).
VARIATION: With a strong class, ask them to find other items people wear, such as nose rings and tongue studs.

❷ Remind students that, as with other Papers, not all question types appear in every exam, but they have to be prepared for them in case they do. This also applies, for example, to lexical reference questions (*What does 'it' refer to on line X?*) – see the next Unit for more on this and the main focus on multiple-choice questions. Highlight the point that this is not a test of vocabulary, reminding the class that the Paper is called Reading and therefore tests reading skills – one of which is being able to infer meaning from context. Vocabulary is tested in some parts of Paper 3 Use of English.
NOTE: This may be a good point to explain that First Certificate is perhaps different from other exams they may have taken in that Papers 1, 4 and 5 (in particular) concentrate on just one skill. In Listening, therefore, any reading (of questions) is kept as simple as possible and in Speaking the input is nowadays almost entirely graphic, not written, and they are not being examined on their listening in the oral part. They should therefore ask for repetition if they don't

understand. Paper 2 Writing does contain reading material as input, but again it is relatively simple.

Students study the instructions, which set the scene for the text, and the example question. Remind students again not to be 'distracted' by words in the wrong answers that are also in the text: *unusual* in A, or synonyms that seem to be clues but are not: *dream* in D/*nightmare* in the first line of the text. Point out that contrast and reference backwards or forwards are common types of clue in lexical reference questions, but leave the broader topic of reference words for Unit 11.

They then identify Questions 5 and 7 as this type. Suggest that they make written notes or highlight the relevant parts of the text to show the clues they are using. You could check that they are doing this while they are working on the task. Clues: Q5 following sentences, especially the similar meaning of *explaining* and the contrast with *a little more forcefully*.

Q7 from the beginning of the previous paragraph: *The best thing, convincing, need to be advised*; the rest of the same sentence, particularly *the only solution*.

Go through these with the answers to the exam questions.

ANSWERS: 2D 3A 4B 5A 6C 7B

WORKBOOK: Part 3 pp62–63; Focus On Reading p72.

GRAMMAR: the passive *pp100–101*

❶ Pairs study the example (point out that it is taken from the Reading text on p99) and answer the questions. Check that everyone has the right answers at each stage.

ANSWERS: It is formed by using the appropriate form of the verb 'be', plus the past participle of the main verb, in this case 'keep'. There is no agent given because it is clear from the context. The reason is **b**. You may want to give, or – with a stronger class – elicit, more examples of each reason, particularly for c: 'I have been given some information …', 'It has been suggested that …', 'The chair's been broken' and other ways of avoiding responsibility! In the second part, check on both form and use. Answers: 1 <u>has been thrown out</u> – reason c 2 <u>are politely requested</u> – reason a 3 <u>designed by Versace</u> – reason d 4 <u>shouldn't be worn</u> – reason B

❷ Point out that the present perfect continuous and past perfect continuous are not included here as they are extremely rare, or impossible, in the passive. Ensure that students update their list of examples in the Grammar Reference when they do the infinitive in Unit 11, conditionals in Unit 12 and past modals in Unit 14.

The answers to the questions are used as examples of these tenses in the Grammar Reference on p178.

> Most likely reasons: 1b 2b 3a 4c 5b 6d 7b 8a 9b 10d

❸ Allow time for individuals or pairs to write their answers, then check. Where students have difficulties, put some more examples using the tense in question on the board and elicit the answers.

> **ANSWERS:** 2 were taken/yesterday   3 will be used/in future   4 might be finished/later today
> 5 are asked/at any time   6 is going to be closed down/next year (+ *for ages* for 'going to', rather than 'will')   7 have been opened/since…1997
> 8 was being shown/while   9 had been spent/by then   10 to be made/In those days.

❹ Point out that each of the eight questions focuses on a different passive tense. Take any questions on topic-related vocabulary such as *swimwear*, *catwalk* and *refund*.

> **ANSWERS:** 1 can be bought   2 were told nothing/ were not told anything   3 is being built
> 4 will not be refunded   5 had been promised
> 6 are going to be excited   7 have been caused by
> 8 their collection was being shown

```
C O M M O N   E R R O R S
```
People should be allowed to do what they want. Some transitive verbs are not normally used in the passive. But you may want to point out the change from active to passive with *make*, e.g. *In Britain they make people leave the pubs at 11 o'clock* (active); *In Britain people are made to leave the pubs at 11 o'clock* (passive).

❺ Tell the class they are to write cohesive texts, not isolated sentences, based on the different stages of the process. If necessary, prompt with examples such as *First the person is measured…* feeding in suitable vocabulary such as *pattern* and *design*. Check completed work for accuracy.

FOLLOW-UP: Students discuss or write about processes and sequences of events such as:
1 how an ordinary item of clothing is made, for example a pair of jeans, a suit or a pair of shoes.
2 how something invented by fashion designers becomes internationally popular.

WORKBOOK: The passive pp63–64.

FURTHER PRACTICE: The passive p138.

PHRASAL VERBS: *bring* p101

❶ Pairs use the question as a guide to the meaning of each phrasal verb. Encourage the use of the same tense in each answer as in the question (in order to

provide practice with a range of tenses) and point out that in most cases the object pronoun will come between the verb and its adverb particle (*bring* him *round*). If necessary, go through each stage of the example, eliciting or explaining that *bring round* is similar to 'revive', *was + -ed* shows that the simple past is needed, and *he* before the passive verb must become object pronoun *him* after the active verb.

This is also an exercise in register, in that the language of the questions is more formal than that required in the answers, reflecting both the tendency of many passive sentences to be more formal than active ones and the frequently informal nature of phrasal verbs.

> **ANSWERS:** 2 brought it about   3 are going to bring it up   4 can bring it forward   5 will bring it off   6 brought her up   7 will bring it back
> 8 brought it in   9 are bringing it out
> 10 brought back

❷ Check answers for accuracy.

> **ANSWERS:** 2 The situation was brought about by a mistake.   3 Yes, it is going to be brought up later on.   4 Yes, it can be brought forward to the early afternoon.   5 Yes, I think it'll be brought off somehow.   6 No, she was brought up by her grandmother.   7 Yes, it will be brought back first thing in the morning.
> 8 Yes, it was brought in after the report came out.
> 9 It is being brought out in the New Year.
> 10 Yes, a lot of memories were brought back (by it).

VARIATION: With an advanced class point out that normally only transitive verbs can be used in the passive, which is the case of the ten verbs here. Elicit examples of transitive and intransitive verbs to illustrate the point further.

WORKBOOK: Phrasal verbs *bring* and *come* p61.

VOCABULARY: describing appearance p102

❶ A lot of these are personal preferences, so allow individuals to make up their own minds first. Allow brief discussion of individual words (see 2 below). Begin by revising – preferably by eliciting – more basic vocabulary such as *tall*, *short*, *fat*, *thin*, *ugly*, *pretty*, *beautiful*, *attractive* and any others the class may know. Point out that *pale* and *dark* often collocate with the noun 'complexion' (in the form *has a…complexion*).

❷ When one student has described someone, the partner chooses another, and so on until only two remain. If necessary, give students more information and examples of modifiers/intensifiers, pointing out how the meaning can change according to intonation.

FURTHER PRACTICE: Multiple matching p139.

1 Tell the class to read the advice. Remind students that in the exam there will be no common theme running through the questions. Then play the recording, remembering that each part is played twice consecutively. Go through them, perhaps asking students to expand on them, for example: How reliable is the description of the man in Q1? (It is from eyewitnesses' accounts); Would you wear/buy the shorts in Q2? (Students could say/indicate what they look like); What's special about the umbrella? (It has a blue sky print on the lining), and so on.

ANSWERS: 1A 2C 3A 4B 5C 6B 7A 8A

2 You may want to play the last situation on the recording again, and highlight expressions like 'five foot eight' or 'one metre seventy-five', 'shoulder-length' and further examples of 'fairly' and 'quite'. Students then write their own self-descriptions and give them to you. Give back pieces of paper from students in other parts of the classroom and allow some time for everyone to read and identify the writers. Then tell students to go and talk to the writers, commenting on how accurate their self-descriptions are, and then talking to those who read their own pieces of paper.

VARIATION: If time is short, or you feel students could be embarrassed by discussion of their appearance, stop at the identification stage and ask individuals whose description they have. They could read out the first line for the writer to confirm whether they are correct or not.

WORKBOOK: Focus On Listening p96.

TAPESCRIPT

One
The man the police are looking for is described by witnesses at the scene of the crime as aged about 30, short but heavily-built, with long black hair and a dark complexion. He might have a thin moustache. When last seen he was wearing a brown jacket and dark green trousers. Members of the public are strongly advised not to approach this man, as according to the police he may be armed and dangerous.

Two
I really liked the feel of those 'cause they were made of some nice soft material. The print on them was really trendy and I loved the colours. They were a funny length, though, and they were a bit wide at the ends. I would've liked them shorter, higher up above the knee, and perhaps with straighter legs. They were a bit pricey too, and it'd be cheaper just to cut the legs off a pair of trousers.

Three
…so take shelter where the sky is always blue and the clouds are never grey. Beautifully made with a classic black cotton outer, it opens to reveal the silky blue skies lining inside. There's a metal tip, it's got a strong wooden handle and it extends to well over a metre in diameter when open. Whatever the weather you'll never be gloomy under…

Four
Well it's quite a nice uniform, really. It's dark blue, of course, but made of much better material than the force, er, used to give us. It's warm too, and even though some people think it looks silly the hat does help to keep out the cold when you're after thieves down by the river in January. There are lots of pockets and buttons and things for all the bits and pieces like your radio, a notebook and all the other things you need, particularly when you make an arrest.

Five
What about these then?
Yeah, I agree, those brown leather ones do look good but I don't know whether they'll have them in my size. I'll ask the girl anyway and if they do I'll try 'em on. I'm not gonna make the same mistake as when we were on holiday and buy a pair that's too small, and then have my feet start killing me.

Six
And did you see what she'd done with it at the party on Friday night? She'd obviously dyed it that weird shade of red but as if that wasn't enough she'd gone and put in a blonde streak – right at the front, would you believe. It's about time she had it cut too, she's got split ends all over the place and it doesn't seem to have crossed her mind that…

Seven
This is one I took with lighting directed from a lot further to the right of the camera. I think it gives much more of an impression of depth and highlights her amazing features really well. I've also aimed to capture that characteristic smile of hers, which is something you can only really do if you get the lighting, the angle for the shot and the position of her head just right, and all at the same time.

Eight
How will you recognize me? I'll be wearing a black jumper and a blue skirt, probably with black shoes, and a long navy blue coat. I won't be carrying a handbag but I will've picked up a copy of *The Guardian* by then so that's something else to look out for. I'm fairly tall, about five foot eight, and quite slim. I've got shoulder-length dark hair and brown eyes, but I'm quite pale really. Now what about you…?

WRITING: describing a person *p103*

1 Point out that in an FCE task they will have to do more than just describe, and that the examiners will penalize answers that do not cover all the elements specified in the instructions. Here the two things they have to do are: describe appearance and show how it affected them.

❷ 1 You may want to tell pairs that they are looking for 'typical' errors made by students when describing appearance and clothing, plus three common general ones in the second paragraph. It will be useful for them to write in the corrections on the text as it is going to be used as a model in the following activities.

2 Matching the two parts to the two paragraphs is simple enough, but the importance lies in seeing how each element of the question is given roughly equal coverage in the answer.

ANSWERS: 1 high – tall, and a lovely – and lovely, tooth – teeth, match – fit, dresses – clothes, with a light blue – with light blue, carried – wore, people was – people were, care about – care, Ever since then I am – Ever since then I have been
2 appearance – paragraph 1; what happened – paragraph 2

❸ Give pairs time to study the text and identify examples. All the suggestions have, to varying degrees, been followed.

VARIATION: With a strong class, elicit/suggest more ideas, such as thinking up new metaphors/similes ('white as a sheet', 'thin as a rake', etc.), making descriptions consistent ('a round face with full lips and a broad nose', etc.) unless the writer's aim is to highlight a feature that contrasts with the rest of the appearance.

❹ You may want to discuss these points with the class, or let them read and ask any questions they may have. Encourage them to use their imagination, within the guidelines laid down by the wording, when deciding how to answer questions.
When you look at their completed work, highlight any of their habitual errors and any mistakes involving the use of target language (appearance, dress – particularly verbs like *suit*, *fit*, *wear* and *put on*). Revise these points after work has been checked if weaknesses show up.

NOTE: The instructions say that they will be writing for the teacher, which is quite a common formula in FCE questions, so the style they will choose depends on what you normally regard as appropriate for written work they do for you. Remind them to be consistent once they have chosen.

FOLLOW-UP 1: Ask groups to brainstorm as many possible approaches to this task as they can. This could also be done in subsequent writing tasks to impress upon students the range of possibilities that exists.

FOLLOW-UP 2: To reinforce the work done in the previous unit on narrative tenses, you might want to elicit those used in the final paragraph: past perfect continuous, past simple, past continuous and present perfect.

WORKBOOK: Writing p65; Focus On Writing p80.

SPEAKING and VOCABULARY *p104*

❶ Begin by checking that everyone knows what a 'department store' is: elicit the names of the most famous ones in their country, in London, New York, etc. Be available to take questions on vocabulary, or let them use dictionaries, although some, like *5p off*, will probably need to be explained: 'the price has been reduced by five pence'. Encourage the use of more passive forms such as 'You're not given a receipt in a small shop'.

Go through the answers when pairs have finished categorizing them – associations may depend on local shopping customs.

SUGGESTED ANSWERS: shop assistant c   4th floor c
trolley b   till a, b, c   counter a, c   checkout b
aisle b   try on c   basket b   guarantee c
shopkeeper a   receipt b, c   special offer b, c
own-brand b   5p off b   bargain c
January sales c

❷ Stress that there are likely to be big variations between regions in the UK, town/country, rich/poor areas, as well as among individuals. There are likely to be large variations in other countries too, but certain tendencies can usually be observed and this is what the activity is about.

NOTE: This activity is adapted from 'Shopping habits' in *Cultural Awareness* (Resource Books for Teachers series) by Barry Tomalin and Susan Stempleski, OUP 1993.

FOLLOW-UP 2: Ask the class how people in their country react to being sold poor-quality products or bad service. Do they complain to the staff, take legal action, tell a consumers' organization or do nothing? Suggest groups discuss this, the reasons and whether it is the best thing to do. This activity previews the topic of Listening below.

EXAM STUDY GUIDE *p104*

If students want to know, the number of words regarded as necessary for success at FCE is approximately 5,000 (though not all the meanings of every word). The first part of this activity aims to give students some idea of what the required level is. Ask the class what they notice about the words once you have checked their answers: in very broad terms, the longer words tend to be lower frequency/higher level, with the exception of 'uneconomical' which has both a prefix and a suffix and could appear in, for example, a Use of English word formation task. The activity also presents more topic-related vocabulary.

ANSWERS: 1 a cost b payment c expenditure
2 a buy b purchase c acquire   3 a money
b earnings c remuneration   4 a poor b bankrupt
c impoverished   5 a rich b wealthy c affluent
6 a expensive b uneconomical c extortionate
Students do the second part individually.

FOLLOW-UP: When they have finished, ask the class which are the most popular methods, which they want to try and what other ways they know of or have tried for themselves.

LISTENING *p104*

❶ Refer students briefly to other Part 2 task-types: gaps in notes in Unit 2, completing statements in Unit 4. Remind them that part of the difficulty with them lies in knowing exactly what kind of information is required (and run over the techniques suggested for overcoming this problem). Play the recording twice and then check their answers.

> **ANSWERS:** 1 meat 2 tomorrow/Saturday morning 3 everyone 4 a checkout girl 5 America 6 it's their fault 7 cherry pies 8 twice a month 9 the British 10 they are overpriced/expensive

VARIATION: Help a slow class by telling them the suggested number of words for each question: 1 one 2 two 3 one 4 three 5 one 6 three 7 two 8 three 9 two 10 three
(Stress, however, that the number of words for each answer is a guide only, though they should normally limit the number to three, or at most four.)

❷ Tell pairs to ask and answer these questions, or do them as a class discussion. Don't get too involved with analysis of the grammar of 'wish' at this stage: it is covered in Unit 14. Just point out, if necessary, that it is used here to indicate present regret for past inaction.

WORKBOOK: Part 3 p61; Focus On Listening p96.

TAPESCRIPT

Pres: Today in Consumer Watch we'll be talking to one of life's great complainers. His name is David Walsh and he spends all day in supermarkets like this one, passing judgment on every item from soft fruit to own-brand washing powder, and calls himself a consumers' crusader. Dr Walsh, how did you get involved in this?

Walsh: I think it all started at the meat counter. I asked why British beef was so much more expensive than Australian meat, and was met with this 'take it or leave it' attitude. Then I started looking closely at everything on sale and realized that I wasn't getting value for money. And as for customer service, forget it! Look at this! Only one cake left at 2 pm on Friday and they won't restock the shelves until tomorrow morning – what sort of service is that? I come every day in the hope that they may have pulled their socks up. They haven't managed to get rid of me, but they'd love to.

Pres: Yes, I was going to ask, what do the staff think of you?

Walsh: There's nobody, from the manager on down, who doesn't tremble in terror when I'm in because they don't know what I'll get

up to next. They think I'm mad, but not one of my complaints has ever been unsubstantiated.

Pres: So what sort of reception do you get?

Walsh: Not always as warm as I would like. One manager had the cheek to tell me off for complaining, and one of his staff just laughed in my face, when I asked – she was a checkout girl – when I asked to see her superior. I can't remember what the issue was, but their manner left a lot to be desired.

Pres: But do you get results?

Walsh: Yes, I certainly do. It's not just empty complaining. I shut several stores down by persuading people not to shop there while I was working in America. In another town in the US a manager agreed to assemble his staff, and I walked down the line pointing out those people whose work wasn't good enough. I think they got the sack.

Pres: Don't you feel at all guilty over their dismissal?

Walsh: Not at all. It's their fault because if they are not up to the job, then somebody else should be doing it.

Pres: Tell me, do you ever actually *buy* anything in supermarkets?

Walsh: I make it a rule never to buy more than half a dozen items on my daily visit here, though I must admit that their cherry pies are very good. But I do my main shopping in France. Everything there is so much better and so much cheaper, and I cover my travelling costs on what I save – everything from peppers to kitchen towel is less expensive, so I go twice a month.

Pres: So why do you drive yourself crazy here every day? Could you possibly have become obsessed, a little unbalanced even?

Walsh: It has never crossed my mind that I might be going mad, never once. But this struggle has caused me a lot of stress – some staff have been insulting – but I will still keep coming back, day in, day out. The problem is that we accept whatever is put in front of us without complaint. That's the trouble with us British. Well, not me.

Pres: But don't you get fed up with being so unpopular?

Walsh: Of course I don't like it that they treat me with contempt. The staff think I am a troublemaker because I point out that their shelves aren't restocked often enough, unless it's with expensive items or junk food. And of course I get angry. Above all what really annoys me is when goods are overpriced and the staff couldn't care less about the customers. It's a stressful mission that I've chosen, but somebody's got to do it.

SPEAKING p105

❶ Point out to the class that this activity follows up the theme of the Listening they have just done. Check that groups understand the meaning of *vendetta* and *complaining for the sake of complaining* before they begin. Encourage the use of other arguments on either side, as well as any examples from shopping in their own country. Finally, find out which side the majority of groups sympathized with, and why.

❷ Especially with a weaker class, you may first want to revise the names of shops. Take any questions on what they have to do, but avoid, if possible, discussion of vocabulary items in the materials (the map and shopping list) – the language should be familiar to them at this level. Allow time for them to absorb the ideas in the eight points which follow, explaining and/or giving more examples where necessary. Then give pairs three minutes to do the exam task.

VARIATION: You may want to put students in different pairs than usual, so that they can practise (as in the exam) working with people they do not know well, or at all.

FOLLOW-UP: Discuss how it went: did they have any difficulties? Was there enough/too much time? Did each person speak for roughly the same amount of time? To what extent did pairs agree/disagree, etc.?

❸ Students stay in the same pairs. Encourage complaints about the other items, for instance the oranges are overripe, the dictionary has pages missing, the loaf is stale and you have seen the same floppy disks advertised much more cheaply elsewhere. If necessary, prompt as follows.
What to say: demand money back (and compensation for time, bus fares, etc. wasted?), demand replacement goods, ask for apology.
What shopkeeper/manager might say: the goods were OK when they left the premises, you must have damaged it yourself, no refund on cut-price items/ without receipt/on CDs, credit note only, nothing wrong with the goods, lower price elsewhere no justification for returning, book or CD could have been used or copied, never had any complaints before, '(young) people like you are always…', etc. Threats: encourage discussion of tactics like those used by Walsh in Listening – negative publicity, threatening to have staff sacked, stores closed, etc.

FOLLOW-UP: Students make notes of what they say, as these would be useful for the letter of complaint writing task in Study Check on p107.

WORKBOOK: Focus On Speaking p104.

VOCABULARY: facilities and services p106

❶ This section introduces the topic of services, presents relevant vocabulary and gives more practice with second conditional forms (see Unit 6). You may want to make a link between shops, the topic of the previous pages, and publicly or privately run services here, for example by asking the class what they think the difference is and how they would categorize

some borderline cases like a *service station* which repairs cars (a service) but also sells petrol and other items (a shop).
Elicit the services, focusing on the meanings of potentially confusing terms like *library* and *casualty*.

> **ANSWERS:** 1 post office 2 a hospital/casualty
> 3 garage 4 tourist information office
> 5 job centre 6 police station 7 bank 8 hotel
> 9 library

VARIATION: Also elicit the names of the people who work in these places – although 'jobs' as a topic is covered in Unit 13 – and practise passive forms by asking what other things they might be given at post offices, tourist offices, etc.
Check that everyone has the correct answers to 1–9 before they match the expressions with them. Take any questions on the meanings.

> **ANSWERS:** 1 post office – packages and parcels
> 2 hospital/casualty – the health service 3 garage
> – routine maintenance 4 tourist information
> office – a sightseeing guide 5 job centre – an
> application form 6 police station – a witness
> statement 7 bank – a current account (this
> appears in Use of English on page 107)
> 8 hotel – receptionist and porters 9 library – the
> reference section

❷ This should be done fairly quickly, with students using second conditional and *-ing* forms (as preparation for Grammar below) to ask their partners 'Where would you go if you felt like having a quick snack?', etc. Run through the answers when pairs have finished.

> **ANSWERS:** 1 fast-food restaurant, etc. 2 pub/
> coffee bar/café 3 cinema 4 sports centre
> 5 disco/club 6 hairdresser's 7 art gallery
> 8 indoor swimming pool

VARIATION: Ask the class a few more questions relevant to their age, nationality, etc.: Where would you go if you felt like playing pool/pinball/video games, etc.?

FOLLOW-UP: Tell pairs to write down three words or phrases they associate with all or some of the places mentioned so far. They then report back to the class.

WORKBOOK: Vocabulary p60.

FURTHER PRACTICE: Vocabulary and speaking p137.

GRAMMAR: the gerund/*-ing* form of the verb p106

❶ Point out that any of the eight questions in Vocabulary 2 above would serve as an example of this form and use. Remind them that after a preposition, the verb is always in the *-ing* form (*to* is not a preposition when it forms part of the infinitive – see Common Errors below). Pairs study 1–5 and complete the sentences, although the choice of word is less important than its form. Check answers and elicit more examples, particularly of uses 3, 4 and 5 (1 is basic, while 2 was dealt with in Participle Adjectives in Unit 2).

SUGGESTED ANSWERS: 1 wearing 2 interesting/exciting/amazing, etc. 3 Shopping/Sleeping, etc. 4 cutting 5 doing

2 Students could do this in pairs. All uses from activity 1 are covered. Sentence 1 revises the past perfect continuous from the previous unit and focuses on the irregular -ing form of *lie*. Check the answers and elicit more examples, particularly with prepositions (*interested in*, *chance of*, *danger of*, *keen on*, *no point in*, *good at*, etc. + -ing).

ANSWERS: 1 lying 2 going 3 hiring 4 spending 5 Skating 6 advising 7 collecting 8 boring 9 contacting 10 dialling

3 Whereas in activity 2 students were given the gerund and had to choose the first verb, here they must think of a suitable gerund. Some questions focus on topic-related issues while others require a personalized response, so it is probably best for students to do this activity individually. Encourage, where possible, the addition of more words than just the gerund, although clearly in questions 4 and 6 the most likely answer is one word. Check written work, or – with a strong class – go through the answers orally.

POSSIBLE ANSWERS: 1 delivering letters 2 sitting near the door 3 committing any crime 4 smoking (cigarettes) 5 losing it/having it stolen 6 speaking (to people) 7 going to the seaside 8 eating chocolate 9 stealing it 10 actually living there

COMMON ERRORS

Here, *to* is a preposition, not part of the infinitive. Suggest to students that to check whether *to* is a preposition or not, they try putting a noun after it. If it works (e.g. *I object to lessons at 7 am*), then it is also possible to use -ing: *I object to starting lessons at 7 am.*

4 Pairs first decide that they are all connected with liking and disliking. You may also want to ask which they associate with which, and get students to grade them for intensity. Then they should decide that *fancy*, *dread* and *look forward to* are normally about the future, while *regret* tends to refer to the past. Strong students may point out that *I regret to tell you* relates to the present, but explain that here we are concerned with the use of the gerund and that infinitive patterns are covered in the next unit. The same applies if students mention the forms *like to do*, *hate to see*, etc. Make it clear that *mind* is normally only used in the negative, in questions and conditionals ('*I wouldn't mind (-ing)…*'). Students quickly write their sentences – you may want to do a quick check on what the class likes/hates doing most! – and then work in pairs. Encourage the use of complete sentences in replies, so that students don't

simply answer 'eating' or 'getting up', but say – for example – 'I love eating lots of cream cakes' or 'I really can't stand getting up early in the morning'. If necessary, prompt question forms with examples such as 'What do you really hate doing in the morning?'

WORKBOOK: The -ing form of the verb p63.

USE OF ENGLISH: error correction
p107

1 Students do this task-based advice exercise in pairs, using the exam instructions for guidance on some points but not attempting to do the exam task in 2 at this stage. Be ready to take any questions. Emphasize that the maximum of five correct lines does not include the example lines.

ANSWERS: 2 DO 3 DON'T 4 DO 5 DO 6 DON'T 7 DON'T 8 DO 9 DON'T

2 Tell students to watch out for incorrect uses of passives and gerunds, and to avoid marking correct uses as wrong. Students do this individually. When they have decided, go through the answers with the class and discuss any new vocabulary items.

ANSWERS: 1 too 2 being 3 most 4 ✓ 5 though 6 the 7 have 8 ✓ 9 of 10 to 11 ✓ 12 what 13 for 14 is 15 ✓

VARIATION: With a weak class you might want to help them by telling them there are four correct lines out of fifteen in this particular text.

WORKBOOK: Error correction p64; Focus On Use of English p88.

FURTHER PRACTICE: Error correction p138.

STUDY CHECK *p107*

1 Students do these in pairs, using verb + gerund structures where possible.

FOLLOW-UP: Students think of more everyday places and situations, and continue as above.

2 Students work individually, writing their answers to practise passives (less likely in spoken language in situations like these) and verbs + gerunds. Check their work, and possibly ask the class which of the services they have mentioned they like most and least.

3 If you set this letter for homework, you may first want them to write their plans in class.
Here is some advice you can give them:
• Think back to your discussion in Speaking on page 105.
• Decide whether you'd prefer to write about a real event or an imaginary one.
• Make a plan based on what took place and what you want to happen.
• Use contrast links like a*lthough*, *while*, *whereas*, *even though* and *despite*.
• As this is a formal letter, include lots of passive forms.

Encourage students to use passive forms of as many of the 'points to include' as possible.

Here are some more points:
- They told you it was in perfect condition.
- They gave you a receipt.
- You found out they had overcharged you.
- A different, less polite, assistant spoke to you.

Students now do Unit Test 10 on p177 of this book. The answers are on p215.

VOCABULARY *p108*

❶ Having three correct answers out of four enables students to spend most of their time concentrating on what is right and only a little on rejecting what is wrong, unlike some exercises of this type where only one is correct. The incorrect word is then activated by students using it in sentences of their own.

Elicit the answers, the reason why each is right or wrong and example sentences. Highlight the topic-related words used in the sentences themselves: *flight, ferries, seaside*. The expression *more and more* in the example question previews this form in the text below (*hotter and hotter*), as do several of the words in the options (*air conditioning, balcony, sunstroke, occupants, visitors, guests, manager, tour operator's rep*). Focus on 'campsite' as some languages have adopted 'camping' as a countable noun with this meaning. Ask students what/who they 'pay' (bills, people) and what they 'pay for' (services, etc.).

> **ANSWERS:** 1 book, pay for, reserve 2 air conditioning, a balcony, a fan 3 holidaymakers, tourists, travellers 4 beach, coast, shore 5 journey, ride, trip 6 getting sun-tanned, in the sun, sunbathing 7 gifts, presents, souvenirs 8 guests, occupants, visitors 9 manager, tour operator's rep, travel agent

❷ They should talk here only about imaginary disasters, as they will have the opportunity later on to tell their own stories of holiday nightmares. Eliciting answers may bring up some useful vocabulary on types of weather, crime, etc.

WORKBOOK: Vocabulary p66.

READING: gapped text *pp108–109*

Point out that this Reading section looks at missing paragraphs, while the Reading later in this Unit focuses on missing sentences.

❶ Students work individually on this, checking their answers with their partners when they finish. Then elicit answers.

> **POSSIBLE ANSWERS:** 1 Majorca (Spain), July, early afternoon 2 A woman was stuck on the balcony in the heat when the door locked from the inside (point out that *latch* is an example of a word that can be understood from the context) 3 **a** made the ritual noises and gestures but implied it was somehow her fault **b** thought it was funny; said it wasn't the first time **c** said (half-heartedly) she would warn other tourists

FOLLOW-UP: Here are some more questions you could ask: 'How was the problem solved?' (She communicated her predicament to people in the street using sign language.); 'What would be a good title for the text?' ('Trapped on the balcony', 'Hotel inferno', etc.).

❷ Remind the class to look both for language links and the sequence of events as clues to replacing the paragraphs. Here the emphasis is on the events, with reference words highlighted in the second Reading section of this Unit. Students underline as they go along.

> **SUGGESTED ANSWERS:** (text) I thought of dropping something; I kept shouting for help; my cries reached a girl; once more she passed by; a porter came to free me; I swore I would never again (paragraphs) promised to warn other visitors; I began to call for help; I was able to signal that I was locked out; I couldn't ring; The porter… assured me that it had happened before; She shrugged her shoulders and walked on.

Go through the answers to the exam task as a class, eliciting further clues in the text.

> **ANSWERS:** 1C 2E 3B 4H 5D 6G 7A Not needed: F

❸ This activity provides practice with past conditional forms, presented in Unit 12, and should be done in pairs. Suggest they think about:
– the door   – the window   – the next balcony
– the room below   – the room above   – the people in the street.

If necessary, prompt with further suggestions such as: using the table to break the door or window, climbing onto the next balcony, lowering a message to the rooms below, communicating better with people in the street, not panicking.

FOLLOW-UP: Points for class discussion might include: suddenly realizing the value of learning the local language; dependency on tour operators; apparently thinking about the insurance situation rather than the actual injuries that could be inflicted on local people, etc.

❹ Sentences (which will be needed in the Revision section) should be done individually and checked for accuracy.

WORKBOOK: Focus On Reading p72.

FURTHER PRACTICE: Gapped text p143.

GRAMMAR: reported speech *p110*

1 Refer the class back to the Reading text (the example sentence is in the paragraph after gap 6) and tell them to work individually, then elicit the answers.

ANSWERS:
2 (after gap 7) I swore I <u>would</u> never again <u>close</u> the door of a hotel balcony behind me (future simple/conditional)
3 (para F) she…shouted back that she <u>was going to get</u> help (*going to* future/*going to* past)
4 (para G) The porter…assured me that it <u>had happened</u> before (present perfect/past perfect)

2 Tell the class to use the examples above as clues as they discuss what happens in pairs; then elicit.

ANSWERS: – present continuous: past continuous – present perfect continuous: past perfect continuous – past continuous: past perfect continuous – past perfect: past perfect – can: could – will: would – would/should/could: no change – must: had to – may: might

VARIATION: As you elicit the changes, build up a table on the board.

3 Students read individually. Check understanding and elicit more examples.

1 Students work in pairs, writing in whichever is missing: the direct or reported speech version, plus the function that is expressed. Point out that they must use each function once only. Elicit answers.

ANSWERS: b He complained that he was fed up with that room. Statement.   c Can you let me know today, please? Request.   d She advised me to buy a flat there. Advice.   e Where did you go last week? *wh*- question.   f He told him to take the cases down to reception. Order.   g I'm going to leave right away. Intention.

2 Differences:

ANSWERS: 1 tomorrow/the next day   2 this/that
3 today/the same day   4 here/there
5 last week/the week before   6 bring/take
7 now/right away

FOLLOW-UP: Point out that in b we would still report 'this' room if the reporting conversation occurred in the same place. Explain that these differences usually only occur when the time and/or place really has changed.

4 Students work individually, then check in pairs. Elicit answers.

POSSIBLE ANSWERS:
1 She admitted that she didn't think much of the food.
2 He advised them to give out free local maps to the guests.
3 She enquired/asked whether they had similar accommodation in Italy.
4 He complained that it was the worst flight he'd ever been on.
5 They refused to pay extra for deckchairs.
6 They requested taxis from the airport.
7 He told them he had thoroughly enjoyed the holiday.
8 She threatened to take them to court if they didn't refund her money.
9 He promised to tell them to come the following year.
10 She asked him to tell his staff how wonderful they'd been.

FOLLOW-UP: Here are ten more sentences. Students decide on the original comments.
1 She advised them to get on that bus.
2 He admitted he had left it at home.
3 He asked/enquired where they were supposed to put all that luggage.
4 She refused to sit next to him.
5 He requested them to wake him when they got there.
6 She complained that it was the worst journey she had ever been on.
7 They enquired whether there was another train that night.
8 She told him not to drive on the left.
9 He promised not to tell anyone what she had told him the night before.
10 She threatened to get angry if he did that again.

POSSIBLE ANSWERS:
1 'Perhaps you should get on this bus.'
2 'Yes, I'm afraid I left it at home.'
3 'Where are we supposed to put all this luggage?'
4 'No, I won't sit next to you.'
5 'Would you wake me when we get there, please?'
6 'This is the worst journey I've ever been on.'
7 'Is there another train tonight?'
8 'Don't drive on the left!'
9 'I won't tell anyone what you told me last night.'
10 'Don't do that again or I'll get very angry.'

COMMON ERRORS

I asked her where she was going. Interrogative word order is not used when a question is reported.

5 Go through the instructions with the class and refer them back to some of the questions in Reading 1 p108 as a useful framework for their story. When they have finished the role play, check the sentences

Student B has written and then tell them to change over, so that Student A becomes the journalist.

WORKBOOK: Reported speech pp69–70.

FURTHER PRACTICE: Impersonal reporting p142.

USE OF ENGLISH: key word transformations *p111*

❶ This Part 3 exercise also revises important and in some cases difficult structures, many of which appear frequently in FCE papers. Students work alone on the transformations, identifying reporting functions and, if necessary, checking them against the examples in activity 3 on p110. They could compare with their partners when they have finished. Go through the answers with the class.

> **ANSWERS:**
> 2 asked; request; *if*: if he could stay there
> 3 admitted; statement; *that* + change to past perfect: had gone there on his
> 4 told; order; infinitive: never to mention that
> 5 advised; advice; infinitive: advised Joe to tell
> 6 asked; *wh-* question; *what* + change to past simple: what time that pub closed
> 7 reminded; advice; infinitive: reminded Steve to ask for
> 8 said; intention; *that* + change to past continuous: they were going the next
> 9 warned; advice; infinitive: us not to touch that
> 10 ordered; order; infinitive: to show him what was

❷ Elicit answers to this question, which previews the Grammar section later in this Unit.

> **ANSWERS:** Questions 4, 5, 7, 9, 10

WORKBOOK: Multiple choice cloze p70; Focus On Use of English p88.

FURTHER PRACTICE: Key word transformations p142.

LISTENING *p112*

❶ Students work in pairs, possibly with dictionaries. Elicit these (all used in the recording) and more expressions connected with the seaside (watersports, resort nightlife, etc.) and countryside (plants, fish, animals, etc.).

> **ANSWERS:** a sand, coastline, tide, waves, shore, spray b stream, peaks, river-bank, valley, inland, waterfall, undergrowth

❷ Remind the class how valuable the introduction is in terms of setting the scene for the recording, and the importance of making at least mental notes about the subject before they listen whenever they do this kind of exercise. Give the class a couple of minutes to jot down their ideas, and then elicit as many as possible – reinforcing the point that there is a tremendous amount of useful work that can be done even before the tape starts.

VARIATION: With a weaker class, prompt with general headings such as the weather, where to stay, what to do, meeting people, sports, eating and drinking.

Play the recording twice and then check their answers.

> **ANSWERS:** 1T 2F 3F 4T 5F 6F 7F

❸ Pairs respond to the text. Ask the class for their ideas when they have finished.

WORKBOOK: Part 1 p67; Focus On Listening p96.

TAPESCRIPT

Jill: OK, Steve, what's your idea of the perfect holiday? Just imagine you can choose anywhere in the brochures and go where you like, all expenses paid. What kind of place would you choose?

Steve: Oh, I think it would have to be somewhere with sun, sea and mountains. A place with crystal-clear blue water, a rocky coast with white spray flying all over the place, lots of very green grass with loads of multi-coloured wild flowers mixed in, and as a backdrop some towering peaks that stay white on top all year round.

Jill: So what would you do there apart from admire the views?

Steve: Lots and lots of walks, right up into the mountains and valleys. First, though, I'd explore the coastline, finding my way round the shore and over the rocks, dodging the waves as the tide rose and gradually discovering what lay below as it went out.

Jill: And the countryside?

Steve: Well, after a day or two I'd head inland, maybe following a river upstream. It would be full from the snow melt and there'd be salmon leaping up the waterfalls. You'd see birds of prey circling high up and all kinds of creatures rushing about in the dense undergrowth, from rabbits and lizards to deer and wild boar. As the day got hotter I'd find a slow-moving pool to cool off in, with the plants and flowers on the river-bank reflected on the surface and the water sparkling in the sunlight.

Jill: Sounds wonderful, but wouldn't you get lonely after a while?

Steve: Ah, I was coming to that! As I got nearer the source, high up in the mountains, I'd come to an unspoilt little village where the people are so friendly and the food out of this world. I'd stay at a cosy pub, sampling the local drinks in front of a log fire, as it would get quite chilly at night up there. I'd watch the amazing sunset and then the billions of stars, waking up next morning to dawn across the mountains and sea. That's the perfect holiday, wouldn't you agree?

Jill: Mmm, well, there are certainly parts that sound great but really I dream of something a bit different. For a start it would have to be somewhere where the sun always shines, where it's hot all the time…

Steve: Me too…

Jill: Yes, but mountains and valleys are all very well, very pretty and all that, but really they always seem to attract clouds and rain and stuff, don't they?

Steve: But you need to cool off from time to time…

Jill: Sure, but I'd much rather take a dip in the sea, and if you don't like hot weather you might as well stay at home anyway, right? No, I'd much rather be on a great big beach with acres of soft sand and the chance to do some watersports. Doing some windsurfing and water-skiing and trying something else I've always wanted to do: surfing. I'd love to try those really big waves – can you imagine the feeling if you're on a board actually inside the perfect wave, with a white sheet of water tumbling right in front of you? Beats paddling about in streams any day!

Steve: Yeah, but I wouldn't be looking for excitement, I'd just want to relax.

Jill: Oh, I'd be doing plenty of that too, don't you worry! Apart from the beach there'd be long, lazy evenings sipping cool drinks and watching the world go by from a leafy terrace bar on the promenade. There would be people from every country you can think of, all looking their healthy best and there just to have fun. I'd make friends and we'd go to the very best restaurants, trying every kind of ethnic food you can imagine, then on to the most fantastic disco you've ever seen, with music, lights and a swimming pool to keep you partying till sunrise. Then, after the best coffee you've ever tasted it would be back to the kind of hotel room that makes you feel you're in your own private palace. And that would be just day one!

FURTHER PRACTICE: Vocabulary and speaking p141.

SPEAKING p112–113

This is a main exam focus on Part 2 of Speaking. It should always follow the Listening above as the recording acts, to some extent, as a model for this activity.

❶ Let the class read the first paragraph silently, then ask questions about the procedure (*How many photos will you see altogether?*, etc.) and timing to check comprehension. Students fill in the table in pairs.

> **ANSWERS:** all SHOULD except: 4 He or she will have to talk about them later, and you about his or hers. 9 It's somebody else's turn!

❷ ❸ The instructions are similar to those used in the exam, and the guidance for Students A and B prompts the likely sequence and interaction that would follow. Monitor the conversations and be on

hand to offer advice and supply language where needed, but without interrupting as the interlocutor is unlikely to do so in the exam.

VARIATION 1: With a weaker class, you might want to give fuller prompts as follows:
Student A *They both show lovely places, with sunshine.*
While in the first picture there is…, the second one is of…, or There's nobody in the first picture, whereas in the second there are some people on the beach and…
It seems to be a…, They might be having…, It looks as if they are doing …
It's where you see…, It's how you feel when… greener, sunnier, more exciting,
If you were at a seaside resort you could …, but in the countryside …
Student B: *because there are… and I could…*

VARIATION 2: If you feel that the A students may have difficulty in speaking for a full minute, you could suggest that the B students prompt them by asking questions such as these: *What would you do in the place shown in photo 1? What couldn't you do? What about photo 2?* But point out that in the exam the examiner would do this – not the other candidate.

WORKBOOK: Focus On Speaking p104.

VOCABULARY: British and American English p114

Elicit the answers and, if there is time, ask for more UK/US words – especially those associated with travelling: *petrol/gas*, etc. Focus on the potential for misunderstandings ('Two peoples divided by a common language'). Ask why US words are more likely to be understood in Britain than UK words in North America (American films, TV programmes?).

> **ANSWERS:** (UK form first): railway/railroad, holiday/vacation, pavement/sidewalk, queue/line, motorway/freeway, underground/subway, lorry/truck, lift/elevator, aeroplane/airplane

FOLLOW-UP: Pairs ask each other how they would travel in the US and UK (e.g. *How would you get from Chicago to LA?*), using words from the list in their replies where they can (*I'd hitch a ride on a truck along the freeway*, etc.).

READING: gapped text p114–115

❶ Point out that a key word here is 'generally', as there are always going to be exceptions to overall tendencies. Students work alone and then talk about their answers with their partners.
  They also discuss the two questions about queue jumping. Then look at each situation as a class.

VARIATION: Do this as a cultural awareness task, comparing similarities and differences between the students' culture and that of the UK/US. Here are some more situations.
Paying in a supermarket.   Checking in at an airport.
Buying food in a burger restaurant.   Cashing a cheque in a bank.   Ordering a drink in a bar.

Getting stamps at a post office.   Waiting for the lift in a building.   Going into a nightclub.

❷ Students work alone on the exam task and underline as they go along. Go through both the answers and the linking words with the class.

> **ANSWERS:** 1C, 2F, 3H, 4A, 5G, 6B, 7D
> Not needed: E
> A <u>Such research</u> B <u>Arriving passengers</u> C <u>It's</u>
> D <u>complaints stopped.</u> F <u>It is not how long you have to wait that bothers you, it is how long you think you had to wait.</u>   G <u>more modern example</u>
> H <u>all of them</u>
> 1 <u>is not</u> 2 <u>This seemingly obvious principle</u>
> 3 <u>640 people</u> 4 <u>the study</u> 5 <u>in the 1950s</u>
> 6 <u>Those with luggage</u> 7 <u>To deal with the complaints</u>

VARIATION: With a weaker class, draw the two kinds of queue on the board and elicit the name of each before they start the exam task.

FOLLOW-UP: Ask if they noticed any other American forms, for example *check* (bags) for *check in* in the UK.

❸ Elicit more reference words, pointing out that they can refer forwards as well as backwards. If there is time, refer students to other texts to underline them/note them down. Ask the class what they refer to. Others might include:
Backward: the these those he she him her they
them mine yours his hers its ours theirs some many one another such each every other either neither both so (I think so) not (I hope not) then there in this way the above the former the latter
Forward: below the following this these

> **ANSWERS:**
> Sentence H: Them = *640 people*.
> line 33: Those = *Arriving passengers* (Sentence B).

❹ Students imagine the situations and tell their partners what they would think, say and do.

WORKBOOK: Part 3 pp68–69; Focus On Reading p72.

GRAMMAR: the infinitive *p116*

This section (and Writing) brings in a lot of 'Places' vocabulary. Point out that the focus is on verbs that are or can be followed by the infinitive, with and without *to*. Students read to themselves. Elicit more examples of each. Point out that *help* can also be followed by the infinitive without *to* – *He helped them to do it/He helped them do it* – and that many of these verbs can take *that* + clause forms: – *It appears that the necklace has been stolen.*

❶ Students work in pairs. Check as a class.

> **ANSWERS:** 1 offered/agreed   2 to make
> 3 let them   4 advised/warned people   5 forgot
> 6 saw/heard them   7 promised   8 managed

Give/elicit more examples. An authentic instance of *meant* meaning 'involved' can be found after gap 6 in the *You are how you wait* text on p115. You may also want to focus on the differences in meaning of verbs of perception (*see, feel, watch, hear, smell, notice,* etc.) when they are followed by the infinitive (*I saw her cross the bridge* = the whole action) as opposed to the *-ing* form (*I saw her crossing the bridge* = part of the action).

VARIATION: With a strong class, elicit or explain the small difference in meaning with *hate, love,* etc.:
I hate saying this, but it's not my turn. (it often happens)
I hate to say this, but it's not my turn. (one particular occasion)

> **COMMON ERRORS**
>
> *They don't usually make you wait long. To* is not used after the object of *make* when used with the sense of 'compel'.

❷ Tell the class to imagine the situation for each one and decide on the answers with their partners. Then elicit the answers and more examples.

> **ANSWERS:**
> 1 She was walking but stood still and had a conversation.
> 2 Don't forget to do something in the future.
> 3 Make an effort: something that may not be possible.
> 4 To be sorry about what you are going to have to say.
> 5 Remember to do something in the future.
> 6 We changed activity.

❸ When pairs have finished, elicit some of the answers.

FOLLOW-UP: Here are some more that pairs could discuss:
• What speaking another language lets you do.
• What you mean to do after the lesson.
• What your partner should go on doing.

WORKBOOK: Infinitive and gerund p69.

WRITING: describing a place *p117*

❶ Students work individually. Possible title: 'A town I know'. The task instructions here say 'cross it out' rather than 'write it next to the number', etc. as the text will be used for further tasks and as a model. Go through the answers with the class when they have worked them out alone.

> **ANSWERS:** 0 ✓   00 by   1 is   2 ✓   3 a   4 of
> 5 at   6 also   7 from   8 any   9 ✓   10 for
> 11 too   12 ✓   13 been   14 the   15 ✓

❷ Students work in pairs. Elicit answers when they have finished.

ANSWERS: 3 peninsula, river, seaside, mountains
4 Liverpool, Wallasey, New Brighton, North Wales
5 motorway, rail, air, sea, underground, tunnels,
ferry   6 higher-technology industries and offices
(elicit the meaning of *commute*)   7 docks and
shipbuilding industries   8 outskirts, districts, town
centre, suburbs   9 estates, terraced houses,
detached houses, semi-detached houses
10 unemployment, drug abuse   11 musicians,
actors, sports people   12 Birkenhead Park,
Tranmere Rovers

❸ This is a Writing Part 2 task. Students work
individually, referring back to the text as a model.
Elicit their answers to 1 before students proceed, and
possibly look at their plans in 2 before they start
writing. Remind students at stage 4 always to leave
time at the end of their writing to check their work
thoroughly. Collect in their articles when they have
finished and mark according to the exam criteria.

WORKBOOK: Writing p71; Focus On Writing p80.

STUDY CHECK *p117*

❶ Students work alone, as these are personal
responses. Check their written work for accuracy.

POSSIBLE ANSWERS:
2 I thanked him for letting me back in, but told him
   I didn't think it was very funny.
3 I exclaimed that I had been stuck there for hours
   and that his adjustments certainly hadn't
   prevented it.
4 I admitted that I didn't/don't know what I
   would've done if they hadn't helped me.

❷ Students work in pairs. Student A would ask B,
for instance, *What have you started to do recently?*
and then write down B's reply, possibly *She told me
that she'd started learning French*. Then they would
move on to the next question.

FOLLOW-UP 1: Tell students to ask and answer more
questions using verb + infinitive or *-ing* forms that
they have practised.

FOLLOW-UP 2: Here is an optional further writing task
with a descriptive element:
Follow these Writing Part 2 instructions and the
advice below:
*Your teacher has asked you to write about a village,
town or city that you once visited or lived in. Describe
this place and say why you particularly liked it. Write
your composition.*
Try to include some of these:
• how it made you feel
• what you liked to do there, or enjoyed doing
• what you remember doing there
• something you attempted, began or learnt to do
  there
• what you saw people doing there
• what people there said to you, and you said to
  them.

Remind students that they must answer both parts of
the question: i.e. describe *and* give reasons, examples,
etc. You could give more prompts using grammar
and/or vocabulary from this Unit if you wish.

**Students now do Unit Test 11 on p178 of this book.
The answers are on p216.**

12 Getting on well

SPEAKING and VOCABULARY *p118*

❶ Tell the class to think about these questions (they focus on the content of the Reading text to follow) and discuss them in pairs. Then elicit answers, allowing a short class discussion to develop if opinions differ. This might be a good point to bring in *-ship* words such as *friendship* and *relationship*.

❷ Students work individually. There may be a lot of words that are new, although for students from some countries many of them will be cognates. Care needs to be taken, though, with possible false friends such as *sensible* and *nervous*. If there is time, ask the class which are opposites or near-opposites (*sociable* and *shy*, for example), and which form them by using an affix, like *in*sincere and care*less*. Point out that some affixes do not produce the opposite meaning (*helpful/helpless*, etc.). Dictionaries would be useful here; otherwise you will need to be on hand to answer the many queries on meaning that are likely to come up. Expressions in Reading are previewed.

FOLLOW-UP: Here are some more possible adjectives: careful ambitious calm quiet hard-working lazy cautious well-dressed polite strong friendly rude.

❸ Students work in pairs. Be ready to answer questions on more subtle differences in meaning, such as *self-confident* and *aggressive*.

VARIATION: Students, working alone, decide which words in the list other people would use about them, and which they would use about their partners. Encourage students to be diplomatic, especially if they are a mixed-nationality class with widely different cultural values. Then they compare both lists with their partners' and try to explain any differences. Point out the value, particularly to less self-confident students, of finding out they have qualities they had never previously imagined!

FURTHER PRACTICE: Vocabulary and speaking p145.

READING: gapped text and multiple choice *pp118–119*

❶ Students read the text alone. Elicit the answers.

> **ANSWERS:** a a magazine for young teenagers
> b to give advice on making and keeping friends

❷ Allow students to study the instructions, examples and explanation. Students read the first two paragraphs alone and decide on the answer to the question in pairs.

> **ANSWERS:** *Your best friend; enjoying the same activities, having the same outlook on life, sharing similar experiences; It may be the result of*

> **ANSWERS:** 1F 2B 3D 4A 5C 6E Not needed: G

VARIATION: Revise the importance of finding both content and language links as clues to working out Reading Part 3 tasks. See the 'jumbled paragraphs' exam focus in Unit 1.

FOLLOW-UP: Consider the notion of the topic sentence at greater length.

❸ The multiple choice (Reading Part 2) activity encourages learners to write their own question stems. The language elicited in Questions 1–4 also has a specific language point in each case:
• Q1 recycles the 'X is someone who' form from the text
• Q2 previews the present + zero conditional
• Q3 previews the present + modal form in Conditionals
• Q4 introduces a question form (*Where is X taken from?*) often needed for comprehension of exam instructions.
The activity could be done in pairs, with a class discussion of the answers to follow.

> **POSSIBLE ANSWERS:**
> Q2 your friends for help
> Q3 time with someone of the opposite sex
> Q4 is this text taken from?

VARIATION: If the class are finding any of the questions difficult, prompt by giving more of the sentence.

❹ Before pairs do this, it might be a good idea to elicit/revise the main points of the text. Before 1, for example: 'How does the text say you can make friends?' Answer: 'By enjoying the same activities'.

VARIATION: If you think it is necessary for your students, prompt with suggestions like:
1 getting a job, going out more, learning English!
2 sharing good times and bad times; telling and keeping secrets
3 changing interests; moving home or school/going to university; fancying the same boy/girl

WORKBOOK: Part 2 p76; Focus On Reading p72.

GRAMMAR: conditionals (0) *p120*

Before you start, you may want to elicit and revise the forms and uses of the first and second conditionals from Unit 6.

❶ 1 Go through the explanation and elicit the answer to the question (present simple). Give a few more examples, perhaps on the board, including scientific laws such as *If metals get hot, they expand*, *A plant dies if it has no water* and/or 'universal truths' of the *If you really love someone it shows* variety. Then elicit more, possibly putting the best on the board.

2 Focus attention on the example and the explanation. Give examples and elicit more: song lyrics can be a useful source of this structure. Point out that the *if-* clause does not necessarily have to come first: *Give me a call if you feel at all lonely*, etc. is equally possible.

② Tell the class to do the exercise in pairs, then go through as a class.

> **ANSWERS:** 1b present 2d present 3a imperative
> 4c present 5e imperative

③ This exercise uses the transformation format of Paper 3 Part 3. Students work individually and check their answers with their partners. Go through as a class.

> **ANSWERS:** 1 feel better if I talk 2 if you don't go
> 3 continue if we don't 4 give you information if
> you 5 all doors if there is

> **C O M M O N   E R R O R S**
>
> *If I buy a ticket, I could win. Will/shall/'ll* are not normally used to refer to the future in the *if-* clause.

④ This gives slightly freer practice with each form. In three of them the clauses have changed position. Elicit oral answers or tell them to write them. If they do this, check their work.

WORKBOOK: Conditionals p77.

Conditionals (3 and mixed) *pp120–121*

① This section presents and practises the third and mixed conditionals, moving from concept questions through controlled practice to freer practice. Start by eliciting the answers to Questions 1–6.

> **ANSWERS:** 1 No 2 No 3 Third or Past Conditional
> 4 To talk about a hypothetical situation in the past
> 5 past perfect/*would have* + past participle. When comparing with the L1 structure (question 6) it might be worth checking whether it is a common form, as although there may be a direct equivalent to the English pattern it may tend to be replaced by a simpler construction in everyday situations – which some students may try to transfer to English.

②

> **ANSWERS:**
> 1 *would* (neg) + *have* +   wouldn't have/'ve; we'd
>   past participle +
>   past perfect
> 2 past perfect + modal   she'd; might've
>   (*might*) + *have* +
>   past participle
> 3 modal (*could*) + *have*   could've; hadn't
>   + past participle +
>   past perfect (neg)

Give several models of the contracted forms complete clauses or sentences), as plenty of ex is needed for accurate recognition to be achiev Fluency of production may not be needed at this level, but it is vital that students learn to recogniz them.

③ As with zero forms, some learners may be surprised to find combinations that do not fit neatly into the traditional third conditional pattern.

> **ANSWERS:** past perfect + conditional; conditional continuous + past perfect

Past perfect refers to the past, conditional forms to the present. Give and elicit more examples.

④ Focus on the idea of regret in examples such as those in activities 2 (sentences 1 and 3) and 3 (1st sentence). Point out that all the answers require third or mixed conditionals as presented above. This activity uses the format of Use of English Part 3. Students write their answers alone, check them with their partners and then with the class.

> **ANSWERS:** 1 have ('ve) warned you if I 2 if he
> hadn't (had not) told 3 would have (would've)
> spent more time 4 have ('ve) seen her again if
> 5 would ('d) still be living together 6 would ('d)
> understand if she had (she'd)

⑤ Remind the class that the *if-* clause can come first or second in the sentence, as shown by the two examples. Students work alone: some individuals may feel inhibited from writing freely here if they know they will have to show what they have written to other students, so use your discretion as to whether they should check in pairs or as a class. You may prefer to collect in their work for correction.

> **POSSIBLE ANSWERS:**
> 1 If I hadn't forgotten/If I'd remembered to do it they wouldn't have got angry.
> 2 If I'd gone to the party I would've (I'd have) met somebody I like.
> 3 If I hadn't missed the last bus I wouldn't still be walking home/I'd be home by now.
> 4 If he/she hadn't seen me with somebody else he/she wouldn't have got so jealous.
> 5 If I'd told him/her the truth it might have hurt him/her, so I didn't tell him/her.
> 6 If I had asked him/her to dance, he/she might not have left with somebody else.
> 7 If I hadn't wrongly accused him/her (of...), we would still be friends.
> 8 If I'd remembered/hadn't forgotten to post the letter I would have got the job.

⑥ Students work in pairs, identifying with the characters in the pictures. If necessary, give examples to start them off: *I would've felt lonely/left out*, etc., *I would've gone home, I would've told the others not to be so unfriendly, I'd be feeling angry*, etc.

WORKBOOK: Conditionals p78.

WRITING: a formal letter *p122*

❶❷❸ The aim of this task is to produce a Writing Part 1 transactional letter while also practising report writing, character adjectives, zero conditionals and other language from this Unit. Students begin by reading the letter individually, then work in pairs for 2. They write their own plans in activity 2 and then work together again to brainstorm vocabulary (2) and produce some initial sentences (4), before doing the exam task. Collect in their work once they have corrected each other's letters.

VARIATION: Elicit or give further examples of zero conditionals such as *S/he does not complain if s/he has to work late* or *If the children are having a good time, s/he is happy.*

WORKBOOK: Writing p79; Focus On Writing p80.

READING: multiple matching *p123*

❶ Point out the usefulness of always reading the example paragraph in Reading Parts 1 and 3, and of thinking about the content of opening paragraphs of texts in general as a way of setting up expectations of what follows. Ask the class (or get pairs to discuss) the reasons why the children they did not choose are likely to be less successful, without reading any further into the text.

❷ Students work individually. Check the answers.

> **ANSWERS:** 1E 2F 3G 4A 5B 6D 7C Not needed: H

❸ Pairs discuss the questions, giving reasons and examples to justify their opinions about themselves and each other.

VARIATION: With a strong class, elicit the terms used in the text for some of these, e.g. 'emotional management' for changing your own emotions, and 'empathy' for sharing feelings. Point out how both expressions are explained in the text, reminding students to look out for explanations whenever they come across new words – rather than giving up and thinking 'I don't know that one'.

FOLLOW-UP: Pairs (and then possibly the class) discuss any people they know who are particularly good or bad at any of the three things mentioned. They also talk about how this affects these people's lives.

WORKBOOK: Focus On Reading p72.

LISTENING *p124*

❶ The section begins with a task-based focus on skills students will need for Part 1 of FCE Listening, following up the earlier focuses on this section. Students write their answers individually, check with their partners and then with the class.

> **ANSWERS:** 1 information 2 relationship
> 3 feelings 4 emphatically 5 attention
> 6 indication(s) 7 unrelated 8 useful
> 9 impression 10 choice

❷ Check that everyone understands the adjectives used in the questions, and then play the tape twice. Students do the exam-style multiple choice questions individually. Check the answers.

> **ANSWERS:** 1A, 2A, 3A, 4B, 5A, 6C

TAPESCRIPT

One
Well what amazes me is that there's people who really do take these things seriously – I mean everyone knows that they're all written in the office to look as though, as if they'd been sent in by readers, by making up the kind of things they reckon some people might have problems with, when in fact they just have staff who sit around dreaming up these things and passing it across the desk to dear Mary or whoever happens to be the resident phoney. I sometimes wonder just what kind of people actually read this stuff.

Two
Man: Hello Cathy.
Woman: Hi.
Man: Everything's OK?
Woman: Yes, fine. Jane's had a bit of a cold but she's just about thrown it off now.
Man: And how's Paul? No more accidents, I hope.
Woman: Now you know that could've happened anywhere, so please let's not go into that again, Barry.
Man: If you insist. Now where are they? If I'm only allowed to see them once a fortnight I don't want to be wasting time hanging around waiting for them to appear.
Woman: They'll be here in a moment, don't worry.

Three
Woman: Yes, I know it's not always going to be easy, but let's at least give it a go – there's nothing to lose and, you never know, it might just work out. You can have both upstairs rooms if you want, so any time you want to be on your own you've in effect got your very own place. What do you think?
Man: Well, I don't know really.

Four
I think you have to realize that when something like that happens your whole life seems to fall apart. You can't sleep until it's nearly time to get up and when you wake up you wish you hadn't 'cos the pain starts all over again and you know it'll be there all day. No matter what you do you just can't get rid of it, you just can't concentrate on anything else for long enough because as soon as your thoughts run free – even for a second – you're right back to thinking about her and that awful, horrible feeling of loss cuts right into you even worse than before.

Five

You mean did I get involved when I was still too young? Well, maybe I did miss out on a lot of things the others were doing, like all the parties and the discos and even things like just going down to the park or the shops with everyone – but deep down I know I wouldn't have missed it for the world. It was all there – me shaking like a leaf when we first went out; getting to know each other bit by bit; starting to trust another person with your feelings; the world suddenly seemed more bearable. So if you're asking me if it was worth it, my answer has to be yes – it was.

Six

Boy: Are you at the same school as your sister?
Girl: No, I'm at the convent.
Boy: Why's that?
Girl: Oh it's because when we moved here I was already settled in and my Mum didn't want to take me away from all my friends again, so I stayed.
Boy: Don't you miss her?
Girl: Well, I suppose I do a bit.

WORKBOOK: Part 4 p75; Focus On Listening p96.

GRAMMAR: short replies *pp124–125*

❶ Students study the examples and then do the activity in pairs.

> **ANSWERS:** 2f 3a 4e 5b 6d

VARIATION: Give teacher-class or student-student oral practice of the example exchanges and items 1–6 when the answers have been checked.

COMMON ERRORS

> *I think so that I've met him before. So* is used only in short replies. The correct form is: *I think (that) I've met him before.*

❷ Students fill in their own answers, then do as a teacher-class exchange, avoiding statements of disagreement if possible: there should be enough students who agree with each statement for the point to be made.

> **ANSWERS:** 1 So do I.   2 So would I.   3 Neither do I.   4 So did I.   5 Neither have I.   6 So do I. 7 Neither can I.   8 So am I. (The class might also answer in the plural: *So do we*, etc.)

❸ This further practice activity also brings in 'family' vocabulary.

WORKBOOK: Vocabulary p74.

FOLLOW-UP: With an older class, give them this cultural awareness activity which focuses on similarities and differences that may exist in dating customs. Make sure everyone understands *dating* and *dates*. Students write their answers and check with their partners.

1 Here are some dating customs in countries such as the UK, US and Australia. Say which are similar in your country by answering *So…* or *Neither…*, as in the example. If they are different, put *We are*, *We aren't* or *We don't*.

1 Young women and men often meet
each other at parties.   *So do we*.......
2 They usually have their first dates
in their early teens.   ....
3 They, not their families, choose who
they go out with.   ....
4 They are usually about the same age
as each other.   ....
5 They are not always from the same
economic, religious or ethnic group.   ....
6 They usually decide together where
they are going to go.   ....
7 When they go out, they are not
accompanied by a member of
the family.   ....
8 The man and the woman often pay
half each for everything.   ....

2 Now think about your parents' generation in your country. Answer Questions 1–8 about them in the past, for example:
1 *…So did they…*   2 *…They didn't!…*

Elicit the answers:

> **ANSWERS:** 1 2 So do we/We don't   3 So do we/ We don't   4 So are we/We aren't   5 Neither are we/We are   6 So do we/We don't   7 Neither are we/We are   8 So do we/We don't
> 2 3 So did they/They didn't   4 So were they/They weren't   5 Neither were they/They were   6 So did they/They didn't   7 Neither were they/They were   8 So did they/They didn't

FURTHER PRACTICE: Short replies p146.

SPEAKING *p125*

❶ Students look at both pictures. It is important that students consider the points alone, choosing what is important to them personally. They will have a chance to argue about their choices in 2!

❷ Students do the exam task in pairs, using the suggested expressions where appropriate but without making the dialogue unrealistic by overdoing them.

VARIATION: When students first read the instructions, ask them which are the key words. You may decide on *party*, *organize* and *success*. Remind students to do this whenever they read new instructions in order to understand exactly what they have to do.

FOLLOW-UP 1: Ask the class when they have finished which were the most popular features of a good party, and why.

FOLLOW-UP 2: With an older class, give them the following instructions:

1 It is the morning after the party and the house is in a terrible mess. In the column on the left are some of the things (A–F) that have happened; on the right (1–6) are comments that people might make about them. Match the two.

A Somebody used the fruit bowl as an ashtray.	1 *Where have the CDs gone?*
B An ornament is lying on the floor in pieces.	2 *How could anyone be so stupid?*
C Somebody behaved very badly.	3 *I'm never going to do that again.*
D You have an awful headache.	4 *It's the last time I invite him to a party.*
E There were too few glasses and cups.	5 *How did this get broken?*
F Some things have disappeared.	6 *If we'd used paper ones, we would've had enough.*

ANSWERS: A2 B5 C4 D3 E6 FA

Imagine the scene and talk to your partner, using 1–6 (stress the underlined words) and comments of your own. Mention other things that have gone wrong and also some of the good things about the party, using, for example: *Do you remember…? Did you see…?* or *Wasn't it funny when…?*

2 You only have a few hours to clean and tidy everything. Decide with your partner what to do. Choose some of these to talk about:
• how you feel
• which room(s) you will start with
• what must be tidied up first
• who will do what, and in what order
• what you will do with all the rubbish
• what to do with the left-over food and drinks
• how you will clean everything
• what to do about any damage.

WORKBOOK: Focus On Speaking p104.

USE OF ENGLISH: key word transformations *p126*

❶ Allow some time for the class to study the information and fill in the gaps. Check the answers.

ANSWERS: 1 zero 2 third 3 mixed 4 negative 5 opposite

Elicit more linking words like *because* and expressions like *as a result of*.

❷ It is best to check after the first two that pairs have understood. Check their written answers have followed the instructions, especially regarding the number of words.

ANSWERS:
2 <u>by pressing</u>; zero; *lock if you press*
3 <u>because</u>; <u>didn't wake</u>/<u>didn't hear</u>; third; *I'd/ I would've woken up*
4 <u>The reason</u>; <u>bit</u>/<u>was</u>; third; *wouldn't have bitten him*; <u>hadn't been</u>
5 <u>as a result</u>; <u>wrote</u>; third; *had written more slowly*; <u>wouldn't have made</u>
6 <u>owing to</u>; <u>was</u>; third; <u>hadn't been</u>; *would've been able to*
7 <u>because</u>; <u>didn't save</u>; mixed; <u>had saved</u>/*working he <u>would have</u> some*
8 <u>or</u>; <u>told</u>/<u>might have married</u>; third; *if you <u>hadn't told</u>*
9 <u>Eating</u>; zero; *eat too much it makes*
10 <u>because</u>; <u>couldn't play</u>; third; *it hadn't rained we*; <u>would've been able</u>

VARIATION: Students do activity 2 in two stages. First go through each question, asking which words should be underlined and which kind of conditional used. Then, in pairs, they write the second sentences. Alternatively they underline, choose the conditional type and answer the question.

WORKBOOK: Open cloze p78; Focus On Use of English p88.

STUDY CHECK *p127*

❶ Students work individually, thinking back to events they remember and what happened as a result of them. Allow time for everyone to note down at least six of these. Then check their written work for accuracy. You could ask for volunteers to tell the class about any significant incidents.

You may want to give more examples, such as:
fell off bicycle   broke collar bone
went to disco   met Fran
If I hadn't fallen off my bicycle, I wouldn't have broken my collar bone.
If I hadn't gone to the disco, I wouldn't have met/be going out with Fran.

FOLLOW-UP: Point out to the class that in the exam (and other situations), being able to use the third conditional gives them another conversational 'dimension', which is particularly useful if they are asked a direct question about experiences ('Have you ever done…?') and want to keep talking even if they haven't by answering: 'No, but if I had…'.

❷ You might want to give a few examples first, and when pairs have finished elicit some of their statements, giving your response using *so* and *neither*.

❸ 1 Elicit key words from the instructions, especially those relating to the context, the purpose and the intended reader, as well as the need to deal with both personality and ability to get on with others. Focus on the final points about number of words and appropriacy.

2 Elicit opinions about the questions (the answers are all 'yes'). Ask the class what happens if they don't follow instructions like these and refer them back to Unit 5 (report writing) if they don't know or can't remember.

❹ Give the class plenty of time to think about these questions and then compare ideas with their partners, before going through them as a class.

ANSWERS:
His personality: paragraphs 1 and 2; his ability to get on with others: paragraphs 2 and 3.
Suggested 'positive': lively/adventurous/good sense of humour/ready smile/sports/spends time on his own/reading/makes friends/adaptable/team player/fair play/quick and enquiring mind/good listener and asker/good company.
Suggested 'negative': hard to know his thoughts and feelings/overenthusiastic/noisy/lack of interest in some conversations.
Contrast words; *however, even if, although*

FOLLOW-UP: Here are two more questions for students to answer:
Which of the positive points are the most important to you?
What would be the ideal family for Alan to stay with?

❺ Go through the advice point by point, eliciting more examples of language from the texts.
Students write individually. Check each student's work once pairs have done so.

Students now do Unit Test 12 on p179 of this book. The answers are on p216. Then they do Progress Test 3 on p191 of this book. The answers are on p217.

13 Come rain or shine

SPEAKING *p128*

❶ Elicit the names to go with the pictures: any other violent weather forms (especially those featured in recent films) and the damage they cause, if possible using phrasal verbs such as *blown down*, *turned over*, *cut off* and so on. Elicit brief personal stories for the next questions and then ask if and why they are becoming more frequent, prompting with 'climate change' or 'El Niño' (without going too far into global warming, ocean currents, etc. at this stage) if necessary.

> **ANSWERS:** storm/thunder and lightning – fire, loss of power supplies; tornado – destruction of trees, houses etc.; fog – poor visibility leading to road accidents; heavy snow – blocked roads, isolated villages, etc.

❷ Encourage pairs to say why they wouldn't like to be there: what could/might happen, etc. When they have finished, pairs report back to the class.

READING: multiple choice *pp128-129*

❶ These could be done orally, with a strong class, or else in writing. Students should by this stage be familiar with many of these points but the important thing is getting the sequence right. With an advanced class you may want to make it clear that to some extent the points summarize what has already been covered. Be ready to take any questions as it is important that students understand everything in a–i.

> **ANSWERS:** 2 i 3 e 4 g 5 c 6 f 7 a 8 h 9 d
> Suggested reasons:
> i The aim of three of the possible answers is to distract you from the correct one.
> e The information you need to find in the text is normally* in the same order as the questions.
> g It is better to make up your own mind what the text really says.
> c In this way you start from your impression, not from the ideas in three wrong answers.
> f This gives you a double check on whether your answer is right or not.
> a These are two very common kinds of wrong answer.
> h You get no marks for giving either no answer or a wrong answer, and you could be right.

The first question should be done individually, with a couple of minutes to think about it, before they go on to work in pairs. Then elicit the suggestions that the class found useful, or surprising (such as not being penalized for giving a wrong answer, which may not be the case in their country's educational system).

❷ Before they read, you could focus on the topic of the text with a question such as:
What do you think mountain climbers do in a thunderstorm?
Allow two minutes maximum for the gist question, pointing out that they may encounter a question on text purpose in the exam.

> **ANSWER:** D

❸ For the example, focus attention on 1 *On July 24, lightning on Petits Charmoz caused* only, pointing out that the first paragraph contains the relevant information to complete the statement.

> **ANSWERS:** 2 second and third paragraphs
> 3 fourth paragraph   4 fifth paragraph
> 5 sixth paragraph   6 eighth paragraph
> 7 eighth paragraph

The rest of the advice here continues taking students through the suggested steps in activity 1. It should be done individually, and then checked with the class.

> **ANSWERS:** 2B 3C 4D 5C 6D 7B

Go through the reasons why each alternative answer is right or wrong.

> **SUGGESTED ANSWERS:**
> 2 A 'even the bravest are afraid'
>   B 'bangs that deafen you','make danger…'
>   C 'claims relatively few lives'
>   D This is not suggested in the text.
> 3 A 'flashes' are a kind of light
>   B 'standing straight on end' means vertical
>   C 'a sound like bees flying around'
>   D The noise is not really caused by bees.
> 4 A The text does not suggest this.
>   B This 'should protect people'
>   C 'a good place in an emergency'
>   D 'as long as…at least one metre away'
> 5 A There is no evidence for this.
>   B 'all too often', not all climbers
>   C 'effects of panic', 'forget even the…'
>   D They have accidents, but do not always die.
> 6 A They have differing opinions on this.
>   B They warn climbers to avoid them.
>   C They do not say.
>   D They suggest carrying them.
> 7 A 'they tend to attract lightning'
>   B 'towards the ground'
>   C There is no mention of injury or worse.
>   D 'even melt jewellery' only

4 Tell pairs to work as 'language detectives' (younger students particularly like the term!). Go through meanings – and the clues to them – when they have finished.

VARIATION: With a strong class, elicit a secondary meaning of *summit*.

5 Students work in pairs. Do a quick round-up of ideas with the class afterwards.

WORKBOOK: Part 1 pp84–85; Focus On Reading p72.

VOCABULARY: the weather *p130*

1 Elicit students' answers. Add the temperatures in other cities if they are more relevant to the class.

2 Prompt if necessary with words like *freezing*, *cool*, *mild*, *sweltering*. Elicit synonyms for the extremes, such as *bitterly cold*, *icy* or *frosty* and *scorching*, *boiling* or *blistering*. Discussion of what constitutes 'hot' and so forth could go on for some time. Ask the class for a consensus when pairs have finished.

3 Quickly elicit the answers to these, together with the part of speech for potentially confusing ones such as *blow* and *hail*.

> **POSSIBLE ANSWERS:** cloud **c**, **d** (n) humid **b** (adj) pour **c** (v) storm **c**, **d**, **e** (n) drizzle **c** (n, v) mist **a** (n) wet **c** (n – the wet, adj) breeze **e** (n) blow **e** (v) chilly **a** (adj) bright **f** (adj) ice **a** (n) sleet **a**, **c**, **d** (n, v) shine **f**, **b** (n, v) fog **a** (n) hail **a** (n, v) damp **c** (n, adj) frost **a** (n) clear **f** (v, adj)

If there is time, students could write example sentences, noting the part of speech, e.g. *Showers are common in the mountains*: 'shower' – noun.

> ### COMMON ERRORS
>
> *Open the window please, I'm* (or *I feel/I'm feeling*) *hot*. Many languages use the equivalent of the verb *have* to describe sensations such as feeling hot, cold, hungry, thirsty, etc., but in English we use the verbs *be* or *feel*. Perhaps point out that we can also say *I have a cold*, but that this refers to a specific illness.

GRAMMAR: *so/such … that* *p130*

1 Allow time for students to look at the examples – both taken from the Reading text – and then check the answers: *so* is followed by an adjective or an adverb (and then a *that* clause); *such* is followed by a noun (with *a* if it is countable) or noun group (and then a *that* clause).

2 This activity practises both target structures as well as common collocations. Students work alone and then check in pairs. Go through the correct answers with the class, possibly pointing out the risk of mistakes such as 'high snow' or 'strong rain' if those are the collocations in their first language(s). Elicit the meaning of *overturned* in Question 6 as a preview to Phrasal Verbs with *turn* on the next page.

> **ANSWERS:** 2 clear sky   3 snow, deep
> 4 low temperatures   5 fog, thick *or* rain, heavy
> 6 wind, hard   7 ice, thin   8 heavy rain *or* heavy snow

3 Students write their own sentences. Check their work and elicit more examples of extreme weather conditions in their country.

> **POSSIBLE ANSWERS:** 1 that climbers get lost
> 2 that we went to the beach   3 that houses have to be very solid   4 that you can't see the end of the street   5 that the sun never shines   6 that villages are cut off   7 that boats sometimes sink

WORKBOOK: *so/such … that* p85.

GRAMMAR: adjective order *p130*

1 Let students read the introduction and elicit more examples of categories 1–6, stressing that these are tendencies, not rules. Also point out that the terms themselves are fairly elastic, for example 'material' could include 'electric' in *electric shock* from the Reading text, and the categorizing of some adjectives can be a matter of opinion (for example, whether *tall* is in category 1 or 2). Students work in pairs to answer the six questions. Elicit more groups of adjectives, but remind students that there are not usually more than three before any one noun. Ways of avoiding this (see the Further Practice) include using *made of* (*a delightful old Victorian house made of brick*), *from* (*a lovely little silver statue from Argentina*), *with* (*a useful Swiss mountaineering knife with several blades*) or a clause (*a nasty jagged rock splinter, which was protruding*). Point out that compound nouns (see Unit 7) like *climbing boots* and *lightning conductor* are not separated by adjectives.

> **POSSIBLE ANSWERS:** a opinion (1), size (2)
> b shape (2), material (5)   c size (2), age (2)
> d age (2), origin (4)   e colour (3), material (5), purpose (6)   f opinion (1), size (2), material (5)

2 Students work in pairs. Go through the answers with the class.

> **ANSWERS:** 1 correct   2 nasty black clouds
> 3 dramatic red Aegean sunset   4 freezing cold school bus   5 beautiful clear blue sky
> 6 unpleasant thick grey fog

WORKBOOK: Adjective order p86.

FURTHER PRACTICE: Adjective position p149.

PHRASAL VERBS: *turn* *p131*

1 The example is taken from the Reading text. Remind the class that many phrasal verbs have more than one meaning, but some are more common than others. First Certificate students will be expected to know verbs such as the ones in this exercise. Students work in pairs. Go through the answers, eliciting any more meanings students might know, such as *switch* *off* or *produce* for *turn out*. The form *turn out to be* also appears in the Listening recording on the next page.

> **ANSWERS:** 1 turned back c 2 turned into g
> 3 turned up f 4 turned down h 5 turned off d
> 6 turned out a 7 turned on b 8 turned over e

2 If necessary, prompt with examples such as 'A light breeze turned into a raging storm', 'It turned out to be the worst in living memory', 'We turned back as soon as we saw the clouds', 'We kept the radio turned on for weather forecasts', 'It had been turned off so we weren't expecting the change in weather', 'The boat nearly turned over', 'I turned down the offer of a lifeboat', 'Another boat nearby disappeared but it turned up the day after'.

WORKBOOK: Phrasal verbs: *turn* p83.

USE OF ENGLISH: open cloze *p131*

Apart from developing the skills needed for Paper 3 Part 2, this exercise practises grammar and vocabulary from the unit, as well as revising superlatives.

1 Allow a few minutes for students to discuss these questions without looking at the text, then elicit answers.

2 Allow much less time for them to find the answers.

> **ANSWERS:** wettest – Cherrapunji in India; driest – Atacama Desert; sunniest – eastern Sahara; hottest – Sahara; coldest – Vostok in Antarctica

3 Students work individually and then check in pairs. Go through the text with the class.

> **ANSWERS:** 1 from 2 ever 3 so 4 in 5 with
> 6 into 7 however, though 8 such 9 hand
> 10 a, per 11 which 12 that 13 course
> 14 rises 15 where

WORKBOOK: Focus On Use of English p88.

FURTHER PRACTICE: Open cloze p149.

LISTENING *p132*

1 You may want to begin by eliciting the differences in approach between doing reading and listening multiple-choice questions. Students work alone on the activity, writing in their answers. Then they check with their partners. Go through the advice with the class, answering any questions they may have.

> **ANSWERS:** 2H 3C 4B 5F 6G 7A 8E

2 Ask the class about their local equivalent to the British Met Office and where most people get their weather forecasts from: TV, radio, press, etc. Perhaps also ask if the weather is a popular topic of conversation in their country and why/why not. Students then do the exam task individually. Play the recording twice.

> **ANSWERS:** 1C 2A 3B (point out that the meaning of *so that* makes C impossible) 4C 5A 6B 7B

3 Pairs discuss. Find out how forecasts can help – for example – farmers or people in the tourist industry. This is also an introduction to the topic of Jobs in the second part of the Unit. Encourage students to talk about how they keep cool in summer and warm in winter, how extremes can affect this and possibly also upset their daily routine (snowfalls making it impossible to get to school or work, etc.).

WORKBOOK: Part 4 p83; Focus On Listening p96.

TAPESCRIPT

Colin: For many years, I used to think that the national interest in the weather was a dull British obsession, rather like the state of their health was a French obsession, but now I realize it's not true at all. In these damp and misty islands, the weather and its unpredictability is actually quite an interesting subject, as I found out when I visited our weatherman, Tony Targett, at the Bristol Weather Centre. He, like other forecasters, is actually an employee of the Meteorological Office and doing the TV forecast is only part of his work. Tony, what else does the Met Office do?

Tony: Well, there are a lot of interest groups that have a serious concern about the weather and will pay us for early information. Not just the obvious ones like the National Rivers Authority which need to be told about rainfall; but the police, the highways authorities and the airports, and also some less likely interest groups.

Colin: For instance?

Tony: Well, would you believe that the supermarkets buy weather advice in order to change their window display on the basis of what will sell more? Then there's the pigeon fanciers who time their races, especially the cross-Channel ones, with a careful ear to the forecast advice. And, importantly for everyone, the big power firms take advice from us on expected temperatures so that they can estimate demand for electricity.

Colin: So where does all the information come from? Is it all from satellites nowadays?

Tony: Some of it, yes. We get on-screen advice direct from the polar orbiting satellite and from Meteosat, hanging in fixed orbit over Nigeria. But there are also weather stations and radio operators on vessels in the Atlantic, as well as radar – which shows us exactly where the rain is.

Colin: But what about for more local information, in particular as it affects driving conditions?

Tony: Oh, what really helps there are the sensors we've now got on many roads. They give us an on-screen prediction of when precisely ice will form on the surface, often in the

frost that's already there, which of course they had forecast for that location nine hours earlier.

Colin: I have noticed, though, that an awful lot of your reports seem to be coming from Canada and the United States. It's all interesting stuff, but how exactly does it help us?

Tony: Well what you have to realize is that most of the British weather comes from the west, so knowing what is happening on the east coast of North America will often turn out to be relevant here 24 hours later.

Colin: So really with all this information nowadays there's no excuse for ever getting the forecast wrong, is there?

Tony: Oh, I wouldn't go that far! The Met Office is quite pleased if 85% of its forecasts are right and…

Colin: Only 85%! Whenever I'm sitting in downtown Boston, for example, the local radio seems to be able to tell you at 2p.m. that there will be 'rain in downtown Boston at 2.15p.m.', and shortly after it starts to rain. Why the difference?

Tony: Well, the reason of course is that on the eastern edge of a populated continent the weather systems have been tracked coming across information points for some time, and accuracy is to be expected. In the UK, on the other hand, the weather systems which influence us most frequently have usually come flying across the Atlantic. And the Atlantic, though it has its information points, obviously doesn't have as many of them as the USA and Canada.

SPEAKING *p133*

❶ Point out that the ability to paraphrase and ask other people for help with words are real-world skills that form part of communicative competence, and will be seen as such by examiners if the techniques are used appropriately and effectively.

This exercise also introduces more topic-related vocabulary and gives further practice with *so … that* and *turn*. Highlight the pronunciation of *drought*, and of possible cognates such as *hurricane*, *tornado* or *avalanche*, as they might be pronounced quite differently in the students' first language(s). Go through the answers with the class.

ANSWERS: 1 umbrella 2 drought 3 shelter
4 soaked 5 damp 6 melt 7 rise 8 shiver
9 hurricane 10 tornado 11 avalanche
12 heatwave

❷ Students work in pairs. Be available to answer questions on the meanings of the words, which should be useful for students when they come to do activity 3. They continue with words of their own, which need not necessarily be related to the topic of weather.

❸ Students continue in pairs. This activity includes a cultural awareness element, and a link forward to the topic of jobs. If there is time, discuss the answers as a class.

VOCABULARY: jobs *p134*

First check that everyone understands the meaning of *skills*. You may want to give an example, such as *A doctor has to treat sick people, possibly in a hospital. He or she needs patience and concern for others*. Answer any questions on vocabulary while pairs are working. All the names of jobs will be needed later in the unit.

WORKBOOK: Vocabulary p82.

FURTHER PRACTICE: Vocabulary p148.

READING: multiple matching *p134–135*

❶ These questions could be talked about in pairs, groups or as a class. The aim is to get students thinking about the main points of the text to follow.

FOLLOW-UP: Also ask which countries and which jobs they would choose, and why.

❷ Let the class read the introduction and then focus on the example (0) and the relevant part of the text (end of D – Work your Way Around the World) for the clue: *how to become a barmaid or barman*, emphasizing the fact that in this exam task-type the clues are definitely not in the same order as the questions. Then tell students to answer them individually.

ANSWERS: 1E 2C 3D 4E 5B 6A 7C 8E 9 and 10 C/D 11 and 12 A/D 13 and 14 B/D

❸ Students do this first in pairs or groups, then report back to the class.

FOLLOW-UP: Ask the class what other information they would like books like these to give.

WORKBOOK: Focus On Reading p72.

WRITING: a letter of application *p136*

❶ Check that everyone understands the advertisement. For many students the names of the jobs will be cognates, but it may be best to check this and give examples of what they do where necessary.

VARIATION: If students have any difficulty choosing a job, let them interpret *administrators*, *staff* and *technicians*, for example, very broadly and point out that they could be just temporary jobs rather than permanent careers.

❷ Students read the letter first for overall meaning. You might want to ask some general comprehension questions such as 'Do you think her application has a good chance of success?' When they have filled in the gaps on their own, elicit the answers. Focus on features such as the formulaic use of the present continuous in *I am writing* followed by *to* to express purpose, and the mixture of past and perfect verb forms, thus revising the grammar input from Unit 9. Point out the tentative use of the conditional in Question 9, rather than an over-confident 'will'.

ANSWERS: 1 am writing   2 was born   3 have
been living/have lived   4 passed   5 lived/had
lived   6 moved   7 have had   8 working
9 would be   10 hearing

3 From the tense focus of 2, activity 3 moves on to
concentrate on style/register. Pairs find the more
formal expressions in the text. Elicit the answers.

ANSWERS: 1 job – position   2 as well as – in
addition to   3 because – owing to the fact that
4 give – provide with   5 really good – excellent
6 very much – particularly   7 free – available
8 go to – attend   9 please write soon – I look
forward to hearing from you

4 This activity looks at the content. Pairs write their
answers to the questions as they relate to the sample
letter above. Elicit answers when they have finished.

ANSWERS: 1 Recruitment Specialists. No.   2 To
apply for a job. Secretarial Assistant.
3 'International Jobs' magazine, October.   4 19.
Four temporary secretarial positions.   5 Work with
people from different countries. Like to work hard.
6 CV   7 *Yours faithfully*   8 Quite formal

5 Students work alone. Collect in their completed
work, including letter plans.

WORKBOOK: Writing p87; Focus On Writing p80.

USE OF ENGLISH: error correction
p137

1 Check that everyone understands the terminology
(*articles*, *reflexive pronouns*, etc.) and give examples if
necessary. Tell students to read through the text once
for gist, and to ask (or use their dictionaries) if they
have any vocabulary questions – some of the
expressions used could be useful to them in the Study
Check at the end of the unit. Students work alone
and then check their answers in pairs. Elicit the
answers and the grammatical type of mistake in each
case.

ANSWERS: 0 by   00 ✓   1 a   2 only   3 ✓   4 of
5 being   6 also   7 such   8 for   9 ever   10 to
11 ✓   12 ✓   13 as   14 yourself   15 the
0 preposition   1 article with uncountable
2 adverb   4 preposition   5 verb form   6 adverb
7 pronoun   8 preposition   9 adverb   10 verb
form   13 conjunction   14 reflexive pronoun
15 article with uncountable

VARIATION: If the class have by now done a lot of
exam-style error correction tasks, elicit the most
common kinds of mistakes before they read the first
paragraph.

2 Students, possibly working in pairs, answer the
questions about job hunting in their own country.

WORKBOOK: Error correction p86; Focus On Use of
English p88.

STUDY CHECK *p137*

1 You could bring copies of some more ads from
the press into the class for students to use as model
texts. Students do the exercise alone. Check their
completed written work.

2 These are the kind of notes often used with texts
in Writing Part 1 of the exam. Stress that these are to
refer to their partners. Look at their work when they
have finished.

3 Students work individually on their plans and
letters. You may want to check their plans before
they write the letter. Part 4 gives further practice with
learner training (reasons for mistakes). Collect in their
work when they have finished.

**Students now do Unit Test 13 on p180 of this book.
The answers are on p216.**

14 Making a better world

SPEAKING *p138*

❶ Each of the four pictures illustrates a way in which people try to protect the environment. Point out that many of the words used in the eight aims appear in the reading text and will also be useful later in the Unit. Explain any that students may find difficult. Do this as a whole-class activity, telling the class to concentrate on the people's direct aims rather than subsidiary ones (such as using a bicycle in the hope that less road construction will therefore become necessary).

> **ANSWERS:**
> organic shopper – eat chemical-free food, discourage the use of artificial fertilizers;
> anti-road building campaigners – stop the construction of roads, protect the countryside;
> cyclist – avoid using fuel, avoid polluting the air;
> bottle-bank user – reduce waste, recycle used material

❷ Pairs or groups discuss how successful they think each of the activities in the pictures is, particularly with reference to the two main aims of each one. Encourage discussion of why some are or are not common in the students' own country, if necessary suggesting reasons such as media coverage (or lack of it), effectiveness of direct action, people's attitudes to new roads, provision of cycle lanes in cities, facilities for (and evaluation of the usefulness of) recycling, availability of organic food.

❸ Encourage groups to come up with environmental protection measures that exist in their country or possibly that they have seen in TV programmes about other countries, e.g. organic gardening, avoiding packaged products, eating less – or no – meat, not using aerosols, using less water, insulating the house.

FOLLOW-UP: Ask them 'How could *you* help?' Get them to say what they have done, do or could do, perhaps in the form of suggestions to the rest of the group, e.g. 'Why not use vegetable waste from the kitchen as a fertilizer for house plants?'

READING: multiple matching *p138–139*

❶ Remind students that none of the key words on the exam paper will be underlined. Begin by eliciting the connection between 'danger' and 'accident' and expressions in D: *risk* and *fall*. Students, working in pairs, then underline what they consider to be the key words in each of 1–15. Students then read the text and answer the questions, working individually. Go through the answers and then take any questions,

particularly on environment-related vocabulary and forms used to express opinions, which is a main language focus of this Unit.

> **ANSWERS:** 1C 2B 3D 4D 5/6A, C 7D 8C 9B 10D 11C 12A 13/14C, D 15B

VARIATION: When they have finished underlining, look at (or ask them to tell you) their choice of words before they continue: these should be mainly content expressions like *car*, *tourism* and *other countries*, but there may also be some significant structural forms such as *no longer*.

❷ Pairs or groups discuss this, giving reasons in each case.

WORKBOOK: Part 2 pp92–93; Focus On Reading p72.

GRAMMAR: past modals *p140*

❶ Point out that the example is taken from the Reading text. Highlight the form but not the meaning, as this is the purpose of the activity which follows. When students have matched 1–4 with a–d, go through the answers with the class. Point out that *might* can be both uses a and b.

> **ANSWERS:** 1d 2c 3a 4b

Mention the use of *may have done*, *ought to have done*, *couldn't have done*, etc. as alternatives.

VARIATION: With a weaker class, you may first want to do a quick revision of the use of modals in the present.

❷ Students do this in pairs. Allow a minute or two for them to re-read section D in Reading, as the context is important if time is not to be wasted on alternative answers of varying degrees of implausibility. Check the answers, possibly eliciting the use (a–d from activity 1) as well.

> **ANSWERS:** 1f 2d 3e 4a 5b 6c

❸ Remind the class that they have to compare and contrast a pair of pictures in FCE Speaking Part 2, and point out that they may want to say what might/ must, etc. have happened in the two cases as part of this. When pairs have finished, ask the class for a range of opinions.

WORKBOOK: Past modals p93.

C O M M O N   E R R O R S

They must have found her, mustn't they? The first modal auxiliary verb is repeated in the question tag. This example also practises past modals from p140.

FURTHER PRACTICE: Question tags p152.

GRAMMAR: *wish/if only* *pp140–141*

The example is taken from the Reading text and the task type throughout activities 1, 2 and 3 is that of Use of English Part 3.

1 If the class already know this structure, elicit some more examples, e.g. *She wishes she had an older sister. If only cars didn't need roads.* If not, tell them to study the Grammar Reference before doing so. Then they do the six transformation sentences individually, comparing their answers with their partners and, finally, with the class.

ANSWERS: 1 wish (that) you had 2 wish (that) city life was/were 3 only I could go 4 wish (that) you were 5 wish (that) you could/were able to 6 only I didn't have

2 This activity uses some of the language from 1, but the transformation process is the reverse: i.e. from *wish/if only* to other forms. Point out to the class that this is both to practise the structures and because exam Use of English questions might require transformation either to or from the target structure of this section. This activity is best done in pairs, as some of the questions are quite difficult.

ANSWERS: 1 pity people didn't take 2 silly of you to throw 3 regret not warning them 4 are sorry they ever started 5 a mistake not to tell 6 a shame (that) you could

3 Do this the same way as 1. Point out that *I wish I would…* is not possible; neither are other forms with the same person as subject of both verbs.

ANSWERS: 1 wish (that) he wouldn't 2 wish (that) you would 3 only she would 4 wish (that) you would stop 5 wish (that) he would 6 only you wouldn't keep (you may at this point want to focus on *keep [on] doing*)

COMMON ERRORS

It's time we found a solution to this problem. As with *wish* (and *I'd rather*) we use a verb in a past tense to refer to the present or future after *it's time* when it means somebody should have done something before (see past modals above).

4 Students do these alone, then compare with their partners. Stress the need to avoid just repeating the verbs and other words from the situations in their wishes. Elicit a variety of answers for each.

POSSIBLE ANSWERS: (*if only* is also possible throughout):
1 I wish I had enough money/could afford it.
2 I wish I hadn't eaten those (mussels, etc.).
3 I wish I'd learned some of the language before I arrived here.
4 I wish they'd shut up and listen.
5 I wish I'd checked to see I had my bus money.
6 I wish s/he'd stop doing that.
7 I wish we didn't have to study it.
8 I wish I hadn't left them in the car.

WORKBOOK: *wish/if only* pp93–94.

VOCABULARY: the environment *p142*

1 This activity, which should be done in pairs or groups, prepares students for some of the vocabulary they will hear in Listening and need in Writing. Explain any terms they find difficult.

ANSWERS:
Positive – wildlife protection, conservation, concern for animal welfare, lower energy consumption, green awareness
Negative – forest fires, acid rain, global warming, oil slick, exhaust fumes, overfishing, radioactivity, greenhouse effect, destruction of rain forests, dumping waste at sea, carbon monoxide, destruction of the ozone layer, species facing extinction

2 Elicit answers, ensuring that all the expressions are discussed (the same applies in 3 below).

3 Elicit answers and, where appropriate, ask for recent news stories about them to illustrate both the dangers and any remedies.

LISTENING *p142*

1 This activity aims to stimulate thought on what students will hear on the recording. Whether their choice of a given cause is the same as the speaker's is largely irrelevant, though if it does happen it will probably be encouraging for the student. You may wish to point this out to the class, so that there is no sense of 'failure' if their choices do not coincide with the speakers'. Tell students that the recording will not be played until activity 2.

POSSIBLE ANSWERS: A motor vehicles, industry B dumping rubbish, sewage C burning fossil fuels, deforestation D pesticides, genetic engineering E power station leaks, nuclear waste dumping F need for timber, clearance for livestock farming

2 Play the recording twice, allow a minute for students to check their answers and then go through them with the class.

ANSWERS: 1D 2C 3B 4F 5A Not needed: E

VARIATION: With some classes, you may want to discuss the issues mentioned by the speakers 2–5 as preparation for Writing below.

❸ Play the recording once or twice more, depending on the level of the class. Remind students to write down very brief notes for each point, as they would if this were a Listening Part 2 task. Check the answers and tell the class to keep their notes, as they will need them in Writing below.

> **SUGGESTED ANSWERS:** (Speaker 1) cows/cattle, humans/people (Speaker 2) sea level, temperature (Speaker 3) rubbish/garbage (Speaker 4) forests, animals, plants; Siberia, the Amazon, Malaysia (Speaker 5) hot and sunny weather, lots of traffic; coughing, red/streaming eyes, hospitals full, deaths of old people

WORKBOOK: Focus On Listening p96.

TAPESCRIPT

One
I think one of the biggest threats to our health comes from attempts to interfere with nature, as we saw when they starting feeding animal remains to cattle, which after all are vegetarians. The result, as we know only too well, was BSE, mad cow disease, and its human form CJD. And now there's all this genetically modified stuff flooding into our supermarkets from the US. I know the aim is to create plants that are more productive and resistant to disease but my fear is that however good the intentions, it is only a matter of time before something goes badly wrong and we have a mass outbreak of something awful.

Two
What really worries me is all these strange things like hurricanes and tornadoes in places where they didn't use to happen. There's been a lot about El Niño, this huge mass of warm water that moves across the South Pacific and causes droughts and then there are warnings about the rise in sea level causing entire island groups like the Maldives to disappear. And I read the other day that an increase of just one degree centigrade would be the equivalent of moving all the plants 500 kilometres to the south. Even if that happened over a period of 50 years it would still be twice as fast as vegetation can adapt to different temperatures by evolution.

Three
I got really angry when I heard how much rubbish they were still dumping there and I saw all those seals and dolphins that had been poisoned. Now whenever there's a storm we get loads of garbage from deep-water sites washed up on the beach. It's just so incredibly selfish and short-sighted and I'm delighted when there's the occasional victory against the big boys, as when Shell tried to sink that oil platform – the Brent Spar, I think it was called – in the Atlantic, and Greenpeace made them back off. It gave me a good feeling, that.

Four
I feel passionately that we must do something to save it. Over half of it has already gone, and with it vast amounts of animal and plant life as entire ecosystems are destroyed. And it's not just the tropical areas which, important though they are, account for only a third of the earth's total. The biggest in the world are in Siberia and government inaction has led to more and more trees being cut down there as multinational companies turn their attentions to parts of the world where their destruction of the natural environment gets far less negative publicity than it does in areas like the Amazon and Malaysia. It must stop, it really must.

Five
As far as I'm concerned there's no doubt at all: the reason all three of my kids have asthma is the stuff they have to breathe in every day. It's worst when the weather's hot and sunny, like it was last July, and when there's lots of traffic. Sometimes when that horrible brown cloud is hanging over the city I start coughing too, and there was one day when our eyes were streaming and all red. When there's smog like that the hospitals are full of people with chest trouble, and I know of at least one old person who died of it. If something isn't done soon we'll all have to wear gas masks just to stay alive.

WRITING: a discursive composition
pp142–143

NOTE: You may want first to refer students back to Writing in Unit 3, which looks at the 'balanced discussion' type of discursive composition.

❶ Students work in pairs. Many of these expressions will, of course, be familiar to them, but in these cases the important thing is that students are clear about what they are used for. Remind students that *too* usually goes at the end of a clause or sentence, never at the beginning.

> **ANSWERS:** 1b 2d 3a 4c

VARIATION: With a weaker class, you may want to contextualize the new expressions by giving spoken or written examples in use, although activity 2 provides in-context practice with some of them.

❷ It is essential that students learn where in the sentence to put these expressions and what punctuation is needed, especially with expressions like *however*. Students write their answer individually or in pairs.

> **SUGGESTED ANSWERS:** 1 Nobody has taken any notice of the problem.   2 They knew exactly what they were doing.   3 We are rapidly approaching crisis point.   4 There are several reasons why I believe this.   5 We have tried many different solutions.   6 If we leave it any longer it will be too late.

VARIATION: You may want them to keep to the topic of the environment here, or if – particularly in the case of younger learners – this is not likely to prove easy for them, the topic could be broadened to include other areas.

3 This introductory activity gives further practice with gist-reading and also aims to raise students awareness of the importance of studying – and following – instructions carefully. The point of the activity is that students can lose a lot of marks in the exam if they misinterpret (through carelessness, over-enthusiasm for a particular topic or even trying to fit a rehearsed text to the title) individual words or phrases in the instructions.

> **ANSWER:** a

4 The aim of the task is to practise adding information to justify the choice of dangers, using the linking expressions as a guide to the type (result, contrast, etc.) that it is best to include. Remind students of the 180-word limit in this type of task. The dangers they write about (on land, in the air, and in the water) can be chosen, if they wish, from among those discussed by speakers in Listening above, so students should be able to write about some of the points they heard, using their notes from Listening 3. Check their completed written work, particularly for ideas that reflect the logic of the introductions and linking expressions.

5 Students write their own complete texts, based on the question 'What do you think is the biggest danger to the world's environment and what should we do about it?'. Allow plenty of time for students, working individually, to note down their answers to the six questions. You may want to look at these, or elicit some from the class. If they are weak on paragraphing, refer them to the first and last points of the seven recommended for inclusion. They then write up their compositions, bearing in mind these seven points.

FOLLOW-UP: When you are correcting their work, give special credit for the correct use of the grammar from this Unit (past modals, *wish*, linking expressions).

WORKBOOK: Writing p95; Focus On Writing p80.

VOCABULARY and SPEAKING p144

1 The words in this activity have been chosen to reflect approximately the level of animal vocabulary that is expected at this level, and include items featured in Listening below. Knowledge of 'easier' items like *dog, cat, cow*, etc. is assumed but students can show that they know them in activity 2. Allow plenty of time for useful discussion on categories, particularly where doubts might exist (dolphins, whales, tortoises, etc.). Go through the lists when they have finished, checking pronunciation of potentially confusing items like *wolf, bear, whale, salmon, toad, wasp*, etc.

> **ANSWERS:**
> 1 Mammals: rabbit, wolf, bear, camel, ox, goat, fox, donkey, whale, rat, dolphin
> 2 Birds: goose, pigeon, hen, eagle
> 3 Fish: salmon, shark, sardine, goldfish
> 4 Reptiles/amphibians: snake, lizard, crocodile, frog, toad, tortoise
> 5 Insects: ant, mosquito, bee, wasp, cockroach

VARIATION: With a weak class, it might help if you tell them – before they begin the activity – how many go into each category: 1 – 11, 2 – 4, 3 – 4, 4 – 6, 5 – 5.

2 Students continue in groups. Their choice of words will obviously depend on a range of factors, not least of which will be the animals that are particularly significant in their culture (see activity 3 below).

> **POSSIBLE ANSWERS:** 1 dog, cat, cow   2 chicken, turkey, canary   3 cod, tuna, sole   4 turtle, alligator, chameleon   5 beetle, butterfly, moth

VARIATION: With a more advanced class, you could also elicit other categories like marsupials (kangaroos, opossums, etc.) or crustaceans (crabs, lobsters, etc.).

3 The answers here will vary, and many of the animals can go into more than one category. For the question about b, prompt by asking whether they are rare because it isn't their natural habitat or because of hunting, destruction, etc. This activity should provide plenty of opportunities for discussion of topics like zoos, circuses, meat-eating, livestock transportation, the exploitation of animals, bullfighting and so on.

VARIATION: With a strong class you could encourage discussion of possible differences in attitudes towards animals in, for example, northern and southern Europe, or the USA and Latin America, and the likely reasons for them.

4 Do this quickly, avoiding more than two (the list for *tail*, for instance, could go on and on).

> **POSSIBLE ANSWERS:** tail: rabbit, lizard; wings: pigeon, wasp; claws: bear, eagle; shell: tortoise, cockroach; sting: bee, wasp; horns: ox; hump: camel; fins: shark, salmon; beak: eagle, hen; poison: snake; fur: rabbit; hair: wolf, camel

VARIATION: Depending on level, you could also put some more words on the board, such as scales, webbed feet or hoofs, and continue as before.

WORKBOOK: Vocabulary pp90–91.

LISTENING pp144–145

1 In Unit 8 (page 86), students were advised not to jump to conclusions about the answer when they hear likely-sounding vocabulary items (you may want to remind them of this), whereas here they are warned against inferring opinions too quickly. Let pairs study the questions, exam questions and text transcript, then elicit the answers.

ANSWERS: 1A 2B

2 Play the recording twice. Students answer the questions individually. Go through the answers and highlight some of the expressions used for giving opinions, agreeing and making suggestions (*Well, as far as I can tell...*, *of course I agree that...*, *How about...?*), etc. for Speaking below. Focus on the use of *wish* in 7, which may have led to some mistakes. Point out that the last three texts are all about pets, which is the subject of Speaking, and that the dialogue in 8 could be a mini-model for their own discussion. Take any vocabulary questions, particularly those related to the theme of the Unit.

ANSWERS: 1C 2A 3A 4C 5C 6C 7C 8B

WORKBOOK: Part 4 p91; Focus On Listening p96.

TAPESCRIPT

One

Man: Yes, I should know what that is just by seeing the way it flies, after all I did spend a lot of time bird-watching when we lived near the mountains and I used to see a lot of big birds of prey a bit like that one.

Boy: So is it a golden eagle, or what?

Man: Er, well, as far as I can tell it is, but to be absolutely positive I'll check it against the diagrams in that book of mine once we get back home. Can you wait till then?

Boy: Yes, OK.

Two

Man: Well, of course I agree that in places like that they haven't got enough room, but at least they get well fed, whereas in the wild they might go weeks without a meal...

Woman: Nobody's saying there's anything wrong with what they eat, it's just that having a full stomach doesn't mean they're happy, does it? If we lock them up in cages they get depressed and die young instead of...

Man: But look what happens to those in the forest or wherever they live: most of them get eaten by some bigger animal when they're just weeks or months old, which gives them a much shorter life than in the zoo, doesn't it?

Three

The most annoying sound in the world must be that of a neighbour's dog barking, because as a noise it is sudden and often loud, it's irregular and it achieves nothing. As a dog-owner myself, I've found the best way to deal with this is by not rewarding, rather than punishing. The thing to do is to give the dog its bowl in the usual way, but then blow a whistle and remove the meal. Repeat this three or four times a week until the dog makes an association between the whistle and no food. From then on, you can stop it barking by blowing the whistle, as the dog will come to associate bad behaviour with the whistle and non-reward.

Four

We're determined to stop this evil trade. These poor animals are being packed into lorries without enough room even to turn round and then shipped across the Channel in all weathers. Then they have to travel hundreds of miles abroad, often without being properly fed and watered, until they reach their final destination – which probably doesn't meet even the low minimum standards laid down in this country. So if we have to sell to foreign markets why on earth don't we kill the poor creatures here, and just send the meat?

Five

They're bullies and cowards, and deserve everything they get. I've seen one of those fat guys on a horse lean over and hit someone with his whip, then ride off laughing. Then he'll join up with several dozen of his equally nasty mates and go chasing after a single terrified fox, which they'll all enjoy watching being killed by a pack of dogs specially trained for the job. It makes me sick, and if the only way to stop 'em is by direct action then that's what we're gonna have to do.

Six

Boy: What do you think we should do about them while we're away on holiday?

Girl: I'll ask Linda to call round to the house and feed them every afternoon.

Boy: But they'd be outside, wouldn't they?

Girl: Oh, I'm sure they'd come in if she called them.

Boy: But what if they'd wandered off into someone else's garden?

Girl: Have you ever seen them climb those fences? They'd be back here in seconds!

Seven

It must be great having a dog of your own, one you can take out for walks every day, that you can look after and that looks after you by becoming a good friend you can always talk to. I wish I could have one but my mum won't let me, she says our flat's too small and anyway she'd end up taking care of it. She said the same when I asked her if I could have a rabbit and even though I promised I would do all the work she still said 'no'. Then Sally said I could have one of her white mice, so I took a cute little one called Jerry home with me and hid him in my room. I suppose mum will find out one day. I just hope I'm not around when she does!

Eight

Man: Let's get her a great big dog. One that'll look after the house for her, scare off any unwanted visitors.

Woman: Oh come on, Nick, she's a little old lady! It would be knocking her over all the time, and how's she supposed to take it out for walks? I think she'd be much better off with a cat.

Man:	Well I know she loves ours but doesn't she get ill and start sneezing whenever he's around?
Woman:	Hmm, that's true. But I'm still not going along with the idea of getting her some huge guard dog. How about something smaller, one that she can actually control?
Man:	That's probably the best idea, yes.

SPEAKING p145

Begin by explaining that in the exam the instructions will be spoken, not written, but that they will be given some form of visual material to work with. Tell them to read the suggestions before they start the task and then talk for about three minutes. You may want to monitor pairs as they speak, giving feedback when they have finished.

WORKBOOK: Focus On Speaking p104.

USE OF ENGLISH multiple-choice cloze p146

Allow time for students to look back at the linking expressions as they are tested in questions 1, 3, 11 and 13, and also to re-read the explanation of collocations in activity 1 on p21. They then work through the exam task individually. Go through the answers, making a note of any difficulties with linking expressions, relative pronouns and lexis such as job/work, etc. for possible remedial work.

ANSWERS: 1C 2B 3A 4C 5B 6C 7B 8B 9B 10A 11A 12D 13B 14C 15B

FOLLOW-UP: Ask the class for their opinions on the content of the text. What kind of video might suit other animals, such as cats or horses?

WORKBOOK: Word formation p94; Focus On Use of English p88.

FURTHER PRACTICE: Multiple-choice cloze p152.

STUDY CHECK pp146–147

❶ Tell students that these are to be done individually and, to avoid inhibiting them, that they won't have to show them to anyone else if they don't want to. Elicit some answers from volunteers only, but do look at written answers and check for accuracy.

FOLLOW-UP: Tell pairs or groups to decide which is the most popular wish in each of categories 1–4. Then they compare with others, and possibly the class.

Students talk about only those wishes they want to discuss. Comparing with other groups could be done as a class survey, with one member of each interviewing another group to find out which were their most popular (revealed) wishes. Groups then re-form and compare data, before reporting to the class as a whole. Alternatively, elicit each group's top wishes directly.

❷ This is a Writing Part 1 transactional letter activity. Remind the class that the notes are prompts they may or may not want to use, but that they should try and rephrase them slightly if they do. Elicit the style of the letter from the penfriend (informal) and point out that students should reply in a similar way. When marking, reward the successful use of linking words, good expression of opinion and use of vocabulary from this Unit.

EXAM STUDY GUIDE

1 Students work individually. Elicit answers and reasons.

POSSIBLE ANSWERS:
a GOOD: it may be quite a long time since you last studied some points. (Point out the need to start revising, in a relaxed way, well before the exam date.)
b GOOD: you need to be familiar with many different kinds of English.
c BAD: in the Speaking paper you will be speaking with another (non-native) candidate.
d BAD: there is too much to revise, and you should relax the day before.
e GOOD: you may find they have the same problem and/or can suggest solutions.
f BAD: you don't know what the questions will be and the examiners will penalize it anyway. (Point out, though, that it's fine to memorize phrases, such as 'Looking forward to hearing from you' for letter writing.)
g GOOD: you are concentrating on the essential points and a second look will help you

2 Students work alone. Elicit choices and make a note of the most frequently mentioned grammar points as a possible guide to areas that the class as a whole needs to revise.

3 Remind the class that they may need to look in more than one part of the book for large areas such as phrasal verbs, and for details on the different parts of the exam.

Students now do Unit Test 14 on p181 of this book. The answers are on p216.

15 Doing your best

SPEAKING p148

1 Encourage groups to recall names of friends, other classmates and teachers, and to describe the classrooms as they remember them. They could also talk about their feelings, as they remember them, when they first started school. Suggest that they talk about both subjective differences (everything seeming much smaller than it did at the time, etc.) and objective ones (new equipment, classroom layout, teaching methods, etc.).

2 Still in groups, students guess which person is doing which job and give reasons.

The people in the photos are:

a David Beckham (footballer)
b Bill Clinton (politician)
c Kate Winslet (actor/actress)
d Naomi Campbell (model)

VARIATION: They use the pictures to guess about future appearance: 'He looks fit and healthy, so he's probably still quite slim'.

3 Students work in pairs, comparing predictions about what will be the most lasting memories. Encourage the telling of anecdotes about things that have happened during the course involving individuals, the class and things in the room, including cassette players and OHPs.

4 Again in pairs, they talk about their classmates. You may want to extend this to include yourself and the head teacher or director of studies, but naturally this is entirely up to you!

READING: multiple matching
pp148–149

1 You may want to start by referring the class back to a Part 1 task with headings, such as the one on p18 (as well as the advice which applies to both heading and summary types). Students work alone, underlining the parts of the paragraph that correspond to each of a–c. Check their answers before they go on to the exam task.

> **SUGGESTED ANSWERS:** a because she wanted
> b to tell   c good news

> **ANSWERS:** 1D 2G 3B 4A 5E 6C Not needed: F

VARIATION: With some classes you could tell them to do the same with the rest of the sentences and paragraphs, and check their work after you have gone through the exam task answers, but this will

take more time so in most cases it is probably best – especially if the exam is close and they need to practise timing – for them to do the task in the ordinary way. In that case they could underline after they have finished the task and had their work checked.

2 Allow time for students to study the context of each of the words in the four groups, then ask individuals or pairs for the answers. Also elicit the meaning of *High School* (UK school for 11–18 year-olds, US 15–18).

> **ANSWERS:** 1 Both relate to former pupils at a school.   2 Both relate to senior pupils (*sixth-form* = final year[s] of secondary school; 'sixth-form student' is a common adjectival form)   3 All are 'bosses' of a school   4 All are (physical) parts of a school. Check especially for understanding of *career* – to some students the L1 cognate may mean 'university course'.

FOLLOW-UP: Ask the class the meaning of the expression *attends a school reunion* (the line below the heading). The question highlights two 'false friends' in one clause: some students may confuse *attend* 'pay attention to', perhaps using the false cognate 'assist' instead, while *reunion* can be taken to mean the same as the word in their own language, i.e. 'meeting' in general.

VARIATION: As the Reading text is entirely about a girls' school, if you are teaching an all-boys or mixed class you may want to ask them whether they would expect any differences if a similar reunion took place at their school, and why.

WORKBOOK: Part 4 pp100–101; Focus On Reading p72.

COMMON ERRORS

She came across the old school photo. The phrasal verb *come across* comprises an intransitive verb and a preposition, and therefore cannot be separated by an object, in this case the noun group *the old school photo.*

VOCABULARY: education p150

1 You could also ask the class to put these in order, from nursery (pre-school) for the youngest, through infant school, junior school (both primary), secondary and university. Ask students the corresponding ages in their country, including the age when most students leave university (which may well be higher than the 21 that is common in the UK).

Then ask where you would find each kind of person
(there may be some overlap between pupil/student
at secondary school), taking care with possible 'false
friends' and explaining in more detail where
necessary what a 'professor' is.

You may want to encourage more discussion of the
two types (public school – fee-paying, entrance exam;
private school – fee-paying, no entrance exam),
possibly with examples (some students may have
heard of places like Eton). Ask about the proportion
of children that go to each type in the students'
country, and ask whether those from the fee-paying
sector are in a privileged position for university entry
and getting jobs (and, if so, what they think of that).

VARIATION: An alternative approach, especially for
students in the UK is as follows:
Which of these are free? fee-paying? Which of them
have entrance exams?
state school boarding school private school
comprehensive school public school grammar school

❷ NOTE: The term *arts* for history, etc. may seem
strange to some students, who may expect the word
to be something like *humanities*.

You may want to prompt with examples – e.g. history,
maths, sociology, economics, geography, modern
languages, physics – and ask students to put them
into groups 1, 2 and 3 (ANSWERS: Arts – history,
geography, modern languages. Science – maths,
physics. Social sciences – sociology, economics).

VARIATION 1: With older students, point out that the
category each subject falls into will determine the
name of the degree awarded (see 3 below).

VARIATION 2: You may want to elicit more of each
type of subject, drilling pronunciation where
necessary. Note: sciences are covered in Unit 3 (p34).

FOLLOW-UP: Ask why they think the subjects they
mention are so popular, and compare/contrast with
the situation in the UK (at the time of writing, Media
Studies is extremely popular, while Modern
Languages is in rapid decline).

❸ These abbreviations may need expanding to give
the class more clues (approximate ages when
obtained in brackets): General Certificate of
Secondary Education (16), Advanced Level (18),
Bachelor of Arts/Bachelor of Science (21), Master of
Arts/Master of Science (over 21), Doctor of
Philosophy (over 21), for advanced research.

❹ These expressions can be pitfalls, often owing to
first language interference (students may think 'pass'
= take, etc.), and making mistakes with them in the
Speaking or Writing part of the exam is not a good
idea. You may want to do this task by saying 'Three
of these mean the same, as do another two, while
two more mean the opposite of each other', or by
looking at each one in turn.

VARIATION: Reinforce the meanings by going through
the exam dates, the students' plans for each paper
and what any of them will do if they don't actually
pass this time!

WORKBOOK: Vocabulary p98.

FURTHER PRACTICE: Vocabulary and speaking p155.

GRAMMAR: expressing purpose *p150*

Point out that the first example comes from the
Reading text (Sentence F) before students read the
explanation. Take any questions on vocabulary
relevant to the topic, such as *marks*, *degree*, *Latin*,
answer sheets, and *cheating*. Then elicit more
examples. Begin with the use of the infinitive to
express purpose, which many students may not have
been aware of. Their first language may require a
preposition + infinitive to do the same.

❶ Students work alone, writing short endings for
the sentences. Encourage the use of expressions from
Vocabulary. Check their written work for accuracy.

❷ As in 1, but emphasize the difference in register.
Take vocabulary questions (*prospectus*, *website*,
members of staff, *college regulations*, *documents*).

You'll get a good grade if you work hard. Point out that *in case* does not mean 'if'. They may believe this because of a false friend from their first language, or as a result of seeing English signs saying 'In case of fire break glass', or similar. This formal use means 'if' because the expression is *in case of*, not just *in case*. Elicit or give more simple examples of the difference between *in case* and *if*: *Take your coat if it's cold/Take your coat in case it's cold*, etc.

❸ These could be discussed in pairs: *They go to university to learn/in order to do research*, etc. Encourage the use of both 'so as not to' and 'in case' for *shopping lists* (with 'forget something'), and 'in case' with *insurance*, *take notes* and *spare pen*.

WORKBOOK: Expressing purpose p102.

GRAMMAR: *have something done*
p151

❶ Students study the two examples, as well as the context of sentence **a**. Ask the class what tense they both are (past perfect) and the difference: **a** means somebody else was paid to do our hair for us, while **b** means we did it ourselves. Point out that we can say who did it (*by hairdressers*), as in activity 2 below, or – if this is obvious or irrelevant – we can omit the agent, as in activity 3.

VARIATION: With a more advanced class, elicit or introduce at this point the informal variant *get*, as in *we'd got our hair done*. You may also want to focus on *have something done* meaning that something belonging to the subject has been somehow affected, as in *she had her application rejected*, *he had his nose broken* and so on.

❷ Students do this in pairs. The aim is to heighten awareness of meaning and to differentiate between potentially confusing forms.

> **ANSWERS:** 1c 2a 3b

FOLLOW-UP: Elicit or drill the meaning using other tenses, e.g. 'You'll have your work marked by the teacher' – *The teacher will mark your work.*

❸ This could be done as a written activity, or – with a strong class – orally. Help out with any vocabulary difficulties.

> **SUGGESTED ANSWERS:** (*in order to* and *so as to* as possible variations) 1 to have a room painted
> 2 to have a dress made 3 to have the lights fixed
> 4 to have the grass cut 5 to have their eyes tested 6 to have their teeth checked 7 to have their photo taken 8 to have it delivered
> 9 to have them educated

VARIATION: With a weak class, guide them to the best verb for each situation.

❹ Students do this individually. Their answers may vary according to their age and the culture they are from.

> **ANSWERS:** (*my own* is also possible throughout):
> 1 I cook my meals myself (I cook my own meals)/
> My mother/father cooks my meals/I have my meals cooked (if they always eat out or have servants!)
> 2 I wash my socks myself/I have my socks washed, etc. 3 I have my shoes mended. 4 I shampoo my hair myself/I have my hair shampooed
> 5 I photocopy important papers/I have important papers photocopied/My father, etc. 6 I clean my room myself/I have my room cleaned/My mother, etc. cleans my room 7 I make my bed myself/I have my bed made/My mother, etc. 8 I correct my own homework/I have my homework corrected/My partner, etc. 9 I have my clothes dry-cleaned (or my mother, etc. has my clothes dry-cleaned)
> 10 I have electrical equipment repaired (or possibly I repair, My brother, etc. repairs)

Students, working alone, then add *by my mother*, *by my wife/husband/girlfriend/boyfriend*, etc.

FOLLOW-UP: It might be interesting to ask for a show of hands on each of these, to see who is (according to the students) doing the housework!

FURTHER PRACTICE: Causative verbs p156.

USE OF ENGLISH: key word transformations *p151*

Students do these individually.

> **ANSWERS:** 1 in order to/in order that I could
> 2 have your mark sheet filled 3 so as not to have
> 4 in case there isn't 5 had the book sent
> 6 turned it down in 7 must have my watch mended 8 have our written work marked
> 9 so as not to 10 can have your certificate collected

VARIATION: Before students start, point out that the following questions test purpose links: 1, 3, 4, 6, 9, while these test causative *have*: 2, 5, 7, 8, 10.

WORKBOOK: Error correction p102; Focus On Use of English p88.

FURTHER PRACTICE: Key word transformations p156.

LISTENING *p152*

❶ Point out that A–F are all popular ideas about language learning that may or may not be supported by the facts. Remind groups that they can 'agree to disagree', as in Part 3 of FCE Speaking. Do not go into the arguments at this stage, as some of them feature on the recording in Listening.

Current thinking would give a qualified 'no' to all the statements. In the case of D (which is the 'extra letter' not on the recording), the reasoning would be that although students can only learn the language they are exposed to, they certainly do not acquire everything they read or hear. Nor, conversely, are they limited to this as they use their internal learning systems to work out rules, patterns and relationships in language, and go on to produce forms of their own. They can also acquire a tremendous amount of language from non-classroom sources, particularly if they follow the advice in the Exam Study Guide sections and elsewhere in this book on how to get more practice with English.

VARIATION: With an advanced class, focus on the topic by asking them to think about how they learned their first language as a child. Ask what similarities and differences there are between the way they learned it and the way they have learnt English. This could be done as a class discussion, in groups or in pairs. You may want to prompt with some of the following:

Similarities – imitation and practice, learning grammar in a certain order, acquiring language though exposure to simplified input, learning through interaction, feedback from parent/teacher, learning effectively when relaxed and in no hurry, etc.
Differences – L2 need to speak straight away (in L1 no need for the first couple of years), knowledge of first language (helps when talking about language, but there may be first language interference), greater general knowledge and reasoning ability when older, possible shyness when speaking (unlike a small child), etc.

2 Students have already spent a lot of time thinking about the questions, so go straight into playing the recording twice, while they work individually. Check their answers.

ANSWERS: 1A 2F 3C 4B 5E Not needed: D
---

3 If and where necessary, remind groups of points made by the speakers on the recording. Finish by discussing the answers to the two questions together as a class, bearing in mind that one aim of this activity – through what the speakers say – is to boost students' confidence in themselves and the methodology underlying the course they have followed.

WORKBOOK: Focus On Listening p96.

TAPESCRIPT

One
It certainly seems that no matter how well adults master a second language, their pronunciation and choice of words is still a little different from that of native speakers, or those who began it at an early age. But where the aim is basic communicative ability, older students can be more efficient learners. According to some studies, those who began in early adolescence do as well, in the end, as those whose first lessons in the language were at primary school.

Two
The point here is that there's quite a lot of research to show that students are no less accurate when they are speaking to someone of the same language level than when they are in conversation

with more advanced learners or native speakers. And if they're doing the right tasks in the right way they also tend to correct each other when they're working in pairs or groups.

Three
What we've found is that this may be the case where the aim of the lessons is to teach students *about* the language – things like grammar rules, lists of vocabulary and so on – just as it is when other things are taught in an academic way. When the emphasis is more on what they can *do* with the language, though, it seems that learners of very mixed abilities can be equally successful, particularly in speaking and listening.

Four
They're a natural part of learning either a first or a second language, and often show that a learner – a child or an adult – is trying something new out, is experimenting to see if he or she's got a word or phrase right. That's not to say, of course, that if a student keeps on making the same ones, or if they make communication difficult, that we shouldn't say so. But the idea that they lead to bad habits and should be stamped out does seem very old-fashioned nowadays.

Five
This may be true in part, but children who rarely do so still manage to learn, and there's no evidence that those who do so a lot learn any faster. It is more likely that they develop their own rules and then test these in speech. How else can we account for a child coming out with language they couldn't possibly have heard before, things like 'Look me!' or 'I sawed my little brother'?

WRITING: set books *p152–153*

NOTE 1: At the end of this section there is a writing activity that is equally suitable for students who have not read, and do not intend reading, a set book.

NOTE 2: Before the class do this activity, it might be worthwhile to check the names of these books in the students' first language, in case they have read one or more of them but do not recognize the English title.

1 Students work in pairs. You may want to give some brief background on some of the books or their authors, although if they understand the titles and study the covers there should be enough information for them to form opinions about which they would like to read. When they have finished, ask the class for a show of hands on those who have read them in English or their own language. Then ask which books they would most like to read and make a note for future reference.

2 Not many candidates choose to write about the set books, which is a pity given the advantages mentioned in the second paragraph of the text – and others, such as developing the reading habit – so it may be worthwhile encouraging more of your students at least to try reading one or more of them. In any event, tell the class to work through the activity, which focuses on many of the most important words concerning the set books questions. It is also a useful exercise in itself, using the C-test technique to concentrate on vocabulary relevant to the topic of the unit. Students could do this individually or in pairs. Go through the answers and take any questions, particularly from students who intend to answer (or want to have the option of answering) Question 5 in the exam.

> **ANSWERS:** 1 number   2 regulations   3 simplified   4 collections   5 advantages   6 choice   7 subject   8 familiar   9 vocabulary   10 neither   11 general   12 compositions   13 depth   14 overall   15 characters

❸   Point out that it is not essential to read the book three times, but it certainly helps. Nor do students have to follow every one of suggestions a–j, or do so in any strict order, but these answers may be useful.

> **ANSWERS:** c between 2 and 3   d after 2   e during 2   f during 3   g between 2 and 3   h between 1 and 2   i during 2   j during 2

Discuss these as a class, asking (in more advanced classes, particularly) for more ideas, such as reading any published notes on the book, or checking out Internet discussion groups formed to talk about the book or its author.

❹   Let pairs discuss these before they write them out. Then go over the answers with the class. Number 5 may be a particular problem in some countries, where books of 'prepared answers' to possible questions exist. Students are sometimes forced to learn these off by heart and are then expected to try to tailor them to the exam question when they actually take FCE. If necessary, point out that the examiners are aware of this and penalize 'writing' of this sort severely. Elicit more 'Don'ts', such as repeating themselves, especially in the concluding paragraph; or stating the obvious, like 'Shakespeare is a famous writer'. You could also elicit some 'Don'ts' about pre-exam work, such as not spending too much time preparing the set book question if it means neglecting other areas of language learning.

> **POSSIBLE ANSWERS:**
> 1 Don't misspell the title of the book or the name of the author.
> 2 Don't write about other books written by the same author.
> 3 Don't do Question 5 on the exam paper if you don't like it, even if you've read the book.
> 4 Don't include irrelevant quotations just because you've memorized them.
> 5 Don't try to write 'prepared' answers that you may have studied before the exam.
> 6 Don't pretend you've read a book if you haven't!

VARIATION: Ask for a reason for each of the above.

> **SUGGESTED ANSWERS:**
> 1 It gives the impression you haven't paid much attention to the book.
> 2 You lose marks if you don't follow the instructions.
> 3 You don't have to do it and you might get more marks if you do another one.
> 4 You can lose marks if you include things that have nothing to do with the topic.
> 5 You will lose a lot of marks if the examiners see that you have tried to fit a prepared answer to the question.
> 6 The examiners will notice, so answer another question!

❺   Students work in pairs. When they have finished, you may want to refer them back to the Unit where each task-type is dealt with, as they will have to use their more general writing skills, too.

> **ANSWERS:** 1 a the book in general b letter
> 2 a the setting b opinion composition
> 3 a a relationship, the story b narrative/opinion composition   4 a an event b narrative composition
> 5 a the book in general b article
> 6 a a character b descriptive/opinion composition
> 7 a the story, characters b report

VARIATION: With a strong class, elicit more topics such as the title, the beginning or end, the atmosphere, the message or an object that plays a significant part in the story.

❻   All students can do this activity. When marking, penalize any non-adherence to the instructions, such as simply going through the plot of the book.

WORKBOOK: Writing p103; Focus On Writing p80.

VOCABULARY: First Certificate *p154*

❶   Students do these in pairs or groups. If they have worked with past papers or books of practice tests they should be familiar with some of these. If you have examples, show them to the class. Ask which one is only given to Candidates for Paper 5 (the marks sheet).

> **ANSWERS:** a entry form   b answer sheet, marks sheet, question paper   c results slip, certificate

The answer sheet is for students to write their answers on, or transfer them from the question paper. The results slip is sent to the student's home as soon as the Local Secretary has details of the Candidates' grades. The marks sheet is sent to students, who hand it to the examiners at the beginning of the oral part of the exam. The certificate shows the grade awarded and is to be collected by the student some time after the results slip has arrived. The entry form is the original application to do the exam. The question paper contains texts, questions and, in Paper 2, space for the Candidate's answers.

FOLLOW-UP: Ask which of a, b or c they associate each of these with:
grade 'A' fees absent syllabus closing date withdraw borderline pass refund
Go through the answers, mentioning that *absent* and *withdrawn* appear on answer sheets (for the Supervisor to mark, but students may want to discuss them). Check that everyone understands them, and that they (or their parents) have dealt with practical matters such as *fees* before the *closing date*.

> **ANSWERS:** a fees, syllabus, closing date, withdraw, refund   b absent   c grade 'A', borderline pass

❷ Allow time for students to discuss these, then make sure everyone understands all of them. They are important because they all appear in the instructions to candidates on the question papers for the written parts of the exam – including Listening, which follows below.

> **ANSWERS:** booklet – all the pages of the question paper, Candidate Number – a number given by UCLES (before the exam) to each candidate, blank page – page in the booklet without any text, turn over – go on to the next page in the booklet, soft pencil – one that writes easily (B or HB), eraser – item of stationery made of rubber, additional materials – extra things like the answer sheet, eraser and pencil, Centre Number – reference number of the place where the exams take place, quoted on correspondence with candidates, printed pages – booklet pages containing text, approx. – approximately, used on question paper as in 'Approx. 40 minutes'

FOLLOW-UP: Ask the class who these people are:
the Candidate the Local Secretary the Supervisor the Interlocutor the Assessor.
Local Secretary, *Assessor* and *Interlocutor* may not be high-frequency expressions, but they are used on documents given to the candidate (the first one on correspondence from UCLES, the last two on the Paper 5 mark sheet).

> **ANSWERS:** Candidate – the student taking the exam, Local Secretary – the person in the students' city/country who organizes the exam on behalf of UCLES, Supervisor – the person present at the exam sitting who distributes question papers, plays the tapes, etc., Interlocutor – the examiner in Paper 5 who speaks to the Candidates, Assessor – the non-speaking examiner in Paper 5 who listens and marks.

❸ Some of these may be used in the students' first language, so it may be advisable to check which before proceeding. Give pairs a minute or so to match abbreviations and meanings, bearing in mind that some are very easy (when, as here, the full forms are given – perhaps less so if students come across them in, for example a Writing Part 1 input text). It may also be worth checking that they know what FCE and UCLES stand for (and the meaning of 'stand for').

> **ANSWERS:** e.g. – for example, etc. – and so on (*et cetera*), info. – information, esp. – especially, i.e. – that is, NB – note well, max. – maximum, PS – postscript, No. – number, incl. – including, min. – minimum

VARIATION: With an advanced class, present and/or elicit more, such as misc. (miscellaneous), PTO (please turn over), ASAP (as soon as possible), etc.

WORKBOOK: Vocabulary p99.

FURTHER PRACTICE: Reading p157.

LISTENING *p154*

❶ These words are all used in the Listening text, and may be useful when students come to discuss exams in Speaking. Point out that *award* can be a noun or a verb. Elicit answers when pairs have discussed them. You might also want to highlight the pronunciation of 'myths' (it may be a cognate) so that students have a better chance of recognizing it when they hear it.

> **ANSWERS:** fairness – being reasonable, according to accepted ideas of what is right, standard – level of quality, perform – general level of work on the day of the exam, confidence – belief in one's own ability to do well, award – give a mark or grade

❷ This activity focuses attention on the content of the recording, which compares aspects of present-day and more traditional exams. Students' experiences of testing in their own country may tend to be of the traditional sort. Encourage discussion of all exams, especially of their mother tongue and any other foreign languages apart from English that they may have studied.

❸ If necessary, refer students back to Grammar on p150. Play the recording twice while students write their answers in (as near as possible to) exam conditions.

> **SUGGESTED ANSWERS:** 1 why   2 the examiner   3 mistakes   4 artificial/boring   5 writing   6 easier   7 pass/get higher grades   8 sex, race (or) religion   9 more than one   10 success

FOLLOW-UP: Focus on the advice given at the end of the recording, possibly by asking students what was said: think about timing (see p157), build up confidence and imagine success.

❹ Tell the class that the information on the recording applies not only to FCE but also to most other English language exams – including CAE and Proficiency, which might well be the next step some of them want to take. Encourage students to use the Index of Exam Task-types in their revision, too.

WORKBOOK: Part 2 p100; Focus On Listening p96.

TAPESCRIPT

Exams have changed. Few of them, nowadays, test abilities that nobody needs outside the exam room. Instead, students' skills are assessed in circumstances as similar as possible to those in the real world.

Tests of writing, for instance, now usually say why and how students should do a text, as well as who for – rather than just being told 'Write 150 words about your school'. Speaking tests, too, have changed. Gone are instructions like 'Ask me a question using the future continuous'.

In modern exams they are much more like real-world communication in which people give each other information in order to achieve an aim. In some cases this means discussing it with other candidates rather than with the examiner, which can help create a much more relaxed atmosphere. And as with writing skills the marking is becoming more positive: in other words, rewarding what the student does well rather than taking marks off for mistakes.

Reading and listening tests have also changed, with the use of texts similar to those that learners might meet in everyday situations, rather than the artificial or boring comprehension 'passages' of old. And reading, these days, means they are being tested on just that – reading. Not a mixture of different things, as in the old 'read this text and then write your answers' type of exercise, which made it impossible for examiners to separate reading ability and writing ability. No, nowadays each part of an exam is a 'pure' test of each skill, so that 'speaking' tests speaking – not listening; 'writing' tests writing – not reading; and so on.

But, despite all these improvements, some students remain suspicious of exams, often because of myths that have grown up over the years. One is the belief that the exam is getting harder, or easier in December, or whatever. In fact the exam boards make sure that the standard remains the same, year after year and exam after exam. They do this by pre-testing the exam material with real students, by getting examiners to practise marking with sample answers and videotaped oral exams, and by comparing the marking with that from previous years. If more students do pass, or are awarded higher grades, it's because more students have performed better.

Then there's the story that the exam's easier in one country or another, when in reality the same standard applies everywhere and great care is taken in the choice of topics and situations, so that nobody is at a disadvantage because of their sex, race, religion or whatever.

Complete fairness is also the aim in the marking and candidates really needn't worry about things like whether the examiner will like what they have written, or what happens if the examiner's having an off day – for the simple reason that more than one checks every piece of work. And the truth is they really *want* students to pass, so that if for instance there's a borderline score, one that's just below the pass mark, they'll mark that candidate's exam papers all over again – just in case.

And yet we still hear people saying 'Good luck!' to students before they take an exam, as if their success or otherwise is something totally outside their control, when in fact it's all up to them. What candidates should be doing is thinking about practical aspects like timing, building up their confidence and – above all – imagining success, like an athlete does. Which, as every sports person knows, is the key to making sure it happens.

SPEAKING p155

1 Remind students that in the exam the instructions will be spoken, not written, but that they will be given some form of visual material to work with. As in Unit 14, students could work with new partners for this task, as they will probably do in the exam. They should talk for about three minutes. Tell any students who have left school / university to say which would have been most popular, etc. when they were still in full-time education. The artwork shows a PC with Internet connection, TV and video, satellite TV, CD ROM and educational game, audio-cassette, and a reading room.

2 Remind students that the examiners do not want to hear candidates saying the same things they said in Part 3, so the conversation must move on to other aspects of the topic. Do not get students to answer questions **a–d** at this stage. Take the class through the example, pointing out that other questions are possible.

> **SUGGESTED ANSWERS:** 1 Who do you speak to in Part 4? 2 How long does Part 4 last? 4 What should you do if you don't understand something? 4 Why should you speak clearly? 5 What is the purpose of Part 4? 6 Do you have to agree with what the other person says? 7 What happens if you don't say anything? 8 What should you do while the other candidate is speaking? 9 How long should you speak for? 10 What will the examiners say at the end?

VARIATION: If students are still weak on asking questions, revise *Wh-* questions from Unit 9, as 1–10 here all practise the forms presented there.

3 This begins a roleplay in which groups of four practise the exam format of Part 4. It should help to demystify the oral and make students more aware of important features, such as the need to avoid short answers, for both candidates to speak sufficiently for an assessment to be made and the difficulties that examiners can face if students do not speak clearly and work cooperatively with their partners. Point out that 'fluency' means the ability to speak smoothly and easily, with little or no hesitation.

Before they start, elicit more questions that the 'examiners' could ask and/or put some of these on the board:
What are the differences between school and university? Where would you most like to study?

Do you think you are given too much homework?
Are there too many exams where you study?
What is the purpose of education in your country?
What changes would you like to make?
Explain, though, that the choice of questions will depend to some extent on the candidates themselves, for instance whether they are at school or university, or working – in which case many of the questions will have to be asked in the past tense. Remind students not to ask the examiners to comment on their performance at the end of the exam (as in FCE). Encourage the use of expressions of opinion (see Unit 14) and agreement/disagreement, stressing the fact that as in Part 3 they can 'agree to disagree', putting forward their own views and drawing on their own experiences to justify what they say, while taking into account the other person's contribution.

4 These dialogues simulate conversations that often take place after a real exam. Tell the 'Examiners' to make notes on strong/weak points (encourage them to make constructive suggestions). Point out that the Assessor has the final say on marks if they can't agree on marks.

5 You may want to take a note of the marks, and compare them against your own previous assessments. When groups have finished talking, get them to report back to the class – not on individuals but on any significant difficulties. Then ask the class to suggest solutions.

VARIATION: With an advanced class, you could bring in another stage: the examiners' meeting, where they discuss the most common problems overall and put forward recommendations both for candidates and examiners. The candidates, meanwhile, discuss how the orals were conducted and suggest improvements. A class discussion between the two sides could then follow.

FOLLOW-UP: If the activities in 3–5 work well, you may want to use them with other parts of the Speaking exam. Parts 2 and 3 will require materials such as photos, which will need to be prepared before the class, and the 'examiners' will need to be familiarized with these before the activity begins.

WORKBOOK: Focus On Speaking p104.

USE OF ENGLISH: word formation
p156

You may want to refer students back to Units 3 and 6 for affixes, Unit 6 for spelling changes, Unit 8 for present and past participles in Word Formation, as well as 'compound words' in Unit 7. Focus on the example and point out that the word given could also be WORK, which of course gives the compound *homework*, too. Students then do the exam task individually. Go through the answers, emphasizing the points made by the text about the night before the exam.

> **ANSWERS:** 1 revision/revising 2 useful
> 3 advisable 4 studying 5 desperately
> 6 headache 7 musician 8 sleepy 9 nervous
> 10 determination

VARIATION: Ask which answers are which type: participles – 1 (if 'revising'), 4; internal spelling changes – 3, 5; compounds – 0, 6; affixes – the rest.
WORKBOOK: Focus On Use of English p88.

EXAM STUDY GUIDE *p157*

Students read the introduction. You may want to give them this example:
In Reading there are four parts, each with about the same number of marks and the time allowed is 75 minutes. You might decide to leave about 5 minutes at the end for checking and divide the rest of the time equally among the four parts, so for Part 1 you would write 17 under 'Minutes'. If, though, you sometimes leave questions unanswered and come back to them at the end, you might want to leave more time, so you might put '15', or even less.

Ask any questions the students may have, and then get them to fill in the spaces in the 'Minutes' column. They should have access to past papers or a book of practice tests while they do this, as they may not be able to identify every task-type from its number or description. If this is not possible, quickly show the class each part from papers or books of your own before they begin.

They should work individually, as the answers are very much a matter of personal choice and preferred working style. When they have finished, ask for the general opinion on the timing of each part, asking them if anything in the table surprised them. You may want to highlight some interesting features, such as the advisability of not spending too long on individual questions in Reading Part 1 (only one mark each), the equal marks for Parts 1 and 2 of Writing, and the high value in terms of marks of Use of English Part 3, particularly in comparison with Part 5.

If class time allows, do each of these papers under exam conditions. Remind them how essential it is to finish all parts of the paper, and how damaging it can be to get stuck on individual questions. While they are working, you might want to give reminders of how much time is left, but point out the importance of having a reliable watch on the day of the exam! When time is up, check who's finished and who hasn't, and find out which part(s) of the paper held people up. Ask the class to suggest reasons and solutions.

An alternative approach, in a class where a consensus exists on the timing of each part, is to tell them which point they should have reached at certain times while they are working. Get them also to note down on the question paper the time when they finished each part so that you can check later how they were progressing against the clock. You may even wish to develop a class dynamic whereby most or all students finish sections, turn pages and finish the paper at about the same time.

You might also want to tell them that scores on each paper are adjusted to give a mark out of 40, so the maximum possible is 200 marks (otherwise some might jump to the conclusion that Writing, for example, carries fewer total marks than other papers). They need to score about 60% to pass with a Grade C.

STUDY CHECK *p157*

1 Encourage the use of grammar from p150 and question forms from p155 and be ready to answer any queries about the place, starting times, lunchtime (between the written papers) and essential items to take with them: pens, pencils, sharpener, eraser – and, of course, a reliable watch. Some may want to take food and drinks for the breaks between papers.

2 Begin by eliciting common 'report language' such as *He has made steady progress but still needs to take more care with…* Point out that this is a fairly light-hearted sort of end-of-course activity, but that they may like to compare their observations, when they have finished, with what they put in Exam Study Guide in Unit 1 (p17). Make it clear that partners must justify any observations they make by giving reasons and examples. You could look through the students' work and add a brief 'headteacher's comment' at the bottom of each report.

FOLLOW-UP: If there is time for further practice, ask them to choose another title from Writing 5 on page 153. If they have read a set book they can write about that; if not they could write about any other book they have read, or – if they have not read much – substitute the word *film* for *book* in most of the titles and write about that instead. Tell them to check their work for their six most common mistakes when they finish.

Students now do Unit Test 15 on p182 of this book. The answers are on p216.
Then they do Progress Test 4 on p195 of this book. The answers are on p217.

Exam Revision Section Key

PAPER 1 READING

Part 1 multiple matching

Instructions: extra   beginning

❶ 1 the title
2 the instructions
3 the list of summaries
To form a first impression of what you are going to read and to get an idea of the main points.
The example heading.

❷ Quickly.
Because the aim is to get the general idea
a The example heading.
b Each heading as you choose it.
So as not to spend any more time on it.

❸ heading
paragraph

❹ order
flashbacks

Part 2 multiple choice

Instructions: best   text

❶ Maybe that part of the text is not tested.

❷ To form a mental picture of the situation.

❸ Whether you can work out meaning from context.

❹ 1 answers
2 line
3 mind
4 nearest/closest
5 evidence/proof
6 wrong
7 text
8 contradicts
9 crossing
10 guess

Part 3 gapped text

Instructions: removed   fits   one

❶ The main idea. Which part of the text it belongs to.

❷ vocabulary   after   result   sequence   contrast

❸ a The main events in both text and paragraphs.
b The words that link the sentences to the main text.

❹ it, the, this, those, such, them, etc.

Part 4 multiple matching

Instructions: choose   once   any

❶ Possible questions:
2 What should you do first?
3 How should you read the text the first time?
4 What should you underline?
5 What is the purpose of the example?
6 What should you do when you read the text again?
7 Can a section be the right answer more than once?
8 Can a question have answers in more than one section?
9 What should you do if you can't find an answer?
10 How many marks do you get for a correct answer?

❷ look   find   words   underline

PAPER 2 WRITING

Part 1 transactional letter

❶ has   three   information/facts   give   make   address   not/never

❷ 1 Study the instructions and the materials and decide on the appropriate style and aim.
2 Highlight the key words in the text and in the notes.
3 Make a plan, with a purpose for each paragraph.
4 Note down some useful expressions.

❸ a one
b linked to text
c advertisement
d company
e formal/semi-formal
f to complain

❹ 1 ending   2 paragraphs   3 writing   4 sentences
5 reader   6 words   7 notes   8 relevant
9 grammar/structures   10 instructions

❺ All suggestions followed.

Part 2 choice of task

❶ 4, 1, 2, 120, 180, 50, 45.

❷ who   why   what   which

❸ 1 a magazine b title c involve d attention
e formal f opinions g describe h think
2 Key words – international music magazine/stars/influence/pop music/article.
3 All suggestions followed.

❹ 1 Possible answers:
a Write notes on your ideas under each of the headings.
b Decide on the order of the sections.
c Think of a heading for each section.
d Divide the report into sections.
Suggested order: d, c, b, a or d, b, c, a
2 Key words – international charity/living conditions/elderly people/report/your country.
3 Suggested answer – Living conditions among the elderly.
4 All techniques used except 11.

❺ 1 a a given beginning or ending
b the first or the third
c the stages in the story
d too many events
e the reader want to
f where and when
g the main characters
h main stage of the story
i direct speech
j time links
k an explanation
l a good title
2 Words you have to use: beginning or end. Third person. Presumably to win the competition.
3 'Short sight, long sentence', 'Look before you steal', etc.
4 Suggested answers:
(e) 2nd sentence; (f) before they retired; (g) Philippa and Ned/partnership; (i) "It'll be nice … .";
(j) no sooner, meanwhile, at that moment, as, etc.;
(k) surprise/explanation: police station.

6 1 Best wishes, love from, Yours

2 Yours faithfully, Yours sincerely

3 I am writing to apply for, position, in addition to, owing to the fact that, provide you with a reference from my current employers, I look forward to hearing from you.

4 The title of the job you want, where and when you heard about it, your age, relevant experience, languages spoken, why you want the job, why you would do it well, when you are available for interview and to start work, whether you are enclosing anything (e.g. CV).

5 phrasal verbs, contracted forms, very short sentences, informal or slang expressions, friendly tone.

6 To describe actions and feelings, a letter, an English-speaking penfriend.

7 Suggested answers: doesn't, got out, came down, this thing, Please write soon.

7 1 Discursive: for and against

2 Make a note of your opinion, imagine what someone who disagrees would say and note that down too.

3 You might end up writing very long and involved sentences, with a high risk of making mistakes.

4 A short introductory paragraph, points on one side in the next paragraph, points on the other side in the one after that, finally a short concluding paragraph containing your opinion.

5 Semi-formal or formal

6 Words in the instructions

7 Possible answers:
a firstly, to begin with, to sum up, etc;
b also, moreover, besides, etc;
c however, while, etc;
d so, consequently, etc.

8 As suggested in 4; semi-formal; However (c), as well as (b), On the positive side (a), In addition to (b), besides (b), On the other hand (c), First of all (a), Secondly (a), Finally (a), To sum up (a), but (c)

PAPER 3 USE OF ENGLISH

Part 1 multiple-choice cloze

Instructions: text space

1 narrow escape – 3; take turns – 1; badly made – 4; keen on – 2.

2 1B type 3; 2A type 2; 3C type 2; 4A type 1; 5D type 1; 6D type 4

Part 2 open cloze

Instructions: of one

1 instructions, title, example, gaps, text, gist, missing, end, clues, answer, sheet, print, handwriting, blank, next, questions, easier, guess, check, makes.

2 1 There are always 15 plus the example.
2 There are never any contracted forms as answers.
3 Correct
4 It makes no difference
5 Correct
6 Correct
7 200-250 is the norm.
8 You only ever get one mark, and not even that if either of them is wrong.
9 Reference words are quite often tested.
10 Part 3 has the most marks in Paper 3.

Part 3 key word transformations

Instructions: similar change five.

1 never: put too many/too few words, cross out words in sentences, change/leave out key word
always try to: spell correctly, look for two marks
Q How many questions are there? A 10
Q If an answer is partly right what happens? A 1 mark is possible.

2 All 2 words.

3 The question will probably test reported speech. A reporting verb.

Part 4 error correction

Instructions: each some tick word two

1 Possible answers:
1 To get the general idea.
2 They may introduce the topic.
3 The instructions do not ask you to do this.
4 They can help give more context.
5 There will only be one error per line.
6 There will not be this many correct lines.
7 There will not be 13 or more incorrect lines.
8 To check that everything makes sense.

2 1 nobody: double negative
2 the: no article required
3 to: no preposition required
4 too: repetition of meaning
5 of: no object present
6 herself: not reflexive
7 can: incorrect modal verb
8 what: incorrect relative pronoun
9 though: incorrect conjunction
10 him: repetition of pronoun

Part 5 word formation

Instructions: capitals same

1 1 Read the text for gist.
2 Part of speech; whether it is negative.
3 All the different forms of it that you can think of.
4 Whether any internal spelling changes are needed.
5 Guess from among the words you noted down.
6 Check that the words you have added make sense in the context of the text as a whole.

2 Example answers: disappear, interview, retake, overeat, misuse, useless, scientist, acceptable, kindness, wonderful

3 Example answers:
Useful, misuse, user, uselessly, overuse, etc.
Disappear, appearance, apparently, disappearance, reappear, etc.
Overdo, underdo, outdo, undo, redo, etc.
Building, builder, rebuild, buildup, etc.
Helpful, helplessly, helper, helpfulness, helping, etc.
Direction, director, indirectly, misdirect, directness, etc.
Friendship, unfriendly, friendless, befriend, friendliness, etc.
Children, childish, childhood, childishness, childless, etc.

4 Possible answers: amazed/amazing, shocked/shocking, bored/boring, tempted/tempting, etc.

5 teacup, haircut, breakdown, toothpaste, loudspeaker, doorstep, handwriting, sightseeing, timetable, earthquake, headache, rainfall, schoolchild, birthday setback.

PAPER 4 LISTENING

Part 1 multiple choice

Instructions: eight   best

❶ 1 You both read and hear the questions.
2 Separate texts: problems with one doesn't affect the others.
3 The situation is described in an introductory sentence.

❷ 1 form an idea of what you will hear.
2 the place, people and what they are doing.
3 you are listening to.
4 every word you hear.
5 a word from it on the recording.
6 your mind about the correct answer.

❸ 1 d 2 e 3 a 4 b 5 c

Part 2 note taking/blank filling

Instructions: complete

❶ Possible questions:
1 If you are not sure what to do, should you ask the teacher before you listen?
2 Should you study all four parts before Part 1 begins?
3 Should you try to predict the content of the text from the questions?
4 If you find a part of the recording difficult, should you stop listening and wait for it to be played again?

❷ One. One, two or three.

❸ Possible answers:
1 Study the questions to form an idea of what you are likely to hear.
2 Underline the key words in the questions that you might hear on the recording.
3 Listen out for information in the same order as in the questions.
4 If you hear key words, pay attention.
5 If you spend too long on one question you may miss some information.
6 Do not try to use different words from those you hear.
7 Never give more than one answer to a question.
8 Do not stop listening while you are writing your answers.
9 Write quickly so that you are ready for the next point.
10 Check your answers for correct grammar and spelling.

Part 3 multiple matching

Instructions: five   choose   once   letter

❶ Possible answers:
A patient, hospital, medicine, illness, pain, operation
B food, cook, vegetables, meat, fish, roast
C land, weather, crops, animals, feed, plough
D prison, sentence, innocent, guilty, fine, release
E plane, fly, wings, air, ground, clouds
F school, pupils, class, homework, test, exams

❷ Possible answers:
1 When do you hear a piece for the second time? After you have heard all the others once.
2 What connection is there between the pieces? They might share the same function or subject.
3 How should you use the introduction? To predict the aspect of the topic and the language.
4 What do you do with the extra answer? Nothing – you don't use it.
5 When should you decide on your final answers? When you have heard everything twice.

Part 4 selection from two or three answers

Instructions: true, false, Yes, No, best, writing
Questions and answers will be student specific.

PAPER 5 SPEAKING

Part 1 interview

❶ 1 1 examiner   6 examiner   11 present
      2 three   7 part   12 past
      3 greeting   8 candidate   13 future
      4 mark   9 questions   14 simple
      5 name   10 relax   15 continuous

2 home town, family, work/study, leisure, future plans.

3 1 ✔ 2 ✔ 3 ✘ 4 ✘ 5 ✔

Part 2 individual long turn

❶ four   two

❷ Statements 2, 4, 8, 10.

❸ Possible answers:
1 The two pictures show … , In both pictures … , In the first picture as well as the second …
2 While in the first picture … , Whereas in this picture … , On the one hand this picture shows …
3 It looks as if … , It seems to me that … , I would say that …
4 I'd prefer … , I'd rather … , I'd be happier …
5 It's a sort of … , It's what you use to … , It's where … .

Part 3 collaborative task

❶ 1 candidate, three
2 problem, making, reaching decisions.
3 photo, diagram, drawing, map, advertisement etc.

❷ 1 A 2 B 3 A 4 C

❸ Possible answers:
1 You should study the materials carefully before you begin.
2 You should take turns with the other candidate, speaking for about the same amount of time.
3 If the other candidate is talking too much, you can politely interrupt.
4 Try to avoid periods of silence during the task.
5 You don't have to agree with everything your partner says. The examiner will tell you whether you have to agree or not about decisions, plans, solutions, etc.

Part 4 three-way discussion

❶ Part 4 continues the same topic as Part 3, but focusing on different aspects of it.

❷ 1 Who do. You speak to the examiner and Candidate B.
2 How long. Usually about four minutes.
3 What should. Ask the examiner to clarify or repeat it.
4 Do you. No, you can disagree if you like.
5 What should. Listen carefully to his or her opinions.
6 How long. About the same amount of time as Candidate B.
7 What will. They'll just say 'thank you' and 'goodbye'.

❸ Asking to repeat: Sorry, what did you say? Do you think you could say that again? etc.
Encouraging: What did you feel about this? What worried you most about that? etc.

❹ 1 structures   3 link   5 tasks
    2 vocabulary   4 Communicate   6 clearly

Further Practice

UNIT 1

LEAD-IN

1 What is the difference between fitness and health?

2 In no more than two minutes, make one list of things you can do to make you fit, and another for things that make you healthy.

Do any of them fall into both lists?

VOCABULARY and SPEAKING

1 Match the following verbs to their definitions:

1	snore	A	sleep later than intended
2	doze	B	breathe noisily while asleep
3	nap	C	sleep lightly
4	oversleep	D	fall asleep (often in a chair)
5	lie in	E	stay in bed later than usual
6	nod off	F	have a short sleep.

2 Using the following words as appropriate, describe to a partner exactly how to make a bed:

mattress	quilt
sheet	bedspread
pillow	duvet
blanket	pillowcase

Do you both make beds in the same way? If not, how do you differ?

What kind of beds have you got at home? Single, double, bunk beds, twin beds? And your partner?

3 A friend of yours is suffering from insomnia, or sleeplessness. Discuss with your partner the best advice for somebody with this problem. Here are some suggestions:

- a hot milky drink
- meditation
- sleeping tablets
- more exercise
- sleeping with the window open
- moving or changing the bed

GRAMMAR: present tenses

1 The present continuous is formed by using the present of *be* plus the present participle of the verb, which is always pronounced as a full syllable /ɪŋ/.

1 Complete rules a–d for present participle spelling and write an example for b, c and d. Use the following once each: *y   e   ie   ee*

   a Most verbs which end in ..... lose this letter and add *-ing* instead, e.g. *have -> having.*

   b Verbs ending in ..... , however, do not lose a letter, e.g. ....

   c For verbs that end in ..... , *-ing* is added, e.g. ....

   d If a verb ends in ..... , we use the letters *-ying* instead, e.g. ....

2 Choose from these words to complete rules a–e for present participle consonants. There is one word that you do not need to use.

   first   second   one   two   either

   a One-syllable verbs which end in ...... vowel letter plus a consonant double the final consonant, e.g. *sit -> sitting.*

   b One-syllable verbs ending in ...... vowel letters plus a consonant do not double the final consonant, e.g. *heat -> heating.*

   c One-syllable verbs ending in ...... *w, x* or *y* do not double the final consonant, e.g. *know -> knowing; fix -> fixing; stay -> staying.*

   d Some two-syllable verbs that end in ...... vowel letter plus a consonant double the final consonant, e.g. *regret -> regretting.*

   e Two-syllable verbs that are stressed on the ...... syllable do not double the final consonant, e.g. *open -> opening.*

2 Use the present continuous forms of these verbs to write as many sentences as you can about 1–6, as in the examples. Try to use each verb at least once.

hope	shop	~~copy~~	see	cry	plan
stop	leave	slam	chat	~~use~~	~~go~~
dance	play	begin	lie	carry	phone
smile	~~get~~	cheat	study	~~sit~~	~~write~~

1 What is happening right now: ... *Everyone is writing* ...

2 Temporary situations: ... *I'm using a different pen today* ...

3 Situations that are changing: ... *My spelling is getting better* ...

4 Future intentions and plans: ... *I'm going to Sara's house later* ...

5 Annoying things that often happen: ... *He's always copying my answers* ...

USE OF ENGLISH: key word transformations

In each of 1–10, two of the three sentences have similar meanings. Which are they?

1 a They never stop making that awful noise.
   b They often make that awful noise.
   c They are always making that awful noise.

2 a We want enough room for two people.
   b We want a room for two people.
   c We want accommodation for two people.

3 a She's got a date with him at nine outside the cinema.
   b She's meeting him at nine outside the cinema.
   c She's with him at nine outside the cinema.

4 a He lives in the city but he is coming from the country.
   b He lives in the city but he was born in the country.
   c He lives in the city but he comes from the country.

5 a There's a little left in the bottle.
   b There's not enough left in the bottle.
   c The bottle isn't quite empty.

6 a You should get a lot more exercise.
   b You should exercise a lot more.
   c You should write a lot more exercises.

7 a I'll collect them at the station at 5.30.
   b I'm collecting them at the station at 5.30.
   c I've arranged to collect them at the station at 5.30.

8 a I'm thinking of going to the match on Friday.
   b I'm going to the match on Friday.
   c I think I might go to the match on Friday.

9 a I'm not seeing him any more.
   b He's disappeared completely.
   c I've stopped going out with him.

10 a She has a lot of fun.
   b She's having a really good time.
   c She's enjoying herself a lot.

PRONUNCIATION

❶ Read the following passage and do the two exercises which follow.

I was already out of <u>breath</u> when I arrived at the fitness <u>suite</u>. I'd <u>put</u> on a lot of <u>weight</u> now I was at home again – my mum <u>fed</u> me <u>sweet</u> things at every meal plus <u>two</u> or three snacks at intervals throughout the <u>day</u>. Not fancying an aerobics course surrounded by beautiful people in exercise <u>suits</u>, I <u>took</u> the easier <u>route</u> to a <u>new</u> slim me – the machines. Ten minutes later I was covered in <u>sweat</u>, I <u>could</u> hardly <u>breathe</u> and I had an <u>ache</u> all over.

1 Divide the 16 underlined words into five groups according to the vowel sound in each one.

1 ....
   ....
2 ....
   ....
3 ....
   ....
4 ....
   ....
5 ....
   ....

2 Find all the words of two or three syllables and divide them into four groups according to the way they are stressed. The patterns are:

a ☐☐   b ☐☐   c ☐☐☐   d ☐☐☐

❷ The following short poem is in the form known as a limerick. Limericks always have five lines with similar patterns of stress and rhyme.

Read the limerick aloud and then mark the stressed syllables. Underline the words that rhyme.

A teacher who lived in Japan
Was Cambridge exams' greatest fan.
She told all her classes:
'I want lots of passes,
So study as hard as you can.'

Now choose suitable words from the list to complete the other two limericks. Pay attention to the number of syllables and the stress in each line, and to the rhyme pattern.

> visit impressed known horses see invited
> famous pigeons interest wanted choir cows
> declares hoped orchestra bats claims liar
> believed after used asked singer without

1 *A cowboy .... a guest*
   To .... his ranch in the west.
   He .... his resources
   To buy lots of ....
   And .... that his guest was ....

2 *A soprano who sings in the ....*
   Now .... she can sing even higher
   .... really trying
   Like .... do when flying.
   (She's .... as a terrible ....)

WRITING

You are not happy about a particular situation in your home and have decided to write to a magazine about it.

Either   Imagine you are a parent. Write to describe the lifestyle of your daughter or son, saying what is wrong with it and why it annoys you. Ask for advice about how to change the situation.

Or   Imagine you are a teenager. Write to describe the problems you are having with your parents concerning your lifestyle and the restrictions they are placing on it. Ask for advice about sorting things out.

5-MINUTE ACTIVITIES

In rooms where space allows, choose one student as 'instructor' and have a mini exercise class, with the instructior giving precise instructions for different exercises (e.g. 'Touch your toes', 'Stretch your right arm above your head' etc.).

DISCUSSION

❶ What kind of things keep you awake at night?

❷ Do you have the same dream regularly? Do other people have similar dreams?

❸ Do you ever have nightmares? What about?

UNIT 2

VOCABULARY

❶ Imagine you have just seen a ghost. Write down as many words as you can connected with:

the ghost	e.g. *frightening*
the feeling it produced	e.g. *fear*
how you felt	e.g. *frightened*

Compare your list with other students' ideas.

❷ Use the following words to complete the sentences. You will need each word twice.

harm   risk   danger

1 I could have got here more quickly by walking across the ice, but I didn't want to take the ....

2 If you follow the instructions, you shouldn't come to any ....

3 The rollercoaster is frightening, but passengers are never really in ....

4 James didn't know the robber had a gun and by the time he realised the .... it was too late.

5 The boy had been eating berries from the trees, but fortunately they didn't do him any ....

6 Your health is at .... if you smoke.

❸ Complete the following table:

Noun	Adjective
danger	dangerous
harm	....
safety	....
risk	....
hazard	....

What prefix must be added to *safe* to make the opposite?   ....

What suffix must be added to *harm* to make it mean *safe*?   ....

❹ What do you think of people who take risks? Are they brave or are they crazy?

Which of the following adjectives are positive words to describe somebody, and which are negative?

fearless	*foolish*
reckless	*courageous*
heroic	*daring*
adventurous	*brave*

GRAMMAR: nouns and verbs

❶ Words like *ride*, *claim* and *twist* can be used either as nouns or as verbs, for example:

They queued for almost an hour for a ride on the rollercoaster.
Some would prefer to ride a bicycle.

Use each of these words in two of the sentences below, once as a verb and once as a noun:

plan question reply

1 For the .... to succeed, we all need to work hard.

2 Would you please .... to the above address.

3 Few people would .... the importance of a healthy diet.

4 I'm sorry, could you repeat the .... please?

5 We don't .... to build on that land.

6 I wrote to them but we still haven't had any ....

❷ Now make pairs of sentences of your own in the same way, using these words:

answer notice book fish paint turn

❸ Words like *record* can also be used in both ways, but when they are used as nouns the first syllable is stressed; when they are used as verbs the second syllable is stressed:

There's been a huge increase in the number of visitors.
At that point the speed of the ride starts to increase.

Practise saying these words, once as a noun and once as a verb:

perfect, rebel, present, export, contrast, desert

❹ Some words have a different consonant sound, depending on whether they are being used as nouns or verbs:

People are not housed in a train.

When it is a verb, the 's' in *house* is pronounced /z/; as a noun the sound is /s/.
Other words change from /f/ to /v/, as shown by the spelling:

The book was on the top shelf. /f/
They are going to shelve the plan. /v/

What are the verbs formed from the following nouns? How are they pronounced?

1 *use* 2 *belief* 3 *advice* 4 *proof*

❺ Study the words below. Using the pronunciation shown, think of a sentence for each one.

Examples: <u>con</u>vict   *The escaped convict was caught by the police.*
grief /f/   *Her sudden death caused grief everywhere.*

1 suspect	5 emphasize /z/	9 protest
2 halve /v/	6 object	10 decrease
3 contract	7 import	
4 progress	8 abuse /s/	

USE OF ENGLISH: multiple-choice cloze

Choose the best answer A, B, C or D to complete the collocation or phrasal verb.

1 Let's hire some mountain bikes and go ...... (A in B for C by D to) a ride.

2 I've heard that Funworld Park ...... (A demands B asks C claims D charges) £20 admission per person.

3 The best way to get ...... (A through B off C out D round) the problem is to buy a new one.

4 The driver lost ...... (A control B command C power D rule) of the car and it crashed into a wall.

5 The train went round a ...... (A keen B sharp C cutting D strong) bend in the track.

6 It will take him time to get ...... (A by B back C over D away) her and find someone else.

7 His new film is a first ...... (A level B rate C standard D degree) adventure story which cost ...... (A much B far C well D many) over $100 million to make.

8 At the age of 82, she is making her final ...... (A appearance B performance C role D part) before she ...... (A withdraws B retires C resigns D departs) from acting.

9 The star received his acting ...... (A award B present C gift D reward) at the ceremony, to ...... (A high B strong C heavy D loud) applause from the audience.

10 Their negative comments ...... (A wounded B injured C hurt D damaged) his feelings and in the end they got him ...... (A out B down C away D back) so much that he left.

PRONUNCIATION

1 Look at the following words and mark the stressed syllables.

monster	rollercoaster
terror	afraid
cinema	creature
hazard	mammoth

How are the unstressed syllables pronounced?

2 Now find the same unstressed sound in the following phrases:

1 starts to run

2 drops of blood

3 terrified but unharmed

4 more frightening than he thought

5 skull and crossbones

6 thinks he can win

3 In the following sentences, mark the stressed syllables and underline all the words and syllables that contain the same unstressed sound as the words in 1 and 2.

1 This rollercoaster's really going to impress Julia.
2 Richard backed away from the enormous spider with a cry of horror.
3 Fortunately, not many people ever have to face a really life-threatening experience.
4 Marmaduke had the uncomfortable feeling that he was being observed by invisible watchers.

Check your answers and practise reading the sentences quickly.

When you are confident, try repeating the sentences without looking at the text.

4 The following is a famous English tongue-twister that contains a lot of examples of the same unstressed sound.

Peter Piper picked a peck of pickled pepper.
If Peter Piper picked a peck of pickled pepper,
where's the peck of pickled pepper Peter Piper
picked?

(A *peck* was an old measure, equivalent to about nine litres.)

Mark all the examples of the sound and then try to say the tongue twister as quickly as you can.

5 Listen to the following short passage. The first time you hear it, follow the text and pay special attention to the pronunciation of unstressed syllables and words. The second time you hear it, read along with it very quietly, trying to match what you say to what you hear. Finally, try to read the passage aloud by yourself.

> Trevor can still remember the night that he thought he saw a ghost. It'd been a very dark and thundery evening and he went to bed early. However, he couldn't get to sleep and at about twelve o'clock he got up and looked out of the window. The sky was lit from time to time by flashes of lightning and in one particularly brilliant flash he saw what seemed to be a ghostly figure crossing the lawn. As he watched, the figure turned and appeared to be pointing at something. Then it disappeared from view. When the lightning flashed again, the figure had gone.

WRITING

1 Write a paragraph about an occasion when you felt very frightened. You should mention:

- when it happened
- where you were
- what frightened you
- how you felt
- whether you were really in danger.

2 Think of someone you know or have heard about who has done something really dangerous. Write a brief account of what they did, saying:

- who it was
- what they did
- why they did it
- your opinion of their action.

3 Imagine you have designed a new fairground ride to be the scariest in the country. Write an advertisement for the ride, giving a suitable name for it and saying what makes it so frightening. You may include an illustration if you wish.

4 Write a letter to a friend who likes horror stories, recommending a book you have read. Say what it is about (without giving away the ending!) and why you think they will enjoy it.

5 A friend of yours has been asked to make a speech and is very worried about speaking in public. Write a letter to your friend, giving advice on how to overcome their fears.

5-MINUTE ACTIVITIES

❶ Compare these two sentences:

When he saw the spider, his blood ran cold.

When he saw the enormous black spider with its eight long hairy legs and glowing red eyes, his blood ran cold.

Which is more interesting?

In pairs or small groups, replace the word *spider* with each of the following words and add more descriptive words and phrases. Try to make your descriptions as frightening as possible!

monster   cave   dagger   cliff   snake

❷ Horrible Consequences

This is a game for the whole class.

- Take a blank sheet of paper.
- At the top, write *One dark night .... met*
- (Write somebody's name in the gap)
- Fold the paper over and pass it to the next student.
- Under the folded part of the paper you receive describe somebody or something frightening (e.g. a monster with ten heads).
- Fold and pass on the paper.
- Write *They went to ....* (Use your imagination!)
- Fold and pass on the paper.
- Write *And then they ....* (What happened next?)
- Fold and pass on the paper.
- Write *And the consequence was ....* (What was the outcome of the story?)
- Fold and pass on the paper.
- Open the paper and read out the story.

DISCUSSION

❶ In pairs or small groups, discuss what you think Trevor saw in the passage on page 113. Was it really a ghost or was there a more rational explanation?

Decide on an ending for the story and tell the rest of the class your version.

❷ Would you spend the night alone in a house if you had been told that it was haunted?
If not, would it make a difference if you were paid £10? £100? £10,000?

❸ Consider the following actions and discuss whether somebody doing them would be brave or foolish, and why.

1 Rushing into a burning house to rescue a cat.

2 Going on a rollercoaster despite being afraid of heights.

3 Rowing across the Atlantic on your own.

4 Agreeing to be buried alive for 24 hours to raise money for charity.

UNIT 3

VOCABULARY

❶ Can you complete the following table? (Be careful with *sun* and *moon*!)

Noun	Adjective
astronomy	astronomical
sun	....
moon	....
planet	....
universe	....

❷ Use words from the table in activity 1 to complete the following sentences:

1 Earth is one of the .... in the .... System.

2 The .... is 96,000,000 miles away from the earth.

3 .... is the name we give to the study of the stars.

4 There is a famous .... telescope at Jodrell Bank.

5 Neil Armstrong was the first man to walk on the ....

6 There may be life on other planets in the ....

❸ Divide the following words into three groups. Can you give each group a name?

ray	foundation
rectangle	multiplication
viaduct	laser
energy	subtract
plus	dam
cylinder	magnet
pyramid	reflection
minus	tunnel

❹ You will often come across the old system of measurements used in Britain, the United States and other English-speaking countries. Divide the following according to what they measure and arrange them in order, from smallest to largest.

inch stone ton gallon pound yard pint
foot ounce mile

Distance	Weight	Liquids
.... = 2.5cms	.... = 28.3g	.... = 0.5l
.... = 30.5cms	.... = 0.45kg	.... = 4.5l
.... = 0.92m	.... = 6.35kg	
.... = 1.6kms	.... = 1016kg	

GRAMMAR: *too* and *enough*

① Look at these three sentences:
1 *The changes will be too big.*
2 *The changes will be big enough.*
3 *The changes will be very big.*

In which case, 1, 2 or 3, do we know that the speaker:
a thinks the changes are sufficient?
b thinks the changes are excessive?

② What part of speech is *big* in sentence 2 above?

What part of speech is *time* in this sentence?

   There will be enough time.

What do you notice about the position of *enough*?

What do you think is the rule for where we put *enough*?

③ Look at pairs of sentences 1–4 below.

Is there any difference in meaning between the sentences with *too* and the sentences with *enough*?

What do you notice about the position of *too* in all of the sentences?

1 *It's too old.*	*It isn't new enough.*
2 *It's too slow for me.*	*It isn't fast enough for me.*
3 *It's too heavy to carry.*	*It isn't light enough to carry.*
4 *There's too little progress.*	*There isn't enough progress.*

④ Use *too* or *enough* to complete these sentences. Add nouns, adjectives and infinitives as appropriate. The first one has been done as an example.

1 My little brother can't reach the switch.

   He isn't ....*tall enough*....

2 The science lesson only lasts half an hour.

   It isn't ....

3 I couldn't possibly afford that PC.

   It's ....

4 She needs five disks but she's only got four.

   She hasn't got ....

5 I would walk to the shop but it's five miles away.

   The shop is ....

6 John can't go because he's still got flu.

   John isn't ....

7 The job takes a day but we've only got an hour.

   We've got ....

8 This room is so dark that I can't read.

   There's not ....

9 We won't get there in time to see the others.

   We'll be ....

10 I couldn't concentrate because it was so noisy.

   There was ....

⑤ Think of things that you can or cannot do at your age. Write sentences with *too* and *enough*.

   Examples: *I'm fifteen so I'm too young to drive a car.*
   I'm eighteen so I'm old enough to vote.

USE OF ENGLISH: open cloze

Fill in the spaces in sentences 1–10 by using each of these words once only. There is one word you do not need to use.

who on a an rid will across it can one spite which by anything himself

1 We went from .... shop to another before we finally decided which to buy.

2 Is that the man .... sold you this thing?

3 When she worked in the laboratory she was paid only a few pounds .... hour.

4 The red light came on, ... meant that something had gone wrong.

5 Was there .... unusual about the experiment he was doing?

6 When are you going to get .... of that useless old machine and buy a new one?

7 In .... of all my warnings, he tried to fix the video .... instead of getting a professional to do it.

8 You need to spend .... little time thinking about this before you .... make a proper decision.

9 There's a good science programme .... TV tonight, followed .... a discussion of the topic.

10 We must get the message .... that .... is dangerous to ignore the instructions.

READING

1 Working with a partner or in groups, try to arrange the following inventions in chronological order from earliest to most recent.

- electric shaver
- fire extinguisher
- electric iron
- air-conditioning
- escalator
- Kleenex tissues.

Now read the text to check your answers.

ELECTRIC SHAVER

The first electric shaver was developed by an American, Colonel Jacob Schick, who marketed the first model in 1931. After a slow start, the shavers caught on and by the end of the 1930s were selling in their millions each year.

FIRE EXTINGUISHER

In 1816 Captain George Manby from Norfolk in the United Kingdom developed a fire extinguisher which worked using compressed air. Later, models using chemical reactions were introduced and were similar to those in use today.

ELECTRIC IRON

The electric iron was originally invented in 1882 by a New Yorker, Henry W Seeley, but it was of little use at the time as homes of that period were not connected to an electricity supply!

AIR-CONDITIONING

An American, Willis Carrier, invented air-conditioning in 1911 after studying how humidity was controlled at a Brooklyn printing firm. His system both cooled air and removed its humidity and is still in use today.

ESCALATOR

The escalator was invented in 1892, though it was not given its name until 1899. It was invented by two Americans, Jesse W Reno and George H Wheeler. The original design was for a moving slope, but as this proved rather dangerous, it was replaced with a model using rotating steps.

KLEENEX TISSUES

The first disposable paper handkerchiefs were produced in 1924 by the Kimberley-Clark Company in the USA, under the name of Celluwipes. They were later renamed Kleenex-Kerchiefs, which was then shortened to Kleenex. The early ones, however, were actually sold as face wipes for women.

---

2 Look back at the text to find the answers to the following questions. You have a maximum of two minutes to do this. One of the inventions is not used.

Which invention:

1 solved two problems at once? ....

2 was not very safe at first? ....

3 took a few years to become popular? ....

4 originally worked in a different way from modern versions? ....

5 could not be taken advantage of at first? ....

3 Read this text about William Herschel, from which five sentences have been removed. Decide where each sentence should go and underline all the information that helped you to decide. There is one extra sentence that you do not need to use.

William Herschel

In the eighteenth century, it occurred to astronomers that there might be some sort of pattern to the vast number of stars they could see. (1) .... William Herschel was the first astronomer to look for a pattern, and he found the correct one. He identified a new planet – the first to be found in historical times – and also worked out that the sun was moving in space.

Born in Germany, William Herschel worked in England as a musician and became a naturalized Briton. He spent all his spare time studying astronomy, using home-made telescopes. On 13 March 1781, he saw an object much further away from the earth than the planet Saturn. (2) .... Soon, however, it was decided that the object was a planet. This came as a surprise to astronomers and upset long-held beliefs. (3) ....

(4) .... He was able to give up his music career and spend the rest of his life as an astronomer. He had originally wanted to name his discovery after George III, the king of England at the time. (5) .... Nevertheless, King George was flattered and Herschel, by then famous, was appointed King's Astronomer and given a yearly salary.

A At first he thought it might be a comet as it moved slowly among the stars.

B Other astronomers persuaded him to call it Uranus, after one of the Greek gods.

C They thought that the stars might move in the same way as the planets moved round the sun.

D They were, it turned out, separate galaxies like our own.

E From earliest times, they had recognized five planets plus the sun and moon.

F With this discovery, Herschel's fortunes changed.

WRITING

1 The twentieth century saw a rapid growth in the entertainment industry. What do you think will be the best development during the twenty first century? Write two paragraphs, one about home entertainment and one about mass entertainment.

2 If you could make just one important discovery or invention, what would it be and why?

3 Write a short science fiction story ending like this: *That was when I realised that the aliens were not so very different from humans.*

5-MINUTE ACTIVITIES

1 Can you unscramble the following inventions and discoveries and link them to the people below? The first letters are given.

1 FL**I**T	5 TRI**M**INSKI
2 HELPENOTE	6 LINI**P**LINCE
3 EVILIS**T**ONE	7 OR**A**DI
4 MU**R**DIA	8 HOTPOTSEA**T**

a Guglielmo Marconi   ....

b Marie Curie   ....

c Alexander Graham Bell   ....

d Scribonius Largus   ....

e Mary Quant   ....

f John Logie Baird   ....

g Alexander Fleming   ....

h Elisha Graves Otis   ....

2 Working in pairs, think of an invention you would like to see on the market – it can be as unusual as you wish! Take turns to explain briefly what it would do and approximately how it would work (e.g. clockwork, electricity etc.).

DISCUSSION

1 Imagine that Earth has to be evacuated and you are preparing to leave for the nearest habitable planet in a small escape craft, with very limited room for supplies. Make a list of the six most important things you are going to take with you to help you survive on the alien planet. If you could take six people with different professions, who would you take? Compare your list with other students and be prepared to explain your choices.

UNIT 4

LEAD-IN

1 Why do people take up hobbies? Do you think people nowadays are spending more or less time on them? Why?

2 Quickly note down all the hobbies: you have had in the past … you have now … you would like to take up in the future.

For each one, say why you took it up, or would like to do so.

VOCABULARY and SPEAKING

1 Write the adjectives formed from these nouns:

safety   amusement   risk   excitement   cruelty fun (take care!)   *entertainment   enjoyment silliness   boredom   reward   unpleasantness relaxation   health   challenge   exhaustion*

2 Form the names of hobbies by matching these verbs with the nouns below.

playing   collecting   taking   going riding   keeping

.... photographs   .... cards

.... fit   stamp ....

.... fishing   horse ....

3 Say what you think of the hobbies in activity 2 by using words from 1 (and any opposites that you know, e.g. *safe – dangerous*).

Now do the same with these:

gardening   drawing   folk dancing painting pictures   modern dancing collecting coins   playing computer games dressmaking   drama   surfing   cookery camping   skateboarding   sailing   singing

Which of the words in 1 would you use for your favourite hobby? Are there any other words you would use to describe it?

4 Which of these words, in your opinion, are positive words to describe a piece of music, and which are negative?

loud   rhythmic   melodic   sentimental   catchy restful   romantic   traditional   stirring   spiritual soft   tuneless   nostalgic   deafening

Which of the adjectives above would you use to describe each of these kinds of music?

folk   rap   lullaby   country   blues   hymn metal   pop   march   salsa   anthem   jazz

GRAMMAR: comparatives using *the ..., the ...*

The richer they get, the greedier they become.

❶ To show the link between two things, or qualities, you can use two comparatives after *the*, separated by a comma. In the example this is done with two adjectives, but two adverbs or a mixture of adjective and adverb are also possible:

> *The harder you work, the better you feel.*
> *The louder they play, the happier their fans are.*

Another common pattern uses *more* + noun, *less* + noun, or a mixture of both:

> *The more tickets they sell, the more money they make.*
> *The less food you eat, the less weight you put on.*
> *The more I see those people, the less I like them.*

Sometimes the verb *to be* is left out of one or both parts of the sentence. In some cases with *better*, the subject and verb can also omitted. Look at these examples and suggest what has been left out:

1 *The bigger the festival, the more bands there are.*
2 *The more famous the bands, the higher the prices.*
3 *In my opinion, the longer the concert is, the better.*
4 *What time should we leave? The sooner, the better.*

❷ Use a comparative form to complete each of these sentences.

1 The sooner you finish your homework, ... you can go out.
2 The more time people spend watching TV, ... they have to do other things.
3 The later I go to bed at night, ... the next morning.
4 The more effort you make, ... the results.
5 The bigger the cities get, ... countryside there is.
6 The more expensive the clothes, ... the quality.
7 The more I read in English, ... I will learn.
8 The more people who go to the party, ...

❸ Use comparative forms to complete both clauses in these sentences.

1 The .... there are, the .... the traffic becomes.
2 The .... the book, the .... I like it.
3 The .... the weather, ... go to the seaside.

4 The .... somebody is, ... popular he or she is.
5 The .... time I spend alone, ... I feel.
6 The .... meal, ... I enjoy it.
7 The .... tourists there are, ... , I'm afraid.
8 The .... we finish this, ... for everyone.

❹ Complete these sentences about yourself.

1 The later I stay in bed in the morning, ...
2 The more homework I do, ...
3 The more time I spend with my best friend, ...
4 The longer the holidays, ...
5 The more English I learn, ...
6 The sooner I get a (new) job, ...
7 The more I see my favourite band, ...
8 The less free time I have, ...
9 The more I watch the news on TV, ...
10 The older I get, ...

USE OF ENGLISH: word formation

For sentences 1–10, use the word given in capitals at the end of the line to form a word that fits.

1 My favourite .... of classical music are Mozart, Beethoven and Bach.   (COMPOSE)
2 Jimmy's brother is the .... in that rock band I was telling you about.   (GUITAR)
3 This is a purely .... piece of music with no singing in it at all.   (INSTRUMENT)
4 It was the best live .... I have ever seen.   (PERFORM)
5 Not many .... sing and play at the same time, but she's an exception.   (DRUM)
6 Sit at the same distance from both .... to get the best sound quality. (LOUD)
7 She's a brilliant .... , but she prefers painting and drawing.   (MUSIC)
8 My mother said the volume was .... and asked me to turn it down.   (DEAF)
9 Tonight's live .... includes a world-famous jazz band from Chicago.   (ENTERTAIN)
10 They had practised a lot so their music was .... and pleasant.   (TUNE)

Further Practice

PRONUNCIATION

❶ Look at the following list of things you might do in your spare time.

- read a book
- watch a film
- go for a walk
- paint a picture
- have a rest

In each example, the last sound of the first word is linked to *a* without a pause so that each phrase is pronounced like one word, e.g. *watchafilm* or *havarest*.

This always happens in English where the final consonant sound of one word in a phrase is followed by a vowel sound at the beginning of the next.

Mark the links in the following sentences and then practise saying them quickly and naturally.

1. He spends a lot of time listening to these old rock albums.
2. She found an interesting collection of stamps in the strange old man's attic.
3. Pete opened the box and spread out its contents ready for the game.
4. For this game you need a set of chessmen and a board.
5. The referee went over to find out if the player was hurt or not.

❷ Look at the question below:

Is chess a sport or a game?

How many links are there like those in 1 above?

What is the difference between the link between *sport* and *or* and the one between *or* and *a*?

Mark the links in the following passage and practise saying it.

> My father always went for a walk after our evening meal. He generally wore a rather old blazer and strolled as far as the River Ouse. I think he liked to be by himself for a while.

❸ In activity 2 above, you had an example of a sound that is not usually pronounced being pronounced where the next word began with a vowel.

Now look at these phrases and mark the links.

> *a new album*
> *now and then*
> *I know a good gallery*

The *w*, which is usually silent, is pronounced before a vowel in the next word. Even if there is no written *w*, words ending in a similar sound will link to the next word in the same way.

Mark the links in these sentences:

> *Are you a keen gardener?*
> *The match was so exciting.*
> *I think he had to go out.*
> *What do I have to do next?*

❹ The same thing happens with words ending in *y* or with a similar sound.

Mark the links in the following:

> *The day of the match.*
> *Why are you here?*
> *That's very interesting.*
> *Most people enjoy a good book.*
> *I enjoy a good book too.*

❺ Listen to the following conversation, mark the links and then practise it with a partner.

Jack Hi!
Jill   Hi, how are you?
Jack Fine. How are your art classes going?
Jill   Not bad – I've even managed to produce some acceptable portraits of the other students.
Jack Great. I've got a new hobby, too. I've taken up bird-watching.
Jill   Really? It's always sounded a bit boring to me.
Jack No, I thought it might be, but it isn't. I spotted a really interesting bird the other day and I think I could really get to enjoy it, as I learn more about it.
Jill   Hm … maybe … I think I'll stick to art.

WRITING

❶ You have just taken up a new leisure interest and are very excited about it. Write a letter to a friend to tell her/him about it. Explain:

- what the interest is
- why you took it up
- what you particularly like about it

❷ Think of a game that you enjoy playing, and write a clear set of instructions for somebody who has never played it before. It could be a board game, a card game or a computer game, for example.

❸ *It's much better for you to go out and do some sport than to sit at home with a book.*
Do you agree?

❹ You have been asked to produce a tourist leaflet with details of the leisure activities available in your area.

You should include information on:

- activities/facilities available
- location
- times
- prices, etc.

5-MINUTE ACTIVITIES

❶ Think of a famous singer, musician or songwriter and, without naming the person, describe her or him for the other students to guess. You could mention:

- age
- appearance
- particular musical talent
- hits, etc.

❷ Your teacher has an unusual hobby. Take turns to ask questions to find out what it is, e.g.

- indoors or outdoors?
- special equipment?
- training?

❸ Think of the title of a well-known book and act it without words for other students to guess. You can either act the whole title at once or do it word by word.

DISCUSSION

❶ Do you think everyone should have a hobby? What are the advantages of having other interests besides your work or studies?

❷ *Computers and computer games are anti-social.* Do you agree?

❸ Your grandparents probably had very little leisure time. Do you think this made them happier? What changes do you think there will be in the amount of time available for leisure in the future?

❹ An education centre in your town is planning to run a series of classes for adults called 'Make the most of your spare time'. They can offer four of the following:

- car maintenance
- computing skills
- English lessons
- yoga
- cookery
- First Aid
- pottery
- photography

In small groups, try to agree on a final list of four courses. Bear in mind that the centre wants to attract adults of all ages.

UNIT 5

LEAD-IN

❶ Where do you live: a flat in the city, a house in the suburbs, a cottage in the country, or somewhere quite different?

What are the main differences between these kinds of home? What are the advantages and disadvantages of each?

❷ What kind of building would be your ideal home and where would it be?

VOCABULARY

❶ Think of these rooms in your home. For each one, write down the names of as many things in it as you can.

*the living room   the bathroom   the kitchen
your bedroom*

Now write down all the extra things you would like to have in each room.

Compare your lists with your partner.

What are the other main rooms or parts of your home? What is there in each one?

❷ Use the following to form as many compounds (one word or two) as you can by choosing from the words below:

1 .... basket   3 .... pan

2 .... bowl   4 .... pot

coffee   fruit   shopping   frying   laundry   sugar
sauce   wastepaper   goldfish   flower   picnic
soup   salad   tea

Which of these do you have at home? In which room? Can you think of any more compounds you can form using the four words?

❸ 1 Look at the list of places on the right and decide where the people on the left would stay or live.

1	a camper	a	a cell
2	a king or queen	b	a cabin
3	a soldier	c	a tent
4	a ship's passenger	d	a chalet
5	a business traveller	e	a villa
6	a prisoner	f	a motel
7	a wealthy tourist	g	a barracks
8	a skier	h	a palace

2 Look again at the eight places and imagine spending a night there. Put them in order, from the most to the least comfortable. In each case, what furniture and other objects would you have in the place where you were sleeping?

Further Practice

GRAMMAR: *used to*

❶ Match the underlined expressions in 1–3 with uses a, b and c.

1 I <u>used to</u> tidy my room every day.
2 I'm <u>getting used to</u> tidying my room.
3 I'm <u>used to</u> tidying my room.

a for something you are accustomed to
b for a past habit or action which no longer happens
c for the process of becoming accustomed to something

Which form of the verb follows each of 1–3?

❷ Use the correct form of each of these verbs to fill in the gaps in 1–8.

hear   cook   find   have   get   spend   sleep share

1 After a while you get used to ...... on the ground, without a bed or pillows.

2 I used to ...... a really good can-opener but I must have lost it somewhere.

3 I don't think I'll ever get used to ...... insects everywhere, even in my clothes.

4 I didn't use to like ...... my own food but now I enjoy making soup.

5 I was in the Scouts so I'm used to ...... a tent with other people.

6 It takes a while to get used to ...... the sounds of the country at night.

7 As a child I got used to ...... the night outside when it was very hot.

8 It's always raining where I come from so I'm used to ...... wet all the time!

Can you identify the situation that the speakers in sentences 1–8 are in?

❸ Read this text and replace expressions 1–8 with the correct form of *used to* or *get used to*.

When we first moved to England there were a lot of things I had to (1) <u>become accustomed to</u> very quickly. There were the differences that everyone notices, like the grey skies and the rain, the green fields and the hills; but also less immediately obvious things that I (2) <u>wasn't familiar with,</u> such as the much longer spring and autumn than we had at home, and the different songs that the birds sing. Most noticeable of all, though, was the lack of light in winter. I don't think I'll ever (3) <u>find it normal to go</u> to school in the morning in the pitch dark, or to seeing dusk begin at half past three in the afternoon. You notice it even more, of course, when you live a long way away from the bright lights of the city centre. Back home we (4) <u>always went out</u> in the evening, even in winter, because there were lots of people in the streets and you would often see someone you

knew. Here, though, almost everyone stays in. Nowadays I'm (5) <u>gradually adapting to</u> spending more time at home, but that's not too difficult because the television is very good. I (6) <u>never enjoyed</u> it before we came here, but on British TV there are lots of programmes for young people. Something else that I (7) <u>no longer feel is strange</u> is living in a house rather than a flat, and I know my parents appreciate being able to leave the car right outside the front door, rather than spending half an hour looking for somewhere to park, as they (8) <u>normally had to</u> do.

❹ An English-speaking person of your age is coming to live in your town or city. What difficulties do you think he or she will have? Write as many sentences as you can using *used to*.

Examples: *She won't be used to the higher temperatures.*
He'll have to get used to traffic coming from the left.

USE OF ENGLISH: error correction

Study each of sentences 1–12. Some of the sentences are correct, and some have a word which should not be there. If a sentence is correct, put a tick (✔) at the end of the line. If a sentence has a word which should not be there, write the word at the end of the line. The first two sentences have been done as examples.

1 Last month I gave to my room a completely new look. ....*to*.......

2 I wanted to make the best possible use of all the available space. ....✔.......

3 First I got rid of the table and many other furniture that I never used. ....

4 I also threw out the carpet, even although it was quite a new one. ....

5 Next I replaced the thick curtains with some much more lighter ones. ....

6 I moved my desk and seat so that they were nearer in the window. ....

7 Then I put my bed where the table, the chairs and the desk used to be. ....

8 I'd got some new bookshelves, so I put them at the end of the bed. ....

9 There was being a gap in the middle shelves, so I put my TV there. ....

10 I placed a few of plants, which should flower in the summer, on top. ....

11 Finally, I put the CDs I listen often to when I'm studying on my desk. ....

12 I didn't use to have enough room for all my things, but I do now. ....

PRONUNCIATION

❶ Peter and Jane, a newly-married couple, are discussing arrangements for their house-warming party. Listen to the conversation and underline the main stresses in what Jane says.

P Do you think the party should be on a Friday?
J No, I think Saturday would be better.
P But people may be too busy on a Saturday.
J Yes, but on a Friday evening they'll be too tired.
P OK. Are we inviting everyone who came to the wedding?
J Not all of them, no.
P Right, just the ones we really like! What time shall we say? About eight?
J I think nine would be better.
P OK. Shall we put all the food out in the dining-room, you know, like a buffet?
J No. Let's have a barbecue.

❷ Work with a partner and ask each other the following questions. Reply to each one with the correct information, using stress as in activity 1.

1 Are you English?
2 Were you born in the United States?
3 Did you take First Certificate last year?
4 Did you start learning English when you were a baby?
5 Are you a film star?

❸ Look at the main stress in the following answers and write a question for each one.

1 ....
No, <u>my</u> flat's in London.

2 ....
No, my flat's in <u>London</u>.

3 ....
No, my bedroom's <u>downstairs</u>.

4 ....
No, it was my <u>neighbour's</u> cat.

5 ....
No, it was my neighbour's <u>cat</u>.

❹ Listen and mark the contrastive stress:

1 I don't like the brown cushions, but I do like the blue ones.

2 I won't be at home tomorrow, but I will be there on Sunday.

Now read the following sentences in the same way:

1 The house hasn't got a garden, but it has got a garage.

2 James wasn't at the party, but I did see his brother.

3 I don't fancy going to New York, but I would like to live in California.

4 I can't afford a detached house, but I could manage a small flat.

5 I don't live in Edinburgh now, but I used to live there.

WRITING

❶ *Modern homes are not as attractive as the homes of the past.* Do you agree?

❷ What are the advantages and disadvantages of living in the centre of a large city?

❸ You are going to study in England and have just received your host family's address.
Write to the family to introduce yourself and asking anything you want to know about your accommodation.

5-MINUTE ACTIVITIES

❶ Working in teams, write down as many things as possible in five minutes that you would expect to find in a living-room.

❷ You and your partner are neighbours but you don't get on and you have finally decided to discuss all your problems and differences.

Role-play your 'discussion'. (You can either end up by reaching a solution to your problems or by swearing never to speak to each other again.)

❸ You and your partner are looking for a flatmate. Write an advertisement with a description of the flat and saying what kind of person you are looking for.

DISCUSSION

❶ Imagine you are about to move house. What kind of place would you like to move to? What are the most important features of a home –

• type of accommodation
• size
• location
• price?

List the ten most important things for you, in order of priority, and compare your list with other students'.

❷ Is it better for elderly relatives to live with their family or to live in sheltered accommodation?

❸ What are the advantages and disadvantages of owning your own home?

UNIT 6

LEAD-IN

1 What were your favourite things to eat and drink when you were a child? Do you still like them?

2 What are your favourites now? How are they cooked? What words would you use to describe their taste?

VOCABULARY and SPEAKING

1 Form as many new words as you can from these base words, in each case noting the part of speech.

Example: FRESH
             freshness (adj.),
             freshen (v.),
             freshly (adv.),
             refresh (v.),
             refreshment (n.),
             refreshing (adj.),
             unrefreshing (neg. adj.).

1 cook   ....
2 heat   ....
3 appear   ....
4 sweet   ....
5 excite   ....
6 prepare   ....
7 taste   ....
8 digest   ....

2 Write the opposites of the following.

1 fresh bread   6 mild cheese
2 tender meat   7 raw vegetables
3 a rare steak   8 flavoured crisps
4 fizzy drinks   9 sliced fruit
5 dry wine   10 a hard-boiled egg

Now decide, in each case, which of the alternatives for 2–10 you prefer (or whether you don't like either!).

3 Form phrases by adding the past participle of the verbs on the left to the nouns on the right. Some of the nouns can be used more than once.

chop	beat		cheese	butter
peel	slice		onions	milk
melt	grate		melon	apples
skim	mince		beef	eggs

Can you think of a dish that is made with each?

GRAMMAR: *no matter what, whatever, etc.*

No matter where you buy one, what you get will be basically the same thing.

1 We use *no matter* when something is always the case. In this sentence it means that changing the place where you buy one would make no difference; the result would still be the same.

Instead of where, we can also use *who, what, how, which* or *when*. Use one of these words to complete each of examples 1–5.

1 No matter ...... of these two desserts you choose, I'm sure you'll enjoy it.
2 No matter ...... they are, they can wait their turn like anyone else.
3 No matter ...... you ring, weekends included, we'll bring you a delicious pizza.
4 No matter ...... much she eats, she never puts on any weight.
5 No matter ...... the experts say, I think this tastes wonderful.

2 Another way of saying 'it doesn't matter where', 'it doesn't matter who', etc. is to use *wherever, whoever, whatever, however, whichever* or *whenever*. Choose from these words to complete examples 1–5.

1 I don't know the chef's name, but ...... he is he's done a great job.
2 Remember she's a vegetarian, so ...... happens don't put any lamb on her plate.
3 .... I'm a bit hungry, I eat a bar of chocolate.
4 A Big Mac always tastes exactly the same, in ...... country you buy it.
5 .... often I eat, I never get tired of it.

3 Expand these notes to form complete sentences.

Example: matter/where/I go/always/think/her
        No matter where I go, I always think of her.

1 matter/how hard/work/I never seem/finish
2 this foreign food/delicious/whatever/is
3 wherever/I go/always/take/dog with me
4 I want/best/meal/menu/however/expensive/is
5 whenever/you want/go out/just give me/ring
6 don't let anyone/rude to you/matter/who/is
7 you can phone/here/matter/what time/get home
8 matter/which dress/wears/always/looks lovely

❶ The headings have been removed from the following article about apples. Choose a suitable heading for each paragraph from the list below. There is one extra heading that you do not need to use.

A Apples in earlier times
B Apple selection
C Traditional remedies
D Less juice, more sugar
E Tasty apple recipes
F A valuable food
G Keeping them at their best

❷ Look back at the text and find words or phrases that mean:

1 something eaten between larger meals   ....

2 satisfying   ....

3 mature   ....

4 cooked in liquid   ....

5 a fruit and vegetable seller   ....

6 keeping something in good condition   ....

7 increased in strength   ....

APPLES

1

A fresh apple is the ideal healthy snack – easy to carry, filling, juicy and refreshing. Some varieties are a good source of vitamin C, which helps to maintain the immune system. Apples are also relatively low in calories and contain a high proportion of fructose. This simple sugar, which is sweeter than sucrose – the main component of sugar cane – is metabolised slowly and so helps to control blood sugar levels.

2

In herbal medicine, ripe, uncooked apples have long been given to treat constipation, while the stewed fruit can be eaten for diarrhoea and gastro-enteritis. Apples are also used in external treatments for skin complaints.

3

People have eaten fresh and dried apples since the Stone Age, and they were popular with the Egyptians as long ago as the twelfth century BC. Valuing the fruit for its durability, early settlers planted apples as one of their first crops in the New World.

4

Look for apples that are firm to the touch, with no brown bruises. Large apples are more likely to be overripe than smaller ones. Local fruits in Britain are at their best – in flavour, scent and texture – when they ripen in the autumn. Some 50 or so varieties are grown commercially in Britain, but only a tiny proportion of these are widely available. However, it is worth seeking out the traditional, old-fashioned types. They may be less regular in size and shape, but their flavours and texture will reward the effort.

5

Unless they have been imported, apples bought out of season will have been stored in a cool environment where the oxygen balance has been chemically lowered. This halts the natural maturing processes, so they can be kept for several months without going soft. When they are again exposed to normal temperatures and oxygen levels – on a greengrocer's or a supermarket's shelves – they continue to mature and may quickly go soft.

6

Drying is one of the oldest forms of fruit preservation. The medieval housewife would hang strings of apple rings from the rafters, but today the slices are exposed to the fumes of burning sulphur to prevent them from browning, and then dried in the sun on wire trays. As moisture is lost, natural sugars become concentrated, which is why athletes value dried apples as a source of carbohydrate that is quickly converted to energy. Weight for weight, however, dried apples contain six times more calories than dried ones.

USE OF ENGLISH: word formation

For sentences 1–10 use the word given in capitals at the end of the line to form a word that fits in the space.

1 Cook the vegetables in a saucepan containing two litres of .... water. **BOIL**

2 Serve the two dishes .... , one on a plate and another in a bowl. **SEPARATE**

3 She likes to drink pure lemon juice .... with a little honey. **SWEET**

4 Add the two ingredients together and then put the .... into a pan. **MIX**

5 The .... of ready meals has increased enormously in recent years. **CONSUME**

6 Pour the oil .... into a small cup, making sure you don't spill any. **CARE**

7 Stir in the frying pan using a long-handled .... spoon. **WOOD**

8 Leave the soup .... to cook for ten minutes, then put the lid on. **COVER**

9 When the sauce begins to .... , remove from the heat and serve. **THICK**

10 If the meat is still .... cooked, turn the heat up a little. **SUFFICIENT**

Were there any changes in the part of speech?

WRITING

❶ Think of a special festival or occasion in your country and describe the food that is eaten on this day. You should mention:

- the type of food
- how it is prepared
- where and when it is eaten
- who makes it and who eats it.

❷ Describe a visit to a restaurant which was either very enjoyable or a disaster. Say

- where you went
- who you went with
- what was good or bad about the meal and service.

❸ A friend of yours will be living in your home while you are on holiday. Write a letter to your friend saying which shops are best for different foods and also mentioning any food which is a speciality of your area.

❹ *It is much healthier to be a vegetarian.* Do you agree?

5-MINUTE ACTIVITIES

❶ What is your favourite fruit or vegetable? Without naming it, describe it to another student. You can mention its flavour, scent, texture, how you eat it, etc. and let the other student guess what it is.

❷ 'It's as easy as boiling an egg.'
Going around the class, describe each individual step involved in boiling an egg, from the hen to the first mouthful.

❸ Can you unscramble the names of these fruits?

1 apenetogram ....
2 ogman ....
3 partugfire ....
4 metronewla ....
5 spryraber ....
6 cepha ....
7 ocripta ....
8 pipeplane ....

Now make up anagrams for eight vegetables and get your partner to work them out.

❹ You are going to the supermarket to buy food for the week. Taking it in turns around the class, add items to your list. For example, the first student says:

'I'm going to the supermarket to buy some rice.'

The next student says:

'I'm going to the supermarket to buy some rice and a cauliflower.'

The next

'I'm going to the supermarket to buy some rice, a cauliflower and some sugar.'

And so on.

This is a test of memory, so you are not allowed to write anything down!

When a student cannot remember the list so far, he or she is out.

DISCUSSION

❶ Do you think food should be produced naturally or by using chemicals such as fertilizers and pesticides?

❷ Imagine if you were going to live on a previously uninhabited island for a year. The island has fertile soil, some animal life and fish in the sea, so you will be able to grow food and hunt for it. Discuss what ten things you would take with you to ensure you had a balanced diet.

UNIT 7

1 Write down the names of:

1 three team sports

....

2 three water sports

....

3 three indoor sports

....

4 three snow/ice sports

....

5 three athletics events (field)

....

6 three athletics events (track)

....

2 Which of those in activity 1 above are Olympic sports and which are not?

Can you think of any sports that are not at present Olympic events but which you think should be included?

VOCABULARY

1 For each of these groups of three words, name the sport and add more related words of your own.

	Sport	More words:
1 serve net table	....	....
2 tyres pedals sprint	....	....
3 penalty corner header	....	....
4 crawl stroke length	....	....
5 gloves round knockout	....	....
6 club green hole	....	....

7 goal ice stick	....	....
8 saddle gallop jockey	....	....
9 sails crew mast	....	....
10 doubles racket set	....	....

2 1 Form compound nouns by matching the sports on the left with the locations on the right.

1	cricket	a	course
2	basketball	b	slope
3	wrestling	c	pitch
4	hurdles	d	ring
5	snowboarding	e	track
6	golf	f	pool
7	roller-skating	g	court
8	diving	h	rink

Can you think of more sports played in each of these places?

2 Which sports do you associate with each of these people?

referee   umpire   starter   judge

What do they do in these sports?

3 Form compound nouns associated with sports using each of these words as often as you can.

1	racing	6	jump
2	ball	7	record
3	ice	8	line
4	goal	9	board
5	water	10	player

GRAMMAR: prepositional phrases with *at*, *by* and *on*

Here are some more prepositional phrases from the Reading and Listening texts:

- *At rest, most people only need to supply the muscles with about three units of oxygen per minute.*
- *This is equivalent to a total impact of more than five million kilograms ..... by the time the race is over.*
- *The staff were, on the whole, very helpful and the snack bar did a great plate of chips.*

❶ For each of 1–15, complete the underlined phrase by using one of these prepositions:

   at   by   on

1 She is   far the best runner this country has ever produced.

2 The match was so violent that the two teams appeared to be   war with each other.

3 Marathon runners need to know the route   heart because they can't carry maps.

4 There will be no second chance so you must win this race   all costs.

5 He obviously did it   purpose so he deserved to be shown the red card.

6 Their clothes and footwear are all made   hand to ensure a perfect fit.

7 If the game finishes   time we should be home by half past five.

8 My partner was injured early on in the race, so I had to complete it   my own.

9   first sight he seemed a bit weak, but during the competition his strength became apparent.

10 I met the champion, quite   chance, when we were both on holiday in Ibiza.

11 He's playing in Italy   present, but he's likely to move back to Brazil soon.

12 The cyclist took him   surprise.

13 He's been   the phone for a whole hour, trying to get them to sell him a ticket.

14 When the favourite was beaten, the commentator was   a loss for something to say.

15 The previous champion's name was   the tip of my tongue but I couldn't quite recall it.

❷ Complete each of the answers to questions 1–10 by using a prepositional phrase from activity 1 above.

Example: 'Are you going out with anybody?'
       'No, not at present.'

1 'Did you arrive a little bit late?'
   'No, I got there exactly ....'

2 'Had you arranged to see her there?'
   'No, we met up completely ....'

3 'Could I speak to the Team Coach, please?'
   'I'm sorry but right now she's ....' .

4 'How on earth did he get past you in the last few metres?'
   'Well, he took me ....'

5 'Can't you remember the name of the last team to win it twice?'
   'Ooh, it's ....'

6 'Is it really true that she deliberately hurt her?'
   'Yes, I'm afraid she did it ....'

7 'Are all tennis rackets mass produced nowadays?'
   'No, these are made ....'

8 'Was the moment you won the championship the best ever?'
   'Yes, it was .... the best'.

9 'Did you have any help with building the boat?'
   'No, I did it all ....'

10 'How do you manage to remember all those tiny details?'
   'Oh, I learn them ....'

❸ Write a sentence containing each of the four phrases from activity 1 not used in activity 2.

USE OF ENGLISH: error correction

Study each of sentences 1–10. Some of the sentences are correct, and some have a word which should not be there. If a sentence is correct, put a tick (✔) at the end of the line. If a sentence has a word which should not be there, write the word at the end of the line.

1 He kicked the other player in an attempt to injure him.

2 Martina Hingis, who won the title two years ago, is injured.

3 Players who breaking these rules will be disqualified.

4 Most people can prefer watching a sport to taking part.

5 The match that started earlier should be finished by now.

6 Darts, is a game played mainly in pubs, has been popular in Britain for many years.

7 When United lost again, their fans whistled in the disgust.

8 We might not be playing this evening because of the weather.

9 The problem what we had was that the other team was better.

10 It's very much in the fashion for athletes to advertise trainers.

❶ How many sports can you think of that are played on a court?

What do they have in common?

❷ Read the following text about real tennis and answer the multiple choice questions that follow.

 Real Tennis

One of the oldest of all court games, real tennis is also known by a host of other names including court tennis and royal tennis. The game is thought to have been devised by French monks in the eleventh century. In the Middle Ages it was played by the nobility and even by royalty (hence the alternative names of royal tennis and court tennis). Among the most famous players was Henry VIII of England, who had a real tennis court built at Hampton Court Palace near London in 1530.

The heyday of real tennis was during the seventeenth and eighteenth centuries, but in reality it was played only by a few, just as it is now. However, from this noble game evolved many more popular court sports, such as lawn tennis. Real tennis lovers have long maintained that their sport is the greatest of all court games, but they have been the lucky ones who have had the chance to play. Real tennis remains exclusive – most courts are in England but there are a few in the United States, Australia and France. The premier governing body of the game is the Tennis and Rackets Association, which was formed as recently as 1907. The major trophy to be won in international real tennis competition is the World Championship.

Games can be between individuals or pairs; both women and men play and frequently pair up to form mixed doubles teams. The object of the game is to win points by hitting a ball over a net into the opponent's part of the court. But that is where the simplicity ends – of all games, including cricket and baseball, none is more complicated than real tennis.

No two real tennis courts are identical. They are, however, all enclosed by four walls and must have:

◆ a net that hangs across the centre of the court;
◆ a sloping roof down one side of the court off which the ball has to be served at the start of each point;
◆ another sloping roof at one end of the court;
◆ an open area usually covered by netting at the opposite end, over which there is yet another sloping roof.

Once a player has served (service only takes place from one end of the court), an opponent tries to return the ball over the net. The ball is only allowed to bounce once but may be struck off one of the sloping roofs or the enclosing walls. Points are won when an opponent is unable to return the ball or hits it into the net.

Real tennis rules and courts take a lot of understanding but once mastered they can produce a truly stimulating game. Real tennis is often likened to chess played with balls. Hard hitting counts for little; subtlety is the most important thing – hitting the relatively heavy ball into corners, and bouncing it off sloping roofs and into inaccessible little spots are the essential tactics.

1 Why is real tennis sometimes known as 'royal' or 'court' tennis?
   A It was invented by the French nobility.
   B It was the favourite sport of Henry VIII.
   C It was played by monarchs.
   D It was popular with monks.

2 During the seventeenth and eighteenth centuries, real tennis was played by
   A about the same proportion of the population as today.
   B fewer people than in the Middle Ages.
   C a larger number of ordinary people than nowadays.
   D more monks than nobles.

3 What do real tennis lovers say about the game?
   A It is a better sport than other court games.
   B It is played on a longer court than lawn tennis.
   C Luck plays a bigger part in it than in other court games.
   D It should remain an exclusive sport.

4 What do we learn about the rules of real tennis?
   A Cricket and baseball are more complicated.
   B Real tennis is the least complicated court game.
   C There should be two people in each team.
   D The rules appear very simple at first.

5 What do we learn about real tennis courts?
   A There is a sloping roof on every side.
   B There are differences between individual courts.
   C The net is closer to one end than the other.
   D All four walls are the same length.

6 To be good at real tennis, players must be
   A able to hit the ball really hard.
   B good at playing chess.
   C very strong to cope with the heavy ball.
   D skilled at placing the ball.

WRITING

1 *Playing sports is a healthy activity, but watching them is a waste of time*. Do you agree?

2 Choose a sport that interests you or that is unusual, and describe it. You should mention:

- its history
- where it is played
- how it is played
- the equipment needed
- any famous competitions or championships.

3 You have been given tickets to an important international match.

Write a letter to a friend with details of the event and try to persuade her/him to accompany you.

5-MINUTE ACTIVITIES

1 Your teacher will give you the name of a piece of sports equipment. Without naming it, describe it for the rest of the class to guess.

2 In two teams try to complete the following as quickly as possible.

Name two sports that:

1 involve horses
2 are played with rackets
3 are played with bats
4 have participants going backwards
5 are played with wooden mallets

DISCUSSION

1 Do you think team games such as football are more enjoyable than individual sports such as skiing? Why? Why not?

2 Your teacher has asked you to write a composition about the following statement:

Footballers and other professional sports players do not deserve the huge amounts of money that they are paid.

You should state whether you agree or disagree with this statement, explaining your reasons clearly. Write your **composition**.

3 Real tennis was described as an 'exclusive' sport. What sports are considered to be exclusive in your country? Should governments try to make all sports available to all people?

UNIT 8

VOCABULARY and SPEAKING

1 Match the art form in column A with an example in column B and the person in column C.

A
a portrait painting
an abstract painting
an Impressionist painting
a play
an opera
a ballet

B	**C**
Don Giovanni	Tchaikovsky
Macbeth	da Vinci
Guernica	Mozart
Sleeping Beauty	Monet
Mona Lisa/Giaconda	Picasso
Water-lilies	Shakespeare

Can you think of more examples for each of the six forms in column A?

2 What do these people in television and/or radio do?

interviewer   commentator   announcer   presenter
newscaster   foreign correspondent   reporter
weatherman/woman

3 Match the extracts below with each of these types of newspaper text:

review   editorial   news item   advertisement

'We strongly believe that the Government should take immediate action to end this crisis'.

'This must surely be her best performance since she appeared in that TV serial many years ago'.

'Book by midnight tonight and you'll save over half the usual fare to many destinations'.

'A 15-year-old boy has been rescued from a small boat after it capsized in heavy seas'.

Now write four similar extracts that might appear this week in an English-language newspaper in your country.

GRAMMAR: present perfect or past simple?

1 Some of these sentences contain a mistake with a verb tense. Tick (✔) those which are right and correct those that are wrong.

1 I've seen a really good play on television last night.
2 I saw him go into the theatre just a second ago.
3 Recently there were several incidents like that.
4 Did you ever see any paintings by Goya?
5 In modern times, nothing like that happened.
6 Since I was born there have been all kinds of changes.
7 I've watched more films this month than I've seen all last year.
8 That boring series began over a year ago but it didn't finish yet.
9 We didn't have television at school when I've been a boy.
10 I've already asked her to tape the film I told you about earlier.

2 Form sentences by joining clauses 1–6 with a–f.

1 She first went to see a play
2 The curtain's gone up
3 I spoke to the director
4 The newspaper reviews said it was funny,
5 I've seen better performances than that,
6 She's had many more leading roles

a but it hasn't made me laugh yet.
b when I met her in the bar.
c since that first appearance on stage.
d although it wasn't the worst ever.
e when she was a schoolgirl.
f at least three times already.

Which cultural activity do sentences 1–6 describe?

3 Fill in the gaps with the present perfect or past simple form of the verb in brackets.

Then fill in your answers to the questions.

1 What .... (you see) on TV since last week?
   ....

2 Which programmes .... (you enjoy) most this week?
   ....

3 Why .... (you like) them so much?
   ....

4 Which programmes .... (you not enjoy) so far this week?
   ....

5 Why .... (you not like) them?
   ....

6 Which programmes .... (you enjoy) last week?
   ....

7 Where .... (you watch) them?
   ....

8 Who .... (you watch) them with?
   ....

9 What .... (be) the best programme so far this year?
   ....

10 When .... (you see) it?
   ....

4 Ask your partner the questions in activity 3 above. Then ask more questions using the present perfect or past simple, for example:

- *What else have you seen on TV? Have you missed any programmes?*
- *Have you seen any good music programmes/films/comedies?*
- *What did you like best about it/them? What made you laugh most?*

USE OF ENGLISH: multiple-choice cloze

Choose the best answer A, B, C or D to complete the collocation or phrasal verb.

1 Take the stairs up to the first ...... (A stage B floor C storey D deck) of the National Gallery, where you will find world-famous paintings and other ...... (A works B jobs C acts D labours) of art.

2 Objects that are valued for their beauty ...... (A instead B not C rather D preferably) than their usefulness are sometimes referred to as examples of ...... (A pure B good C top D fine) art.

3 *February 23*, Antonio Caminero's new ...... (A smash B hit C record D strike) play, was fiercely...... (A criticized B judged C treated D commented) at first, but now it is attracting huge ...... (A spectators B public C audiences D attendance) every night.

4 By far the best ...... (A set B scene C view D shot) in this play is where the four main ...... (A characters B persons C speakers D roles) have a conversation which seems taken from ...... (A true B proper C genuine D real) life.

5 With that new satellite ...... (A bowl B plate C saucer D dish) on the roof, we can ...... (A grip B catch C get hold of D pick up) hundreds of TV ...... (A routes B channels C canals D providers) from all over the world.

1 Think of some famous artists of the past. What do you thinks their lives were like?

What do you know about Michelangelo?

2 Read the following text about Michelangelo, from which six sentences have been removed. Replace the sentences in the correct gaps. There is one extra sentence which you do not need to use.

MICHELANGELO
the businessman

When the Sistine Chapel in the Vatican was renovated and reopened to the public in 1994 in all its former glory, for many people it called to mind a common image of Michelangelo. They pictured him alone, lying
5 on his back with a paintbrush in his hand and creating his own personal masterpiece on the ceiling. (1) .... It turns out that the Renaissance artist, far from working in isolation as so often imagined, was running a highly organized business.
10 New records found in archives in Florence and Pisa show that Michelangelo was fanatically attentive to detail. (2) .... Around 480 years ago he was the managing director of a small to medium-sized company – his workshop – that, over time, had some very
15 demanding chairmen: the popes. A man of cultivated tastes, Michelangelo travelled business class (by mule) or first class (by horse), dressed fashionably in black, drank good wine and liked to eat Florentine pears.
   The romantic myth that he worked by himself fits our
20 idea of the creative artist, but, in fact, Michelangelo hardly ever worked alone. (3) .... Similarly, about twenty helped carve the marble tombs in the Medici Chapel in Florence and over the eighteen years he spent building the Laurentian Library there, he supervised a
25 crew of at least two hundred.
   We know about his helpers because every week he recorded the names, days worked and wages of every employee. (4) .... These included The Fly, The Carrot and The Thief.
30 Michelangelo's employees benefited from flexible holidays, good pay and job security. Many were employed for ten, twenty, thirty or more years – remarkable at the end of the Middle Ages, given that era's life expectancy.
35 (5) .... But when Francesco da Sangallo turned out poor quality carving, his boss reduced his pay, noting, 'I don't want to give him more, if he does not produce what he promised.'
   Michelangelo made modifications as necessary,
40 altering designs, colours and so on, and solved problems as they arose. He visited his production lines every day, working almost every Saturday and most holidays. (6) .... To oversee the carvers working at the Laurentian Library, he wrote, required 'a hundred eyes'.
45 As with many other business people, there were occasional faults in Michelangelo's managerial style, but he was enormously successful in getting the best from himself and his colleagues. In his lifetime he delivered total customer satisfaction and he has been
50 doing so ever since.

A His close relationship with his staff guaranteed quality control.

B This kind of business has always been profitable.

C In fact, this is by no means correct.

D Like many business executives, he checked on all details and interested himself in all aspects of his company.

E Most were so familiar that he called them by nicknames.

F At least thirteen people helped him paint the Sistine ceiling.

G They also illustrate Michelangelo the businessman.

3 Look at the following words and phrases from the text and decide which option best gives their meaning in this context.

1 renovated (line 1)
  A completely rebuilt
  B made like new
  C redesigned

2 in isolation (line 8)
  A by himself
  B with others
  C for nothing

3 cultivated (line 15)
  A simple and uneducated
  B animal loving
  C used to good-living

4 myth (line 19)
  A religious story
  B fairy tale
  C mistaken belief

5 carve (line 22)
  A dig out
  B cut into shape
  C slice up

6 era (line 34)
  A people
  B time
  C workforce

7 modifications (line 39)
  A changes
  B plans
  C decisions

8 oversee (line 43)
  A work with
  B look at
  C supervise

WRITING

1 Who is your favourite actor of all time? Write a brief description of them, with details of their career and why you think they are so good.

2 Write a letter to a friend who is considering a career as an actor, saying whether you think it is a good idea and offering some advice, for example pay prospects, job security.

3 An international magazine is producing a special issue on the world's press. Write an article for the magazine about newspapers in your country. You should mention:

- what newspapers there are
- whether they are local or national
- how often they are printed: daily?
                                              weekly?
- which have the biggest circulation
- how seriously they report news/how sensational they are
- how much freedom they have

5-MINUTE ACTIVITIES

1 Look at the following headlines and try to imagine the story behind them. Choose one headline and make brief notes so that you can report the item for the TV news.

THEATRE COMPANY JOBS SHOCK

Museum art theft – two arrested

Hollywood stars' marriage breakdown

SCULPTURE SHOCKS ART CRITICS

NEW PLAY FLOPS IN NEW YORK

Opera lovers ticket anger

2 Can you unscramble these Shakespeare characters?

1 THEMAL   ....

2 CHEMBAT   ....

3 TOLHOLE   ....

4 EMOOR   ....

5 LUIJUS SARACE   ....

All the above characters give their names to the titles of plays. Who is missing? ....

Which one said 'To be or not to be … ?' ....

Can you name three more of Shakespeare's plays?

3 Divide the following into poets and novelists.

Charles Dickens
W.H. Auden
John Keats
Jane Austen
William Wordsworth
Mary Shelley
James Joyce
Virginia Woolf
John Milton
W.B. Yeats

Can you name at least one poem or novel by each one?

DISCUSSION

1 Preserving old buildings and works of art costs a lot of money.

Do you think the money should come from:

- governments?
- entrance fees?
- donations?
- somewhere else?

Or do you think it's a waste of money that could be used for something else?

2 If you were organizing an exhibition of the greatest works of art in the world, which six items should definitely be included?

Discuss this with a partner or a group of other students and draw up a list.

3 Do you think the media should be free to report absolutely everything?

UNIT 9

❶ Write down the names of all the kinds of criminal you can think of, e.g. *thief*.

Write down the names of the crimes they commit, e.g. *theft*.

Now write the punishment you think suitable for each crime, e.g. *prison*.

❷ Write down all the means of transport you have ever used, e.g. *bicycle*.

Now put them in order, from the one you enjoy most to the one you like least.

VOCABULARY

❶ Which of these words:

- are the names of crimes?
- are often associated with these crimes?
- are normally associated with cars and driving?

  *wreck   weapon   ransom   chase   captive
  hostage   crashing   hijacking   kidnapping
  racing*

Now fill in the gaps, using each of the words above once. There is one you do not need to use.

In a recent case, two men were accused of (1)............. a businessman and demanding a (2)............. of £5 million from his employers, a major oil company. When the police found him, the (3)............ executive had been held (4).......... for over two months. One of the men managed to get away, (5).............. a powerful BMW at gunpoint and opening fire on the police during the car (6) .... that followed. Eventually he lost control of the vehicle, (7) .... into a wall, and although he escaped virtually uninjured from the (8).............. , he was cornered by heavily armed police. Realizing that there was no escape, he threw down his (9).............. , an automatic pistol, and slowly raised his hands.

❷ When you fly abroad, in what order do you go through, or past, the following (some may be needed twice)?

boarding gate	*passport control*
check-in desk	*baggage reclaim*
customs	*arrivals hall*
security scanners	*departure lounge*
aircraft cabin	

Which of these are in the 'landside' part of the airport (i.e. open to the general public) and which are 'airside' (for passengers and staff only)?

❸ Put these in order of size, from the smallest to the biggest:

  coach   motorbike   van   lorry   moped

Can you think of a general term for all five?

Which of these do we *ride* and which do we *drive*?

At what age can you legally ride/drive each of them in your country?

❹ What general word can we use for all the following?

  *trawler   liner   powerboat   barge   rowing boat
  tanker   ferry   submarine   yacht   lifeboat*

Which of the above:

1 travels underwater? ....
2 carries hundreds of people across oceans? ....
3 rescues people? ....
4 transports goods on canals? ....
5 catches fish? ....
6 takes passengers and cars short distances? ....
7 goes very fast? ....
8 is propelled by using oars? ....
9 is propelled by sails? ....
10 carries a cargo of oil or other liquid? ....

Whereabouts in your country would you be likely to see some or all of these?

GRAMMAR: *yes/no* questions

Questions which can be answered 'Yes' or 'No' are called *yes/no* questions, as these are answers that you might expect if you ask someone, for example: 'Are you feeling hungry?' Other answers are of course possible, such as 'A bit', 'Not yet' or something longer, but they are still likely to be affirmatives or negatives of some sort.

❶ Use each of these words once to fill in the gaps in these rules. There is one you do not need to use.

Has Did Is Are Used Can Does Had Will

1 When the *yes/no* question has an auxiliary verb, put this first. Next put the subject, and finally the main verb:

...... *you staying with friends?*

...... *she spoken to you yet?*

2 When it has more than one auxiliary verb, the first one goes at the beginning. After that comes the subject, and then the other verbs:

...... *he been drinking earlier?*

...... *they be staying long?*

3 When there is no auxiliary verb, put the appropriate form of *do* before the subject, and then the infinitive without *to* of the main verb (this is necessary even where the main verb is *do*):

...... *she live near here now?*

...... *he do another job before?*

4 With the verb *be* or modal verbs you don't need to use *do*. Just put the verb at the beginning, immediately before the subject:

...... *he the man you saw?*

...... *you see him now?*

❷ Write suitable questions for these answers:

1 ....

No, I'm a bit older than her.

2 ....

Yes, I can. I learnt how to when I was a child.

3 ....

No, I live with my family.

4 ....

Yes, I'm going to do the exam in June.

5 ....

No, I won't be at home then.

6 ....

Yes, I've been learning it for a few years.

7 ....

No, I haven't, but I'd like to try it.

8 ....

Yes, I did. I had a really good time there.

9 ....

No, I hadn't. I'd done *wh-* questions before, though.

10 ....

Yes, I used to. But that was a long time ago.

11 ....

No, not unless she says she's sorry.

12 ....

Yes, I would. In fact I'd love to go there.

❸ Think of six *yes/no* questions about yourself that you would like to answer, for example:

Do you know how to drive a car?
Have you ever been on a long sea voyage?

Write them down and then give them to your partner to ask you. Give full answers, as in activity 2 above.

USE OF ENGLISH: open cloze

Fill in the spaces in sentences 1–8 by using each of these words once only. There is one word you do not need to use.

in which took once just time than on could had was what until back soon sooner

1 Our plane .... off at nine, but .... before that we had seen your flight landing.

2 He took the car straight ...... to the garage ...... he realized what a poor repair job they had done.

3 The ship had no .... left the calm blue waters of the harbour .... a terrible storm struck it.

4 At first she .... remember nothing of the incident, but by the .... she left hospital the memories had returned and she .... able to tell the police about it.

5 As .... as he was arrested, he told the police exactly .... had happened, ... made the inspector's enquiries much easier.

6 He told everyone, ... his release from prison, that he .... been away on holiday for six months, but few people were taken .... by his story.

❶ Have you or any of your friends or relatives ever witnessed a crime? What happened?

❷ Read the following report of a crime from a local paper. The headings have been removed. Choose the best heading for each paragraph from the list that follows. There is one extra heading that you do not need to use.

A Painful evidence
B Taken by surprise
C Police fight rise in thefts
D Woken in the small hours
E An unproductive intrusion
F Back to work
G Setting a trap
H Struggle in the dark
I A successful getaway

English teacher has a go

Brave language teacher Ann Masters, 45, tackled an intruder at her home last night but was eventually obliged to let him go.

1 ....

Mrs Masters, who teaches English as a foreign language at a local language school, was awakened at 2.00 a.m. by her son, Nick, opening her bedroom door. Informed in a nervous whisper that there was someone outside in the garden, Mrs Masters slipped on a dressing-gown and went downstairs, followed by her husband.

2 ....

Having opened the front door, Mrs Masters checked the drive and then along the passage which led down the side of the house to the back garden. This passage was the only means of access to the garden, and Mrs Masters reasoned that if she waited at the front of the house, she could catch the intruder on his way out.

3 ....

After a few minutes she heard footsteps from the direction of the garden and a figure appeared at the end of the passage. The last thing he was expecting as he made his escape was to be suddenly confronted by a middle-aged woman in a dressing-gown.

4 ....

Mrs Masters brought her knee up into the intruder's stomach and grabbed hold of his arms. They swayed together in the blackness of the passageway for a few minutes while Mrs Masters called out to her husband that she had caught the man. Desperate to get away, the intruder, who was considerably taller and heavier than his attacker, battled to break free from her grip. 'He really put up a fight,' she said.

5 ....

Finally, he managed to throw Mrs Masters to the ground and run off up the drive to the street. Mr Masters, followed by Nick, arrived on the scene too late to be of assistance, having gone to the back door to check the garden. He gave chase but was not quick enough to catch the intruder.

6 ....

Going back into the house, Mrs Masters called the police, who arrived a few minutes later. While she was waiting, she realized that the little finger on her left hand had been broken in the struggle, and this information was included in the radio message to patrol cars in the area. 'The injury increased the seriousness of the offence,' explained the officers.

7 ....

According to the police, there had been several reports of thefts from garden sheds in the neighbourhood and various items such as garden tools and lawnmowers had been stolen. In this case, the would-be thief was out of luck – Mrs Masters' shed was securely locked and he had doubtless received a nasty shock into the bargain.

8 ....

Mrs Masters received treatment for her broken finger, which required surgery but was hardly, she said, a major injury. This morning she was off to school as usual with her arm in a sling and an interesting story to tell her students.

WRITING

1 The heading in the reading exercise that you did not need was

Police fight rise in thefts

Write another paragraph for the story for which this is the heading.

2 A student magazine is producing an issue focusing on crime. You have been asked to contribute an article about a famous criminal.

Write the article, including information on

- the criminal
- the crime(s)
- the punishment (if they were caught)
- how they should be punished (if they were not)
- the victim(s) of the crime

3 *Criminals seem to be getting younger and younger.*

Write a report on the increase in the number of young offenders, and suggest suitable ways of punishing them and preventing them from offending again.

4 *The most famous crime in history.*

What do you think is the most famous, or infamous, crime that has ever been committed?

Write about the events leading up to the crime, the crime itself and what happened afterwards.

5-MINUTE ACTIVITIES

1 Working in teams, try to think of as many crimes as you can that are connected with some kind of transport. They can be modern day crimes or crimes that were more common in the past.

2 Your teacher is a well-known criminal. Take it in turns to ask questions to find out who. You can *only* ask questions which can be answered with '*Yes*' or '*No*'.

3 In pairs or groups, plan the perfect murder. You will need to decide on

- the victim
- the weapon
- the time
- the place
- your alibi

DISCUSSION

1 In some countries, such as the USA, Mrs Masters would probably have had a gun in the house.

Do you think citizens should have the right carry arms?

What difference do you think it would have made in Mrs Masters' case if she had had a gun?

2 What punishments do you think would have been appropriate

- if the intruder had not injured Mrs Masters?
- for the crime he actually committed?
- for Mrs Masters if she had injured the intruder in the fight?
- for Mrs Masters if she had shot and killed the intruder?

3 If somebody is found guilty of murder,

- should they be sentenced to death?
- is life imprisonment more appropriate?
- should 'life' mean life or simply a long time?

Are some cases of murder more serious than others?

4 If somebody commits a crime while they are abroad, should they serve their sentence in the country concerned or should their embassy try to arrange their return to their own country?

UNIT 10

1 Make a list of all the kinds of shop you can think of, e.g. *a florist*.

Now write down next to each one what it sells or does, e.g. *sells flowers*.

2 Now draw up a list of services, together with what they do, e.g. *a library lends books*.

VOCABULARY and SPEAKING

1 For each group of objects, say where you would find them and add more items.

Example:
cakes, pastries, pies   ....*baker's*.........
doughnuts, bread, rolls, biscuits ....

1 plaice, cod, salmon   ....
   ....

2 scissors, comb, mirror   ....
   ....

3 plug, wire, switch   ....
   ....

4 cheques, notes, safe   ....
   ....

5 brochures, timetables, tickets   ....
   ....

6 tools, engine oil, spare parts   ....
   ....

7 leads, goldfish, catfood   ....
   ....

8 drill, brush, anaesthetic   ....
   ....

2 Which of these qualities do you look for when you are buying clothes, food and electrical equipment (such as a CD player or computer)?

*cheap to buy   freshness   reliability   good fit
quick to prepare   powerful   good sound quality
nice colour   well-known brand   easy to repair
good tastes   excellent design   quality material
free extras   easily upgraded   cheap to run*

Clothes	Food	Electrical equipment
....	....	....
....	....	....
....	....	....
....	....	....
....	....	....
....	....	....

Now, for each item, put the things you look for in order: from most to least important.

3 On which part, or parts, of the body do people wear these accessories?

1 necklace   ....   6 earrings   ....
2 watch   ....   7 rings   ....
3 bracelet   ....   8 braces   ....
4 hairband   ....   9 cuff-links   ....
5 pendant   ....   10 belt   ....

What material is each usually made of?

4 Put these items into three groups: summer clothes, winter clothes and nightclothes.

*gloves   scarf   shorts   overcoat   nightie
sandals   dressing-gown   t-shirt   pyjamas
sunhat   boots   slippers*

Summer	Winter	Night
....	....	....
....	....	....
....	....	....
....	....	....

Can you add more to each group?

GRAMMAR: the passive

❶ In some situations, it is quite natural to use the passive in everyday conversation. For 1–8, fill in the gaps using a passive form of the verb plus the details suggested in brackets.

1 I .... (*be born*) in .... (place of birth) on .... (date).

2 I .... (*bring up*) in .... (town or district).

3 I .... (*educate*) at .... (school).

4 I .... (*teach*) by .... , ... and .... (names of teachers).

5 I .... (*show*) how to .... (skill, sport, hobby) by .... (name).

6 My favourite song is .... , which .... (*sing*) by .... (name).

7 My favourite book is .... , which .... (*write*) by .... (name).

8 My favourite TV programme is .... , which .... (*show*) on .... (days).

❷ Often, however, we try to avoid using the passive when we are speaking as it can sound rather impersonal and formal. Rewrite these sentences using active forms of the passive verbs.

Example: I'm not given enough pocket money.
My parents don't give me enough pocket money.

1 I was told by one of the neighbours about the robbery in the post office.

2 You aren't going to be criticized by anyone if you change your mind.

3 He had been warned about that many times by me and my sister.

4 Some nice things will be bought by us when we get to those shops.

5 My younger brother and I are taken to school in the car every morning.

6 Those old toys and games used to be played with by me.

7 Lots of different kinds of clothes are being worn in this classroom.

8 Quite a bit of money has been given to me by my grandparents.

9 That disco might be checked out by us if it's not too expensive.

10 I was being helped when that rude customer started shouting.

❸ For questions 1–6, complete the second sentence so that it has a similar meaning to the first sentence, using the word given. Do not change the word given. You must use between two and five words, including the word given. All the questions require a change from passive to active.

1 Excuse me, aren't you employed by the council?
work

Excuse me, ... the council?

2 You are advised not to do that again.
better

You .... that again.

3 The service given by the bank has improved lately.
improvements

The bank .... service lately.

4 They're not even allowed to wear earrings at that school.
let

That school .... wear earrings.

5 We are being transferred to different premises next month.
moving

They .... to different premises next month.

6 The law on unfair competition is being changed.
changes

They .... the law on unfair competition.

USE OF ENGLISH: error correction

Study each of sentences 1–10. Some of the sentences are correct, and some have a word which should not be there. If a sentence is correct, put a tick (✔) at the end of the line. If a sentence has a word which should not be there, write the word at the end of the line.

1 I'm sorry to bring in bad news, but I'm afraid the party's off.

2 The matter was already being looked into when your letter was received.

3 We really enjoyed to going shopping in New York.

4 He's been being told for years not to dress like that.

5 Where possible, I avoid buy goods that are not clearly labelled.

6 Such a small mark probably won't be noticed by anyone at all.

7 A new version of that song has been brought out by a Chilean singer.

8 I can't stand waiting to be served in places like this.

9 They might not been get the surprise they were promised.

10 I really feel like have a night out with my friends.

Read the four texts about famous people and their image. Choose from the four people

A Charles Atlas
B Marilyn Monroe
C Elvis Presley
D Lesley Hornsby

the one you think best fits each question 1–12. You can use each person more than once.

Which text mentions someone		
whose image was copied by others in the same profession?	1	......
whose image appealed particularly to those unhappy with their appearance?	2	......
who deliberately changed their image?	3	......
whose image reflected developments in society?	4	......
whose image is marketed in many different ways?	5	......
whose image depended on looking young?	6	......
who persuaded people to buy their image?	7	......
who particularly appealed to young people?	8	......
whose image was specially developed for films?	9	......
whose image had two different aspects?	10	......
who developed their image after an unpleasant event?	11	......
whose image was developed by others?	12	......

Twentieth Century Images

A CHARLES ATLAS

One of the most familiar masculine ideals for the American male of the 1950s was the Charles Atlas figure. The Italian-born body-builder came to the States as a skinny young immigrant but, following an incident in which a man at the beach kicked sand in his face and stole his girlfriend, he swore he would build up his body so that such a thing could never happen again. By the time he was thirty, he had improved his physique so much that he was described as 'America's Most Perfectly Developed Man' and, together with an advertising man called Charles Ronan, he began marketing a programme of exercises and advice on nutrition. The body-building course was available by mail order. It was enormously popular with men who were desperate to appear 'masculine' with broad shoulders and huge muscles, and who were convinced that this would make them more attractive to women.

B MARILYN MONROE

Walk down any high street anywhere in the western world and there will be Marilyn Monroe – on posters and greetings cards, T-shirts, dresses and advertisements of all kinds. Since her death, at least as much as during her life, the image of Marilyn Monroe has fuelled fantasies. For at least one generation of Americans, she was the perfect physical model of a woman, but also one who could be easily hurt. Born Norma Jean Baker, she had an unhappy childhood and married very young. She started working as a model and then moved into cinema, where her studio established her as a sex goddess. She married twice more, but never found the love and protection she needed. She died, apparently by committing suicide, in her thirties.

C ELVIS PRESLEY

In his films and stage appearances, Elvis Presley presented an image which was the direct result of the cultural changes that had been taking place throughout the twentieth century. It challenged people's expectations about identity and body language, and for almost the first time this challenge came from a white American source. It also came at the same time as the development of a distinct teenage culture, and with Elvis the teenage audience realized that it could now express its own identity. Parental objections to Elvis and his image only made him more attractive to the young, and he became the model for a whole generation.

D LESLEY HORNSBY

Better known as Twiggy, Lesley Hornsby was voted 'Face of the Year' by a British newspaper in 1966. She was then a sixteen-year-old model weighing 41kg, and her nickname was the result of her slender, boyish, rather stick-like figure. She was, however, ideally suited to the clothes of the period. With her short, slightly masculine haircut she was the perfect image of the childish look that miniskirts, high waists, short or very long hair and schoolgirlish fashions gave women in the mid-1960s. She became the most sought-after and most imitated model of the time, and later appeared in several films.

Who do you think is the 'Face of the Year' for this year? Think of one male and one female. What kind of image do they have?

WRITING

1 Imagine that your company is about to launch a new product.

Write a report on the product, mentioning the following:

- a description of the product
- the market it will appeal to (e.g. age group)
- the price
- where and how it should be advertised.

2 You are going into politics and are about to start fighting your first election.

Think about your character and physical appearance and what you think you should change or develop about them to give you maximum appeal to voters.

3 A friend of yours has asked for advice on choosing a bank.

Write a letter to your friend about the qualities you would look for in an ideal bank, including the services they offer, their security, what they do with your money (investments, etc.) and anything else you consider important.

5-MINUTE ACTIVITIES

1 Work with a partner. One of you is a bank manager, the other a customer who would like to borrow £500. The bank manager wants to know what the money is for, how easily it can be repaid, etc. The customer does their best to persuade the bank manager to lend them the money.

2 You are about to open a new shop. In pairs or groups, discuss what you are going to sell, the location of the shop, what you will display in it and how, how much stock you should buy, etc.

3 You and a colleague have just interviewed three people for a job.

- One was badly dressed but very well-qualified.
- One was smart and seemed efficient but was very boring.
- One was very well-qualified and experienced but nearly at retirement age.

Which one will get the job?

DISCUSSION

1 Marilyn Monroe appeared to have everything – beauty, fame, money, adoration – but was never really happy.

Think of some of the people who have been famous in your lifetime.

How do you think fame has affected them? Do you think their image is close to their real personality?

2 How do people try to make themselves more attractive? Think of as many different ways as you can.

How many of them would you be prepared to try yourself?

Do you prefer people to see 'the real you' or do you try to improve on nature?

Do you think people should grow old gracefully or try to delay the ageing process?

3 Can you judge people by their appearance?

What do you think you can tell about someone's character and lifestyle from the way they look?

4 If you were meeting somebody for the first time, what five pieces of information about them would be most helpful in giving you an idea of their character (for example, knowing what newspaper they read)?

5 How high is the cost of living in your country?

How long does an average worker have to work to afford a CD, a new suit, a small car, a house, etc.?

Do you think money is becoming obsolete? How do people usually pay for things in your country?

UNIT 11

1 Write down the names of six countries that are popular with tourists, e.g. *France*.
Now, for each one, write at least two tourist attractions, e.g. *the Eiffel Tower*.

2 What are the main tourist attractions in your country?

Think of examples in some or all of these categories:

- history
- art
- geography
- wildlife
- architecture
- folk traditions
- entertainment
- relaxation

VOCABULARY and SPEAKING

1 Think of two very different regions of your country, for example the mountains and the flat areas, the forests and the coast, or the countryside and the capital city. Put their names at the top of the columns and then decide which of these words you would use to talk or write about each:

*wild   agricultural   mountainous   rocky
densely-populated   barren   arid   hilly
industrial   poor   upland   fertile   wet   lowland
coastal   rural   unspoilt   urban   rugged
developed   alpine   rich   marshy*

....	....
....	....
....	....
....	....
....	....
....	....
....	....

Now compare your list with what your partner has written.

2 Look at the numbers below. Write one of the following next to each number:

- highest mountain
- speed limit
- people's average height
- people's average weight
- a special day
- percentage living in cities
- country's population
- summer temperature
- a famous year
- telephone code
- country's area
- unit of currency

28°C .... 00 44 ....

£1 .... 1m 72cm ....

130kph .... Jan 1st ....

1492 .... 2,874m ....

65kg .... 9,965,000 ....

91,945km² .... 30% ....

Now write each of the numbers above in full.

Example: 28°C = *twenty-eight degrees centigrade.*

3 Write the approximate equivalents in your country for each of the figures in activity 2 above, both in numbers and words.

4 1 Write these numbers and signs next to the words below:

$\div$ 0.21   ¼   =   +   ⅝ $\times$ $-$ ⅔

equals	....
add/plus	....
minus/subtract	....
two-thirds	....
five-eighths	....
nought point two one	....
divided by	....
a quarter	....
times/multiplied by	....

2 Do these sums:

Six multiplied by four, divided by twelve, equals	....
Five plus three minus two, divided by three, equals	....
Add three to five, multiply by four and divide by two. What do you get?	....
Add two and a half and one point five. What do you get?	....

Now write the sums in numbers.

GRAMMAR: impersonal reporting

It is estimated that a quarter of all tourists suffer some kind of accident.

1 We use the impersonal form *it* + passive + *that* to indicate that something is an opinion held by certain people. This could be because:

a you may not know who these people are;

b you might not want to say who they are, *or* you may not be sure that what they say is true.

Study sentences 1–4. Which of them are impersonal forms? In each case, say whether you think **a** or **b** is the reason for the use of impersonal.

1 Health experts recommend that you have vaccinations before visiting certain countries.

2 It is recommended that you have vaccinations before visiting certain countries.

3 He stole something from a shop while he was on holiday.

4 It was claimed that he stole something from a shop while he was on holiday.

2 Rewrite these sentences using *It* plus an impersonal form.

1 Everyone expects that she will become the new Minister of Tourism.

2 Some people have suggested that the development has done more harm than good.

3 Officials have confirmed that the project will go ahead.

4 People used to assume that new roads were good for the country.

5 The local people felt that one supermarket in the village was quite enough.

3 Another way of reporting impersonally is to use the passive of the reporting verb plus the full infinitive. This infinitive is often *be, have* or the perfect infinitive (*to have* + past participle):

It is understood to be the only one of the islands which is inhabited.
The four people are reported to have disappeared in the forest.

For 1–6, complete the second sentence so that it means the same as the first sentence.

1 The authorities know that the local wildlife is in danger.

The local wildlife .... in danger.

2 Everyone believes that the factory has polluted the beaches.

The factory .... the beaches.

3 Some people say the council is planning to build more flats.

The council .... to build more flats.

4 Many feel that the development has spoilt this part of the coast.

The development .... this part of the coast.

5 There are reliable reports that water levels have fallen yet again.

Water levels .... fallen yet again.

USE OF ENGLISH: key word transformations

In each of 1–5, two of the three sentences have similar meanings. Which are they?

1 a 'I arrived here yesterday,' said James.
   b James said that he had arrived there the day before.
   c Yesterday, James said that he had arrived there.

2 a They have stopped to buy drinks in that shop.
   b They don't buy drinks in that shop any more.
   c They have stopped buying drinks in that shop.

3 a Carmen asked Joe to go back there the following summer.
   b 'Are you coming back here next summer?' Carmen said to Joe.
   c Carmen asked Joe if he was going back there the following summer.

4 a Nearly everybody believes the new museum will be good for the town.
   b Most people in the town expect the new museum will be good.
   c The new museum is generally expected to be good for the town.

5 a We can do nothing until they are proved to have been responsible.
   b Until it has been proved that they are responsible, we can do nothing.
   c We cannot do anything until we have proved that they are responsible.

1 What is the top tourist destination in your country? Is it a man-made attraction or is it natural?

If you were travelling around the world, what would you want to visit in each continent? (Try to think of at least two man-made and two natural attractions for each one.)

2 Read the following article about the terracotta warriors of Xi'an, in China. The headings of the paragraphs have been removed. Choose from the headings A-G below the one you think best fits each paragraph. There is one extra heading you do not need to use.

A Ready for battle
B Perfectly preserved
C The ruler's final resting place
D A return to popularity
E Discovered by chance
F A memorable experience
G An army of individuals

Xi'an's Terracotta Warriors

1 ....

One of the greatest cities in the history of civilization, Xi'an had become little more than a small provincial town before the discovery of its terracotta warriors. Since then, it has become one of the most important tourist destinations in the world and its prosperity has increased correspondingly.

2 ....

The world-famous terracotta warriors were unearthed in 1974 by local farmers who were digging a well. The army of soldiers made out of baked clay turned out to be one of the most important archaeological finds of the twentieth century.

3 ....

The warriors were made to protect the tomb of the First Emperor, Qin Shihuang, which lies beneath a hill 1.5 km away. Work on the tomb began in 246 BC as soon as the Emperor came to power, and records say that it is filled with model palaces and even a model of China itself, with rivers of mercury that can actually be made to flow. As yet, however, the tomb remains unexplored and there is no confirmation of these wonders.

4 ....

So far, interest has focused instead on the life-size soldiers lined up in wide ditches to the east. They stand in military formation and have some armour but no helmets (which were reserved for officers). They did, however, originally carry real weapons, made of metal, which were stolen by robbers soon after the Emperor's death.

5 ....

The statues themselves were made of local clay. No two faces are alike – each is a personal portrait. Each body was made separately. The legs are solid, but the rest is hollow, with hands and head added later. Details such as beards and ears were sculpted afterwards, then the whole was brightly painted. It is uncertain quite why so much trouble was taken, but one theory is that the different faces, many of which belong to what have become minority races, are a celebration of the first unification of China.

6 ....

In addition to the foot soldiers, tourists can see horses and chariots. Examples of all the finds are on display in separate exhibition halls which allow closer inspection than is possible with the majority of figures in the ditches. It is forbidden to photograph or video the main army but photography is permitted elsewhere. There is no doubt that a visit to the Warriors of Xi'an is the highlight of their tour for many visitors to China.

WRITING

1 Write a tourist leaflet for your town or region, outlining the main places of interest and trying to make everything sound as attractive as possible.

2 The number of tourists in Kingstown has been increasing in the last two or three years. In a survey carried out by the local tourist board, the following views were expressed.

> 'In summer, our lives are a misery. The tourists seem to forget that not everybody is on holiday. They are out in the streets making a noise until all hours, and there's also a lot of noise from all the new discos and clubs that have opened for them. Not to mention the litter everywhere ...'
> (Janet Smith-Carpenter, local resident)

> 'Well, of course, it's been very good for business. We were fully booked almost the whole of the summer and we've had more guests for the rest of the year, too. Not all the hotels offer a good service, though – I think some of them tend to exploit the tourists.'
> (Tom Charles, hotel owner)

> 'We've had problems with traffic – the town isn't really designed for lots of cars and there isn't enough parking. There's been an increase in crime, too – tourists are easy targets for pickpockets and we've arrested a number of holidaymakers for shoplifting.'
> (Angela Bradley, police officer)

> 'We sell a lot more, of course, during the tourist season, but we've had more problems with shoplifting recently, too.'
> (Graham Barnes, shopkeeper)

> 'I welcome the extra customers, of course, but I think some of our local regulars tend to avoid the restaurant in summer – they don't like the crowds.'
> (Mary James, restaurant owner)

Write a report based on the comments above on the increase in tourism in Kingstown, and suggest what the tourist board should do to improve the situation in future.

3 *Travel broadens the mind.* Do you agree?

5-MINUTE ACTIVITIES

1 This game can be played in groups or by the whole class.

- Your teacher will whisper something to one student.
- In a whisper the student reports what the teacher said to the next student, saying 'He/She said that ...'
- The next student puts the information back into direct speech and whispers it to the next student.
- This student uses indirect speech and so on alternately.
- The last student should repeat the information aloud, using direct speech. How close is what they say to the teacher's original words?

2 Your teacher will start this game with the name of a city, country, river, mountain, etc. and nominate a student to follow. This student must say the name of another location which begins with the last letter of the teacher's word. The game continues around the room and any student who cannot think of anywhere or who hesitates too long is out. The winner is the one who lasts longest.

3 Draw six columns on a piece of paper and write TRAVEL across the top, one letter at the top of each column. Down the side, write the following categories: COUNTRY CITY RIVER LAKE/SEA. In the time limit set by your teacher, try to write one name in each category which begins with the letter at the top of the column.

When the time is up, compare answers and score one point for any answer not shared with another student.

DISCUSSION

1 Would you want to spend your holiday visiting historical sites such as Xi'an? What are the advantages and disadvantages of the following types of holiday and holiday activities?

- sightseeing
- trekking
- lying on the beach
- learning a new skill (e.g. cooking, horseriding, painting)
- staying at home and relaxing
- skiing
- visiting friends and family

What other ways of spending your holidays can you think of?

2 Tourism is becoming increasingly popular; big international hotels and branches of Macdonald's can be found in almost every major city. Do you think there is a serious danger that eventually all countries will be the same?

3 Litter dropped by tourists is now a major problem on the slopes of Mount Everest and many people are trying to promote 'green' tourism, or 'ecotourism' as it is sometimes called. What are the positive and negative effects of tourism on individual towns and regions, and on the environment in general?

UNIT 12

LEAD-IN

1 Make a list of your relatives, starting with those closest to you. In each case, note down their relationship to you (sister, cousin, etc.).

2 For each of the people in 1, write as many character adjectives (*generous, practical*, etc.) as you can think of to describe them.

VOCABULARY and SPEAKING

1 Match these adjectives with the people described below:

boastful   protective   considerate   spiteful
hot-blooded   outgoing   self-conscious   forgetful
indecisive   pessimistic

Someone who:

1 never remembers to do things

2 always thinks that the worst will happen

3 takes into account the wishes and feelings of other people

4 is shy and always thinks that everyone is looking at them

5 is always telling everybody how wonderful he or she is

6 expresses feelings of anger or love very quickly and easily

7 can never make their mind up about anything

8 is friendly and open in their behaviour

9 likes to harm or annoy other people, especially in little ways

10 prevents other people from being harmed.

Can you think of people in films or TV programmes who fit each of these descriptions?

2 Put these characteristics into two groups, those you personally think are positive and those you think are negative.

kindness   ruthlessness   creativity   patriotism
optimism   imagination   patience   tolerance
arrogance   determination   pride   hypocrisy
courage   vanity   truthfulness   snobbishness
calmness

3 For each of these people, which of the characteristics from activity 2 would you expect them to have?

Example: artist – *creativity, imagination, patience, sensitivity.*

1 primary school teacher   ....

2 top sportsman/woman   ....

3 policeman/policewoman   ....

4 famous pop singer   ....

5 politician   ....

6 research scientist   ....

7 priest   ....

8 gangster   ....

4 We use these expressions to describe our relationship (or lack of it) with other people. Put them into two categories: positive or negative feelings towards someone.

*not get on   have a lot of respect   be fond
not be sure   can't stand the sight   look up
have a high opinion   look down   be a bit scared
think the world   feel sorry   have a lot in common
be fed up   couldn't care less   in love*

Positive	Negative
....	....
....	....
....	....
....	....
....	....

Now use these expressions once each about people you know or have met. Add a preposition in each case.

Example: get on well
        I get on well with my younger brother.

© Oxford University Press   **Further Practice**

GRAMMAR: short replies

❶ There is another way to avoid repetition using *so:*

Speaker A: *'Do you understand?'*
Speaker B: *'I think so.'*

This means *'I think that I understand'*. We can use *so* in this way after the following:

believe expect guess hope imagine
suppose think be afraid

Reply to 1–8, using each of these expressions once followed by so.

Example: 'Is he really going to be the new boss?'
.........*'I believe so.'*......

1 'She should be out of hospital in a few days.'

....

2 'Does she live near you?'

....

3 'Is it true there's been an accident?'

....

4 'I know you're tired but won't you come with us?'

....

5 'It looks like they're going to win, doesn't it?'

....

6 'The other one, apparently, is her brother.'

....

7 'I would say there are forty thousand people here.'

....

8 'He must be the guy the police are after.'

....

❷ Reply to 1–6 in the negative using *so* or *not*.

Examples: 'Haven't you ever been to her house before?'

'I don't think so.'...

'It's getting very late. It looks like they're not coming.'

'I guess not.'.........

1 'I know it's midnight but can't you let us in?'

....

2 'You don't think he's got lost, do you?'

....

3 'Will any of his friends be there?'

....

4 'You don't mind if I drive, do you?'

....

5 'Isn't there anywhere else we can go?'

....

6 'It can't be long till we take the exam, can it?'

....

❸ Work in pairs. Think of famous people whose relationships are in the news. Ask your partner six questions. He or she answers using 'so' or 'not' as in activities 1 and 2 above.

Example: A: *Isn't (that singer) getting married again?*
B: *I don't think so.*

USE OF ENGLISH: word formation

For sentences 1–8, use the word given in capitals at the end of each line to form a word that best fits in the gap.

1 The very poorest people in that part
of town are .... on   DEPEND
the help and .... of   GENEROUS
their neighbours, many of whom are
also quite poor.

2 She is popular with all her classmates
because of the .... of   WARM
her .... , so we will miss   PERSON
her at lot when she leaves.

3 No matter how close brothers and sisters
are, ... between   JEALOUS
them can sometimes lead to certain
.... in their   DIFFICULT
relationship.

4 Claire was .... accused   FAIR
of saying things behind Jane's back, despite
the fact that she had always shown great
.... to her friends.   LOYAL

5 Because of her .... to   PATIENT
get to the party, she completely forgot
to make any .... for   ARRANGE
getting home later on.

6 What I find most ....   ANNOY
about him is the fact that he totally
lacks the qualities, such as
.... and kindness, that   SELFISH
he so much admires in others.

7 The school used to think he was
.... but then they   INTELLIGENT
realized his poor work was the
result of .... , and   LAZY
that in fact he was quite clever.

8 She is a highly .... child   SENSE
who is easily hurt by cruel comments
by other pupils, and finds her extreme
.... very difficult to   SHY
overcome.

PRONUNCIATION

❶ Listen to the pronunciation of these conditional sentences:

If I had known that before, I would have /I might have /I could have/ I wouldn't have/ I mightn't have/ I couldn't have come home.

Practise saying the sentences quickly, without looking at the written form.

❷ Finish these sentences in a suitable way. Do *not* write anything down.

Try to use *could* and *might* as well as *would*.

1   If I'd known what he was like, ...

2   If Peter had been less selfish, ...

3   If we hadn't been friends for such a long time, ...

4   If his mother hadn't interfered, ...

5   If Marjorie hadn't passed the exam, ...

6   If I hadn't had my family to turn to, ...

❸ Stephen was a terrible student:

- he was always late for classes
- he never had the right books
- he never did his homework
- he went out every night
- he didn't do any revision
- he didn't listen to his teacher's advice

and he failed his exam!

Say what Stephen *should* or *shouldn't have* done.

❹ Yesterday morning you had to meet your friend at the airport very early in the morning and you made a big effort to be there on time. When you arrived at the airport, you discovered that the plane's arrival had been delayed for two hours.

Think of all the things you did to make sure you were at the airport on time and then say what in fact you needn't have done.

WRITING

❶ Who was your first best friend?

- Where did you meet?
- What attracted you to each other?
- What was he or she like?
- Do you still keep in touch?

❷ *It is better to come from a large family than to be an only child.* Do you agree?

❸ Write a story which begins or ends with the words *If only Pat had told me the truth at once, it would never have happened.*

5-MINUTE ACTIVITIES

❶ Work in pairs or small groups. You are discussing plans for a wedding – the parents want a big celebration but the couple want a small wedding.

Consider points such as cost, tradition and so on and try to reach a compromise.

❷ Your teacher will tell a member of the class something and the student must say whether or not this is also true for them. For example:

T: 'I'd love to go to the moon one day.'
S: 'Oh, so would I.'   *or*   'Really? I wouldn't.'

The student then gives a similar piece of information to the next student and so on.

Try to answer without hesitating.

And try to vary the verbs you use to make the next student think!

DISCUSSION

❶ What changes have there been in the structure of family life in your country since your great-grandparents' time?

Do you think these changes have been for the better?

❷ In many countries it is now acceptable for couples to live together without getting married. Do you think this is a good idea?

❸ What are the features of a successful relationship?

- What should the couple have in common?
- Do opposites attract?
- Do arranged marriage have more chance of success than those based on romantic love?

❹ Who do you think is more important, your friends or your family? In what circumstances might you prefer to talk to a friend than a member of your family? Are there times when it is more helpful to talk to a stranger?

UNIT 13

LEAD-IN

1 Write down all the kinds of weather which occur in your country.

Now write down those that do not normally occur in your country.

2 Make a list of jobs – full-time, part-time and temporary – that you would like to do.

Now write a list of jobs that you would *never* want to do.

VOCABULARY

1 Which of these adjectives give a positive impression of a job, and which a negative impression?

*dangerous   demanding   socially useful
repetitive   worthwhile   responsible   stressful
dead-end   rewarding   poorly paid   secure
glamorous*

Positive	Negative
....	....
....	....
....	....
....	....
....	....
....	....

Which of the above adjectives describe these jobs? You can use more than one for each job.

airline pilot	clerk
firefighter	tax inspector
software designer	novelist
waiter	psychiatrist
driving instructor	civil engineer
architect	plumber
model	

2 Who gets what? Match these forms of payment with the people below. There is one you do not need to use.

salary   pension   tip   fees   bonus   dole interest   wages   royalties   winnings commission

1 A person who does an unskilled temporary job and is paid weekly, in cash.

2 A rock band who receive money every time their music is played on the radio.

3 People who are unemployed and receive money from the government.

4 A music teacher who is paid by parents for each private lesson she gives to children.

5 A porter who is given money by hotel guests to thank him for his service.

6 Someone who has a steady job and is paid monthly, through a bank.

7 A salesman who is paid according to the number of sales that he makes.

8 Old people who have retired and receive money from the state or a former employer.

9 Somebody who receives a percentage of the money they have invested.

10 An employee who is given an extra payment as a present or as a reward.

Which of these people, do you think, are likely to be well paid and which not?

3 Form the names of jobs from these base words:

*act   farm   jewel   reception   garden   electric
accounts   manage   surgery   law   sail   execute*

Which do you think is the highest paid and which the lowest paid in your country?

4 Match these extreme weather conditions with the consequences on the right.

1	sub-zero temperatures	a	floods
2	torrential rain	b	drought
3	dense fog	c	forest fires
4	blizzards	d	poor visibility
5	below-average rainfall	e	blocked roads
6	lightning strike	f	burst water pipes

Find at least one job in Vocabulary 1 or 3 that is affected by each of these consequences.

GRAMMAR: adjective position

The mountaineer, who was alone, waited for the storm to die down.

❶ Some adjectives, such as *alone* and *glad,* cannot go before a noun. Instead, we put them after a verb as in the example above. Match the expressions on the left with those that have a similar meaning on the right.

1 A frightened person.
2 A sleeping person.
3 A living person.
4 A happy person.
5 A sick person.

a A person who is asleep.
b A person who is content.
c A person who is ill.
d A person who is alive.
e A person who is afraid.

❷ To avoid putting too many adjectives before a noun we can use a relative clause:

He was wearing a light blue nylon jacket, which was waterproof.

We can also use *from, with* or *made of*:

Fresh green olive oil <u>from</u> Spain.
A lovely new detached house <u>with</u> three bedrooms.
Some lovely old winter clothes <u>made of</u> wool.

Using one of these forms, rewrite each of these sentences so that they sound more natural.

1 a tall slim Norwegian football player
2 a pretty little stone country cottage
3 a beautiful old South American folk song
4 cute little red and white furry animals
5 a new two-speed Japanese video recorder
6 a shabby old blue denim jacket
7 heavy black Atlantic rain clouds
8 a delightful warm sunny Spring morning

❸ Some common adjectives go directly after measurement nouns:

ten feet wide
two metres deep
five centimetres thick

When we use these complete phrases as adjectives, they become singular:

a ten-foot wide gap
a two-metre deep pool
a five-centimetre thick board

Write the names for the following in the same way:

1 A report consisting of 20 pages.
2 A coin worth one pound.
3 A girl who is fourteen years old.
4 A lesson which lasts two hours.
5 A flight which takes 90 minutes.
6 A break of ten minutes.
7 A glass that contains half a litre.

8 A race run over 2000 metres.
9 A temperature of 40 degrees.
10 A sumo wrestler weighing 100 kilos.

❹ Make the necessary corrections or improvements to these sentences:

1 My awake sister said she had heard footsteps.
2 He carried some hundred dollars bills with him.
3 We saw the magnificent 5000-metre white Andean mountains.
4 It's only a five-minutes walk to the school from here.
5 The table won't fit in that room: it must be at least five long metres.
6 The ashamed boy said he was very sorry.
7 Use of English is a five-parts exam paper.
8 She's six tall feet – the same height as her husband.

USE OF ENGLISH: open cloze

Fill in the spaces in sentences 1–6.

1 In the morning it had been .... wet that the road looked like a river, but fortunately it turned .... much better in the evening, ... was when were having a party in the garden.

2 In his first job, he didn't even make .... money to pay the rent, ... he had to move to the capital city in .... to earn a decent wage.

3 We .... almost certainly be there by now if we .... listened to the weather forecast on the radio, but you turned it .... just as they were starting to talk about snowfalls.

4 It was .... a long working day, sometimes reaching fifteen hours, ... some of the staff were unable to carry .... doing their jobs.

5 Sarah told me she .... spoken to you and that she .... definitely try to arrange an appointment .... soon as possible.

6 The helicopter crew managed .... rescue two people, but they said that .... there was an improvement in the weather conditions they would be unlikely to find .... else.

PRONUNCIATION

1 Listen to these two sentences:

1 It isn't raining, is it? (falling intonation on tag)
2 It isn't raining, is it? (rising intonation on tag)

Which intonation pattern shows that the speaker doesn't think it's raining?

Complete the following with a tag question, then say each one, first with an intonation which shows that you are sure about what you are saying, then to show some doubt.

1 The forecast was good, ... ?

2 It's not going to snow again, ... ?

3 We won't need an umbrella, ... ?

4 The rainy season hasn't started yet, ... ?

5 Everybody's brought a raincoat, ... ?

6 They didn't forecast thunderstorms, ... ?

7 You haven't brought your sunglasses, ... ?

8 You can't always predict the weather, ... ?

2 Now look at the tag questions used to show surprise or irritation:

Oh, you're a meteorologist, are you?
You arrived late again, did you?

How do they differ from the usual tag questions in activity 1?

What is the intonation pattern – rising or falling? Listen and check.

Complete the following to show surprise or irritation:

1 He's working as a dustman, ... ?

2 He's got a new secretary, ... ?

3 She took over as manager yesterday, ... ?

4 She'll be in charge of this department, ... ?

5 They're all doing overtime, ... ?

6 We're all being made redundant, ... ?

7 Rex had copies made of the report, ... ?

8 He's a world-famous surgeon, ... ?

3 Listen to how these short answers show surprise or irritation.

A I used to work in the same department as you.
B Oh, you did, did you?
A Yes, I was junior to you then, of course.
B Oh, you were, were you?
A But I'm taking over as managing director next week.
B Oh, you are, are you?
A And I'm afraid you're going to be out of a job.
B Oh, I am, am I?

Work with a partner.

Take turns to say something intended to surprise or irritate, and respond appropriately.

WRITING

1 Describe a day in your life when the weather played an important part.

2 Write a story which ends with the words
... and outside, the snow continued to fall.

3 Think of a retired person you know and the job they used to do.

Describe what the job involved and explain how things have changed for somebody starting the same kind of job today.

5-MINUTE ACTIVITIES

1 Work in pairs or groups to produce the news stories behind the following headlines:

FLOODS THREATEN TOWN CENTRE

Britain suffering severe drought – it's official!

VILLAGES CUT OFF BY BLIZZARD

GALES strike south

Heatwave set to continue say forecasters

2 Match the beginnings and endings of these English sayings and try to work out what they mean:

1	All work and no play	A	but it pours.
2	Too many cooks	B	blames his tools.
3	It never rains	C	does not make a summer.
4	One swallow	D	makes Jack a dull boy.
5	A Jack of all trades	E	is master of none.
6	Make hay	F	while the sun shines.
7	A bad workman	G	spoil the broth.

Are any of them the same in your language?

DISCUSSION

1 A nearby river has burst its banks after torrential rain and the floodwater is threatening your house.

What things will you move upstairs out of harm's way?

2 When you think back to your childhood, does the weather seem to have been better or worse then? How do you think the weather is changing?

3 Farmers, sailors and others whose jobs are closely connected with the weather often have their own methods of forecasting it. How many examples can you think of? Do you think they work?

UNIT 14

❶ In a maximum of five minutes, write down the names of all the creatures you can think of that:

- fly
- swim
- walk, run or crawl.

❷ Which creatures have you – or members of your family – ever kept as pets?

Are there any other kinds of pet you would like to have? Why?

VOCABULARY

❶ Match the names for the adult and the young of eight different creatures:

sheep	calves	kittens	birds	horses	lambs
chicks	piglets	puppies	cubs	cows	foxes
cats	dogs	foals	pigs		

Which of the above pairs of animals live in these places? There are two pairs you do not need to use.

sty   nest   kennel   stables   shed   den   basket

❷ Which creatures make these noises?

bark	roar	howl	grunt	growl
hiss	quack	hoot	snort	buzz
squeal	bleat	croak	squawk	neigh
snarl	purr	whine		

Which of these are sometimes used to refer to sounds that people make? What do they mean?

❸ Match these animals with the collective nouns below. There is one you do not need to use.

fish   lizards   wolves   buffalo   birds   insects

A swarm of ....   A pack of ....

A herd of ....   A flock of ....

A shoal of ....

Think of more creatures that can be used with each collective noun:

Example: *a swarm of bees.*

❹ Choose from these words to fill in the gaps and match the underlined idioms in 1–8 with meanings a-h below.

birds   fish   crocodile   bull   duck   cat   crow   bee

1 He'll really <u>let the .... out of the bag</u> if he tells anyone.

2 The company's <u>a real lame ....</u> now that it has no cash to invest.

3 He <u>shed .... tears</u> when his ex-wife's marriage broke up.

4 From here to the coast, it's 50 kilometres <u>as the .... flies</u>.

5 I'll do some revision while I'm waiting and <u>kill two .... with one stone</u>.

6 It's time you <u>took the .... by the horns</u> and asked her what she's up to.

7 Now he's got that flashy car he really thinks he's <u>the ....'s knees</u>.

8 I know you're missing him but <u>there are plenty more .... in the sea</u>!

a in a straight line

b an organization in financial difficulties

c superior to other people

d achieve two aims though one action

e reveal the secret

f lots of other possible boy/girlfriends exist

g faced up to a difficulty courageously

h pretended to be very sad

GRAMMAR: question tags

❶ We add a question tag to a statement when we expect the other person to agree with us, or confirm what we are saying. Questions tags are common in spoken English and are also used in informal writing such as letters to friends. Study these rules and fill in the gaps with an appropriate word from the list:

pronouns   first   affirmative   suggestions   main negative   same   modals

1 We form tags by using the verb *be*, the auxiliaries *do* or *have*, or .... such as *can* or *must*, plus the subject pronoun. We add this to the end of an affirmative or negative statement.

2 With an affirmative statement, we normally use the contracted form of a(n) .... tag:

Those animals are becoming rare, aren't they?

3 With a negative statement, we use a(n) .... tag:

There won't be any countryside left, will there?

4 If the statement has *be*, an auxiliary or a modal in it, we use a form of the .... word in the tag:

You weren't at the meeting, were you?
She has already decided what to do, hasn't she?
They shouldn't build on that land, should they?

5 If there is only a(n) .... verb in the statement, we use a form of *do* in the tag:

They cut down the entire forest, didn't they?

6 With negative adverbs and .... , we use an affirmative tag:

They've never admitted responsibility, have they?
None of them live in this area any more, do they?

7 To make .... , we use *shall*, not *will*:

I'll tell you what happened, shall I?

8 We use *aren't* in the .... person singular when *am* forms part of an affirmative statement:

I'm always the one everybody blames, aren't I?

❷ For each of 1–9, add a suitable tag.

1 The drought hasn't ended yet, ... ?
2 Too many tourists go there, ... ?
3 Let's join the protesters, ... ?
4 People shouldn't drop litter, ... ?
5 You'd rather see animals in the wild, ... ?
6 Nobody lived there until recently, ... ?
7 I'm stupid to believe everything they say, ... ?
8 There are hardly any eagles left, ... ?
9 They can't have destroyed everything, ... ?

❸ When you reply to a question tag, you answer the statement, not the tag. This means that you confirm an affirmative statement by saying *Yes* and a negative statement by saying *No*:

You're in my brother's class, aren't you? – Yes, I am.
She wasn't at the party, was she? – No, she wasn't.

If the statement is wrong, you do the opposite. If you are disagreeing, you also probably add more information to avoid sounding abrupt or rude:

No, I'm not, I'm in class 3E.
Yes, she was, but she left very early.

Study 1–8 and write questions about your partner by filling in the missing word and then adding a question tag. Then work in pairs, asking and answering each other's questions.

1 You're ..... years old, ... ?
2 You live in .... street, ... ?
3 You're taking First Certificate in .... , ... ?
4 Your favourite colour is .... , ... ?
5 You like .... a lot, ... ?
6 You don't like .... very much, ... ?
7 You were at .... last Saturday, ... ?
8 You'd like to visit .... , ... ?

❹ Write down three more things you know about your partner, and three things you think you know about him or her. Then use question tags to ask each other if the statements are true.

USE OF ENGLISH: multiple-choice cloze

Read the sentences below and decide which word A, B, C or D best fits each gap.

❶ Did you know, for ...... (A chance   B instance   C case   D situation), that if everybody in this country turned off their television ...... (A by   B for   C in   D with) hand instead of using the remote control, it would ...... (A keep   B preserve   C recover   D save) enough electricity to provide all the ...... (A strength   B energy   C force   D pressure) needs of a town with ...... (A an occupation   B a people   C a population   D a settlement) of one hundred thousand?

❷ The huge hole in the Antarctic ozone layer forms every ...... (A south   B southern   C southward   D southwards) spring, when a ...... (A joint   B meeting   C union   D combination) of the first rays from the sun and the ...... (A intense   B powerful   C high   D heavy) cold bring ...... (A over   B up   C about   D out) the unique conditions which have ...... (A caused   B led   C produced   D directed) to man-made chemicals destroying two-thirds of the ozone in the area.

1 Can you think of five characteristics that distinguish birds from other animals?

Can all birds fly?

Which other animals can fly?

Are there any other animals that have beaks?

... or feathers?

... or two legs?

2 You are going to read a text about birds and flying, from which six sentences have been removed. Choose from sentences A–G the one which you think best fits in each gap. There is one extra sentence that you do not need to use.

BIRDS IN FLIGHT

To get into the air and fly, birds have to flap their wings. Among the fastest flappers are ducks, geese and pigeons. (1) .... However, none of these compares with the falcons and swifts, which are the fastest birds known. A falcon swooping down to catch its prey can reach nearly 300 km/h and some swifts may reach speeds even higher than this.

When we consider the speed of flight, it seems all the more remarkable that birds can make a perfect landing on a tiny perch. Clearly the bird has to time its braking precisely enough to land without injury. (2) .... Thus birds have to be able to brake rapidly, but also to keep airborne till the last possible moment.

(3) .... The same parts of the body which can help the bird glide through the air so efficiently during flight are now instinctively used to the opposite effect just before landing.

First the flying bird pulls back into a near-vertical position with its head held high, then beats its wings forward against the direction it is moving in, and lowers and spreads out its tail. (4) .... Wherever possible the bird also flies in below its landing place and then glides up to settle on it. For waterbirds, the webbed feet can also be used as additional brakes.

(5) .... The albatross, for example, an enormous seabird with wings measuring up to 3.5 m from tip to tip, spends most of its time in the air. Landing on the ground is quite a rare event in its life and even when they use all their braking powers, the largest albatrosses are awkward at landing and frequently go head over heels. (6) ....

A The simplest form of flapping flight is seen during take-off.

B If it stops too suddenly, it may crash.

C In spite of having all these methods available, not all birds are guaranteed a graceful landing.

D Finally, the legs are stretched forward and relaxed just enough to cushion the shock of landing.

E Fortunately, they are strongly-built birds and are not usually injured by crash-landings of this sort.

F To do the first of these, all birds have various methods of slowing down.

G Even most of our common, small birds can move as fast as a horse.

3 Look back through the completed text and find:

1 two words that mean 'to move (wings) up and down'

   ....

2 a word to describe flying down very fast

   ....

3 a word to describe how a bird moves through the air without moving its wings

   ....

4 a word used for the place where a bird sits

   ....

5 a word used for a bird or animal hunted for food

   ....

WRITING

1 Many advances in science and technology are made at the cost of the environment. Think of three or four examples and say whether you think each one was worth it, and why.

2 Scientists often use animals in their experiments. Do you think this is justified?

3 Think about some of the environmental problems facing the world today and what is or is not being done about them. Now imagine writing a letter to a child fifty years in the future. Write the letter, saying what people today should or should not have done, and what you wish had been done differently.

5-MINUTE ACTIVITIES

1 Work in teams. See which team can complete the following the fastest.

Name three animals that live

1 in the jungle   ....
2 underground   ....
3 in gardens   ....
4 in the desert   ....
5 in the snow   ....

2 Think about environmental concerns and then note down

- 5 things you wish hadn't happened

  ....
  ....
  ....
  ....
  ....

- 5 things you wish weren't happening

  ....
  ....
  ....
  ....
  ....

- 5 things you wish would happen

  ....
  ....
  ....
  ....
  ....

3 Genetic engineering is making it possible to combine the characteristics of different animals to make new ones.

Think of all the ways in which humans use animals. The work in groups to design the perfect animal – one that will provide humans with food, materials, transport, etc.

DISCUSSION

1 Global warning has caused worldwide flooding. Imagine you are the captain of an immense boat and are able to save certain species of animal from extinction. Which animals would you personally *not* try to save? Why?

2 Many conservationists are trying to protect animals and plants threatened with extinction. Do you think it is important to save them? Are some more important than others?

3 Following a global environmental disaster, you and a few other survivors are left to start life again on a large island without any modern technology or the comforts you have been used to.

What skills would you and the other survivors need to develop first?

What would be your priorities for making life bearable?

What would you personally miss most from your present way of life?

UNIT 15

LEAD-IN

❶ What do/did you like about school? What do/did you dislike about it? Think about:

- the buildings
- the staff
- other students
- school rules
- the timetable
- breaks, sports and other non-study times
- homework
- travelling to and from school.

❷ Write down all the subjects you are studying or used to study at school.

Now put them in order, from those you like/liked best to the ones you like/liked least.

VOCABULARY and SPEAKING

❶ Put these words and phrases associated with school into the four groups below. There are four expressions in each group.

playground	text book	blackboard
head	half-term	register
caretaker	desk	dinner lady
speech day	playing fields	deputy head
canteen	sports day	
gym	assembly	

Staff

....

....

....

....

Places

....

....

....

....

Events

....

....

....

....

Objects

....

....

....

....

Think about the people you have listed under 'Staff'. What are (or, if you've left school, were) their names at your school? How would you describe each one's personality?

❷ Fill in the gaps by using each of these 'school' words once in its correct form. There is one you do not need to use.

*reports   disqualify   expel   truant   suspend
results   absent   punish   year   note   cheat*

On the day of the fourth (1) .... examination, two students were (2) .... , one of whom had previously sent a (3) .... from her parents, the other who is known to have 'played (4) ....' on more than one occasion. During the first part of the test, one pupil was seen looking at another's answer sheet. If it is proved that he was attempting to (5) .... , we shall have no alternative but to (6) .... her from the entire exam. We have also made it clear to any pupils caught copying that we shall (7) .... them for up to two weeks, and that if it happens a second time we shall (8) .... them from the school immediately. The (9) .... of the examination will be known within a week, and will be included in the (10) .... which will, as usual, be sent to parents on the last day of term.

Do you know of any incidents like this? If so, what happened to the person or people involved?

❸ Put the following into two groups: Good Ideas and Bad Ideas.

*single-sex schools   boarding schools
minimum school-leaving age   strict discipline
long school holidays   lots of homework
uniforms   exams   repeating school years*

Good idea:

....

....

....

Bad idea:

....

....

....

Now compare lists with your partner.

❹ Which school subjects are most useful for you to study if you want to be:

- a doctor?
- a computer programmer?
- a teacher?
- a senior manager?
- a television presenter?
- an electrical engineer?
- a banker?
- a film director?
- a social worker?
- a musician?

Are there any subjects taught at school which you think are not useful at all? Why?

GRAMMAR: causative verbs

❶ Instead of *have something done*, we sometimes use the form *get something done*, particularly in less formal situations:

We ought to get the tickets sent here.

Write six sentences about things that you, your family or your friends sometimes get done by somebody else. In each case say why, using *to, in order to* or *so as to*.

Example:

I get my clothes specially made, to make sure they fit well.

Tell your partner about three things you would like to get done for you rather than have to do them yourself. Say why.

❷ To tell someone what to do, we use *get* more often than *have*:

Hey, referee, get your eyes tested!

What would you say in each of these situations? Use *get* plus the verb in brackets.

1 Your sister's alarm clock never works in the morning. (fix)

2 Your little brother's hair is so long he can't see through it. (cut)

3 Someone's shoe has got a hole in it. (repair)

4 Your elder brother is going to wear his best suit to a wedding. (dry clean)

5 A friend's CD ROM drive doesn't seem to be working properly. (check out)

6 Your mother doesn't want to carry everything home from the supermarket. (deliver)

Tell your partner three things you would like to tell members of your family, or friends to do, using *get*.

❸ We can also use either *have something done* or *get something done* for something that happens to us. This event is often unexpected or unpleasant, and beyond our control.

Examples:

We had some things stolen from the car.
I got my fingers trapped in the door.

Rewrite each of these sentences using one of these forms.

1 Although they were poor, their rent increased every six months.

2 If you touch that piece of metal, it'll burn your hand.

3 They turned down her appeal against the decision.

4 Some older girls pulled her hair.

5 After the civil war, many people's property was seized.

6 They took away his driving licence after he nearly killed someone.

7 When he joined the army, they cut his hair really short.

8 A player in their team was sent off for fighting.

9 They would have increased his sentence if they had known about the murder.

❹ Using the forms from 3 above, write down six things that have happened to you, your family or your friends.

Examples: *I once got my jacket caught in the bus doors when they were closing.*

My friend had her picture published in the paper, right next to a story about a robbery.

Now show your partner your sentences, in each case explaining what happened before and after the event.

USE OF ENGLISH: key word transformations

In each of 1–6, two of the three sentences have similar meanings. Which are they?

1 a I'd better that book before the exam.
   b It's a great pity I didn't read that book before the exam.
   c If only I'd read that book before the exam.

2 a We're going to have the house completely rebuilt.
   b Someone's going to rebuild the house completely for us.
   c We're going to rebuild the house completely.

3 a I'm fed up with him criticizing me all the time.
   b I wish he wouldn't keep criticizing me.
   c If only he hadn't been constantly criticizing me.

4 a It's possible that they took the exam last week.
   b If they'd been able to, they would've taken the exam last week.
   c They might have taken the exam last week.

5 a He stole his own car so that he could claim the insurance.
   b In order that he could claim the insurance, he had his car stolen.
   c To claim the insurance on his car, he had somebody steal it.

6 a In case there was a queue, we began our journey early.
   b We set off early because of the risk that there might be a queue.
   c We left the house early if there was a queue.

READING

1 Is FCE preparation part of your school curriculum or are you doing a special course?

How long ago did you enrol for the course?

Did you have to enrol in advance?

How difficult is it to get grants for studying in your country?

2 You are going to read some information about enrolling for courses at a college.

Read the text and then do the multiple-choice questions which follow.

Enrolment Procedure

If you wish to enrol by post, complete the application form at the back and return it with the appropriate fee to the Enrolment Office. Either enclose a cheque made out to the College or enter your credit card details in the space provided.

- It is essential that all sections of the application form are completed.
- If you would like an early acknowledgement of your enrolment, please enclose a stamped addressed envelope.
- Please assume that you have a place unless we notify you to the contrary.
- Telephone and personal applications are also accepted.

We do our best to run all courses advertised, but do need a minimum enrolment – normally 12 – to make them viable. If courses do not reach this minimum number they may be cancelled. Most courses, particularly languages and computer courses, also have a maximum number and early enrolment is advised to avoid disappointment. Course numbers are reviewed two weeks before the start date and courses may be cancelled at that stage if student registrations have not reached double figures.

We will take enrolments at the first meeting of most courses, if places are available. However, students should note that late applications result in delays in producing the college library card and access to computer workstations.

The College receives funds from the government to provide selective help to certain students who have serious financial difficulties or whose access to higher education might be restricted for financial reasons. Those students most likely to qualify for a grant are those with parental or other family responsibilities, those with heavy travel costs, or with other exceptional circumstances.

If a course is cancelled by the College, all student fees will be refunded in full. On most courses, if students withdraw from a course before the first meeting and notify us in writing, fees will be refunded less a 10% administration charge. We regret no fees will be refunded once a course has started. Details will be on your course syllabus.

---

1 If you want to enrol by post
  A you must obtain an application form from the office.
  B you must enclose a stamped addressed envelope.
  C you will not be told if you have a place.
  D you will be contacted about the fees.

2 What is said about the number of students on a course?
  A There is a minimum number for most courses.
  B The maximum is lower for Language and Computer courses.
  C Numbers are fixed before the course starts.
  D Students will be told in advance the number of students on their course.

3 What is said about late applications?
  A They cause problems for students.
  B They are not usually accepted.
  C They are accepted up to two weeks before the course starts.
  D They are accepted if sufficient computers are available.

4 Which of these students may receive financial help?
  A Those who are living with their parents
  B Those who live a long way from the College
  C Those who pass a selection examination
  D Those who register for government help

5 If students wish to obtain a refund of fees, they must
  A notify the College as soon as the course starts.
  B return their copy of the course syllabus.
  C inform the College of the full amount paid.
  D apply by letter before the course starts.

6 This information comes from
  A a newspaper article
  B a student magazine
  C a prospectus
  D a guidebook

WRITING

1 Write a letter to a friend who is about to take an exam, giving advice on revision and the best way to spend the evening before the exam.

2 Write a description of your first day at school.

3 You have been asked to write a report on your school for a student new to the area. Write the report, mentioning the facilities available, the classes, the teachers and any especially good or bad points.

5-MINUTE ACTIVITIES

1 Give a brief oral summary of the set book you have been studying.

2 In pairs or groups act out a major scene from the set book.

3 In pairs or groups, work out a student/teacher charter, saying how students and teachers should behave and what they should do.

DISCUSSION

1 What subjects would you *not* include in the school curriculum and why? And what new subject would you add?

2 What are your favourite revision strategies? Work together to produce a list.

3 *Schooldays are the happiest days of your life.* Do you agree?

4 Your school has received a large donation from a local businesswoman. The following ways of spending the money have been suggested. Discuss the pros and cons of each one and decide which would be the best.
- a swimming pool
- a gym
- a cafeteria
- a minibus
- a sculpture outside the main entrance.

Further Practice Key

UNIT 1

VOCABULARY and SPEAKING

1 1 B 2 C 3 F 4 A 5 E 6 D

GRAMMAR: present tenses

1 1 SUGGESTED ANSWERS:

a e
b ee, see -> seeing
c y, fly -> flying
d ie, lie -> lying

2 a one b two c either d one e first
Not needed: second

USE OF ENGLISH: key word transformations

1 a, c   3 a, b   5 a, c   7 b, c   9 a, c
2 b, c   4 b, c   6 a, b   8 a, c   10 b, c.

PRONUNCIATION

1 1 The groups are:

1 breath fed sweat
2 suite sweet breathe
3 put took could
4 weight day ache
5 two suits route new

2 There are 20 words altogether. The groups are as follows:

a fitness every people minutes later covered hardly over
b arrived again throughout machines
c intervals fancying beautiful exercise
d already aerobics surrounded easier

2 The syllable and stress pattern in these limericks is as follows:

long lines: □ ☐ □ □ ☐ □ □ ☐

short lines: □ ☐ □ □ ☐ ☐

Limerick 1: invited visit used horses hoped impressed

Limerick 2: choir claims without bats known liar

UNIT 2

VOCABULARY

2 1 risk   3 danger   5 harm
2 harm   4 danger   6 risk

3 harm*ful*/*less* safe risky hazard*ous* *un*safe harm*less*

4 POSITIVE: fearless courageous heroic daring adventurous brave
NEGATIVE: foolish reckless

GRAMMAR: nouns and verbs

1 1 plan   3 question   5 plan
2 reply   4 question   6 reply

4 1 use 2 believe 3 advise
4 prove; /s/ and /ʃ/ for nouns, /z/ and /v/ for verbs

USE OF ENGLISH: multiple-choice cloze

1 B   3 D   5 B   7 B, C   9 A, D
2 D   4 A   6 C   8 A, B   10 C, B

PRONUNCIATION

1 The stressed syllables are the first in each word, except for *afraid* which is stressed on the second syllable. All the unstressed syllables contain the schwa sound.

2 1 to 2 of 3 but 4 than 5 and 6 can

3 Stressed syllables:
1 roll, real, press, Jul
2 Rich, back, norm, cry, horr
3 For, not/man(y), peop, face, real, life, (ex)perience
4 Warm, (un)com(fortable), (ob)serve(d), (in)visible, watch

Schwa sounds in:
1 roll<u>e</u>rcoaster Juli<u>a</u>
2 Rich<u>a</u>rd <u>a</u>way fr<u>o</u>m enorm<u>ou</u>s spid<u>er</u> <u>a</u> <u>o</u>f horr<u>o</u>r
3 Fortun<u>a</u>tely ev<u>er</u> t<u>o</u> <u>a</u> threat<u>e</u>ning experi<u>e</u>nce
4 Marm<u>a</u>duke uncomfort<u>a</u>ble th<u>a</u>t w<u>a</u>s <u>o</u>bserved watch<u>er</u>s

UNIT 3

VOCABULARY

1 solar   lunar   planetary   universal

2
1 planets, Solar
2 sun
3 Astronomy
4 astronomical
5 moon
6 universe

3 PHYSICS: energy   laser   magnet   reflection   ray
MATHEMATICS: rectangle   multiplication   plus cylinder   pyramid   subtract   minus
ENGINEERING: viaduct   tunnel   foundation dam

4 DISTANCE: inch   foot   yard   mile
WEIGHT: ounce   pound   stone   ton
LIQUIDS: pint   gallon

GRAMMAR: *too* and *enough*

This section also provides more practice with future forms and *make*.

1 a2   b1

2 adjective, noun, before the noun, before a noun but after an adjective

3 no real difference; always before the adjective

4
2 long enough
3 too expensive
4 enough disks
5 too far away (to walk to)
6 well enough (to go)
7 too little time (to do the job)
8 enough light (to read)
9 too late (to see the others)
10 too much noise (to concentrate)

USE OF ENGLISH: open cloze

1 one	5 anything	9 on by
2 who	6 rid	10 across it
3 an	7 spite himself	Not needed: will
4 which	8 a can	

READING

1
Fire extinguisher	1816	Air-conditioning	1911
Electric iron	1882	Kleenex	1924
Escalator	1892	Electric shaver	1931

2
1 Air-conditioning
2 Escalator
3 Electric shaver
4 Fire extinguisher
5 Electric iron
Not used: Kleenex tissues

3
1 C 'pattern' – C is an example to illustrate this, 'They' refers to 'astronomers'
2 A 'At first' in A contrasts with 'Soon, however,' 'it' refers to 'object'

3 E 'From earliest times' picks up 'long-held beliefs',
'they' refers to 'astronomers'
4 F 'this discovery' refers to 'his new planet', 'changed' leads on to giving up his music career.
5 B 'Other astronomers' contrasts with 'He' (Herschel), 'call' picks up 'name' 'it' refers to 'his discovery'.
Not needed: D

5-MINUTE ACTIVITIES

1
a 7 radio		e 5 miniskirt
b 4 radium		f 3 television
c 2 telephone		g 6 penicillin
d 8 toothpaste		h 1 lift

UNIT 4

VOCABULARY and SPEAKING

1 safe, amusing, risky, exciting, cruel, fun, entertaining, enjoyable, silly, boring, rewarding, unpleasant, relaxing, healthy, challenging, exhausting

2 taking photographs, playing cards, keeping fit, stamp collecting, going fishing, horse riding

GRAMMAR: comparatives using *the ..., the ...*

1
1 festival is
2 bands are; prices are/will be, etc.
3 better it is/will be, etc.
4 we leave; it will be/we'll feel, etc.

2
1 the sooner, the earlier, etc.
2 the less
3 the sleepier, (etc.) I am
4 the better
5 the less
6 the better, higher, etc.
7 the more (vocabulary, etc.)
8 the better, the more fun it will be, etc.

3 SUGGESTED ANSWERS:
1 more cars; worse/heavier
2 more frightening; more
3 hotter/better; the more people
4 more honest/trustworthy; the more
5 more/less; the more relaxed/miserable
6 the bigger/spicier; the more/less
7 more; the worse the noise/mess
8 sooner; the better

4 POSSIBLE ANSWERS:
1 the more tired I feel.
2 the faster I progress.
3 the better I get to know her/him.
4 the more I enjoy them.
5 the easier it becomes.
6 the better.
7 the more I like them.

8 the more things I want to do.
9 the more I realise how lucky I am.
10 the more I enjoy life.

USE OF ENGLISH: word formation

1 composers 5 drummers 9 entertainment
2 guitarist 6 loudspeakers 10 tuneful
3 instrumental 7 musician
4 performance 8 deafening

PRONUNCIATION

1 1 He spends_a lot_of time listening to
these_old_rock_albums.
2 She found_an_interesting collection_of
stamps_in the strange_old man's_attic.
3 Pete_opened the box_and spread_out_its
contents ready for the game.
4 For this game you need_a set_of
chessmen_and_a board.
5 The referee went_over to find_out_if the
player was hurt_or not.

2 Is chess_a sport_or_a game?
The final r is not usually pronounced.

My father_always went for_a walk after_our_evening
meal. He generally wore_a rather_old blazer_and
strolled_as far_as the River_Ouse. I think he liked to
be by himself for_a while

3 a new_album
now_and then
I know_a good gallery.

Are you_a keen gardener?
The match was so_exciting.
I think he had to go_out.
What do_I have to do next?

4 The day_of the match
Why_are you here?
That's very_interesting.
Most people enjoy_a good book.
I_enjoy_a good book too

5 A Hi!
B Hi, how_are you?
A Fine. How_are your_art classes going?
B Not bad – I've_even managed to produce
some_acceptable portraits_of_other students.
A Great. I've got_a new hobby, too. I've taken_up
bird-watching.
B Really? It's_always sounded_a bit boring to me.
A No,_I thought_it might be, but_it_isn't. I
spotted a really_interesting bird the_other
day_and_I think_I could really get_to_enjoy this
hobby_as_I learn more_about_it.
B Hm ... maybe ... I think_I'll stick to_art

UNIT 5

VOCABULARY

2 SUGGESTED ANSWERS: shopping/laundry/
wastepaper/picnic basket; fruit/sugar/goldfish/soup/
salad bowl; frying/saucepan; coffee/flower/teapot

3 1 1c, 2h, 3g, 4b, 5f, 6a, 7e, 8d
2 Possible order: palace, villa, motel, cabin,
chalet, barracks, tent, cell.

GRAMMAR: used to

1 1 b 2 c
3 a; 1 infinitive 2 -ing form 3 -ing form

2 1 sleeping 5 sharing
2 have 6 hearing
3 finding 7 spending
4 cooking 8 getting

Situation: camping in the countryside

3 1 get used to 5 (gradually) getting used to
2 wasn't used to 6 didn't use to enjoy
3 get used to 7 am used to/have got used to
4 used to go out 8 they used to have to

USE OF ENGLISH: error correction

3 many 5 more 7 ✔ 9 being 11 often
4 even 6 in 8 ✔ 10 of 12 ✔

PRONUNCIATION

1 Saturday; Friday; tired; all; no; nine; barbecue

3 1 Is your parents' flat in London? (or other
possessive)
2 Is your flat in New York? (or other location)
3 Is your bedroom upstairs?
4 Was it your cat?
5 Was it your neighbour's dog?

UNIT 6

VOCABULARY and SPEAKING

1 SUGGESTED ANSWERS:
1 cook: cooker (n), cooking (n), cookery (n / adj),
cooked (adj), uncooked (neg adj)
2 heat: heated (adj), unheated (neg adj),
heater (n), heating (n)
3 appear: appearance (n), disappear (v),
disappearance (n), apparent (adj), apparently
(adv)
4 sweet: sweeten (v), sweetened (adj),
unsweetened (neg adj), sweeteners (n),
sweetly (adv)
5 excite: excited (adj), unexcited (neg adj),
excitement (n), excitedly (adv),
excitable (adj)

6 prepare: preparation (n), prepared (adj), unprepared (neg adj), preparatory (adj)

7 taste: tasty (adj), tasteless (neg adj), tasting (n), taster (n)

8 digest: digestion (n), digestive (adj), digestible (adj), indigestible (neg adj)

② 1 stale bread
2 tough meat
3 a well-done steak
4 still/non-fizzy drinks
5 sweet wine
6 mature/strong cheese
7 cooked vegetables
8 plain crisps
9 whole fruit
10 a soft-boiled egg

❸ SUGGESTED ANSWERS: chopped onions, apples; peeled onions, apples; melted cheese, butter; skimmed milk; beaten eggs; sliced onions, melon, apples; grated cheese; minced beef

GRAMMAR: *no matter what, whatever, etc.*

① 1 which 2 who 3 when 4 how 5 what

② 1 whoever   4 whichever
2 whatever   5 However
3 Whenever

❸ SUGGESTED ANSWERS:
1 No matter how hard I work I never seem to finish.
2 This foreign food is delicious, whatever it is.
3 Wherever I go I always take my dog with me.
4 I want the best meal on the menu, however expensive it is.
5 Whenever you want to go out, just give me a ring.
6 Don't let anyone be rude to you, no matter who he/she is.
7 You can phone me here no matter what time you get home.
8 No matter which dress she wears she always looks lovely.

READING

① 1 F 2 C 3 A 4 B 5 G 6 D
Not needed: E

② 1 snack   5 greengrocer
2 filling   6 preservation
3 ripe   7 concentrated
4 stewed

USE OF ENGLISH: word formation

1 boiling: verb -> adjective
2 separately: verb/adjective -> adverb
3 sweetened: adjective/noun-> adjective
4 mixture: verb -> noun
5 consumption: verb -> noun
6 carefully: verb/noun -> adjective -> adverb

7 wooden: noun -> adjective
8 uncovered: verb/noun -> adjective (negative)
9 thicken: adjective -> verb
10 insufficiently: adjective -> adverb (negative)

5-MINUTE ACTIVITIES

❸ 1 pomegranate   5 raspberry
2 mango   6 peach
3 grapefruit   7 apricot
4 watermelon   8 pineapple

UNIT 7

LEAD IN

① POSSIBLE ANSWERS:
1 hockey, rugby, netball
2 windsurfing, water-skiing, canoeing
3 table-tennis, five-a-side football, squash
4 speed skating, skiing, bobsleigh
5 shot put, high jump, javelin
6 1500 metres, relay, sprint

VOCABULARY

① POSSIBLE ANSWERS:
1 table tennis: ball, bat, return, volley, smash, forehand, backhand, doubles, spin, points
2 cycling: tour, handlebars, wheels, brakes, chain, puncture, crash, leader, climb, descent
3 football: foul, goal, net, card, tackle, kick, save, handball, striker, defender, midfielder
4 swimming: backstroke, breaststroke, butterfly, freestyle, medley, dive, turn, breathing
5 boxing: corner, ropes, bell, count, punch, knockdown, jab, uppercut, hook, champion
6 golf: fairway, links, bunker, tee, rough, drive, wood, iron, putt, ball, flag, shot, caddy
7 ice hockey: net, skates, penalty, foul, team, shoot, score, puck, strike, pads, tackle, save
8 horse racing: bridle, reins, whip, spurs, hoof, fence, furlongs, betting, odds, favourite
9 sailing/yachting: water, boat, hull, waves, keel, rudder, cabin, steer, spray, anchor, captain
10 tennis: ball, net, serve, volley, deuce, forehand, backhand, smash, lob, fault, return, love

② 1 1 cricket   pitch: football, rugby, hockey
      2 basketball   court: badminton, tennis, squash
      3 wrestling   ring: boxing, show jumping
      4 hurdles   track: athletics, running
      5 snowboarding slope: skiing, ski jumping, luge
      6 golf   course: race, rowing
      7 roller-skating rink: ice-skating, ice-dancing
      8 diving   pool: swimming

2 referee – football, etc.   umpire – tennis, etc.
starter – marathon, etc.   judge – ice-skating, etc.

❸ POSSIBLE ANSWERS:
1 motor/horse/motorcycle/greyhound racing;
2 foot/basket/volley/handball;
3 ice-hockey/skating/dancing;
4 goalkeeper/kick/post/line;
5 water-ski/skiing/polo/jump;
6 high/long/triple jump;
7 record-holder/breaker/breaking;
8 starting/finishing/winning/base/touchline;
9 surf/dart/diving/skate/snow board;
10 football/basketball/rugby/tennis/badminton player

GRAMMAR: prepositional phrases with *at, by* and *on*

❶
1 by	4 at	7 on	10 by	13 on
2 at	5 on	8 on	11 at	14 at
3 by	6 by	9 At	12 by	15 on

❷
1 on time
2 by chance
3 on the phone
4 by surprise
5 on the tip of my tongue
6 on purpose
7 by hand
8 by far
9 on my own
10 by heart

USE OF ENGLISH: error correction

1 ✔	3 who	5 ✔	7 the	9 what
2 ✔	4 can	6 is	8 ✔	10 the

READING

❶ Court sports include: basketball, real tennis, pelota, rackets, squash, lawn tennis, racketball, fives, badminton, netball, volleyball.
They all involve playing a ball (or a shuttlecock) with the hand or a racket. Kicking is not allowed.

❷ 1 C 2 A 3 A 4 D 5 B 6 D

5-MINUTE ACTIVITIES

❷ POSSIBLE ANSWERS:
1 dressage, show jumping, eventing, horse-racing, polo
2 tennis, real tennis, squash, badminton
3 cricket, baseball, rounders, softball
4 rowing, tug-of-war, abseiling
5 croquet, polo

UNIT 8

VOCABULARY and SPEAKING

❶ a portrait painting: *Mona Lisa/Giaconda*, da Vinci
an abstract painting: Guernica, Picasso
an Impressionist painting: Water-lilies, Monet
a play: Macbeth, Shakespeare
an opera: Don Giovanni, Mozart
a ballet: Sleeping Beauty, Tchaikovsky

❷ POSSIBLE ANSWERS:
interviewer: asks people such as politicians questions
commentator: describes (sports) action as it happens
announcer: says which programmes are coming on
presenter: introduces separate parts of a programme
newscaster: reads the news bulletins
reporter: gives on-the-spot news
foreign correspondent: reports from abroad
weatherman/woman: gives the weather forecast

❸ editorial, review, advertisement, news item

GRAMMAR: present perfect or past simple?

❶
1 I saw
2 ✔
3 there have been
4 Have you ever seen
5 has happened
6 ✔
7 I saw
8 it hasn't finished
9 I was
10 ✔

❷ 1 e 2 f 3 b 4 a 5 d 6 c
Cultural activity: the theatre

❸
1 have you seen
2 have you enjoyed
3 did you like
4 haven't you enjoyed
5 didn't you like
6 did you enjoy
7 did you watch
8 did you watch
9 has been
10 did you see

USE OF ENGLISH: multiple-choice cloze

1 B, A	3 B, A, C	5 D, D, B
2 C, D	4 B, A, D	

READING

❶ Michelangelo (1475–1564) was an Italian artist, architect, sculptor and poet, best known for his painting of the Sistine Chapel ceiling in the Vatican and for his sculpture *David* in Florence. He was also the architect of St Peter's Cathedral in Rome from 1546.

❷ 1 C 2 G 3 F 4 E 5 A 6 D
Not needed: B

❸
1 B	3 C	5 B	7 A
2 A	4 C	6 B	8 C

2 1 Hamlet 3 Othello 5 Julius Caesar
2 Macbeth 4 Romeo

Juliet is missing from the titles.
Hamlet said 'To be or not to be … ?'

3 Poets: W.H. Auden, John Keats,
William Wordsworth, John Milton, W.B. Yeats
Novelists: Charles Dickens, Jane Austen,
Mary Shelley, James Joyce, Virginia Woolf

UNIT 9

VOCABULARY

1 crimes – hijacking, kidnapping; associated with
these – weapon, ransom, captive, hostage;
cars/driving – wreck, chase, crashing, racing.

1 kidnapping	4 hostage	7 crashing
2 ransom	5 hijacking	8 wreck
3 captive	6 chase	9 weapon

Not needed: racing

2 Probable order – check-in desk, passport control,
security scanners, departure lounge, boarding gate,
aircraft cabin, passport control, baggage reclaim,
customs, arrivals hall.
Airside/landside answer: Only check-in desk and
arrivals hall are landside.

3 Smallest to biggest – moped, motorbike, van,
lorry/coach
General term – motor vehicles
Ride – motorbike, moped; Drive – coach, van, lorry
Age – will depend on the laws in the students'
country, but may be in this order: 1 moped
2 motorbike 3 van 4 lorry and coach

4 vessels

1 submarine	6 ferry
2 liner	7 powerboat
3 lifeboat	8 rowing boat
4 barge	9 yacht
5 trawler	10 tanker

GRAMMAR: *yes/no* questions

1 1 Are, Has 2 Had, Will 3 Does, Did 4 Is, Can

2 POSSIBLE ANSWERS:
1 Are you the same age as your partner?
2 Can you play the piano?
3 Do you share a flat with your friends?
4 Are you going to take First Certificate this
summer?
5 Will you be in at nine o'clock?
6 Have you been studying English long?
7 Have you ever eaten Basque food?
8 Did you go to a club at the weekend?
9 Had you studied *yes/no* questions before?
10 Did you use to live in another part of town?
11 Will you speak to her again?
12 Would you like to visit Rome?

USE OF ENGLISH: open cloze

1 took, just	4 could, time, was
2 back, once	5 soon, what, which
3 sooner, than	6 on, had, in

READING

2 1 D 2 G 3 B 4 H 5 I 6 A 7 E 8 F
Not needed: C

1 Possible crimes: hijacking, stowing away, ram-
raiding, joy-riding, smuggling, piracy, drink-driving,
speeding, driving without a seat belt/crash helmet/
licence/insurance, highway robbery (highwaymen),
the Great Train Robbery

UNIT 10

VOCABULARY and SPEAKING

1
1 fishmonger's	5 travel agent's
2 barber's/hairdresser's	6 garage/service station
3 electrical shop	7 pet shop
4 bank	8 dentist's

3
1 neck	5 throat	9 wrists
2 wrist	6 ears	10 waist
3 wrist	7 fingers, toes	
4 head	8 shoulders	

the jewellery – silver, gold or similar;
the others – plastic, leather, elastic, etc.

4 SUGGESTED ANSWERS:
Summer – shorts, sandals, t-shirt, sunhat
Winter – gloves, scarf, overcoat, boots
Night – nightie, dressing-gown, pyjamas, slippers

GRAMMAR: the passive

1 (verbs only – other answers will be student
specific):

1 was born
2 was brought up
3 was educated/have been educated – (Elicit the
difference between continuing and completed
schooling here.)
4 was taught/have been taught/am taught
5 was shown/have been shown/am being shown
6 is sung/was sung
7 was written
8 is shown/is being shown/has been shown

2 1 One of the neighbours told me
2 No-one/Nobody is going to criticize you
3 My sister and I had warned him
4 We'll buy some nice things
5 My parents (for example) take my younger
brother and me
6 I used to play with those
7 People are wearing lots of

8 My grandparents have given me quite
9 We might check out that
10 The shop assistant was helping me when

③ 1 don't you work for
2 had better not do
3 has made improvements to its
4 doesn't even let them
5 are moving us
6 are making changes to

USE OF ENGLISH: error correction

1 in	3 to	5 buy	7 ✔	9 been
2 ✔	4 being	6 ✔	8 ✔	10 have

READING

1 D	3 A	5 B	7 A	9 B	11 A
2 A	4 C	6 D	8 C	10 B	12 B

UNIT 11

VOCABULARY and SPEAKING

② 28°C: the summer temperature, 00–44: the telephone code, £1: the unit of currency, 1m 72cm: people's average height, 130kph: the speed limit, Jan 1st: a special day, 1492: a famous year, 2,874m: the highest mountain, 65kg: people's average weight, 9,965,000: the country's population, 91,945km^2: the country's area, 30%: percentage living in cities

one pound (Sterling) one hundred and thirty kilometres per hour, fourteen ninety-two, sixty-five kilo(gram)s, ninety-one thousand, nine hundred and forty-five square kilometres, oh oh four four/double oh double four, one metre seventy-two (centimetres), January the first/New Year's Day, two thousand eight hundred and seventy-four metres, nine million, nine hundred and sixty-five thousand, thirty per cent

④ 1 equals =, add/plus +, minus/subtract −, two-thirds $\frac{2}{3}$, five-eighths $\frac{5}{8}$, nought point two one 0.21, divided by ÷, a quarter $\frac{1}{4}$, times/multiplied by ×
2 2, 2, 16, 4.

GRAMMAR: impersonal reporting

① 2a 4b

② 1 It is expected that
2 It has been suggested that
3 It has been confirmed that
4 It used to be assumed that
5 It was felt that

③ 1 is known to be
2 is believed to have polluted
3 is said to be planning
4 is felt to have spoilt
5 are reliably reported to have

USE OF ENGLISH: key word transformations

1 a, b 2 b, c 3 b, c 4 a, c 5 a, b

READING

② 1 D 2 E 3 C 4 A 5 G 6 F
Not needed: B

UNIT 12

VOCABULARY and SPEAKING

① 1 forgetful   6 hot-blooded
2 pessimistic   7 indecisive
3 considerate   8 outgoing
4 self-conscious 9 spiteful
5 boastful   10 protective

④ (positive or negative in brackets after each):
not get on (neg), have a lot of respect (pos),
be fond (pos), not be sure (neg),
can't stand the sight (neg), look up (pos),
have a high opinion (pos), look down (neg),
be a bit scared (neg), think the world (pos),
feel sorry (neg?), have a lot in common (pos),
be fed up (neg), couldn't care less (neg), in love (pos)

I don't get on with X, I have a lot of respect for X, I'm fond of X, I'm not sure about X, I can't stand the sight of X, I look up to X, I have a high opinion of X, I look down on X, I'm a bit scared of X, I think the world of X, I feel sorry for X, I've got a lot in common with X, I'm fed up with X, I couldn't care less about X, I'm in love with X

GRAMMAR: short replies

① 1 I hope so   5 I expect so
2 I think so   6 I believe so
3 I'm afraid so   7 I guess so
4 I suppose so   8 I imagine so

USE OF ENGLISH: word formation

1 dependent, generosity
2 warmth, personality
3 jealousy, difficulties
4 unfairly, loyalty
5 impatience, arrangements
6 annoying, unselfishness
7 unintelligent, laziness
8 sensitive, shyness

UNIT 13

VOCABULARY

1 SUGGESTED ANSWERS:
dangerous (neg), demanding (neg or pos),
socially useful (pos), repetitive (neg),
worthwhile (pos), responsible (pos?), stressful (neg),
dead-end (neg), rewarding (pos), poorly paid (neg),
secure (pos), glamorous (pos)

2
1	wages	6	salary
2	royalties	7	commission
3	dole	8	pension
4	fees	9	interest
5	tip	10	bonus

Not needed: winnings

3 actor, farmer, jeweller, receptionist, gardener,
electrician, accountant, manager, surgeon, lawyer,
sailor, executive

4 1f 2a 3d 4d/e 5b 6c
floods – farmers; drought – farmers, gardeners;
forest fires – firefighters; poor visibility – sailors,
airline pilots, driving instructors; blocked roads –
driving instructors; burst water pipes – plumbers.

GRAMMAR: adjective position

1 1 E 2 A 3 D 4 B 5 C

2
1 ... from Norway.
2 ... made of stone.
3 ... from South America.
4 ... which were red and white.
5 ... with two speeds.
6 ... made of denim.
7 ... from the Atlantic.
8 ... (which was) in Spring.

3
1 A 20-page report
2 A one-pound coin.
3 A fourteen-year-old girl
4 A two-hour lesson
5 A 90-minute flight
6 A ten-minute break
7 A half-litre glass
8 A 2000-metre race
9 A 40-degree temperature
10 A 100-kilo sumo wrestler

4
1 My sister, who was awake, or My sister who
  was awake (depending on the number of
  sisters)
2 hundred dollar bills
3 which were 5000 metres high
4 a five-minute walk
5 five metres long
6 The boy, who was ashamed,
7 a five-part exam
8 six feet tall

USE OF ENGLISH: open cloze

1 so, out, which
2 enough, so, order
3 would, had, off
4 such, that, on
5 had, would, as
6 to, until/unless, anyone

PRONUNCIATION

1 The first example (falling intonation on tag)
shows that the speaker doesn't think it's raining.
1 wasn't it?   5 haven't they?
2 is it?   6 did they?
3 will we?   7 have you?
4 has it?   8 can you?

2
1 is he?   5 are they?
2 has he?   6 are we?
3 did she?   7 did he? (not had he?)
4 will she?   8 is he?

5-MINUTE ACTIVITIES

2
1 D Everybody needs to relax.
2 G Too many people working on something get
  in each other's way.
3 A Problems never come singly.
4 C Do not take things for granted too soon.
5 E It is better to do one thing thoroughly.
6 F Take advantage of good conditions while
  they last.
7 B Some people don't accept responsibility for
  their mistakes.

UNIT 14

VOCABULARY

1 (with homes in brackets): sheep/lambs, cows/
calves (shed), kittens/cats (basket), birds/chicks (nest),
horses/foals (stables), piglets/pigs (sty), puppies/dogs
(kennel), cubs/foxes (den)

2 bark- dog; roar – lion, tiger, etc.; howl – wolf,
dog, etc.; grunt – pig; growl – dog, bear, etc.;
hiss – snake; quack – duck; hoot – owl; snort – pig,
boar, etc.; buzz – bees, wasps, etc.; squeal – piglet;
bleat – sheep; croak – frog; squawk – large bird;
neigh – horse; snarl: dog, wolf, lion, etc.; purr – cat;
whine – dog.
People: mostly anger or aggression, but also pain
(howl, squeal), complaint (bleat, whine), laughter
(hoot), contempt (snort), illness (croak).

3 a swarm of insects, a herd of buffalo, a shoal of
fish, a pack of wolves, a flock of birds. Not needed:
lizards

4
1	cat, e	3	crocodile, h	5	birds, d	7	bee, c
2	duck, b	4	crow, a	6	bull, g	8	fish, f

Further Practice Key

GRAMMAR: question tags

①
1 modals
2 negative
3 affirmative
4 same
5 main
6 pronouns
7 suggestions
8 first

②
1 has it
2 don't they
3 shall we
4 should they
5 wouldn't you
6 did they
7 aren't I
8 are there
9 can they

③
1 aren't you
2 don't you
3 aren't you
4 isn't it
5 don't you
6 do you
7 weren't you
8 wouldn't you

USE OF ENGLISH: multiple-choice cloze

① B, A, D, B, C

② B, D, A, C, B

READING

① They can fly; they have wings; they have beaks; they have feathers; they have two legs.

Flightless birds include ostriches, emus, kiwis, rheas, penguins.
Bats, insects and flying fish can all fly. Flying lemurs, flying foxes and a type of African squirrel can glide for long distances.
The duck-billed platypus has a beak, so does an octopus.
Only birds have feathers.
Humans, apes and kangaroos usually walk on two legs.

② 1 G 2 B 3 F 4 D 5 C 6 E
Not needed: A

③
1 flap / beat
2 swooping
3 glides
4 perch
5 prey

UNIT 15

VOCABULARY and SPEAKING

① Staff: deputy head, caretaker, dinner lady, head
Places: playground, playing fields, canteen, gym
Events: assembly, half-term, speech day, sports day
Objects: blackboard, desk, register, text book

②
1 year
2 absent
3 note
4 truant
5 cheat
6 disqualify
7 suspend
8 expel
9 results
10 reports

Not needed: punish

GRAMMAR: causative verbs

②
1 Get your alarm clock fixed!
2 Get your hair cut!
3 Get your shoe repaired!
4 Get it dry cleaned!
5 Get it checked out!
6 Get everything delivered!

③ SUGGEST ANSWERS:
1 … they had their rent increased … .
2 … you'll get your hand burnt.
3 She had her appeal … turned down
4 She had her hair pulled … .
5 … many people had their property seized.
6 He had his driving licence taken away after …
7 … he had his hair cut really short.
8 Their team had a player sent off for fighting.
9 He would have had his sentence increased if …

USE OF ENGLISH: key word transformations

1 b, c   2 a, b   3 a, b   4 a, c   5 b, c   6 a, b

READING

② 1 C 2 A 3 A 4 B 5 D 6 C

Unit Test

UNIT 1

1 Write a single word or phrasal verb that means each of the following:

1 become a member of a club ....
2 healthy and not easily tired ....
3 hit by using the foot ....
4 ability to do something well ....
5 remove by drawing a line through ....
6 difficult, hard or violent ....
7 the only one of its kind ....
8 injure by stretching too much ....
9 hit with the fist (closed hand) ....
10 start doing a hobby or sport ....

2 Fill in the gaps in sentences 1–10 with one of these verbs in either the present simple or the present continuous:

see   get   lift   own   remind   go   leave   stay   close   tire

1 I think she .... better and better at this all the time.
2 They .... the gym once every year for maintenance work.
3 People who train at sea level .... very quickly at high altitude.
4 She's travelling on a scheduled flight which .... at 0830 tomorrow.
5 The weight he .... now is the equivalent of a small car.
6 The club .... the land but we're always playing there.
7 All of us .... to the swimming pool next Saturday.
8 This month I .... at my cousins' house in the country.
9 I'll feel much happier when I .... the finishing line.
10 She .... (always) .... me how much weight I've put on.

3 What do you associate with each of 1–10? Write one of these words next to each:

face   body   arms   hands   legs   feet

1 elbow ....   6 chest ....
2 toes ....   7 lips ....
3 chin ....   8 waist ....
4 thumb ....   9 calf ....
5 thigh ....   10 tummy ....

4 Fill in the gaps in sentences 1–10 with either *many* or *much*.

1 How .... rooms does that hotel have?
2 Have you still got .... work left to do?
3 We didn't have .... money when I was a child.
4 I didn't see .... people when I was out walking.
5 We won't need .... glasses if people aren't thirsty.
6 They didn't give us .... information when we rang.
7 How .... time have we got before the shop closes?
8 There isn't .... evidence that eating it is harmful.
9 They don't catch .... fish in the lake nowadays.
10 On Sundays there never seems to be .... news.

5 Choose one of the expressions in brackets to complete each of the sentences 1–10.

1 I'll do .... (a/some/a piece of) shopping after work.
2 Let me give you .... (an/little/a little) advice about this.
3 The vegetables are served with .... (a/a little/a few) butter.
4 The children catch .... (lots of/plenty of/a great deal of) colds every winter.
5 You need to learn .... (a large number of/a great deal of/large amounts of) words.
6 We've only been there .... (a little/little/a few) times before.
7 I managed to save .... (a/a bit of/an item of) cash during the summer.
8 Your father doesn't have .... (much/many/all) hair to comb these days.
9 For breakfast, I usually have a cup of coffee with .... (a/a piece of/a few) toast.
10 We've got very .... (few/little/small number of) homework to do this weekend.

Unit Test

UNIT 2

❶ Fill in the missing word by re-arranging the words in brackets.

1 A curve, for example in a road or a river, is often called a .... (debn).

2 A .... (tepes) hill is one that goes up or down sharply, not gradually.

3 People often use the word '................' (draces) instead of 'frightened'.

4 The word '................' (crakt) is used for railways, rough roads and running surfaces.

5 If you dive or jump into the sea or a swimming pool, you .... (glupen) into the water.

6 If someone .... (smilac) something, they say it is true although others may not believe them.

7 The appearance of a place, especially beautiful countryside, is called the .... (reynecs).

8 When you are .... (rovesun) about something, you are worried about what might happen.

9 An .... (temtivenns) is something a person buys, or pays into, to try and make a profit.

10 If you do something on purpose, you do it .... (lanylitintone).

❷ Put *a, an* or *the* in each of the gaps. Where no article is needed, leave it blank.

1 We spent the summer sailing round .... Aegean Sea.

2 He's .... honest man who always tells the truth.

3 It was the year when .... Argentina won the World Cup.

4 In the mountains, ... brown bear is quite common.

5 She's studying at university in .... United States.

6 This is a club for .... young: meaning those under 20.

7 She's .... doctor at the general hospital.

8 My brother learnt to play .... piano when he was six.

9 We're staying at .... home today.

10 We have English lessons five times .... week.

❸ Choose the word, A, B, C or D, which best completes the collocation.

1 She's got a summer job as a shop ....
   A helper   B assistant   C server   D waiter

2 That film is sure to .... a prize at the festival.
   A gain   B win   C beat   D score

3 The .... date of the band's new album is July 1.
   A release   B publication   C sale   D out

4 The book .... have all been very positive.
   A reviews   B criticisms   C notices
   D comments

5 The cinema .... loved this film.
   A audience   B spectators   C watchers
   D public

❹ Use the -ed or -ing form of five of these verbs to complete the sentences:

shock   confuse   bore   relax   exhaust

1 Politicians are so .... that every time I hear one speak I go to sleep.

2 We felt .... after a whole day spent walking around the huge adventure park.

3 It was such a .... scene that many people watching the film were afraid to look.

4 I spent a .... day lying on the couch doing nothing but watch TV – it was wonderful!

5 I ended up completely .... because the instructions for the video were not at all clear.

❺ Use one or two words to complete the phrasal verb in each of these sentences.

1 He got .... his bike and stared at the flat tyre.

2 How are you getting .... in your Spanish lessons?

3 She was very upset by what he said but now she's got .... it.

4 Nobody was arrested: the killers have got .... murder.

5 What page have you got .... in that book you're reading?

Unit Test

UNIT 3

1 Write the adjective formed from each of these nouns:

1 chemistry ....

2 science ....

3 physics ....

4 theory ....

5 industry ....

6 power ....

7 basis ....

8 medicine ....

2 Use the word given in capitals at the end of each sentence to form a word that fits in the space in the same sentence.

1 Some people strongly .... being told what to do by a machine. LIKE

2 Many old industries .... a long time ago, and won't return. APPEAR

3 New technology is vital if we want to have high .... growth. ECONOMY

4 The factory has made more goods in a shorter time for less money; in other words .... has risen a lot. PRODUCE

5 The firm is being very .... about the design of its new hardware. SECRET

6 It is becoming .... obvious that changes will have to take place. INCREASE

7 He was a little .... about how to use the complicated new software. SURE

8 It was never .... true that all the work was done by hand. WHOLE

9 He's so .... that sometimes he leaves everything switched on. FORGET

10 That sentence is completely .... ; it makes no sense at all. MEAN

3 Fill in the gaps with the correct form of *do* or *make*.

1 That insect won't .... you any harm.

2 He .... very few mistakes in last week's test.

3 I hope that next term you .... more homework.

4 It took her ages to .... that dress for herself.

5 The ending of that film .... us all cry.

6 They .... a good job when they mended it.

4 In each sentence, form a suitable word using the prefix given.

1 It's not her fault everything always goes wrong for her: she's just un............ .

2 His micro............ wasn't working so he had to shout to make himself heard.

3 On Sundays, I sometimes over............ and don't wake up till very late.

4 The level of the exam is neither elementary nor advanced; it's inter............ .

5 People were becoming im............ because of the long delay.

6 This country is an in............ nation with its own government.

7 If you under............ the cost you will find you don't have enough money.

8 Last year's champion expected to win again and was dis........... when he didn't.

9 That film is just a re............ of the Hitchcock original, and it's not as good.

10 Don't try to trans............ reading texts word for word into your language.

5 Use the correct future form of the verb in brackets to fill in the gaps.

1 That box looks awfully heavy; I .... (help) you carry it if you like.

2 The ferry to the island .... (depart) from Piraeus at noon tomorrow.

3 We .... (get) married at the beginning of September.

4 By the look of those clouds it .... (start) raining quite soon.

5 Have something to eat before you .... (go) out.

6 By this time next year I .... (leave) school and be at university.

7 I'm sure Mum .... (not notice) if we just take a few cakes.

8 While the big match is on I .... (work) hard on that maths exercise.

9 Please let me know as soon as you .... (have) any news.

10 They met at Christmas so soon they .... (go) out together for a whole year.

Unit Tests

Unit Test

UNIT 4

❶ In some of the sentences 1–10, the frequency adverb is in the wrong place. Tick (✔) the sentences which are right and correct those that are wrong.

1 My friends and I normally work together.

2 They go frequently to the same place.

3 You sometimes have to wait here for hours.

4 She often is at home at this time of day.

5 I study seldom after nine in the evening.

6 Always she is telling them not to make a noise.

7 Usually, people notice things like that.

8 We hardly ever do that kind of exercise.

9 There are occasionally some complaints.

10 I need to rarely mention it to her.

❷ Choose the modal verb which best fits each of the sentences 1–10.

1 You look tired; I think you *should/must/have to* have a rest.

2 You *must/need to/have to* stop that immediately or I shall get very angry with you.

3 It's the end of term so you *shouldn't/mustn't/don't have to* do any homework.

4 You *should/ought to/have to* have a licence to drive a car on the roads.

5 I've told you before – you *needn't/mustn't/don't have to* hit your little brother!

6 You *needn't/shouldn't/mustn't* write it all out again if you don't want to.

7 She really *should/must/has got to* take more care but she probably won't.

8 Today's Saturday, so I *oughtn't to/haven't got to/shouldn't* get up early.

9 It's a fantastic song – you *have to/must/need to* hear it as soon as you can!

10 I *shouldn't/mustn't/don't have to* be telling you this, but she fancies you a lot.

❸ Match the expressions in italics in 1–10 with one of the meanings in A–J.

1 I'll *give up* learning to play the piano if I don't improve soon.

2 We've got to go soon so it isn't *worth* starting a new game.

3 His reaction to losing the game was completely *over the top*.

4 You really should *cut down on* the amount you drink.

5 To see who's won, *add up* the value of your houses, hotels and cash.

6 He'll *pull out* of the card game if the bets go too high.

7 The bookshop is going to *branch out* into music and art.

8 The cover of a book can *put off* people who would otherwise read it.

9 We always *pick up* any litter we see in the countryside.

10 If you're too busy to give a pet exercise, *stick to* keeping goldfish.

A calculate the total of

B not change from

C extend interests or activities

D lift from a surface

E discourage

F likely to be a good idea

G exaggerated or excessive

H withdraw from

I stop attempting

J consume less or do less often

❹ Write the comparative and superlative forms of each of these words:

1 silly   ....

2 good   ....

3 bad   ....

4 far   ....

5 little   ....

❺ Complete the second sentence so that it means the same as the first sentence.

1 I can't play the guitar as well as he can.

   He is a .... me.

2 Haven't you got any cheaper tickets?

   Are those .... you've got?

3 You talk far more quickly than Julie.

   You don't talk .... Julie.

4 I've never been to a less exciting concert.

   It was .... I've ever been to.

5 I'd never been so busy before.

   I was .... I'd ever been before.

Unit Test

UNIT 5

❶ In which room are you most likely to find 1–10? Write one of these words next to each:

kitchen   bathroom   bedroom

1 mattress   ....
2 basin   ....
3 microwave   ....
4 dishes   ....
5 sheets   ....
6 linen   ....
7 freezer   ....
8 pillow   ....
9 alarm clock   ....
10 frying pan   ....

❷ Complete sentences 1–10 with the verb in brackets. Use each of these forms at least twice:

past simple   past continuous
used to + infinitive   *would* + infinitive

1 When we arrived at the flat early that morning, everyone .... (sleep).

2 Factory workers .... (live) in terrible conditions, but it's all changed now.

3 Her family were rich and .... (own) property in every part of the city.

4 I used to see him cycling to work every morning and he .... (wave) to me.

5 The land .... (belong) to him and he was always putting up fences.

6 When I was a child, I .... (think) that it would be fun to live in a tent.

7 I .... (watch) TV when suddenly there was a loud knock at the door.

8 We .... (choose) this flat to live in because it is on the ground floor.

9 Every day they began work at dawn and they .... (continue) until nightfall.

10 While you were chatting to the neighbours, I .... (wait) here for you.

❸ Match these verbs with meanings 1–4. There is one word you do not need to use.

swap   shrink   steal   stink   split

1 break into parts   ....
2 smell very bad   ....
3 exchange for something else ....
4 become smaller   ....

❹ Fill in the gaps in the text by using each of these linking expressions once only:

*even though   although   but   despite
however   though*

The first flat we went to see was in a good area, (1) .... it was too far from the nearest Underground station and (2) .... it wasn't expensive we decided it wouldn't suit us. The next one was handy for both buses and trains, and (3) .... its rather old-fashioned appearance it had big windows and inside there was plenty of light. (4) .... , it was on a very noisy street so we thought we would have a look at a few more places, (5) .... we know that we'll never find the perfect home. We can take our time making up our minds, (6) .... , because we don't have to leave the place we're in now until next month.

❺ For each of the meanings 1–10, write a noun or adjective beginning with the letter given.

1 A man who owns a flat and charges other people to live in it.   l..............
2 The money you pay every month to live in a flat.   r..............
3 A small house on its own, probably in the country.   c..............
4 The jobs you do around the home, like cleaning and washing.   h..............
5 A person who pays every month to live in someone else's flat.   t..............
6 A piece of paper that shows how much you must pay for a service.   b..............
7 A small house joined on both sides to other houses.   t..............
8 A person who shares an apartment with you.   f..............
9 A room that is used for both living in and sleeping in.   b..............
10 Any kind of room or building that people can live or stay in.   a..............

Unit Test

UNIT 6

❶ Match these words with 1–10 below. There is one word you do not need to use.

ripe mineral spicy crunchy olive cream bitter mashed salty scrambled french

1 .... lemon
2 .... oil
3 .... water
4 .... apples
5 .... potatoes

6 .... cakes
7 .... fries
8 .... fish
9 .... sweets
10 .... curry

❷ Complete the sentences with the correct form of the verb in brackets.

1 If you continue to work hard, there is little doubt that you .... (pass) the exam.

2 We'd go on holiday more often if we .... (earn) more money.

3 I .... (tell) you what she said if you promise to keep it a secret.

4 If he could improve his spelling, he .... (get) very good marks.

5 If I .... (be) her boyfriend, I would find out where she was last Friday.

6 I hope you .... (let) me know if there's anything you don't agree with.

7 What would you like to have with you if you .... (be) alone on a desert island?

8 If I .... (have) so much homework to do, I'd go out with my friends tonight.

9 There would be less traffic on the roads if everyone .... (work) at home.

10 If I had a small problem like that, I .... (waste) any more time on it.

❸ Put these in order, from the most to the least:

a teaspoonful a cupful a pinch a tablespoonful

❹ Fill each of the gaps with one of these words. There is one word you do not need to use.

bowl loaf stick bar slice

1 A .... of bread
2 A .... of chocolate
3 A .... of soup
4 A .... of pizza

❺ For each of the sentences 1–10, write a conditional sentence using the expression in capitals.

1 This meal can burn if you don't watch the temperature very carefully.   UNLESS
....

2 You've still got a chance, but only if you are more careful in future.   PROVIDED
....

3 Unless we take action now, the countryside will completely disappear.   IF
....

4 You can add vegetables to this dish, but they must be fresh.   AS LONG AS
....

5 Nobody will go to the concert unless they reduce the price of the tickets.   IF
....

6 We won't win this game if we don't start playing as a team.   UNLESS
....

7 Some animals can survive in the desert, but they have to stay underground.   AS LONG AS
....

8 They can go to the park, but only if their elder sister is with them.   PROVIDING
....

9 Don't put up you hand unless your name's not on the list.   IF
....

10 Eating good, tasty food is fine, but don't overdo it!   AS LONG AS
....

❻ Complete this text by using these verbs once each. There is one word you do not need to use.

fry leave pour serve mix warm spread add remove melt grate beat overheat

First, break a couple of eggs into a bowl and (1) .... them well. Next, (2) .... some cheese as finely as possible and (3) .... it to the eggs. Then place a couple of tablespoons of good quality oil in a large pan and (4) .... gently. Alternatively, (5) .... a little butter in the pan – but in either case do not (6) .... as this would spoil the flavour. Meanwhile, (7) .... the eggs and the cheese together, perhaps with a little salt and pepper. When the temperature is right, (8) .... the mixture into the pan and (9) .... to cook for a minute or two. You may want to turn it over and briefly (10) .... the other side, without browning, before you (11) .... it from the heat. Finally, (12) .... it with a little parsley on top.

Unit Test

UNIT 7

1 Form a compound noun or adjective (one word or two, with or without a hyphen) by adding one of these words to each of 1–15. There is one word you do not need to use.

cup	*clock*	*skates*	*point*
race	*games*	*holder*	*centre*
handed	*known*	*friend*	*mate*
attack	*paste*	*ticket*	*board*

1 tea ....
2 bus ....
3 well ....
4 class ....
5 surf ....
6 tooth ....
7 right ....
8 heart ....
9 ice ....
10 alarm ....
11 pen ....
12 boiling ....
13 record ....
14 leisure ....
15 video ....

2 Use relative clauses to rewrite these pairs of sentences as one sentence.

1 Here's the album. You said you wanted to listen to it.

....

2 The girl over there is the one. I was telling you about her.

....

3 This dish comes from Brazil. It's very tasty.

....

4 His motorbike goes even faster than mine. It's a Kawasaki.

....

5 That's the woman. Her husband is in prison.

....

6 Ms Jones is my son's teacher. I spoke to her earlier.

....

7 That's the house. We used to live there.

....

8 My friend Sophia is a very good cook. She loves trying new things.

....

9 It was in 1998. We met for the first time.

....

10 Juan spends every summer near Liverpool. He speaks English very well.

....

3 Write the name of an Olympic sport by forming a compound word using each of 1–8.

1 volley ....
2 ice ....
3 long ....
4 table ....
5 water ....
6 weight ....
7 wind ....
8 pole ....

4 Correct the punctuation errors in these sentences and write the name of the missing punctuation mark(s) at the end of the line.

1 She was always the peoples favourite runner.   ....

2 Can you tell me the way to the sports centre.   ....

3 The youngest student's date of birth is 3586.   ....

4 He said I didn't mean it after he hurt the other player.   ....

5 We don't know who France or Spain is going to win.   ....

5 Write an expression using *in* that means the same as each of 1–6.

1 crying   ....
2 finally   ....
3 especially   ....
4 at risk   ....
5 actually   ....
6 not publicly   ....

6 Choose the right word to complete each of these sentences.

1 I'm sure they .... (*may/can*) play better in the second half.

2 They're losing at the moment but they .... (*can/could*) score later.

3 I think we .... (*can/might*) be in the wrong place altogether.

4 It's only nine o'clock so it .... (*mightn't/can't*) be time to go already!

5 If we leave it any later, we .... (*mightn't/couldn't*) get there before the kick-off.

6 We .... (*can/might*) be looking at the next world champion at this very moment.

Unit Tests

Unit Test

UNIT 8

❶ Complete sentences 1–10 with one of these expressions. There is one you do not need to use.

full-length	subscription
satellite dish	sitcom
soap	update
commercial break	spin-off
foreign correspondent	documentary
broadcast	

1 Following the success of her programmes, she is now making a .... film.

2 The interview with her will be .... to the nation after the nine o'clock news.

3 His experience as a reporter includes working as a .... in 20 countries.

4 Some people who watch that .... every day believe the characters actually exist.

5 He now has his own show; it's a .... from that popular US comedy.

6 If you've got a .... on the roof you can pick up lots more TV channels.

7 The BBC's .... about hunger showed people the reality of life in East Africa.

8 It's a typical .... ; the same characters trying to be funny in the same place every week.

9 With a .... every ten minutes, you spend more time watching the ads than the show.

10 The regular bulletins .... the news every hour and half-hour.

❷ Some of these sentences contain a mistake. Tick those which are right and correct the mistakes.

1 She was at home all this week.

2 I've spoken to him just a minute ago.

3 It's happened twice since January.

4 Hi – have you waited for me long?

5 I've been there once in the last ten years.

6 I never met anyone like her before.

7 Recently he's been working very hard.

8 Have you ever gone to Buenos Aires?

9 I've come here to give this back to you.

10 We've lived here before we moved abroad.

❸ For each of the meanings 1–10, write a word or words beginning with the letter(s) given.

1 The people watching a play in the theatre or a film in a cinema: a...................

2 The place where paintings and drawings are shown to the public: a................... g...................

3 A brilliant example of something, particularly in art, literature or music: m...................

4 A painting, photograph or drawing of a person, often just their face: p...................

5 The sound made by people when they clap at the end of a performance: a...................

6 A collection of pictures or other art forms which people can come to see: e...................

7 The raised platform on which actors in the theatre perform: s...................

8 A drawing that is done quickly, without very much detail: s...................

9 The art of making figures out of solid materials like stone or wood: s...................

10 The different forms of a colour, such as light blue and dark blue: s...................

❹ Complete this dialogue as in the example (0).

Jayne: Hi Liam, I/not see/you for ages.
　　　　(0) *Hi Liam, I haven't seen you for ages.*

Liam: I know, I/be/in South America since November.
　　　　(1) ....

Jayne: You/be/back long?
　　　　(2) ....

Liam: No, I/just come/back. On Tuesday, in fact.
　　　　(3) ....

Jayne: You/get used to/the weather here again yet?
　　　　(4) ....

Liam: No, I/wear/two sweaters ever since I arrived!
　　　　(5) ....

Jayne: So who/see/since you got back?
　　　　(6) ....

Liam: Well, so far I/not have/time to contact anyone.
　　　　(7) ....

Jayne: But you/not stay/with friends for the last couple of days?
　　　　(8) ....

Liam: No, since Tuesday I/live/at home with my family.
　　　　(9) ....

Jayne: Oh, I bet you/already start/taking it easy again!
　　　　(10) ....

① What is the word for someone who:

1 steals another person's property? ....

2 steals things from shops? ....

3 steals money from a bank? ....

4 breaks into a house to steal things? ....

5 kills someone on purpose? ....

6 brings things into the country illegally? ....

7 enjoys damaging public property? ....

8 demands money for the safe release of a person? ....

9 gets money by threatening to reveal secrets about someone? ....

10 uses violent means, such as bombing, for political purposes? ....

② Use the past simple or past perfect form of the verb in brackets to complete 1–8.

1 First he went to the booking office and bought a ticket. Then he .... (get on) the train.

2 When she arrived at the bus stop there was no-one there. The bus .... (go) already.

3 Just after he came out of the stadium he reached for his wallet. It .... (disappear).

4 The jury decided he was guilty of the crime. The judge .... (send) him to prison for it.

5 He got off his bike after crossing the mountains. It .... (take) him two days.

6 After the accident he got out of the car. He .... (break) one of the lights.

7 I suddenly remembered that I'd been there before. The memories .... (be) very pleasant.

8 She quickly opened the envelope from the examination board. She .... (pass)!

③ Complete 1–6 with the past simple or the past perfect continuous forms of the verbs in brackets.

1 We .... (be) extremely tired when we got there because we .... (travel) all day.

2 When we .... (get up) in the morning we realised it .... (snow) all night.

3 As soon as the witness .... (give) evidence it was clear that they .... (not tell) the truth.

4 We .... (wait) in the plane for ages when at last it .... (take off).

5 It .... (be) clear from the figures that someone .... (steal) for many years.

6 A man .... (ask) me how long I .... (stand) there in the queue.

④ Use each of these expressions once only to complete 1–10. There is one you do not need to use.

*first class   emergency exit   terminal   cabin staff
cut-price   luggage labels   hold-up   check-in
boarding card   baggage reclaim   hand luggage*

1 A big airport often has one .... for domestic flights and another for international flights.

2 When you get there, first go to the .... desk of the airline you're flying with.

3 If you have no cases, only .... , you can then got straight to Departures.

4 Otherwise, they will weigh your cases and bags and put .... on them.

5 You'll need to show your .... before you can actually get on the plane.

6 If you're flying on a .... ticket, there'll probably be no food, just a cup of coffee.

7 There is more space next to the .... , which is only used if people have to get out quickly.

8 People travelling .... are given hot meals and maybe a glass of champagne.

9 However you're travelling, though, the .... are usually friendly and helpful.

10 If there is any kind of .... , they will explain the reasons for the delay.

⑤ Complete the sentences with these expressions. There is one you do not need to use.

*afterwards   until   hardly   by the time   than
once*

1 We went for a boat ride round the lake and .... we had a lovely meal.

2 The gang had escaped .... the police arrived on the scene.

3 We decided to walk home .... we realised the last bus had gone.

4 We'd .... started our journey when the car broke down.

5 They had no sooner walked into the bank .... the alarm went off.

Unit Test

❶ Match each of 1–10 with one of these words:

material   size   colours

1 leather   ....
2 tiny   ....
3 fur   ....
4 faded   ....
5 tight   ....
6 woollen   ....
7 striped   ....
8 loose   ....
9 denim   ....
10 patterned   ....

❷ Fill in the gaps with the *–ing* form of a suitable verb.

1 I find that .... exercise helps me eat and sleep better.

2 When I had finished .... in the form, I handed it in.

3 I love .... for a swim when there's no-one else in the pool.

4 Going shopping is one of the most .... things you can do.

5 He denied .... the bank but he was arrested anyway.

6 There's no point in .... all those clothes if you never wear them.

7 I really hate .... to wear my elder sister's old clothes.

8 It's not worth .... money on poor-quality goods like those.

9 There's the travel agency: how about .... a holiday right now?

10 Can you imagine .... the lottery and having all that cash to spend?

❸ Use each of these verbs once only to complete sentences 1–3. There is one word you do not need to use.

fit   match   clash   suit

1 Those shoes don't .... you; they're too small and will damage your feet.

2 I'm afraid her red hair and that bright pink blouse really .... quite horribly.

3 She was carrying a dark blue handbag to .... her blue dress.

❹ Finish these sentences so that the second one means the same as the first.

1 In that shop they always cut the cloth very carefully.
The cloth ....

2 She is shortening the dress for you right now.
The dress ....

3 The tailor measured my father for a new suit.
My father ....

4 We will sell all those new dresses by the weekend.
All those ....

5 They used to sew every button on by hand.
Every button ....

6 I think somebody's already told me that story.
I think I ....

7 Customers may try on clothes before purchasing.
Clothes ....

8 They're going to change the law on shopping hours.
The law ....

9 The assistant was serving me when the bell rang.
I ....

10 They had often talked of building a superstore there.
Building ....

❺ Where would you get, or find, each of 1–10? Use each of the following places once. There is one place you do not need to use.

*library   casualty   department store
solicitor's office   leisure centre   chemist's
bank   post office   travel agent's   supermarket
bookshop*

1 stamps   ....
2 a chequebook   ....
3 legal advice   ....
4 books for sale   ....
5 a trolley   ....
6 the winter sales   ....
7 an indoor pool   ....
8 books to borrow   ....
9 urgent medical assistance   ....
10 prescribed medicines   ....

Unit Test

UNIT 11

1 Complete these sentences using a suitable form of the verb in brackets:

1 We agreed .... (meet) at nine o'clock the next evening.

2 I want them .... (clean up) this mess immediately.

3 I can't stand .... (wait) to be served.

4 I reminded my little brother not .... (go) too close to the edge.

5 They won't let people .... (swim) when there's a red flag flying.

6 Would you mind .... (open) the door for me, please.

7 I remember .... (visit) that village when I was very young.

8 We were lost, so we stopped .... (ask) a policewoman for directions.

9 I meant .... (tell) you we were going away, but I completely forgot.

10 He tried .... (climb) to the top of the mountain, but it was impossible.

2 Rewrite sentences 1–10 in reported speech, using the verb in brackets.

1 'You'd better not spend any more time in the sun, Kate,' said Annie. (advised)

....

2 'Do you have another key?' they said to the woman at reception. (asked)

....

3 'Yes, I broke the mirror in the bathroom,' he said. (admitted)

....

4 'I'll never come back here again,' said the angry tourist. (swore)

....

5 'Don't go into the water on your own,' she said to her children. (told)

....

6 'Which flight are you taking, sir?' the policeman wanted to know. (asked)

....

7 'You ruined our entire holiday,' said Amanda to her boyfriend. (accused)

....

8 'I've had enough of this heat,' she said to her husband. (complained)

....

9 'I'm going home if the weather doesn't improve,' George said. (threatened)

....

10 'Will I ever see her again?' thought the boy. (wondered)

3 Complete sentences 1–15 by using each of the following nouns once only. There is one word you do not need to use.

tourists waves stream coast brochure peaks waterfall shore journey resorts voyage beach souvenirs trip tide undergrowth

1 Buy your .... and other things to take home with you at local shops.

2 The Mediterranean town of Benidorm is one of the biggest holiday .... in Spain.

3 Let's do a quick .... to the shops before they close for lunch.

4 The exhausting .... across the desert took them nearly two weeks.

5 When the .... goes out, you have to walk miles across the sand to reach the sea.

6 As everyone knows, the first and last .... of the Titanic ended in disaster.

7 In summer they rent a flat on the .... , which is much cooler than inland areas.

8 The .... that the travel agency gave us didn't show this factory next to the hotel.

9 The little .... in the hills becomes a deep, wide river as it flows towards the sea.

10 We had to carry our boat round the 10-metre .... and then continue down the river.

11 The animals don't climb the tall trees of the rain forest; they're in the .... down below.

12 We spent nearly all our time on the .... , lying on that lovely soft sand.

13 The huge Atlantic .... were breaking over the small boat, filling it with icy water.

14 At over 3000 metres, the .... of those mountains are covered in snow, even in summer.

15 Walking along the rocky .... , we found a bottle – with a message in it!

Unit Test

UNIT 12

1 For each of adjectives 1–10, choose the opposite from this list. There is one you do not need to use.

generous   stupid   relaxed   interesting
unfriendly   adventurous   bad-tempered
miserable   rough   self-confident   energetic

1 intelligent ....
2 warm ....
3 shy ....
4 nervous ....
5 gentle ....
6 cheerful ....
7 boring ....
8 selfish ....
9 lazy ....
10 easy-going ....

2 Complete these sentences with a suitable form of the verb in brackets:

1 I enjoy myself more if I .... (be) with my friends.

2 I would have gone out with him if he .... (ask) me.

3 If water .... (freeze), it expands.

4 If I had spent less money last year, I .... (save) enough to buy it.

5 Don't tell anyone if I .... (let) you into the secret.

6 She .... (buy) that dress if she'd known it was such poor quality.

7 You can only work properly if you .... (get) enough sleep.

8 If we .... (speak) about this earlier we wouldn't be arguing now.

9 Nobody would've minded if you .... (leave) early yesterday.

10 I .... (lie) on a tropical beach right now if I'd married him.

3 What are the adjectives for these people?

1 A person who belongs to the same family. ....

2 An adult who is not married. ....

3 A person who has promised to marry someone. ....

4 A woman whose husband has died. ....

5 Married people who no longer live together. ....

6 A person who has ended his or her marriage. ....

4 Give short replies (*So do I/I don't*) to these comments:

1 I'm feeling a bit hungry.

....

2 I'd like to have a holiday.

....

3 I haven't got enough money.

....

4 I love eating chocolate.

....

5 I won't be here on Sunday.

....

6 I can't speak Welsh.

....

7 I haven't watched TV today.

....

8 I did all my homework last week.

....

9 I'm going to take FCE in June.

....

10 I must read more in English.

....

11 I don't have to leave yet.

....

12 I hadn't studied this structure before.

....

5 What nouns do we use for these people?

1 Your mother's father. ....
2 Your brother's daughter. ....
3 Your sister's son. ....
4 Your uncle's child. ....
5 Your sister's husband. ....
6 Your brother's wife. ....
7 Your mother's sister. ....
8 Your brother: born some years before you. ....
9 Your sister: born at exactly the same time as you. ....
10 Your husband or wife's mother. ....
11 Your mother's husband by a later marriage. ....
12 Your father's father's father. ....

Unit Test

UNIT 13

❶ Choose the correct collocation.

1 .... rain (heavy/hard/strong)

2 .... skies (light/thin/clear)

3 .... snow (deep/low/strong)

4 .... sunshine (light/bright/clear)

5 .... clouds (dark/hard/strong)

6 .... ice (thick/deep/low)

7 .... showers (occasional/continuous/hard)

8 .... wind (thick/strong/heavy)

9 .... temperatures (mild/light/thin)

10 .... fog (thick/deep/heavy)

11 .... thunder (hard/loud/strong)

12 .... breeze (thin/bright/gentle)

❷ Use *so, such, such a* or *such an* to complete these sentences:

1 My hands were .... cold that I couldn't feel my fingers.

2 There is .... low cloud that no planes can take off.

3 She's got .... little time to do so many jobs.

4 The trees were hit by .... huge hailstones that the fruit was damaged.

5 There was .... awful storm last night that two windows were broken.

6 I'm driving .... slowly because there's ice on the road.

7 There are .... many people who want the job that it isn't worth applying.

8 It's .... cold day that I think I'll stay in bed all morning.

9 We had .... good weather last year that we're going there again.

10 He works .... quickly that he gets the job done in half the time.

❸ Complete 1–12 with one word each. Use these adjectives as many times as you like:

cold   hot   windy   wet   dry

1 In a heatwave, the weather is unusually ....

2 When it drizzles, the weather is rather ....

3 If you are soaked, you are uncomfortably ....

4 You shiver when you are feeling very ....

5 When clothes are damp, they are slightly ....

6 In a hurricane, the weather is extremely ....

7 Frostbite occurs when the weather is very . ...

8 There are often many gusts when it is ....

9 If it is chilly, you will probably feel a bit ....

10 Some metals can melt when they are very ....

11 Floods follow a period of weather that is very ....

12 A drought follows a long period of weather that is very ....

❹ For each of 1–6, put the adjective in brackets in the correct position.

1 a dramatic Arctic sunset (red)

    ....

2 some lovely hot soup (vegetable) ....

    ....

3 an ancient Inca temple (stone)

    ....

4 my leather walking boots (strong)

    ....

5 a warm Caribbean evening (delightful)

    ....

6 an amazing Himalayan mountain (8000-metre)

    ....

❺ What do we call someone who:

1 has just left school? A s............... l...............

2 writes articles for a newspaper? A j...............

3 plays the music in a disco? A d............... j...............

4 serves customers in a shop? A s............ a...............

5 serves drinks in a pub? A b............... *or* b...............

6 teaches people how to ski? A s............. i...............

7 carries out operations on patients? A s...............

8 helps take care of patients? A n...............

9 gives verbal translations? An i...............

10 applies for a job? A c...............

UNIT 14

① Complete 1–12 by using each of the following once only.

forest fires   oil slicks   conservation   rain forests ozone layer   exhaust fumes   global warming carbon monoxide

1 If .... occurs on this scale, the ice caps will melt and the sea level will rise dangerously.

2 Protecting the environment, and the living things in it, is often called ....

3 Much of the pollution in cities is caused by the .... from cars, lorries and buses.

4 One of the most dangerous gases given off by road vehicles is called ....

5 Following the dry weather, huge .... burnt down millions of hectares of trees.

6 Aerosol use has partly destroyed the .... , which protects us from the sun.

7 The .... of the tropics, with their huge variety of plant and animal life, are in danger.

8 If the tanker sinks near the coast, ... will kill birds and fish, and damage beaches.

② Use the modal verb in brackets to rewrite sentences 1–10.

1 I'm sure I told you about this last year. (must)

....

2 It's possible that they didn't tell him. (might)

....

3 Unfortunately, he didn't make a note of the number. (should)

....

4 Nobody answered the phone so I'm certain they weren't in. (can)

....

5 She probably felt very happy when she received the news. (must)

....

6 It was silly of him to tell all his friends about it. (should)

....

7 There's a chance that he's gone away. (may)

....

8 Maybe he didn't get the letter I sent him. (might)

....

9 I bet he wasn't very pleased when his ex-girlfriend turned up. (can)

....

10 I didn't take the exam in December although it was possible for me to do so. (could)

....

③ Write the names of the following creatures:

1 A flying insect which makes honey.   ....

2 A mammal like a big dog, that may attack sheep.   ....

3 A reptile with a shell, that walks very slowly.   ....

4 A flying insect that bites people in summer.   ....

5 A large reptile that likes water and has lots of teeth.   ....

6 A big mammal that is well adapted to deserts.   ....

7 A big fish that, in films at least, attacks people.   ....

8 The world's biggest mammal, which lives in the sea.   ....

④ Match 1–6 with the following sentences. There is one sentence you do not need to use.

But he did.   But I do.   But he didn't.   But he hasn't.   But I don't.   But he won't.   But I'm not.

1 I wish I lived nearer my friends. ....

2 I wish I didn't have to get up early. ....

3 I wish I were a famous singer. ....

4 I wish he'd spoken to me. ....

5 I wish he hadn't said anything. ....

6 I wish he would tell me the truth. ....

⑤ Match these words with 1–6 below. There is one word you do not need to use.

sting   claws   horns   fins   hump   beak   paws

1 bull   ....

2 goldfish   ....

3 wasp   ....

4 pigeon   ....

5 crab   ....

6 rabbit   ....

Unit Test

UNIT 15

❶ Put the following in order of age, from the youngest to the oldest:

*undergraduates   juniors   sixth-form students
infants   nursery children   postgraduates
secondary school pupils*

....

....

❷ Complete the sentences by choosing from the following expressions:

*to   in order to   so as to   in order not to
so as not to   so   so that   in order that   in case*

1 I want to go to university .... I can get a better job.

2 I'll take some of my notes with me .... I get a few moments to study.

3 I always write down new words in context .... forget how to use them.

4 I sometimes talk to my friends in English .... practise for the exam.

5 I went to the library on Tuesday .... borrow that book I told you about.

6 Let's phone the airport .... the flight is delayed.

7 I'm going to buy my ticket now .... waste time in the morning.

8 I left a message for her .... she'll know where we've all gone.

9 It's late, so we'd better turn down the music .... disturb the neighbours.

10 He checked his list again, ... he'd forgotten to get anything.

❸ Write these abbreviations in full:

1 e.g. ....   6 No. ....
2 i.e. ....   7 max. ....
3 NB ....   8 esp. ....
4 PS ....   9 approx. ....
5 etc. ....   10 min. ....

❹ Finish the second sentence so that it means the same as the first sentence.

1 My dress needs to be cleaned before the party.

   I must ....

2 They're going to paint the house for us at the weekend.

   We're going ....

3 He hasn't been to the barber's for over a year.

   He hasn't had ....

4 When we were on holiday, somebody cooked all our meals for us.

   When we were on holiday, we ....

5 Your parents have to sign these documents for you.

   You have to ....

6 It was an important parcel, so I paid a courier to deliver it.

   It was an important parcel, so I had ....

7 Somebody did the garden for us while we were away.

   We ....

8 The manager should tell his staff to throw him out of the club.

   The manager should have ....

9 I paid someone to frame that lovely picture.

   I had ....

10 It's wonderful when someone else cleans your room for you.

   It's wonderful having ....

11 That old keyboard is not worth repairing.

   It is pointless to ....

❺ Complete the following sentences:

1 You should write your name, Centre Number and C.................. N.................. at the top.

2 There may, for example, be three b.................. p.................. and nine printed ones.

3 When the exam has started, you can t.................. o.................. the pages whenever you want.

4 For papers 1, 3 and 4 you must mark your answers on the separate a.................. s.................. .

5 In all three of these papers, use a s.................. p.................. to write your answers.

6 If you make a mistake, use a soft clean e.................. to rub it out.

7 In Paper 2 (Writing) you must write on the q.................. p.................. in ink.

8 When you go into the exam room, you give your m.................. s.................. to the Assessor.

9 Assuming you have passed, your c.................. can be collected some time after that.

1 Multiple choice cloze

For Questions **1–15**, read the text below and decide which word **A**, **B**, **C** or **D** best fits each space. There is an example at the beginning (**0**).

Example:

0	**A**	close	**B**	united	**C**	joined	**(D)**	together

EXAM ADVICE

In Part Three of FCE Speaking you work (**0**) .... with a partner. You have to do a (**1**) .... task which usually (**2**) .... about 3 minutes. One possible task is 'problem (**3**) ....', which means you have to look at some (**4**) .... information and then (**5**) .... the problem with your partner. You may be shown photos, drawings, diagrams, maps, plans, advertisements or computer graphics and it is (**6**) .... that you study them carefully. If necessary, check you know exactly what to do by (**7**) .... asking the examiner to (**8**) .... the instructions or make them clearer.

While you are doing the task, the examiner will probably say very (**9**) .... and you should ask your partner questions and make (**10**) .... if he or she is not saying much. If either of you have any real difficulties the examiner may decide to step in and (**11**) .... Normally, however, you will find plenty to say, which helps the (**12**) .... to give you a fair mark. This mark depends on your success in doing the task by (**13**) .... with your partner, which includes taking (**14**) .... in giving opinions and replying appropriately, although in the end it may be possible to 'agree to (**15**) ....'.

1	**A**	single	**B**	lonely	**C**	unique	**D**	once
2	**A**	exists	**B**	lasts	**C**	stays	**D**	maintains
3	**A**	solving	**B**	working	**C**	making	**D**	finding
4	**A**	optical	**B**	obvious	**C**	noticeable	**D**	visual
5	**A**	argue	**B**	discuss	**C**	talk	**D**	have
6	**A**	essential	**B**	needed	**C**	helpful	**D**	successful
7	**A**	formally	**B**	officially	**C**	politely	**D**	sincerely
8	**A**	insist	**B**	copy	**C**	tell	**D**	repeat
9	**A**	little	**B**	much	**C**	few	**D**	many
10	**A**	ideas	**B**	statements	**C**	speeches	**D**	suggestions
11	**A**	complain	**B**	help	**C**	suggest	**D**	fail
12	**A**	judge	**B**	referee	**C**	assessor	**D**	observer
13	**A**	competing	**B**	struggling	**C**	opposing	**D**	co-operating
14	**A**	changes	**B**	sides	**C**	turns	**D**	sentences
15	**A**	contrast	**B**	disagree	**C**	argue	**D**	object

2 Open cloze

For Questions **16–30**, read the text below and think of the word which best fits each space. Use only **one** word in each space. There is an example at the beginning (**0**).

Example: | **0** | *at* |

FLU AND HOW NOT TO CATCH IT

This winter, in offices and workplaces throughout the country, people are (**0**) .... risk of becoming a health danger to (**16**) .... colleagues. These are the people (**17**) .... , carrying flu but noble to the end, have dragged (**18**) .... into work in spite of the high temperature, headache, sore throat and coughs that they (**19**) .... suffering from. Most experts agree that people with flu (**20**) .... to stay at home, certainly in the case of those (**21**) .... jobs involve public safety – airline pilots, air traffic controllers or train drivers.

A diet rich in vegetables and fruit, good general health and regular exercise may help avoid (**22**) .... illness. Experts are doubtful whether taking lots of vitamin C will (**23**) .... any difference, but reducing stress levels may help. Basic hygiene is certainly important, though, especially in the office. We know that the illness (**24**) .... be passed on from cups and saucers, so do (**25**) .... than simply rinse them under the tap with all the others. Wash them properly (**26**) .... hot water and use disinfectant to clean surfaces. Remember (**27**) .... wash your hands regularly and don't touch your face, (**28**) .... flu enters the body through the eyes, nose or mouth. Other tips on prevention include (**29**) .... rid of cloth handkerchiefs, which provide a home for germs. Change to paper tissues and throw them (**30**) .... afterwards.

3 Key word transformations

For Questions **31–40**, complete the second sentence so that it has a similar meaning to the first sentence, using the word given. **Do not change the word given.** You must use between two and five words, including the word given.

Here is an example:

Example: We have no definite plans to go away.

are

We .*are not definitely planning*. to go away.

---

31   Keyboards like that are too small to use.
     big
     Keyboards like that .... to use.

32   I've never seen such good graphics.
     ever
     These graphics are .... seen.

33   I'll speak to them during our stay here.
     staying
     I'll speak to them .... here.

34   There will be too much data on that disk.
     space
     There .... on that disk.

35 I'm sorry but this game isn't much fun.

enjoying

I'm sorry but .... this game much.

36 Nobody in the team plays as skilfully as she does.

player

She is .... in the team.

37 There is a slow improvement in his condition, say the doctors.

getting

He .... , say the doctors.

38 You shouldn't go to so much trouble.

need

There is .... go to so much trouble.

39 He didn't run fast enough, did he?

too

He .... he?

40 I was less impressed by their performance than I'd hoped.

not

Their performance was .... I'd hoped.

---

4 Word formation

For Questions **41–50**, read the text below. Use the word given in capitals at the end of each line to form a word that fits in the space in the same line. There is an example at the beginning (**0**).

Example: | **0** | *organization* |

STOP THE MUSIC

For six years, an (**0**) .... called Pipedown has been fighting against the   ORGANIZE

music played to us in public places. It has 4000 members (**41**) .... ,   WORLD

including conductors and (**42**) .... , authors and actors. To avoid   VIOLIN

giving the (**43**) .... of being snobbish, the founder, Nigel Rogers,   IMPRESS

points out that the (**44**) .... of Pipedown also includes jazz players,   MEMBER

rock (**45**) .... and folk singers. Their aim, he says, is to get rid of   MUSIC

the recorded music we are forced to listen to, (**46**) .... kind it is,   WHAT

in places like lifts and shops. He suggests people should (**47**) .... to   THREAT

do their shopping (**48**) .... , and that bank customers should inform   ELSE

the manager of their (**49**) .... to withdraw their money if they continue   INTEND

to be subjected, without their (**50**) .... , to that awful canned muzak.   PERMIT

Writing

Write an answer to **one** of the Questions **1–3** in this part. Write your answer in **120–80** words in an appropriate style.

1   Your college magazine is asking readers to write about films they have seen. Write an article describing a film that you have enjoyed watching and explaining why you think other readers would like it.

Write your **article**.

2   The class has been discussing the new technology used in language learning and your teacher has asked you to write a composition, giving your views on this statement:

The changes currently taking place in technology will make it much easier for people to learn languages.

Write your **composition**.

3   Read this extract from a letter you have received from an English-speaking friend:

> The last time we spoke, you said you were expecting to be given quite a bit of money and that you were going to spend it on some records you had always wanted to buy. Which did you get, and why? Please write and tell me all about them.

Write your **letter**, answering your friend's questions and giving details. Do not write any addresses.

Progress Test Two

UNITS 1-8

1 Multiple choice cloze

For Questions **1–15**, read this text and decide which word **A**, **B**, **C** or **D** best fits each gap. There is an example at the beginning (**0**).

Example:

0	**A**	good	**B**	ideal	**C**	model	**D**	suitable

(B ideal is circled)

BREAKFAST CEREAL AND THE BRAIN

The (**0**) .... breakfast, say scientists, is a glass of orange juice, a cup of coffee and a (**1**) .... of cereal. People who start the day (**2**) .... a drink of vitamin C, a dose of caffeine and a (**3**) .... of their favourite cereal are happier and perform better (**4**) .... the morning, Andy Smith, of the University of Bristol, said.

A (**5**) .... of 600 people who were asked to record their breakfast (**6**) .... found that those who regularly ate cereal first (**7**) .... in the morning had a more positive mood compared with those who ate other foods or had (**8**) .... breakfast.

Earlier research had shown that people whose (**9**) .... performance was measured (**10**) .... after eating breakfast of any kind performed 10 per cent better on (**11**) .... of remembering, speed of response and (**12**) .... to concentrate, compared with those given only a cup of decaffeinated coffee.

In (**13**) .... research, Professor Smith said that people who drank four cups of coffee a day performed more (**14**) .... all day than those who drank less. He suggested that sensible employers should (**15**) .... out free coffee or tea.

1	**A**	bowl	**B**	pan	**C**	saucer	**D**	pot
2	**A**	by	**B**	together	**C**	for	**D**	with
3	**A**	amount	**B**	helping	**C**	quantity	**D**	piece
4	**A**	throughout	**B**	while	**C**	along	**D**	when
5	**A**	search	**B**	study	**C**	research	**D**	check
6	**A**	habits	**B**	ways	**C**	traditions	**D**	uses
7	**A**	hour	**B**	time	**C**	point	**D**	thing
8	**A**	none	**B**	no	**C**	not	**D**	nothing
9	**A**	mental	**B**	sensible	**C**	intelligent	**D**	psychological
10	**A**	later	**B**	following	**C**	suddenly	**D**	immediately
11	**A**	examinations	**B**	trials	**C**	tests	**D**	investigations
12	**A**	skill	**B**	ability	**C**	power	**D**	strength
13	**A**	farther	**B**	further	**C**	another	**D**	longer
14	**A**	well	**B**	better	**C**	profitably	**D**	efficiently
15	**A**	put	**B**	get	**C**	give	**D**	throw

2 Key word transformations

For Questions **16–25**, complete the second sentence so that it has a similar meaning to the first sentence, using the word given. **Do not change the word given.** You must use between two and five words, including the word given.

Here is an example:

Example: I last went there two years ago.

        been

        I ....*haven't been there for*..... two years.

---

16   He hasn't got the intelligence to be a programmer.

       intelligent

       He .... to be a programmer.

17   The team members have never been so fit before.

       fitter

       The team members are .... been before.

18   There is a continual rise in the number of club members this year.

       rising

       The number of club members .... this year.

19   Although she was alone she still enjoyed the meal.

       spite

       She still enjoyed the meal .... alone.

20   The only reason I watch this show at all is because I like the dancers.

       watch

       If I didn't like the dancers in this show, I .... at all.

21   Players are allowed to pick up the ball but they must not run with it.

       provided

       Players are allowed to pick up the ball .... run with it.

22   I bet your brother's still watching television.

       must

       You brother .... television.

23   She started to train there over six months ago.

       training

       She .... over six months.

24   Because the sculpture weighed so much, we couldn't carry it.

       heavy

       The sculpture was .... carry.

25   Do you only come here because you're on your own at home?

       if

       Would you come here .... yourself at home?

3 Error correction

For Questions **26–40**, read the text below and look carefully at each line. Some of the lines are correct, and some have a word which should not be there.

If a line is correct, put a tick (✓) **at the end of the line**. If a line has a word which should not be there, write the word at the end of the line. There are two examples at the beginning (**0** and **00**).

A Wet Weekend

0	In my last letter I think I mentioned that we were being thinking	*being*
00	of going to a big pop festival not too far from here. Well, in the	✓
26	end we decided to go because of there were some really good	
27	bands playing and we knew that the atmosphere would be great,	
28	even if the weather wasn't. We set out more early on the Friday	
29	evening, taking us the bus which goes nearest to the	
30	festival site, even although we knew we would have to do the	
31	last couple of miles on the foot. What we didn't expect, though,	
32	was the huge traffic jam that started well before we got anywhere	
33	near at there. We sat in the bus for ages, so by the time we got	
34	off from at the stop it was starting to get dark. Then, of course,	
35	it began raining. Because of the queues at the gates, it took to us	
36	a while for to get in once we arrived at the place, and then we	
37	had to must find somewhere to put up our tent. When at last we	
38	had chosen our spot, in a muddy field with few hundreds of other	
39	campers, we set up the tent and put our things inside - only to	
40	discover that everything was already a damp, and likely to get	
	wet right through as the weekend continued.	

4 Word formation

For questions **41–50**, read the text below. Use the word given in capitals at the end of each line to form a word that fits in the space in the same line. There is an example at the beginning (**0**).

Example: | **0** | *surprising* |

TUNNEL BIKING IN HOLLAND

Everyone knows how keen the Dutch are on cycling. More (**0**) .... , though,   SURPRISE
is their (**41**) .... of riding through the hundreds of kilometres of tunnels   ENJOY
that lie below the surface of the Netherlands, (**42**) .... in Limburg: the one   SPECIAL
hilly province in an (**43**) .... uniformly flat country.   OTHER

The tunnels, some of them dug by the Romans, were (**44**) .... used to mine   ORIGIN
stone by hand. Nowadays the three (**45**) .... miners use power tools, and   REMAIN
the (**46**) .... are closed by steel gates, although cycling guides have a key.   ENTER

It is cold and extremely dark (**47**) .... , so the guides make sure everyone   GROUND
has a working lamp and that (**48**) .... stay close together. Anyone taking   CYCLE
a wrong (**49**) .... would be unlikely to find a way out. The constant 13°   TURN
temperature is fine while (**50**) .... are moving about, but once they stopped   RIDE
they would quickly freeze.

Writing

Answer this Part 1 question.

A friend has written to you asking for information about your local sports centre, which you know quite well.

Study the letter and the advertisement for the sports centre below, on which you have written some notes. Then write back, answering your friend's questions and saying whether you think the sports centre would be suitable or not.

As I think I mentioned in my last letter, I'd love to spend some time at that new sports centre when I come over to stay with you this August. I don't want to do anything that's too organized, so no team sports or anything like that, and I'd rather not be surrounded by lots of people all trying to get super-fit or lose lots of kilos as fast as they can. So if you've been there, could you let me know whether you think there would be any pleasant, relaxing activities that I would enjoy?

Looking forward to hearing from you.

Best wishes

Lee

Woodchurch Sports Centre

- Full-size basketball court — both for teams
- 5-a-side football pitch —
- Large indoor swimming pool
- Weight-training room — everyone building muscles!
- Keep-fit dancing courses
- 4 doubles tennis courts — long wait
- Gentle exercise room
- Outdoor jogging track — OK in summer

Write a **letter** of between **120 and 180** words in an appropriate style. Do not write any addresses.

1 Multiple choice cloze

For Questions **1–15**, read the text below and decide which answer **A**, **B**, **C** or **D** best fits each space. There is an example at the beginning (**0**).

Example:

| **0** | **A** brought | **B** taken | **C** had | **D** given |

THE TRAIN ACROSS CANADA

Until the decision was (**0**) .... to close it in the early 1990s, the Canadian Pacific was for many the world's greatest rail (**1**) .... Built over a hundred years ago at tremendous (**2**) .... cost, it stretched 2,887 miles from Montreal to the Pacific (**3**) .... , crossing dense pine forests, wide-open prairies and massive mountains. The line was cut through (**4**) .... rock by 30,000 men working in huge areas of (**5**) .... country, often in terrible weather conditions.

In many ways, Canada is a nation that was (**6**) .... by railways. Western cities like Calgary would not exist if the trains had not passed (**7**) .... there, and that long thin line was what once (**8**) .... such hugely different places as Newfoundland on the Atlantic with Vancouver on the Pacific. Now, though, it is gone; another victim of air (**9**) .... that is both cheaper and easier. Eastern Canadians, (**10**) .... their American neighbours, do not feel drawn towards the west. When it is (**11**) .... zero in Toronto or Quebec they fly south to the Caribbean rather than freeze in Winnipeg.

Lack of investment, a familiar story in many countries, also (**12**) .... its part. The trains, most of them built of steel in the 1950s, were made to last – but not (**13**) .... as long as that. Maintenance, too, was neglected and breakdowns became (**14**) .... more frequent. Then came the realisation that their diesel engines (**15**) .... the environment far more than buses did.

1	**A** trip	**B** voyage	**C** excursion	**D** journey
2	**A** human	**B** people	**C** labour	**D** man
3	**A** shore	**B** coast	**C** beach	**D** bank
4	**A** firm	**B** strong	**C** deep	**D** solid
5	**A** unknown	**B** uncertain	**C** unexplored	**D** unidentified
6	**A** created	**B** done	**C** invented	**D** set up
7	**A** on	**B** out	**C** away	**D** through
8	**A** related	**B** combined	**C** tied	**D** linked
9	**A** flight	**B** travel	**C** tour	**D** flying
10	**A** unlike	**B** contrasting	**C** different	**D** opposed
11	**A** under	**B** down	**C** below	**D** underneath
12	**A** did	**B** made	**C** played	**D** acted
13	**A** quite	**B** rather	**C** hardly	**D** indeed
14	**A** more	**B** ever	**C** again	**D** often
15	**A** injured	**B** harmed	**C** wounded	**D** hurt

2 Open cloze

For Questions **16–30,** read the text below and think of the word which best fits each space. Use only **one** word in each space. There is an example at the beginning (**0**).

Example: | **0** | *up* |

BEING WATCHED

We like to see murderers and thieves end (**0**) .... in prison. If they are caught as a (**16**) .... of being filmed by security cameras, having their phone calls listened to or their Email messages read, we enjoy (**17**) .... even more. It gives us the comforting feeling (**18**) .... ever-improving technology (**19**) .... just be the weapon we have long been looking for (**20**) .... our war against them. Recent scientific breakthroughs have also (**21**) .... it possible to solve crimes that took place decades (**22**) .... , so that just about any story can be worked out from (**23**) .... ending. This, too, is good news; (**24**) .... it is true it means that there really is (**25**) .... hiding place for the wrongdoer, that the police will always get their man, and that crime cannot pay.

The worrying thing is, of course, that it is not (**26**) .... the criminals who are being watched. All of (**27**) .... have now become the stars of films made in shops, in car parks and in the high street. Records are kept, and sometimes sold, of the numbers we most often phone, while the Emails we like to think (**28**) .... as being private and personal are copied and stored by persons unknown. Some will say this is the price of freedom from crime, that (**29**) .... innocent have nothing to fear. Others believe it is dangerously similar to the argument used by police states (**30**) .... control their citizens.

---

3 Key word transformations

For Questions **31–40,** complete the second sentence so that it has a similar meaning to the first sentence, using the word given. **Do not change the word given.** You must use between two and five words, including the word given.

Here is an example.

Example: I don't need a more powerful PC.

       enough

       My PC .....*is powerful enough for*.... me.

---

31   Playing tennis always makes me feel tired.

     get

     If I .... tired.

32   Perhaps those two women don't really like each other.

     might

     Those two women .... another.

33   I last went there when I was a child.

     been

     I .... I was a child.

34   They were once known everywhere as the top team.

     used

     They .... as the top team.

35 It seems that there is a gradual fall in the number of complaints.

falling

The number of complaints .... , it seems.

36 If they don't improve a lot soon they're bound to lose.

better

They're bound to lose unless .... soon.

37 Please don't shout every time you want a drink.

mind

Would .... every time you want a drink?

38 'Do you know where we are?' he asked me, as the fog closed in.

knew

He asked me if .... , as the fog closed in.

39 They are letting the well-known gang leader out of prison tomorrow.

released

The well-known gang leader .... prison tomorrow.

40 It was only because of your help that I got over the experience.

never

If you hadn't helped .... got over the experience.

4 Error correction

For Questions **41–55**, read the text below and look carefully at each line. Some of the lines are correct, and some have a word which should not be there.

If a line is correct, put a tick (✔) **at the end of the line**. If a line has a word which should not be there, write the word **at the end of the line**. There are two examples at the beginning (**0** and **00**).

A Journey Across America

0	When you last wrote, just after the holidays I think it was, you	✔
00	asked me to tell you about my return at home after we went	*at*
41	our separate ways. Well, the first thing I have tried to do was	
42	to get a lift on the freeway. I was being waiting for what seemed	
43	like hours at the intersection with the main highway to the Twin	
44	Cities, until eventually a truck was stopped. The driver said he	
45	was going to Chicago, so I jumped in and off we went. He was	
46	a friendly sort of guy, and we chatted for hour after an hour as	
47	we crossed on the flat Wisconsin countryside. We stopped only	
48	once, to have the lunch in a roadside diner just like those you	
49	see in the movies. The meal the driver ordered for both of us	
50	was enormous, but when I asked him how much did it cost he	
51	just smiled and said me he was paying. Back on the road, it was	
52	getting hotter, but by half past four we were near of Milwaukee	
53	and there was a pleasant breeze coming off Lake Michigan.	
54	Once we had crossed the Illinois state line, I knew so that we	
55	were getting close, and soon I spotted the most tallest building	
	in America: the Sears Tower.	

5 Writing

Write an answer to **one** of the Questions **1–3** in this part. Write your answer in **120–180** words in an appropriate style.

1   You are spending the summer working for a tourist information service, and have discovered a place that you think would particularly interest young visitors to your country. Your boss would like you to write a report describing it **and** saying why you think it would be popular with younger tourists.

Write your **report**.

2   An English-language magazine in your town has asked readers to send in short stories about their relationships with other people. The story must **end** like this:

After that, I decided that I would never ever speak to that person again.

Write your **story**.

3   Answer **one** of the following two questions based on your reading of **one** of the set books:

Either   **(a)**   Write a **letter** to your penfriend, saying what you think of the book which you have read, and suggesting why you think he or she might enjoy it.

Or   **(b)**   Which part of the book you have read did you like best? Write a **composition**, giving a summary of this part and saying why you liked it so much.

Your answer should contain enough detail to make it clear to someone who may not have read the book.

Progress Test Four

UNITS 1-15

1 Open cloze

For Questions **1–15**, read the text below and think of the word which best fits each space. Use only one word in each space. There is an example at the beginning.

Example: **0** *then*

NOT ENOUGH RAIN IN BRITAIN

If you think we are a group of rain-sodden islands with limitless water supplies, (**0**) .... consider this: (**1**) .... to the European Union and the World Resources Institute in Washington, our 60 million population has no (**2**) .... fresh water per person than South Africa's, we have less per person than sun-baked Spain or France, and parts of Britain are (**3**) .... into areas that are almost semi-desert. But where the water companies want to blame climate and geography (**4**) .... household shortages, the finger is pointing at government and planners who have encouraged us to live (**5**) .... there is least rainfall, and at our lifestyles.

About 250,000 billion litres of water a year fall on Britain, (**6**) .... most of it lands on the hard rocks of northern and western highlands, and relatively little on the majority of people (**7**) .... live in the drier south and east. We use up to twice as (**8**) .... water per person (**9**) .... we did 40 years ago, on gardens, cars, dishwashers, baths and cleaning. The disappearance of heavy industry means far (**10**) .... water is used in coal mining, steel-making or shipbuilding. But intensive agriculture, mainly practised in regions that are (**11**) .... of water, demands much more water at critical times (**12**) .... produce crops suitable for supermarkets.

The water companies are mostly (**13**) .... favour of more reservoirs, and say that only 5 per cent of the water that falls (**14**) .... collected. The Environment Agency, however, has said it will agree to new reservoirs only (**15**) .... every other course of action has been examined in detail.

2 Key word transformations

For Questions **16–25**, complete the second sentence so that it has a similar meaning to the first sentence, using the word given. **Do not change the word given.** You must use between two and five words, including the word given. There is an example at the beginning (**0**).

Example: We are certain this insect is different from that one.

        cannot

        This insect ....*cannot be the same as*.... that one.

---

16   In those days she usually stayed at home in the evenings.

        use

        In those days she .... out in the evenings.

17   There are too many people for so few resources.

        enough

        There are .... many people.

18   They carried on climbing despite such heavy snow.

        although

        They carried on climbing .... heavily.

19   They only sign agreements because they don't have to stick to them.

        if

        They wouldn't sign agreements .... to them.

20   In spite of the expense, the train is still the best way to travel.

        even

        The train is still the best way to travel, ... expensive.

21   If he doesn't have a break immediately, he'll end up exhausted.

        unless

        He'll end up exhausted .... break.

22   Despite his age, he's still working.

        retired

        He .... , despite his age.

23   Unless we get the tickets soon they'll all be sold out.

        if

        The tickets will all be sold out .... them soon.

24   He regrets not studying more before the exam.

        wishes

        He .... before the exam.

25   Your hair really needs cutting.

        must

        You really .... cut.

3 Error correction

For Questions **26–40**, read the text below and look carefully at each line. Some of the lines are correct, and some have a word which should not be there.

If a line is correct, put a tick (✔) **at the end of the line**. If a line has a word which should not be there, write the word **at the end of the line**. There are two examples at the beginning (**0** and **00**).

An Enthusiastic Reader

0	Thank you very much for having sending me the magazines.	*having*
00	Since they arrived the other day I've been so busy reading	✔
26	them that I've hardly had no time to watch television, which	
27	is highly unusual! One of the best things about them is that	
28	they are very great for learning English, particularly the ones	
29	that have articles on subjects what I know something about.	
30	I find those easy to read, because that some of the words are	
31	like words in my first language, and I can usually to work	
32	out the meanings of any new ones without having to look	
33	them up in the dictionary. I should have been started doing	
34	this a long time ago, and I wish I'd mentioned it	
35	sooner. Anyway, while I was reading one of them I came	
36	across by an advertisement for an international edition,	
37	so I've decided that I'm going to write it off and have	
38	it be delivered here every month. In fact I think I'll do	
39	that right now, in case I will miss this month's edition.	
40	Anyway, it's time I have started my homework, so	
	I'd better close. Bye for now.	

4 Word formation

For Questions **41–50**, read the text below. Use the word given in capitals at the end of each line to form a word that fits in the space in the same line. There is an example at the beginning (**0**).

Example: | **0** | *dangerous* |

TORNADOS

Tornados are one of the most (**0**) .... kinds of storm on Earth. Although	DANGER
they do not last long, they can strike with extreme (**41**) .... travelling at	VIOLENT
speeds of up fifty miles per hour. The (**42**) .... of most tornados is about	WIDE
five hundred feet, but in (**43**) .... circumstances they can be up to a mile	EXCEPTION
wide and travel huge (**44**) .... , possibly hundreds of miles. The reasons	DISTANCE
why they spin remain (**45**) .... , but we know that tornados can form	MYSTERY
when columns of air below thunderclouds start rising. Their (**46**) .... is	STRONG
increased by (**47**) .... winds. In the Southern hemisphere, they always spin	CIRCLE
in a (**48**) .... direction, while in the North it is the opposite. At the centre	CLOCK
of the tornado the air (**49**) .... is extremely low, so the wind rushing in	PRESS
at hundreds of miles an hour has the effect of an incredibly (**50**)	POWER
vacuum cleaner on dirt and solid objects on the ground below.	

5 Writing

Answer this Part 1 question.

You are thinking of going to England next summer to study English and you have seen the advertisement below. A friend of yours, who has attended several summer courses, has written some things on it for you to check when you contact them.

Read the advertisement and your friend's notes. Then write to the school, asking about the points that your friend has mentioned as well as any other details you would like to know.

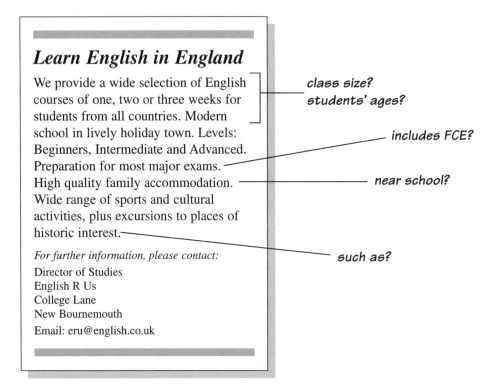

Learn English in England

We provide a wide selection of English courses of one, two or three weeks for students from all countries. Modern school in lively holiday town. Levels: Beginners, Intermediate and Advanced. Preparation for most major exams. High quality family accommodation. Wide range of sports and cultural activities, plus excursions to places of historic interest.

For further information, please contact:
Director of Studies
English R Us
College Lane
New Bournemouth
Email: eru@english.co.uk

class size?
students' ages?

includes FCE?

near school?

such as?

Write a **letter** of between **120 and 180** words in an appropriate style. Do not write any addresses.

Practice Test

PAPER 1   Part 1

You are going to read an article about the indoor sport of snooker. Choose the most suitable heading from the list **A–I** for each part (**1–7**) of the article. There is one extra heading which you do not need to use. There is an example at the beginning (**0**).

A A great spectator sport	**F** Necessary skills
B The name of the game	**G** Variations on a traditional game
C Traditional materials	**H** Overtaking its rival
D Champions and prizes	**I** Outside to inside
E Military origins	

Snooker

0   I

The three main sports played with a stick, or cue – billiards, snooker and pool – all derive from an outdoor game similar to croquet which was played with a mace, a stick which had a flattened end. Louis XI of France (1461–83) decided that the game should be played indoors and he had a special table built. For 300 years billiards, as the new indoor game was called, flourished. The cue, invented in the 19th century, allowed for a greater variety of shots and the mace fell out of favour.

1

Towards the end of the 19th century, a number of new games were played on billiard tables, including life pool and black pool. In life pool, several players each had a ball of a different colour and when their ball was potted (fell into one of the pockets round the table) they lost their 'life' and were out of the game. Black pool was rather different: there were 15 red and one black ball on the table. When a player potted a red he had the chance to pot the black, which was worth more points.

2

Both these games were played in the various colonies of the British Empire and, in 1875, a certain Neville Chamberlain, a junior army officer stationed in India, decided to make things more interesting by combining the two games to form one, with characteristics of both.

3

At the time, a new officer in the army was known in military slang as a snooker. Playing his new game one evening, Chamberlain called his partner a snooker because he had shown his inexperience by missing an easy shot. The term caught on and the game has been known as snooker ever since.

4

Snooker was brought to England in due course but did not outdo billiards in popularity because it was considered a simple potting game with little skill. In the 1920s, Joe Davis, a champion at both games, proved that this was not the case and snooker gradually became the more popular sport.

5

However, it was not until the advent of colour television that snooker really took off. Today it is one of the most popular of all sports televised in Britain. Extended coverage of major tournaments regularly tops the TV popularity charts and leading snooker players have the same celebrity status as soccer and cricket stars.

6

Snooker requires a quick brain as well as co-ordination between hand and eye. The aim of the game is to acquire points either by potting balls or by forcing an opponent into making foul shots: missing completely, for example, or potting colours in the wrong order. To do this effectively, a player needs to be able to calculate angles and place the balls accurately, all with a long thin stick.

7

Snooker cues have always been made of wood. Experiments with aluminium have been unsuccessful. The shaft, or thinner end, is usually made of polished ash or maple, with a heavier wood such as ebony being used to form the butt, or thick end. The leather tip on the shaft is usually stuck on and can be replaced. All players prepare the tip with special chalk before they make a shot to prevent the tip from slipping off the ball.

You are going to read an article about your rights when eating in restaurants. For Questions **8–14**, choose the answer (**A**, **B**, **C** or **D**) which you think fits best according to the text.

YOUR RIGHTS WHEN EATING OUT

While having lunch in an expensive restaurant, I tasted the wine I had ordered. I thought it might be off, so I called the wine waiter. He was most unpleasant at the mere suggestion that something might be wrong. Unwillingly he tasted the wine – and immediately apologized and brought another bottle. 'That's what I call power!' said my guest, but it helped that I knew I was legally in the right. As the customer, you have considerable rights.

If a restaurant fails to provide a table you have booked, they will have broken their contract with you and you can politely threaten to take them to court for the cost of a spoiled evening. They will then usually find you a table. On the other hand, if you let them down, they can take you to court for lost business. In one case, a company booked a table for one o'clock for five people at a popular restaurant, then called to cancel at 1.35 pm on the day, saying their client did not want to eat. When the company refused to pay up, the restaurant owner took them to court and won: the judge decided that, since it was too late to re-book the table, the company should pay for the loss of profit on the meal, plus legal costs. If the owner had had time to use the table, he would not have needed to take them to court.

line 16 The menu is a vital legal document. The price should be included, together with the tax, and the restaurant can be fined up to £5000 for not displaying it outside or immediately inside the door, so that customers know in advance what they are committing themselves to.

It is illegal for any establishment to give a false description of their food. Everything must be what it claims to be. 'Pâté of the house' must actually be made there; fresh fruit salad must consist only of fresh, not tinned, fruit; Welsh lamb must be an animal born or raised in Wales. But a menu does not have to spell out whether 'heart' is that of a calf, a pig or a lamb.

You cannot rely on getting bread and butter free. A restaurant is allowed to make a cover charge – which relates to linen, tableware, salt and pepper, sauces and items like bread or olives – provided it appears on the menu by the door. In theory, if any part of the cover has not been satisfactory (or you have not eaten all the olives), you need only leave what you think the acceptable items are worth. But of course most people do not bother.

If the food is not cooked to your satisfaction, you can insist on the restaurant taking it back and supplying what you ordered. If the food is unfit to eat, you can point out that it is illegal, with a maximum fine of £20,000 and / or up to six months in prison, to supply food 'not of the nature, substance or quality demanded'. If it gives you food poisoning, the restaurant is obliged to pay for the suffering and inconvenience provided you have been to your doctor. If the food is merely not up to a reasonable standard for the money, you can either send it back or pay less than the bill demands. If you do not pay the full price, give your name, address and proof of identity so that you cannot be arrested for leaving without paying.

8 How did the waiter react in the incident with the wine?

    A He brought a replacement at once.

    B He agreed that it was the wrong bottle.

    C He was offended by the initial complaint.

    D He changed the bottle when the guest insisted.

                                                       `8`

9 What does the writer say about table bookings?

    A If a table is not being used, the restaurant must let you have it.

    B If you do not use a booked table you may still have to pay something.

    C Restaurants will usually try to find you a table even if you have not booked.

    D Restaurants cannot take you to court if you cancel a booking by phone.

                                                       `9`

10 What does 'it' refer to in line 16?

    A the restaurant

    B the menu

    C the price

    D the tax

                                                      `10`

11 According to the article, by law restaurants must

    A make homemade dishes in the restaurant.

    B use only fresh fruit for desserts.

    C state which country meat comes from.

    D say what animals are used in meat dishes.

                                                      `11`

12 Restaurants can only ask for a cover charge if

    A it isn't too high.

    B you do not eat everything provided.

    C it includes bread and butter.

    D they display it near the entrance.

                                                      `12`

13 You can claim money from the restaurant if the food

    A is not what you ordered.

    B is not good value.

    C makes you ill.

    D tastes unpleasant.

                                                      `13`

14 What is the purpose of this article?

    A to remind restaurants of their obligations

    B to advise customers about choosing restaurants

    C to inform customers about the laws regarding restaurants

    D to encourage customers to complain about poor service

                                                      `14`

You are going to read a magazine article about a woman who makes perfume. Eight sentences have been removed from the article. Choose from the sentences **A–I** the one which best fits each gap (**15–21**). There is one extra sentence which you do not need to use. There is an example at the beginning (**0**).

At Home with Antonia Bellanca

Nilgin Yusuf talked to the famous perfumier in her seaside home.

With its recipe books, overflowing store cupboards and neatly piled white crockery, this could be any American country kitchen. **0** **I**

The reason for this personalized mark of approval, explains Antonia Bellanca, is that Stewart wears the perfume she created 15 years ago, 'Antonia's Flowers'. **15** It was the first perfume to use 'living flower technology', which reproduces a flower's scent exactly as it exists in nature.

Antonia's Flowers has recently been joined by Antonia's new scent 'Floret', inspired by memories of her Sicilian grandmother's garden on Long Island. **16**

Antonia's journey into the world of perfume wasn't planned. She went to New York to study fine art, but she was too impatient and full of energy to stick at it. When she came across a florist who styled arrangements to look like 15th-century Dutch paintings, her love for flowers was rediscovered. **17**

Customers – who came to include Estée Lauder and Calvin Klein – would often remark on the wonderful smell in the shop and Antonia was inspired to create a perfume that smelt as good

but was available all year round. The perfume, Antonia's Flowers, was an enormous commercial success and has remained so. **18**

A delightfully unlikely perfumier, Antonia can usually be found in dungarees, her dark hair pushed back from her face. She lives in a white cottage in Nantucket Bay with Stephen, her landscape gardener husband of 10 years, seven-year-old Tessie, five-year-old Truman and Rollie the cat. **19** 'I love the salty air, the beach roses, the honeysuckle – even the animal smells,' she says.

The garden has been completely re-landscaped by Stephen. Alongside some strange marble columns left by the previous owners are swings and other play equipment. The children spend long days playing here with friends from the neighbourhood. **20**

Simplicity is the main feature of this charming, relaxed house. Antonia has chosen plain furniture and the pale eggshell colours in which the rooms are decorated are from Martha Stewart's own paint range. **21** From the floral arrangements to the cabinets full of antique perfume bottles and crockery, it feels like the most stylish of family homes.

A
Last year, her perfume empire had a turnover of $2.5 million, achieved without a single advertisement.

B
These large windows flood every room with sunshine, while squashy chairs invite you to relax.

C
Meanwhile, the adults gather round the barbecue, a constant feature of summer life.

D
Antonia remembers these scents of her childhood distinctly – basil as her grandmother cooked, the roses and honeysuckle she would gather up and take to school for her teachers.

E
The flower-based scent is one of those rare perfumes that has made the jump from popular to classic.

F
After a period developing her feel and skills for floral arranging, she opened a florist shop of her own in East Hampton.

G
Every morning, she walks by the sea and woods and breathes in the natural scents around her.

H
This has only 15 shades, but, according to Antonia, everything you would ever need.

I
Except that, alongside the children's drawings on the fridge door, there is a fan letter from famous designer Martha Stewart.

You are going to read September's horoscopes for six different signs. For Questions **22–35**, choose from the signs (**A–F**). Some of the signs may be chosen more than once. When more than one answer is required, these may be given in any order. There is an example at the beginning (**0**).

According to the horoscopes, people with which sign

may have problems early in the month?	**0** C
may be criticized by others over money matters?	**22**
will be popular in their working life?	**23**
may be asked to change their personality?	**24**
will have a successful month financially?	**25**　**26**
will discover early problems have had positive results?	**27**
should change their attitude toward their health?	**28**
will make changes in their working life?	**29**
will find their daily routine altered for the better?	**30**
will meet new people?	**31**　**32**
should forget about past problems?	**33**
should do jobs around the house?	**34**
will not settle matters until the end of the month?	**35**

Your Stars for September

A VIRGO

There's a powerful lunar eclipse this month, which means that your normally well-ordered life gets shaken up in wonderful ways. Some of your old companions need to be dropped in favour of new ones as travel appears on the horizon, and for once you can let others do the worrying while you sit back and relax.

B LIBRA

Physical matters are highlighted this month, but taking a more general approach to your wellbeing may be better than your usual trips to the gym. Emotional attachments to a difficult past are reducing your energy, so sort out where your life is going and with whom. Elsewhere, big plans and small details fall into place, but you'll have to wait until the last week of September to see the full results.

C SCORPIO

Relationships are difficult during the first week of the month, and children – yours or someone else's – make trouble. When things calm down, you'll realise that what had to happen, did happen – and it was for the best. At work, you're a bright shiny star. Colleagues can't get enough of you and queue up to pay you compliments. Enjoy the moment while it lasts.

D TAURUS

This is a month for doing your domestic accounts, getting the car fixed and working in the garden, so it's just as well this is the kind of practical stuff you love. Once that's done we can promise lots of dressing-up and going out – and as you're also making money, you'll have plenty of funds to pay for it. Just watch out for a few sharp remarks from a partner or friend who thinks you should be saving rather than spending.

E GEMINI

Long-standing problems at work can't be put off any longer. You may decide to move your desk or switch jobs entirely. Although this isn't an easy time, by the middle of the month you'll begin to feel you're going in the right direction. Family matters come up, too. Parents and other relatives are putting pressure on you to be the person you stopped being 10 years ago. But this is their problem, not yours.

F CANCER

It's evening class time, and nobody likes signing up more than a Cancerian. Whether you're doing boat building or karate, the important thing is that you'll be meeting like-minded people. Fresh friendships are on the horizon. Money is also a subject dear to Cancerian hearts, and this month you've got lots of it. Now is the time to sell your house.

PAPER 2   Part 1

You **must** answer this question.

1   You are planning a camping holiday in Britain and have been looking for a site near the sea. You have seen an advertisement in an English magazine and have decided to ask for further information.

Read carefully the advertisement and the notes you have made. Then, using this information, write a letter to Sally Peterson. You should cover all the points in your notes. You may add relevant information of your own.

Write a **letter** of between **120** and **180** words in an appropriate style.
Do not write any addresses.

PAPER 2   Part 2

Write an answer to **one** of the Questions **2–5** in this part. Write your answer in **120–180** words in an appropriate style.

2   A group of young people from Britain is coming to your home town for two weeks, and as a member of the local English Club you have been asked to help in preparing an information pack for them.

    You have been given the job of writing a report on the places of historical importance in and around your town.

    Write your **report**, giving details of the sites they should visit, how to reach them, opening times, admission charges, etc.

3   A local English-language magazine has asked for contributions for a special feature called 'Memorable Moments'.

    Write your **article**, describing a moment you will never forget, including details of the events leading up to the moment, why it was so special and what happened afterwards.

4   Your class has been discussing ways of finding out how much students have learnt. Your teacher has now asked you to write a composition, giving your views on the following statement:

    There is too much emphasis on examination results.

    Write your **composition**.

5   Answer **one** of the following two questions based on your reading of one of the set books.

    Either   (a)   Choose a character in the story that you find attractive.
                       Write a **composition**, saying why you like the character and what influence this character has on the development of the story.

    Or   (b)   Write a **composition** describing the setting for the story and saying how the setting is important to the events in the book.

    Your answer should contain enough detail to make it clear to someone who may not have read the book.

PAPER 3   Part 1

For Questions **1–15**, read the text below and decide which answer **A**, **B**, **C** or **D** best fits each space. There is an example at the beginning (**0**).

Example:

| 0 | **A** develop | **B** grow | **C** raise | **D** start |

COCA-COLA

Coca-Cola was invented in 1886 by John Pemberton, a 50-year-old chemist from Atlanta, USA. He decided to (**0**) .... a soft drink to sell as a 'brain tonic'. Working tirelessly in the back room of his drugstore, he produced a (**1**) .... containing, among other things, coca leaves, cola nut oil, sugar and caffeine. (The exact (**2**) .... is still a secret, but the tiny cocaine content was removed in 1903.) A few months later, an assistant (**3**) .... a customer Coca-Cola mixed with soda water by (**4**) .... It was this small addition that (**5**) .... out to be the vital ingredient that made the drink a success.

Coke has always been cleverly marketed. The distinctive (**6**) .... of the bottle was introduced in 1915 to prevent imitations and a 1920s advertising campaign even gave the world Father Christmas as we now know him – with a red and white (**7**) .... , rather than the blue, yellow or green he had often previously worn. Coca-Cola was a major sponsor of the 1984 Olympic Games in Los Angeles, as (**8**) .... as being the Games' 'Official Drink'.

The red and white Coca-Cola logo can be recognised (**9**) .... – a powerful symbol of the American way of life. Coke was the most (**10**) .... distributed mass-produced item in America when World War II broke (**11**) .... and the war provided the (**12**) .... to spread the product into Europe and Asia. When conservative Europeans (**13**) .... about the invasion of modern American values into their ancient cultures, the act of drinking Coke became for the young a (**14**) .... form of rebellion against tradition. Even today, Coke is still (**15**) .... linked with the image of youth.

1	**A** composition	**B** mixture	**C** chemical	**D** drug
2	**A** receipt	**B** menu	**C** recipe	**D** prescription
3	**A** provided	**B** supplied	**C** served	**D** presented
4	**A** error	**B** mistake	**C** wrong	**D** misunder-standing
5	**A** put	**B** picked	**C** turned	**D** set
6	**A** design	**B** pattern	**C** model	**D** representation
7	**A** disguise	**B** clothing	**C** dress	**D** costume
8	**A** long	**B** far	**C** well	**D** soon
9	**A** at times	**B** at once	**C** at all events	**D** at any rate
10	**A** largely	**B** broadly	**C** greatly	**D** widely
11	**A** out	**B** up	**C** through	**D** in
12	**A** possibility	**B** hope	**C** occasion	**D** opportunity
13	**A** blamed	**B** complained	**C** accused	**D** charged
14	**A** fewer	**B** minor	**C** lesser	**D** smaller
15	**A** hardly	**B** rarely	**C** closely	**D** nearly

PAPER 3   Part 2

For Questions **16–30**, read the text below and think of the word which best fits each space. Use only **one** word in each space. There is an example at the beginning (**0**).

Example: | **0** | *one* |

WOOD FROM THE SEA

Many things can be found on the beach, but (**0**) .... of the most useful is wood. Wood that is washed up comes in varying shapes and sizes, (**16**) .... fish-boxes to parts of ships. Most old coastal cottages and houses have (**17**) .... beachwood built into them somewhere and many fishermen have a pile of beachwood from (**18**) .... they can select the required piece for any job in hand.

Not only cut wood, (**19**) .... the trees themselves may end up on the tideline. Torn up by (**20**) .... roots in time of flood or avalanche, (**21**) .... are riverborne and finally seaborne. They (**22**) .... even carry in their roots large rocks. These rocks (**23**) .... sometimes left behind, out of their geological context, to puzzle and intrigue those who come across them. The trees can often be traced back to their source simply (**24**) .... looking at the rings of their trunks. These can then be compared with (**25**) .... of other trees to establish which area they came from.

After being washed by sea and sand, tree roots often take on strange shapes and can look like living creatures (**26**) .... as snakes, and many people use these unusual pieces of art (**27**) .... decorative features in their homes. They can be turned (**28**) .... attractive settings for plants. Or you may see a beachwood tree (**29**) .... used in a garden, perhaps with a bird-table (**30**) .... top of it.

PAPER 3　Part 3

For Questions **31–40**, complete the second sentence so that it has a similar meaning to the first sentence, using the word given. **Do not change the word given.** You must use between two and five words, including the word given.

Here is an example:

Example: I last went there two years ago.

been

I ..*haven't been there for*.. two years.

___

31   Angela regrets not seeing that film.

wishes

Angela .... that film.

32   'Where did you buy your dress?' Janice asked her sister.

where

Janice asked her sister .... dress.

33   My mother wouldn't give me permission to go to the disco.

let

My mother .... to the disco.

34   'Why don't you buy a bigger house, Sue?' said Amos.

should

Amos suggested .... a bigger house.

35   It's possible that the building was burgled after midnight.

may

The building .... after midnight.

36   John's students always respected him.

looked

John .... by his students.

37   'It's your fault the cat died, George,' said Lucy.

blamed

Lucy .... of the cat.

38   Jeremy got sunburnt because he fell asleep on the beach.

if

Jeremy wouldn't have got sunburnt .... asleep on the beach.

39   A phrasebook's a good idea because you might need to ask for directions.

case

A phrasebook's a good idea .... ask for directions.

40   It's impossible to lend you any more money, I'm afraid.

question

Lending you any more money .... , I'm afraid.

PAPER 3   Part 4

For Questions **41–55**, read the text below and look carefully at each line. Some of the lines are correct, and some have a word which should not be there. If a line is correct, put a tick (✔) **at the end of the line**. If a line has a word which should **not** be there, write the word **at the end of the line**. There are two examples at the beginning (**0** and **00**).

LETTER TO AN OLD FRIEND

Dear Costas

0	It was great to see you again after so long and to be able	✔
00	to discuss about all the things we used to do when we were	*about*
41	students together learning the English in London. I hope	
42	you had a good journey home. Did the flight reach to Athens	
43	in time for you to get up your connection? I hope so.	
44	Do you remember I promised to send you that book we talked	
45	about? Well, I've searched in everywhere for it but so far	
46	I haven't managed to find it. As soon as I will do, I'll	
47	put it in the post to you – it's a really exciting story.	
48	And now I'd like to ask you a favour, not for me but for	
49	my sister. She wants to have work in Greece. She doesn't	
50	mind what she does – she would be too happy to work in a	
51	bar or to look after children. So if only you know of	
52	anything, please let us know. She'd like to spend until one	
53	year there from next January, which it should be possible	
54	I think. She has been decided it is the best thing for her.	
55	I'm looking forward to hearing from you soon. Give	
	my regards to your family.	
	Best wishes	
	Mario	

PAPER 3   Part 5

For Questions **56–65**, read the text below. Use the word given in capitals at the end of each line to form a word that fits in the space in the same line. There is an example at the beginning (**0**).

Example: | **0** | *death* |

ALBERT EINSTEIN

On 18th April 1955, the (**0**) .... occurred in Princeton, USA of	DIE
one of the world's (**56**) .... physicists, Albert Einstein, after	LEAD
some years of heart-related (**57**) .... Born in 1879 in Ulm,	ILL
Germany, Einstein's intelligence was not (**58**) .... at school,	NOTICE
but at Zurich University his (**59**) .... skills became obvious	SCIENCE
and he later wrote his famous papers on relativity. These (**60**)	PUBLISH
established his reputation and changed humanity's (**61**)	UNDERSTAND
of the universe. They also (**62**) .... others to build both	ABLE
atomic weapons and nuclear power stations. His work won (**63**)	WORLD
recognition with a Nobel Prize and in 1933 he settled (**64**)	PERMANENT
in America, where his work continued (**65**) .... for the next	INTERRUPT
twenty years.	

PAPER 4   Part 1

You will hear people talking in eight different situations. For Questions **1–8**, choose the best answer **A**, **B** or **C**.

1   You overhear part of a telephone conversation in a language school.
    Who is the woman talking to?

    A   a student

    B   a landlady | 1 |

    C   a teacher

2   Listen to this man talking.
    What is he doing?

    A   threatening to do something

    B   apologising for doing something | 2 |

    C   promising to do something

3   Listen to this conversation between a woman and a man.
    Where did the woman go yesterday?

    A   to a cafe

    B   to a park | 3 |

    C   to a zoo

4   You hear part of a radio programme.
    Where is the presenter?

    A   in the street

    B   in a football ground | 4 |

    C   in a studio

5   Listen to this conversation in the street.
    What are the man and woman talking about?

    A   a dog

    B   a child | 5 |

    C   an elderly man

6   Listen to this woman talking at an airport.
    What is the woman's job?

    A   air traffic controller

    B   airport manager | 6 |

    C   airline pilot

7   Listen to this man talking to a travel agent.
    What does the man want to do?

    A   complain about a holiday

    B   find out the cost of a flight | 7 |

    C   buy a coach ticket

8   Listen to this conversation in an office.
    What is the relationship of the woman to the man?

    A   colleague

    B   boss | 8 |

    C   assistant

PAPER 4   Part 2

You will hear a man talking about an American who lives out in the woods. For Questions **9–18**, complete each of the notes which summarize what he says.

EUSTACE CONWAY

Background:

At age 6: could [____ **9**] accurately.

At age 10: could hunt with [____ and ____ **10**]

At age [____ **11**] : left home to live in woods permanently.

Mother had lived alone in tent with [____ and ____ **12**]

Present life in woods:

Hunts for food

Makes clothes from [____ **13**]

Earns money by visiting [____ **14**]

and by running [____ **15**]

Other activities:

[____ **16**] in New Zealand.

walking in Alps (wearing [____ **17**])

travelling across America [____ **18**]

PAPER 4   Part 3

You will hear five women talking about their schooldays. For Questions **19–23**, choose which of the statements **A–F** is true for each speaker. Use the letters only once. There is one extra letter which you do not need to use.

A   She got very nervous about tests.

Speaker 1 [____ **19**]

B   She enjoyed the meals provided at school.

Speaker 2 [____ **20**]

C   She found one subject quite easy.

Speaker 3 [____ **21**]

D   She liked learning things by heart.

Speaker 4 [____ **22**]

E   She was glad when school ended for the day.

Speaker 5 [____ **23**]

F   She disliked one of the teachers.

PAPER 4   Part 4

You will hear two people discussing the increasing choice available nowadays in the media and in shops.
For Questions **24–30**, decide whether the idea was stated or not and mark Y for **Yes**, or N for **No**.

24	Newspapers take too long to read.	24
25	Book reviews should be read before choosing a book.	25
26	Much of the information on the Internet is useless.	26
27	Few films need to be over three hours long.	27
28	CDs are better value for money than the old albums were.	28
29	We need to learn how to choose.	29
30	Our grandparents were happier with less choice.	30

PAPER 5   Part 1

The interlocutor asks each of the candidates in turn for some personal information, such as:

- Where are you from?
- How long have you been studying English?
- Do you have any hobbies or interests?
- What do you hope to do in the future?

Part 2

(see p213)

Part 3

The interlocutor gives the candidates the illustration below and gives these instructions:

I'm going to show you some ideas for things you could include if you were advertising a language school. I'd like you to choose five of them and put them in order of importance.

library

small class sizes

self-access centre

small shop

friendly teachers

mix of student nationalities

sports facilities

mini bus for trips

Part 4

The interlocutor encourages the candidates to develop the topic from Part 3 by asking questions. For example:

- What are the different ways that you can advertise things?
- Which ways do you think are most effective?
- Which one would you choose to advertise a language school?
- Do you think advertisements always tell the truth?
- Are you influenced by advertisements?
- How do advertisers make their products attractive?

Student A

Student A: Compare and contrast these photographs.
             Which kind of sport appeals to you?

Student B: Have you tried either of these sports?

Student B

Student B: Compare and contrast these photographs.
             Where would you rather be?

Student A: Which do you think is safer?

Unit Tests Key

UNIT 1

1
1 join
2 fit
3 kick
4 skill
5 cross out/off
6 tough
7 unique
8 strain
9 punch
10 take up

2
1 is getting
2 close
3 tire
4 leaves
5 is lifting
6 owns
7 are going
8 am staying
9 see
10 is (always) reminding

3
1 arms   3 face   5 legs   7 face   9 legs
2 feet   4 hands 6 body   8 body   10 body

4
1 many   3 much   5 many   7 much   9 many
2 much   4 many   6 much   8 much   10 much

5
1 some
2 a little
3 a little
4 lots of
5 a large number of
6 a few
7 a bit of
8 much
9 a piece of
10 little

UNIT 2

1
1 bend
2 steep
3 scared
4 track
5 plunge
6 claims
7 scenery
8 nervous
9 investment
10 intentionally

2
1 the   3 –   5 the   7 a   9 –
2 an   4 the 6 the 8 the 10 a

3
1 B   2 B   3 A   4 A   5 A

4
1 boring
2 exhausted
3 shocking
4 relaxing
5 confused

5
1 off
2 on
3 over
4 away with
5 up to

UNIT 3

1
1 chemical
2 scientific
3 physical
4 theoretical
5 industrial
6 powerful
7 basic
8 medical

2
1 dislike
2 disappeared
3 economic
4 productivity
5 secretive
6 increasingly
7 unsure
8 wholly
9 forgetful
10 meaningless

3
1 do
2 made
3 will do
4 make
5 made
6 did

4
1 unlucky
2 microphone
3 oversleep
4 intermediate
5 impatient
6 independent
7 underestimate
8 disappointed
9 remake
10 translate

5
1 'll help
2 departs
3 are getting/are going to get
4 is going to start
5 go
6 'll have left
7 won't notice
8 'll be working
9 have
10 will have been going

UNIT 4

1
1 ✔   5 seldom study   9 ✔
2 frequently go 6 is always   10 rarely need
3 ✔   7 ✔
4 is often   8 ✔

2
1 should   5 mustn't   9 must
2 must   6 needn't   10 shouldn't
3 don't have to 7 should
4 have to   8 haven't got to

3
1 I   3 G   5 A   7 C   9 D
2 F   4 J   6 H   8 E   10 B

4
1 sillier, the silliest   4 further, the furthest
2 better, the best   5 less, the least
3 worse, the worst

5
1 better guitar player/guitarist than
2 the cheapest tickets
3 (nearly) as slowly as
4 the least exciting concert
5 busier than

UNIT 5

1
1 bedroom   5 bedroom   9 bedroom
2 bathroom   6 bedroom   10 kitchen
3 kitchen   7 kitchen
4 kitchen   8 bedroom

2
1 was sleeping
2 used to live
3 owned
4 used to/would wave
5 belonged/used to belong
6 used to think/thought
7 was watching
8 chose
9 would/used to continue
10 was waiting

3
1 split   2 stink   3 swap   4 shrink

4
1 but   4 However
2 although/even though   5 although/even though
3 despite   6 though

5
1 landlord   5 tenant   9 bedsit/bedsitter
2 rent   6 bill   10 accommodation
3 cottage   7 terraced (house)
4 housework   8 flatmate

UNIT 6

1
1 bitter   3 mineral   5 mashed   7 french   9 crunchy
2 olive   4 ripe   6 cream   8 salty   10 spicy

❷ 1 will pass 6 will let
2 earned 7 were
3 will tell 8 didn't have
4 would get 9 worked
5 were 10 would not waste
(contracted forms also possible throughout)

❸ a cupful, a tablespoonful, a teaspoonful, a pinch

❹ 1 loaf 2 bar 3 bowl 4 slice

❺ 1 unless you watch
2 provided you are
3 If we don't take
4 as long as they are fresh
5 if they don't reduce
6 unless we start
7 as long as they stay
8 providing their elder sister is
9 if your name's on
10 as long as you don't overdo it

❻ 1 beat 5 melt 9 leave
2 grate 6 overheat 10 fry
3 add 7 mix 11 remove
4 warm 8 pour 12 serve

UNIT 7

❶ 1 teacup 9 ice skates
2 bus ticket 10 alarm clock
3 well-known 11 penfriend
4 classmate 12 boiling point
5 surfboard 13 record-holder
6 toothpaste 14 leisure centre
7 right-handed 15 video games
8 heart attack

❷ 1 the album (that/which) you said
2 the one (who) I was telling
3 dish, which comes from Brazil, is
4 motorbike, which goes even faster than mine, is
5 woman whose husband
6 Jones, who I spoke to/to whom I spoke earlier, is
7 the house where we used to live.
8 Sophia, who is a very good cook, loves/is a very good cook who loves
9 It was 1998 when we met
10 Juan, who spends every summer near Liverpool, speaks

❸ 1 ball 5 polo/skiing
2 -skating/hockey 6 lifting
3 jump 7 surfing
4 tennis 8 vault

❹ 1 people's – apostrophe
2 centre? – question mark
3 3/5/86 – slash
4 'I didn't mean it' – inverted commas/quotation marks
5 (France or Spain) – brackets

❺ 1 in tears 3 in particular 5 in fact
2 in the end 4 in danger 6 in private

❻ 1 can 3 might 5 mightn't
2 could 4 can't 6 might

UNIT 8

❶ 1 full-length 6 satellite dish
2 broadcast 7 documentary
3 foreign correspondent 8 sitcom
4 soap 9 commercial break
5 spin-off 10 update

❷ 1 She has been 6 I've never met
2 I spoke 7 ✔
3 ✔ 8 ever been
4 have you been waiting 9 ✔
5 ✔ 10 We lived

❸ 1 audience 6 exhibition
2 art gallery 7 stage
3 masterpiece 8 sketch
4 portrait 9 sculpture
5 applause 10 shades

❹ 1 I've been 6 who have you seen
2 Have you been 7 I haven't had
3 I've just come 8 haven't you been staying
4 Have you got used 9 I've been living
5 I've been wearing 10 you've already started

UNIT 9

❶ 1 thief 6 smuggler
2 shoplifter 7 vandal
3 bank robber 8 kidnapper
4 burglar 9 blackmailer
5 murderer 10 terrorist

❷ 1 got on 4 sent 7 were
2 had gone 5 had taken 8 had passed
3 had disappeared 6 had broken

❸ 1 were, had been travelling
2 got up, had been snowing
3 gave, hadn't been telling
4 had been waiting, took off
5 was, had been stealing
6 asked, 'd been standing

❹ 1 terminal 6 cut-price
2 check-in 7 emergency exit
3 hand luggage 8 first class
4 luggage labels 9 cabin staff
5 boarding card 10 hold-up

❺ 1 afterwards 3 once 5 than
2 by the time 4 hardly

UNIT 10

❶ 1 material 5 size 9 material
2 size 6 material 10 colours
3 material 7 colours
4 colours 8 size

❷ 1 doing 6 buying/having, etc.
2 filling 7 having
3 going 8 wasting/spending
4 exciting/boring, etc. 9 booking/arranging
5 robbing 10 winning

❸ 1 fit 2 clash 3 match

❹ 1 is always cut very carefully in that shop.
2 is being shortened for you right now.
3 was measured for a new suit (by the tailor).
4 dresses will be sold by the weekend.
5 used to be sewn on by hand.
6 have ('ve) already been told that story.
7 may be tried on before purchasing.
8 on shopping hours is going to be changed.
9 was being served when the bell rang.
10 a superstore there had often been talked of.

❺ 1 post office 6 department store
2 bank 7 leisure centre
3 solicitor's office 8 library
4 bookshop 9 casualty
5 supermarket 10 chemist's

UNIT 11

①
1 to meet
2 to clean up
3 waiting
4 to go
5 swim
6 opening
7 visiting
8 to ask
9 to tell
10 to climb

②
1 Annie advised Kate not to spend any more time in the sun.
2 They asked the woman at reception if/whether she had another key.
3 He admitted breaking the mirror in the bathroom.
4 The angry tourist swore he would never go back there again.
5 She told her children not to go into the water on their own.
6 The policeman asked him/the man which flight he was taking.
7 Amanda accused her boyfriend of ruining/having ruined their entire holiday.
8 She complained to her husband that she had had enough of the/that heat.
9 George threatened to go home unless the weather improved/if the weather didn't improve.
10 The boy wondered whether/if he would ever see her again.

③
1 souvenirs
2 resorts
3 trip
4 journey
5 tide
6 voyage
7 coast
8 brochure
9 stream
10 waterfall
11 undergrowth
12 beach
13 waves
14 peaks
15 shore

UNIT 12

①
1 stupid
2 unfriendly
3 self-confident
4 relaxed
5 rough
6 miserable
7 interesting
8 generous
9 energetic
10 bad-tempered

②
1 am
2 had asked
3 freezes
4 would have saved
5 let
6 wouldn't have bought
7 get
8 'd spoken
9 'd left
10 'd be lying

(non-contracted forms also possible)

③
1 related
2 single/unmarried
3 engaged
4 widowed
5 separated
6 divorced

④
1 So am I/I'm not.
2 So would I/I wouldn't.
3 Neither have I/I have.
4 So do I/I don't.
5 Neither will I/I will.
6 Neither can I/I can.
7 Neither have I/I have.
8 So did I/I didn't.
9 So am I/I'm not.
10 So must I/I don't have to.
11 Neither do I/I do.
12 Neither had I/I had.

(Note: some of the affirmative answers are very unlikely!)

⑤
1 grandfather
2 niece
3 nephew
4 cousin
5 brother-in-law
6 sister-in-law
7 aunt
8 elder brother
9 twin sister
10 mother-in-law
11 stepfather
12 great-grandfather

UNIT 13

①
1 heavy
2 clear
3 deep
4 bright
5 dark
6 thick
7 occasional
8 strong
9 mild
10 thick
11 loud
12 gentle

②
1 so
2 such
3 so
4 such
5 such an
6 so
7 so
8 such a
9 such
10 so

③
1 hot
2 wet
3 wet
4 cold
5 wet
6 windy
7 cold
8 windy
9 cold
10 hot
11 wet
12 dry/hot

④
1 red Arctic
2 vegetable soup
3 stone temple
4 strong leather
5 delightful warm
6 8000-metre Himalayan

⑤
1 school leaver
2 journalist
3 disc jockey
4 shop assistant
5 barman/barmaid
6 ski instructor
7 surgeon
8 nurse
9 interpreter
10 candidate

UNIT 14

①
1 global warming
2 conservation
3 exhaust fumes
4 carbon monoxide
5 forest fires
6 ozone layer
7 rain forests
8 oil slicks

②
1 I must have told you ...
2 They might not have told him.
3 He should have made ...
4 They can't have been in.
5 She must have felt ...
6 He shouldn't have told ...
7 He may have gone away ...
8 He might not have got ...
9 He can't have been ...
10 I could have taken ...

③
1 bee
2 wolf
3 tortoise
4 mosquito
5 crocodile
6 camel
7 shark
8 whale

④
1 But I don't.
2 But I do.
3 But I'm not.
4 But he didn't.
5 But he did.
6 But he won't.

⑤
1 horns   2 fins   3 sting   4 beak   5 claws   6 paws

UNIT 15

①
1 nursery children
2 infants
3 juniors
4 secondary school pupils
5 sixth-form students
6 undergraduates
7 postgraduates

②
1 so/so that/in order that
2 in case
3 in order not to/so as not to
4 to/in order to/so as to
5 to/in order to/so as to
6 in case
7 in order not to/so as not to
8 so/so that/in order that
9 in order not to/so as not to
10 in case

③
1 for example
2 that is
3 note well
4 postscript (added to letter)
5 and so on
6 number
7 maximum
8 especially
9 approximately
10 minimum

④
1 have my dress cleaned before the party
2 to have the house painted at the weekend
3 his hair cut for over a year
4 had all our meals cooked for us
5 have these documents signed by your parents
6 it delivered by courier
7 had the garden done while we were away
8 him thrown out of the club
9 that lovely picture framed
10 your room cleaned (by someone else)
11 have that old keyboard repaired

⑤
1 Candidate Number
2 blank pages
3 turn over
4 answer sheet
5 soft pencil
6 eraser
7 question paper
8 mark sheet
9 certificate

Progress Tests Key

TEST ONE

1

1 A	4 D	7 C	10 D	13 D
2 B	5 B	8 D	11 B	14 C
3 A	6 A	9 A	12 C	15 B

2
16 their
17 who
18 themselves
19 are
20 ought
21 whose
22 the/this
23 make
24 can
25 more
26 in/with
27 to
28 as/because/since
29 getting
30 away/out

3
31 are not (aren't) big enough
32 the best I've ever
33 while we are staying
34 will not (won't) be enough space
35 I'm not enjoying
36 the most skilful player
37 is slowly getting better
38 no need for you to
39 ran too slowly, didn't
40 not as impressive as

4
41 worldwide
42 violinists
43 impression
44 membership
45 musicians
46 whatever
47 threaten
48 elsewhere
49 intention
50 permission

TEST TWO

1

1 A	4 A	7 D	10 D	13 B
2 D	5 B	8 B	11 C	14 D
3 B	6 A	9 A	12 B	15 C

2
16 is not (isn't) intelligent enough
17 fitter than they have (they've) ever
18 is continually rising/is rising continually
19 in spite of being
20 would not (wouldn't) watch it
21 provided (that) they do not (don't)
22 must still be watching
23 has been training there for
24 too heavy for us to
25 if you weren't (were not) by

3

26 of	29 us	32 ✔	35 to	38 few
27 ✔	30 even	33 at	36 for	39 ✔
28 more	31 the	34 from	37 must	40 a

4
41 enjoyment
42 especially
43 otherwise
44 originally
45 remaining
46 entrances
47 underground
48 cyclists
49 turning
50 riders

TEST THREE

1

1 D	4 D	7 D	10 A	13 A
2 A	5 C	8 D	11 C	14 B
3 B	6 A	9 B	12 C	15 B

2
16 result/consequence
17 it
18 that
19 might/may/could
20 in
21 made
22 ago/earlier/before
23 its/the
24 if
25 no
26 just/only
27 us
28 of
29 the
30 to

3
31 play tennis I always get
32 might not really like one
33 have not (haven't) been there since
34 used to be known everywhere
35 is gradually falling/is falling gradually
36 they get a lot better
37 you mind not shouting
38 I knew where we were
39 is being released from
40 me I would never have

4

41 have	44 was	47 on	50 did	53 ✔
42 being	45 ✔	48 the	51 me	54 so
43 ✔	46 an	49 ✔	52 of	55 most

TEST FOUR

1
1 according
2 more
3 turning
4 for
5 where
6 but/(al)though
7 who
8 much
9 as
10 less
11 short
12 to
13 in
14 is
15 if/when/after

2
16 didn't/did not use to go
17 not enough resources for so
18 although it was snowing so
19 if they had to stick
20 even though it is
21 unless he has an immediate/unless he immediately has a
22 hasn't retired yet/still hasn't retired
23 if we don't get
24 wishes he had studied more
25 must have/get your hair

3

26 no	29 what	32 ✔	35 ✔	38 be
27 ✔	30 that	33 been	36 by	39 will
28 very	31 to	34 ✔	37 it	40 have

4
41 violence
42 width
43 exceptional
44 distances
45 mysterious
46 strength
47 circular
48 clockwise
49 pressure
50 powerful

Practice Test Key

PAPER 1

1 G   2 E   3 B   4 H   5 A   6 F   7 C

8 C   9 B   10 B   11 A   12 D   13 C   14 C

15 E   16 D   17 F   18 A   19 G   20 C   21 H

| 22 D | 24 E | 27 C | 29 E | 31/32 A/F | 34 D |
| 23 C | 25/26 D/F | 28 B | 30 A | | 33 B | 35 B |

PAPER 3

| 1 B | 3 C | 5 C | 7 D | 9 B | 11 A | 13 B | 15 C |
| 2 C | 4 B | 6 A | 8 C | 10 D | 12 D | 14 B | |

16 from	21 they/these	26 such
17 some	22 may/can/might	27 as
18 which	23 are	28 into
19 but	24 by	29 being
20 the/their	25 those	30 on

31 wishes she had seen
32 where she had bought her
33 wouldn't let me go
34 (that) Sue should buy
35 may have been burgled
36 was always looked up to
37 blamed George for the death
38 if he had not/hadn't fallen
39 in case you need to
40 is out of the question

41 the	46 will	51 only
42 to	47 ✔	52 until
43 up	48 ✔	53 it
44 ✔	49 have	54 been
45 in	50 too	55 ✔

56 leading	61 understanding
57 illness	62 enabled
58 noticeable/noticed	63 worldwide
59 scientific	64 permanently
60 publications	65 uninterrupted

PAPER 4

1 B   2 A   3 C   4 B   5 A   6 C   7 B   8 A

9 throw a knife	14 local schools
10 (a) bow (and) arrow(s)	15 (a) summer camp
11 17/seventeen	16 climbing (cliffs)
12 (a) dog (and) (a) gun	17 trainers
13 animal skins	18 on horseback/by horse

19 C   20 F   21 A   22 B   23 D

| 24 YES | 26 YES | 28 NO | 30 NO |
| 25 NO | 27 YES | 29 YES | |

TAPESCRIPTS

PAPER 4   Part 1

1   W: ... Yes, I understand that ... no, no, if she's not well then of course she can't come to classes ... Yes, I'll let all the teachers know and I'll get one of the other students to drop off a copy of next week's social programme on their way home. Thanks for phoning ... I know you'll take good care of her ... Bye ...

2   M: Ah, Brian, I'm glad you're here – I've been meaning to talk to you. It's about this project you're working on. I'm sorry but it's just not up to standard and I'm afraid if things don't improve, I'll get somebody else to take over ... someone who can get things moving a bit faster, with a bit more imagination ... OK?

3   W: Oh, yes, we had a great time.
    M: It wasn't too tiring then?
    W: Oh, I was exhausted! But the kids seemed to have endless energy from the moment we parked the car to the time we got home. I just wanted to sit down with a cup of tea, but they were still on about seeing the lions being fed ... and pretending to be camels ...

4   P: Well ... the atmosphere here's electric ... the roads outside are packed with fans trying to get in ... I gather the police are having a bit of a problem controlling them, but there's been no real trouble ... everyone's been very good-natured so far ... So, with five minutes to kick-off, Barry, what's the feeling back there in the studio? ... who's going to win? ...

5   M: Oh, I'm really sorry! Is he all right?
    W: Yes, I think so, but there could have been a nasty accident. You really should be more careful ... letting him run straight out of the shop like that into the road. You're lucky I didn't run him over. I think he's just frightened, though, not hurt.
    M: I forgot his lead ... Usually he's very quiet ... He's not as young as he was. Honestly, I'm really sorry ...

6   W: Phew! I can't wait to get off duty – I'm exhausted. It's always the same when you get a problem like that – it's not just one delayed flight, it's the way it affects others all through the day. The control tower kept us circling for over 20 minutes before we managed to get down on the far runway. By the time we'd taxied in, the passengers were just desperate to get off.

7   M: Right, so basically you're saying I've got a choice between coach and air?
    TA: Mm, yes.
    M: Well ... I did a coach tour of Austria a couple of years ago. It was OK, but I don't like sitting for long periods, so maybe I should think about the plane. What sort of fare are we looking at? I want to have something left to spend when I'm actually on holiday!

8   W: Yes, I can understand how you feel, but I think you need to discuss it with the head of department. She's really very understanding.
    M: I suppose so.
    W: I mean, I've worked with you for a long time now on one thing or another and I think we're both overdue for promotion. Maybe we should tackle the problem together ...

PAPER 4   Part 2

M: Hi, Annie! Hey, I've just been hearing about this amazing guy in America, a sort of modern Tarzan. I'm thinking of doing an article on him for the college magazine.

W: Hi! Sounds interesting. What does he actually do?

M: Well, his name's Eustace Conway and he lives in the woods in North Carolina with absolutely no modern facilities at all, no money, or at least not for everyday shopping, and completely alone.

W: How long's he been doing it?

M: 20 years! Mind you, we're talking about someone who by the time they were six was able to throw a knife with incredible accuracy. You know, like, enough to kill things.

W: Ugh, nice little boy!

M: Yes, and then when he was 10 he was actually hunting for food using a, you know, a bow and arrow. Apparently he was completely at home in the woods – he used to disappear for days on end and so nobody was very surprised that when he was just 17 he decided to go off and live there all the time.

W: Didn't at least his mother object?

M: Oh, no. She was perfectly happy about it because she'd disappeared off to Alaska when she was younger and lived all by herself in a little tent by a river, with a dog and a gun.

W: Oh!

M: So, anyway, Eustace lives this really simple life, living off the woods by hunting and so forth. He makes all his own clothes, too, just by cutting and sewing animal skins.

W: Sounds revolting ...

M: And when he does have money he spends it on land, so his part of the woods actually belongs to him.

W: Where does he get the money?

M: Oh, well, it's still connected with his lifestyle. He goes into local schools and tells the kids all about it. They just sit there drinking it all in. Oh, and he also organizes a summer camp. That's up at his place and he teaches people how to live like him.

W: OK for a week, perhaps, but 20 years? No, thanks!

M: Well, he's been around a bit, too. He went off to New Zealand climbing cliffs for a while. Oh, yes, and then he's been up in the Alps, walking, and, would you believe it, because he's Eustace Conway he did it in trainers!

W: Hm, I've been up in the Alps, but in proper boots.

M: And then his latest thing was to cross America ...

W: What's special about that?

M: Well, he did it entirely on horseback.

W: Ah, I should have known! Well, it'll make a great article. Now I must rush. See you!

M: See you! Bye!

PAPER 4   Part 3

1   I don't think I was the best of pupils, really. I didn't have a great memory for facts and figures and all that. I got on pretty well with the teachers, though, especially the art teacher. I enjoyed her lessons – maybe because I could actually draw and paint – it just seemed to come naturally. Unlike the other subjects. I suppose I'm just not terribly academic.

2   School wasn't too bad, really, I suppose. I just accepted that you had to go and that was that. I don't think I was much fun to teach, though, and I remember the French mistress – she couldn't stand me and I felt the same way about her. French lessons couldn't end quickly enough for me – all those verbs to learn, not to mention the vocabulary tests. All those years and I still ended up incapable of ordering a cup of coffee in Paris.

3   I don't know about schooldays being the best days of your life, but I quite enjoyed those years. I wasn't a bad pupil – I did what I was told and then went home at the end of the day and did my homework. So the teachers liked me and I used to do well in tests. Mind you, I didn't like them – I was always in a terrible state the night before studying all the stuff until I knew it off by heart.

4   I wasn't a very athletic child, so I found the games lessons a bit of a pain. The games teacher wasn't bad, though – he never tried to make you do things that were really beyond you, never made you look stupid. Maybe if I'd spent less time stuffing myself with school lunches and more time on the hockey pitch I'd be a bit fitter now.

5   Well, I must admit I had a great time at school. There were about five or six of us who were always together. We went home together after school, helped each other with homework, tested each other when we were revising – that sort of thing. I was quite good at memorising stuff. I enjoyed it. I used to sit down on the sofa with something to eat and just get on with it.

PAPER 4   Part 4

M: Honestly! Look at this newspaper – it weighs a ton! You need to be a weightlifter just to pick it up.

W: Well, I suppose at least there's plenty to read, something for everyone.

M: Yes, if you've got several lifetimes to do it in! Papers never used to be that thick. I sometimes think I'm drowning in a sea of words.

W: I know what you mean. Take books. It's impossible to keep up with all the latest ones. I'm sure most people only manage to read the reviews, but there's really no point if you're unlikely to read the book itself.

M: I couldn't agree more. I'd hate to be a writer these days, though I suppose some of them make money.

W: There are more books, but I don't think people – and especially children – read very much these days.

M: Well, they do, but only if it's on a computer screen. There's more useless information available on the Internet than anywhere else. Words, words, words everywhere – it's getting ridiculous.

W: I think there's too much of everything. Films, for example, they're getting longer, too. Personally I find it difficult to sit in a cinema for three or more hours. It might be justified for one or two films, but not for the majority.

M: It's the same with CDs. In the old days an album was about 20 minutes a side. Now CDs are all an hour at least and half of it isn't worth listening to.

W: It's all a matter of having more choice. I mean, compared with our grandparents I suppose we're better off. Take supermarkets, for example, the choice of food and stuff available there.

M: Possibly, in some ways, but more doesn't always mean better, whether it's the media or the local supermarket.

W: No, but at least we have more options. Maybe we're just not used to being selective. OK, often there's a lot of rubbish, but the good stuff's in there somewhere, it still exists – we just have to make more careful choices.

M: I sometimes wonder – maybe we're moving towards a world where only quantity matters, not quality.

W: Possibly, but I think on balance I'd rather have the choice. It must have been very boring for our grandparents having the same things day after day – the same food, the same TV channel, whatever ...

M: Yes, but if you'd never had the choice, you wouldn't miss it.

W: Ah, but I have ...!

UNIVERSITY *of* CAMBRIDGE
Local Examinations Syndicate

SAMPLE

Candidate Name
If not already printed, write name
in CAPITALS and complete the
Candidate No. grid (in pencil).

Candidate's signature

Examination Title

Centre

Centre No.

Candidate No.

Examination Details

Supervisor, please complete the details immediately below (in pencil) as applicable.

|X| If the candidate is ABSENT or has WITHDRAWN shade here ⬜

If a TRANSFERRED CANDIDATE, shade here ⬜ and write the original Centre Number here

Candidate No. grid digits: 0 1 2 3 4 5 6 7 8 9

Candidate Answer Sheet: FCE paper 1 Reading

Use a pencil

Mark ONE letter for each question.

For example, if you think **B** is the right answer to the question, mark your answer sheet like this:

0 | A B D

Change your answer like this:

0 | A B C D

1	A B C D E F G H I
2	A B C D E F G H I
3	A B C D E F G H I
4	A B C D E F G H I
5	A B C D E F G H I

6	A B C D E F G H I
7	A B C D E F G H I
8	A B C D E F G H I
9	A B C D E F G H I
10	A B C D E F G H I
11	A B C D E F G H I
12	A B C D E F G H I
13	A B C D E F G H I
14	A B C D E F G H I
15	A B C D E F G H I
16	A B C D E F G H I
17	A B C D E F G H I
18	A B C D E F G H I
19	A B C D E F G H I
20	A B C D E F G H I

21	A B C D E F G H I
22	A B C D E F G H I
23	A B C D E F G H I
24	A B C D E F G H I
25	A B C D E F G H I
26	A B C D E F G H I
27	A B C D E F G H I
28	A B C D E F G H I
29	A B C D E F G H I
30	A B C D E F G H I
31	A B C D E F G H I
32	A B C D E F G H I
33	A B C D E F G H I
34	A B C D E F G H I
35	A B C D E F G H I

UNIVERSITY of CAMBRIDGE
Local Examinations Syndicate

SAMPLE

Candidate Name
If not already printed, write name in CAPITALS and complete the Candidate No. grid (in pencil).
Candidate's signature

Examination Title

Centre

Supervisor, please complete the details immediately below (in pencil) as applicable.

[X] If the candidate is ABSENT or has WITHDRAWN shade here ⊏⊐

If a TRANSFERRED CANDIDATE, shade here ⊏⊐ and write the original Centre Number here

Centre No.

Candidate No.

Examination Details

0	0	0	0
1	1	1	1
2	2	2	2
3	3	3	3
4	4	4	4
5	5	5	5
6	6	6	6
7	7	7	7
8	8	8	8
9	9	9	9

Candidate Answer Sheet: FCE paper 3 Use of English

Use a pencil

For **Part 1**: Mark ONE letter for each question.

For example, if you think **C** is the right answer to the question, mark your answer sheet like this:

| 0 | A ⊏⊐ B ⊏⊐ C ⊏⊐ ⊏⊐ |

For **Parts 2, 3, 4** and **5**: Write your answers in the spaces next to the numbers like this:

| 0 | *example* |

Part 1				
1	A	B	C	D
2	A	B	C	D
3	A	B	C	D
4	A	B	C	D
5	A	B	C	D
6	A	B	C	D
7	A	B	C	D
8	A	B	C	D
9	A	B	C	D
10	A	B	C	D
11	A	B	C	D
12	A	B	C	D
13	A	B	C	D
14	A	B	C	D
15	A	B	C	D

Part 2	Do not write here
16	⊏⊐ 16 ⊏⊐
17	⊏⊐ 17 ⊏⊐
18	⊏⊐ 18 ⊏⊐
19	⊏⊐ 19 ⊏⊐
20	⊏⊐ 20 ⊏⊐
21	⊏⊐ 21 ⊏⊐
22	⊏⊐ 22 ⊏⊐
23	⊏⊐ 23 ⊏⊐
24	⊏⊐ 24 ⊏⊐
25	⊏⊐ 25 ⊏⊐
26	⊏⊐ 26 ⊏⊐
27	⊏⊐ 27 ⊏⊐
28	⊏⊐ 28 ⊏⊐
29	⊏⊐ 29 ⊏⊐
30	⊏⊐ 30 ⊏⊐

Turn over for Parts 3 - 5 →

FCE-3

DP319/93

©UCLES/K&J

Part 3		Do not write here
31		31 0 1 2
32		32 0 1 2
33		33 0 1 2
34		34 0 1 2
35		35 0 1 2
36		36 0 1 2
37		37 0 1 2
38		38 0 1 2
39		39 0 1 2
40		40 0 1 2

SAMPLE

Part 4		Do not write here
41		41
42		42
43		43
44		44
45		45
46		46
47		47
48		48
49		49
50		50
51		51
52		52
53		53
54		54
55		55

Part 5		Do not write here
56		56
57		57
58		58
59		59
60		60
61		61
62		62
63		63
64		64
65		65

UCLES sample answer sheets

UNIVERSITY *of* CAMBRIDGE
Local Examinations Syndicate

SAMPLE

Candidate Name
If not already printed, write name
in CAPITALS and complete the
Candidate No. grid (in pencil).

Candidate's signature ....

Examination Title

Centre

Supervisor, please complete the details immediately below (in pencil) as applicable.

[X] If the candidate is ABSENT or has WITHDRAWN shade here ▭

If a TRANSFERRED CANDIDATE, shade here ▭   and write the original Centre Number here ▭▭▭▭▭

Centre No.

Candidate No.

0	0	0	0
1	1	1	1
2	2	2	2
3	3	3	3
4	4	4	4
5	5	5	5
6	6	6	6
7	7	7	7
8	8	8	8
9	9	9	9

Examination Details

Candidate Answer Sheet: FCE paper 4 Listening

Mark test version below

A	B	C	D	E
▭	▭	▭	▭	▭

Special arrangements   S ▭   H ▭

Use a pencil

For **Parts 1** and **3**:
Mark ONE letter for
each question.

For example, if you
think **B** is the right
answer to the
question, mark your
answer sheet like this:

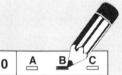

0	A	B	C

For **Parts 2** and **4**:
Write your answers in
the spaces next to the
numbers like this:

0	*example*

Part 1

1	A	B	C
2	A	B	C
3	A	B	C
4	A	B	C
5	A	B	C
6	A	B	C
7	A	B	C
8	A	B	C

Part 3

19	A	B	C	D	E	F
20	A	B	C	D	E	F
21	A	B	C	D	E	F
22	A	B	C	D	E	F
23	A	B	C	D	E	F

Part 2 / Do not write here

9		9
10		10
11		11
12		12
13		13
14		14
15		15
16		16
17		17
18		18

Part 4 / Do not write here

24		24
25		25
26		26
27		27
28		28
29		29
30		30

▭

FCE-4

DP320/94

©UCLES/K&J